The Revolutionary War
Memoirs of
Major General Will

The Revolutionary War Memoirs of Major General William Heath

WILLIAM HEATH

Edited by SEAN M. HEUVEL

McFarland & Company, Inc., Publishers

Jefferson, North Carolina

All images are from the editor's collection unless otherwise noted.

Library of Congress Cataloguing-in-Publication Data

Heath, William, 1737–1814.
[Memoirs of Major General Heath]
The Revolutionary War memoirs of Major General William Heath /
William Heath ; edited by Sean M. Heuvel.
p.   cm.
Includes bibliographical references and index.

ISBN 978-0-7864-7881-1 (softcover : acid free paper) ∞
ISBN 978-1-4766-1737-4 (ebook)

1. Heath, William, 1737–1814.
2. United States—History—Revolution, 1775–1783—Personal narratives.
3. United States—History—Revolution, 1775–1783—Campaigns.
I. Heuvel, Sean M., editor.   II. Title.
E275.H43 2014   973.3'33—dc23   2014032005

British Library cataloguing data are available

On the cover: Major General William Heath engraving by John Rogers
© New York Public Library; Battle of Lexington © Library of Congress

Printed in the United States of America

McFarland & Company, Inc., Publishers
Box 611, Jefferson, North Carolina 28640
www.mcfarlandpub.com

To Maj. Gen. William Heath and
his efforts in bringing about the freedom
and way of life that we enjoy today.

Contents

Preface

As spring blossomed throughout Massachusetts in 1797, Maj. Gen. William Heath of Roxbury was focused on a writing project of great personal importance. The 60-year-old, retired soldier had experienced both success and adversity in America's political and military arenas. Now approaching his twilight years, he pondered how history would remember him. In an April 17 letter to his former commander, Gen. George Washington, Heath wrote, "I am now arrived at threescore years of age, and I know that my glass is nearly run. I am looking back on those scenes through which I have been called to pass, and frequently turn over the numerous orders which I had the honor to receive from you."[1] In the following months, Heath pored over the thousand pages of his wartime daily journal. While it appeared Heath intended to use this writing endeavor to claim a place in American history, some suggested he really meant to use the project to advance his political career in Massachusetts.

Regardless of the memoirs' purpose, compiling such an extensive work was likely a herculean effort. Heath freely admitted that he was not a skilled writer. However, his enthusiasm was surely renewed by a May 20, 1797, letter from his former commander. In it, Washington wrote:

> It gives me great pleasure to hear from yourself, that you are writing memoirs of those transactions which passed under your notice during the Revolutionary War. Having always understood that you were exact, & copious in noting occurrences at the time they happened; a work of this kind will, from the ability, and candor with which I am persuaded they were taken, be uncommonly correct, & interesting.[2]

After completion, Heath's memoirs were printed in August 1798 and distributed widely throughout his native New England. Titled *Memoirs of Major-General Heath, Containing Anecdotes, Details of Skirmishes, Battles, and Other Military Events, During the American War*, the book was published according to an Act of Congress. Ultimately, Heath became one of the few Continental Army generals who thoroughly chronicled his wartime service. Yet, as the decades wore on following Heath's death in 1814, his life and memoirs faded from public view.

Interest in the book was partially rejuvenated in 1901 when Revolutionary War historian William Abbatt edited a revised version.[3] Although it was a noble attempt to re-introduce this historical document, the revision had a number of drawbacks that curtailed its scholarly value. Abbatt included minimal notes and illustrations, and provided limited biographical material as context for the reader. Again, Heath's memoirs were lost to generations until they emerged on the internet. Both the original version and Abbatt's edited revision are now readily accessible online; unfortunately, neither presents Heath's extensive narrative in the best possible light.

Thus, this book is intended to advance Heath's memoirs into the 21st century through the advantages of modern technology and the latest applicable historical research. Readers will find detailed notes on the people, places, and events mentioned in Heath's original writing. Further, the introduction provides a comprehensive biographical overview encompassing the latest scholarly interpretations of Heath's Revolutionary War service. Additionally, nearly 30 illustrations highlight significant people, places, and events in Heath's world—a world I have revisited for several reasons. My connection to Heath began several years ago through some amateur genealogical research on my maternal family's colonial Massachusetts origins. After learning that a Continental Army general named William Heath had hailed from the town of Roxbury, I discovered that I was related to Heath through several familial lines as a distant cousin (a third cousin, nine times removed, to be exact).

I was further intrigued by historians' considerable disagreement about Heath and his military leadership prowess. William Fowler, Jr., described him as a "political general with only modest military abilities," who kept his commission only through his considerable political influence in New England.[4] Bud Hannings argued that Heath lacked aggressiveness as a battlefield commander, while Allen Johnson and Dumas Malone maintained that he "seems to have been a man of solid rather than brilliant parts, and probably a better farmer than a strategist or tactician."[5] Other historians have countered that Heath is an underappreciated Revolutionary War leader who deserves greater recognition. Paul David Nelson noted that he was known as an able logistics officer and as a commander concerned for his men's welfare.[6] Further, William Crafts posited that Heath held important positions throughout the war, noting that while he was never a popular commander, Heath was respected by his contemporaries and honored for his devoted service to the Patriot cause.[7] Infantry officer-turned-historian John Galvin provided what may be the highest praise from a historian: Referencing his work at the Battles of Lexington and Concord, Galvin observed, "Heath's firm grasp of the tactics of the skirmish line and his tendency to see any battle as a series of isolated little fights was just what the provincials needed."[8]

For me, these divergent views concerning Heath's leadership and legacy reinforced the first-person value of his work. By studying the memoirs closely, I drew my own conclusions about this complex Revolutionary War general and invite readers of this revised edition to do the same. An objective examination of Heath's writings does suggest that he was trying to demonstrate his wartime significance for posterity. Heath wrote extensively of the crucial wartime roles that he played, and the high regard in which he was held by political and military associates. For some historians like Richard Blanco, such sentiments give "the impression of a vain and pompous man."[9] Similarly, William Crafts noted that with an apparent desire to avoid egoism by using the personal pronoun, Heath substituted the words "Our General," which magnified rather than diminished the fault.[10] With respect to these views, I believe that Heath sought vindication for earlier mishaps, seeking to establish his legacy. In Heath's mind, he had devoted the prime of his life to the struggle for liberty, sacrificing a great deal for the sake of the cause.[11] Thus, wartime incidents such as the debacle at Fort Independence and his feud with Maj. Gen. Alexander McDougall (described later in this book) were humiliating embarrassments. Ultimately, I believe that the elderly general wrote these memoirs to justify his wartime record.

Whether or not Heath ultimately achieved vindication through these memoirs, they are a vitally important historical artifact from our nation's early history. Since Heath was not an active combat commander, vivid descriptions of battle are minimal in his writing. However, the real value of his memoirs can be found elsewhere. For instance, his rich description of the Continental Army's organizational structure, along with his interactions with high-profile generals like George Washington and Charles Lee, are most informative. Similarly, his correspondence with senior British Army commanders, such as Generals John Burgoyne and William Phillips, provide a fascinating glimpse into the minds of these prominent military leaders. Most importantly, Heath's memoirs give readers a unique insight into the day-to-day operations of the Continental Army.

To develop this book, I studied Heath's original 1798 memoir as well as the 1901 William Abbatt revision closely. I then used the 1901 revision as a foundation to build upon some of Abbatt's original endnotes while adding many more. To give modern readers a feel for Heath's words and personality, I have made only minimal changes to his original writing for this edition. One such change was to modernize the spelling of certain words, such as "candor" instead of "candour," for ease of reading. There are extensive endnotes on individuals Heath mentions, and modern names when needed for ease of identification. To streamline this edition, I have omitted the description of the Battle of Bunker Hill found in Abbatt's 1901 revision, since it was not an engagement in which Heath fought. I have also cut out some sections of non-germane correspondence or lengthy tangents about the weather or other topics unrelated to the war. Lastly, Heath's memoirs are reorganized into chapters chronicling each year of the Revolution. His writings are also sorted by date in order to provide further reading clarity. These changes are not meant to detract from his original writing, but rather to make them more accessible to modern readers. It is my hope that this revised edition will re-introduce this compelling yet underappreciated Revolutionary War leader to a new generation of American history enthusiasts.

Introduction

The American Revolution produced a range of leaders within the Continental Army and its associated militias. During the war, they each had varied degrees of success in shaping their place in history—if they were remembered at all. In some cases, generals such as Nathanael Greene and Daniel Morgan earned lasting fame for their efforts, while others less successful in battle did not. One example of the latter is Maj. Gen. William Heath of Massachusetts. Descended from old New England stock, Heath pursued a career in farming, militia service, and politics prior to the Revolution. While he became one of the Continental Army's most senior commanders, his name does not appear prominently in modern Revolutionary War scholarship. In the few cases where General Heath is mentioned, they usually highlight only his bungled January 1777 attack on Fort Independence in New York, which was intended to support General Washington's actions at Trenton and Princeton.

However, this negative perception of Heath obscures more enduring contributions he made to the Revolutionary cause. These include his leadership during the Battles of Lexington and Concord, his effective management of British General John Burgoyne's Convention Army of surrendered troops, his work in forging a strong alliance with the French Army, and his efforts to recruit and train soldiers for the Continental Army. Further, Heath's significant role in procuring vital supplies and funding for the Continental Army from the New England states is often overlooked. While he did not achieve fame as a brilliant battlefield commander, his skills as an administrator and military diplomat were key to the American war effort. Despite its setbacks and limitations, Heath's Revolutionary War career should be remembered and his "voice" heard once more. What follows is a thorough biographical sketch of General Heath, intended to provide appropriate context and perspective for his memoirs.

Early Years

William Heath was born in March 1737 to Samuel and Elizabeth Payson Heath in Roxbury, Massachusetts, which is now a neighborhood in Boston.[1] His family was of English ancestry and immigrated to Massachusetts in the 1630s. Thus, Heath was among the fifth generation of his family to reside on the homestead developed by his colonial ancestors.[2] Although raised to be a farmer, he took an early interest in military life, which only increased as he grew older. This passion led Heath to "attentively study every military treatise in the English language [that] he could procure."[3] He frequented Henry Knox's Boston bookstore, with its full stock of military texts, and made careful study of the British regulars drilling on Boston Common.[4] Over time, Heath became highly respected among New Englanders for his expertise in military tactics—especially in the tactics of the skirmish.[5] Armed with this knowledge, he enjoyed active militia service and political life as a young adult. Heath represented Roxbury in the Massachusetts General Court in 1761 and again from 1771 to 1774.[6] In 1765, he joined the Ancient and Honorable Artillery Company of Massachusetts, later serving as its commander in 1770.[7] Through his close friendship with Massachusetts Royal Governor Francis Barnard, he also rose steadily in rank to captain in the Suffolk Militia, and eventually became its colonel in a reorganization conducted just prior to the Revolution.[8]

Heath first displayed his public allegiance to the patriot cause around the time of the Boston Massacre. Despite his friendship with key crown officials such as Governor Bernard, Heath was steadfast in his support of the patriot movement. In early 1770, he composed a series of written public addresses using the signature *A Military Countryman*, which called for "the importance of military discipline, and skill in the use of arms, as the only means under heaven that could save the country."[9] He also began organizing and training companies of militia and minutemen for future military service. Following the royal dissolution of the Massachusetts General Court in 1774, Heath was appointed to the patriot-organized Massachusetts Provisional Congress and served on the committees of correspondence and safety. During this time, he figured as a key political and military leader among the Massachusetts patriots, working closely with such notables as Samuel Adams and John Hancock.

On February 7, 1775, the Provisional Congress appointed Heath one of its five brigadier generals. Shortly thereafter, he was the first American general on the scene during the Battles of Lexington and Concord on April 19, later leading the attack on retreating enemy troops serving under the British general, Lord Hugh Percy.[10] While performing his military duties, Heath utilized Dr. Joseph Warren of Bunker Hill fame as a volunteer aide: Throughout the day the pair was inseparable as Heath attempted to impose some semblance of order on the various militia units arriving on the field.[11] Although Heath was certainly active that day providing organizational leadership and guidance to the patriot forces, his strategic worth has been debated—and in some cases diminished—by some modern scholars. Since the patriot militia was more akin to an armed mob than an army, Nathaniel Philbrick and other historians contend that Heath's presence as an American general was more symbolic than tactical.[12] As Philbrick argued, "what Heath provided that afternoon and evening was not tactical and strategic brilliance but legitimacy."[13] However, other historians like David Hackett Fischer and John Galvin assert that Heath supplied important tactical leadership to the patriot forces.[14] As Galvin noted, "Heath's firm grasp of the tactics of the skirmish line and his tendency to see any battle as a series of isolated little fights was just what the provincials needed."[15] Regardless of which interpretation is most authentic, the Battles of Lexington and Concord gave Heath his most successful experience as a battlefield commander. Shortly thereafter, he ordered initial preparations for what evolved into the siege of Boston. However, since his troops were held in reserve during the June 17 Battle of Bunker Hill, he played no active part in that engagement.[16] Even so, on June 20 Heath was promoted to major general of Massachusetts troops, and then appointed a brigadier general in the Continental Army two days later.[17]

Early Revolutionary War Service

For the rest of 1775 and part of early 1776, Heath participated in the siege of Boston, training troops and overseeing the construction of defensive fortifications around the city. Since the Continental Army lacked able engineers, he prevailed upon an old acquaintance, Captain Henry Knox of the Boston Grenadiers, to join the army.[18] Heath later noted in his memoirs that Knox did not need much persuading to join in the cause of liberty.[19] As history records, Henry Knox would go on to earn great fame as the Continental Army's chief of artillery. Following months of skirmishing with the enemy in Boston, culminating in the British withdrawal from that city, Heath was dispatched on March 20, 1776, to assist in the defense of New York City, under the temporary command of Maj. Gen. Israel Putnam.[20] General Washington went on to assume command the following month and did his best to prepare the city for an expected British military invasion.

Following his August 9, 1776, promotion to major general in the Continental Army, Heath was one of three senior officers who voted in a council of war to defend New York City against the imminent British attack.[21] At the time, he was in command of troops posted above King's Bridge, which is located near the modern-day Bronx, with orders to defend the Hudson River above New York.[22] Following the British invasion, Heath remained in command there, and thus did not participate in the Battles of Long Island, Harlem Heights, or White Plains.[23] Believing that Heath had limitations as a battlefield commander, General Washington later decided to post him where little action was expected. Thus, on November 12, 1776, Heath was assigned command of troops defending the Hudson Highlands.[24]

Maj. Gen. William Heath in uniform.

The Battle of Fort Independence

Heath's best opportunity for distinction on the battlefield was lost during his failed January 1777 assault on Fort Independence in New York. To assist in his efforts against the British Army in New Jersey, General

Washington intended to orchestrate what would appear to be an assault on British-occupied New York City. He believed that such a ruse would force the British to evacuate New Jersey in order to adequately defend New York. Therefore, following the American victories at Trenton and Princeton, he ordered Heath to move a force of American troops toward New York in early January 1777.[25] The target of this assault was to be the British-held Fort Independence, located outside the northern reaches of Manhattan in the modern-day Bronx. At the time, it was manned mostly by Hessian mercenary soldiers.

Although Heath's force of roughly 5,000 troops outnumbered the Hessian garrison, the attack quickly stalled following its commencement on January 17. While the American troops were initially successful in overrunning enemy outposts outside of the fort, Heath's demand for the main garrison's surrender yielded little result, and he decided not to press the attack. Since Heath did not expect the Hessians to have many cannons, he was shocked when they fought back with intense artillery barrages. To make matters worse, only news of the initial American success made it to General Washington. Not knowing that the attack had in actuality bogged down, Washington quickly reported the supposed success to the Continental Congress. When reports of Heath's failure made it to General Washington's desk, it proved to be quite an embarrassing episode for both men and for the Continental Army.[26]

Although Heath's troops spent the next few days skirmishing with the enemy, his force had lost both its initiative and the strategic element of surprise. With bad weather looming and British reinforcements under Lord Percy rumored to be on the way, Heath and his subordinate commanders decided to disengage from the assault. When General Washington learned of this sequence of events, he sent a clear letter of condemnation to Heath on February 4, 1777:

> Dear Sir: This letter is in addition to my public one of this date; it is to hint to you, and I do it with concern, that your conduct is censured (and by men of sense and judgment who have been with you on the expedition to Fort Independence) as being fraught with too much caution, by which the Army has been disappointed, and in some degree disgraced.
>
> Your summons, as you did not attempt to fulfill your threats, was not only idle but farcical; and will not fail of turning the laugh exceedingly upon us; these things I mention to you as a friend (for you will perceive that they have composed no part of my public letter). Why you should be so apprehensive of being surrounded, even if Lord Percy had landed; I cannot conceive; you know that landing men, procuring horses, etc. is not the work of an hour, a day, or even a week.[27]

As a result of this censure, Heath was never again placed in command of troops in action. Fellow officers and political superiors in the Continental Congress also expressed dissatisfaction with his leadership. Col. Timothy Pickering, who was then adjutant general of the Continental Army, called the expedition "disgraceful."[28] Meanwhile, in a February 21, 1777, letter to his wife Abigail, John Adams wrote:

> I sincerely wish we could hear more from General Heath. Many persons are extremely dissatisfied with numbers of the general officers of the highest rank... Schuyler, Putnam, Spencer, Heath, are thought by very few to be capable of the great commands they hold. We hear of none of their heroic deeds of arms. I wish they would all resign.[29]

In his defense, Heath countered that he followed proper military protocol in his approach to demanding the fort's surrender. Further, he argued that poor weather, a lack of artillery, and the possibility of intervening British reinforcements all factored in dooming his assault. Most importantly, Heath maintained that his force was comprised entirely of poorly trained militia who could not stand up to professional European soldiers. In a February 6, 1777, letter to General Washington, Heath noted, "every officer [under his command] objected to a storm [of the fort], as they apprehended the militia inadequate to such an enterprise."[30] Heath went on to write:

> No officer could be more anxious to affect something to purpose than I have during the expedition here, or more harassed, perplexed, and fatigued with an undisciplined militia, and if after all this and having taken every step, agreeable to the result of Councils of War, I am to be censured, it is truly discouraging.[31]

In later years, Heath reflected on this episode in his memoirs. He questioned the wisdom of sending minimally trained militiamen into dangerous enemy territory for a span of several days, as he perceived was requested in the original order from General Washington. On that subject, he wrote, "whenever an enterprise is to be attempted in the teeth of the enemy, it should be a *dash* and away."[32] In actuality, it was certainly possible that a more aggressive commander could have overrun Fort Independence as originally envisioned by General Washington. Indeed, the incident demonstrated that Heath was arguably too cautious to be an effective battlefield commander. Ultimately, while Heath did the best job he could under the circumstances, the debacle at Fort Independence represented a low point in his Revolutionary War career.

Supervising the Convention Army

Despite Heath's humiliation following the failure at Fort Independence, he continued to support the cause of independence fully and sought to rebuild his reputation with other assignments in the Continental Army. Following a short leave to visit his family in Roxbury,[33] Heath was ordered to Boston on March 14, 1777, to succeed Maj. Gen. Artemas Ward as commander of the Continental Army's Eastern Department, which encompassed most of New England.[34] He remained in the post until November 1778.[35] A highlight of Heath's tenure was his supervision of General John Burgoyne's Convention Army—British and Hessian prisoners of war who had surrendered following the Battle of Saratoga on October 17, 1777. According to the surrender terms, titled the Convention of Saratoga, the force of 5,900 troops would be sent back to Europe after signing a parole promising that they would no longer participate in the conflict.[36] However, negotiations concerning their status began to stall, and the Convention Army spent over a year in Cambridge, Massachusetts, before being moved to Charlottesville, Virginia, in November 1778.[37]

While the Convention Army was encamped in Cambridge, Heath faced the difficult task of housing that large force adequately while contending with the bitter, arrogant, and petty General Burgoyne, still chafing from his recent surrender. As a prisoner "in misfortune, Burgoyne betrayed a restless spirit, as he found fault with everything, and caviled at the most insignificant trifles."[38] Consequently, Burgoyne complained constantly. He agitated the situation with baseless charges of insolence against Continental Army officers and challenged the modes of transportation given him.[39] General Burgoyne was joined in this effort by his subordinate commanders Maj. Gen. William Phillips and the Hessian general, Baron Friedrich Riedesel.

Such intimidation from high-ranking British and Hessian commanders could have unnerved even the most resolute Continental Army officials. However, while he did it with the utmost respect, Heath consistently stood his ground with Burgoyne and his allies and did not cave in to their petty demands. Most of the correspondence between Burgoyne and Heath during this period was later published, and effectively documents the challenges that Heath faced.[40] Ironically, General Burgoyne was eventually won over by Heath's steadfast approach, gaining his lasting respect. Upon Burgoyne's departure for England on April 5, 1777, "he expressed his utmost satisfaction in respect to the treatment he had personally received from the General [Heath], and promised to remit from England such scarce articles as he should name, for his own use."[41] Heath politely declined the offer, "preferring to submit to the straitened resources of the country in common with his fellow citizens, rather than to avail himself of the advantages, which might result from the politeness of the captive officer."[42]

Following Burgoyne's departure, a division of the captured troops was ordered to move to Vermont, where barracks had been prepared for them in advance. Heath then entered into negotiations with British Maj. Gen. Sir Robert Pigot to provide adequate supplies for this force. When made aware of these negotiations, the Continental Congress passed a resolution on May 22, 1777, that approved highly of Heath's conduct.[43]

Later Revolutionary War Service

Heath remained in the Boston area until early June 1779, when he was ordered by General Washington to join the main army. On June 23, he took command of all troops on the east side of the Hudson River, based near modern-day Peekskill, New York.[44] On June 30, the Continental Congress elected Heath as a commissioner of the board of war, with an annual salary of four thousand dollars and the ability to retain his rank within the army. However, Heath declined this high honor, choosing instead to remain in the field. Thus, he spent the rest of the summer commanding a division that campaigned against British forces that were attacking towns in the Connecticut countryside.[45] On November 28, 1779, General Washington ordered Heath to assume command of all the troops and posts along the Hudson River, which was considered a vital communications link between the New England states and the rest of the country. Along with tending to those duties, he also spent the early part of 1780 lobbying the Massachusetts state government to raise additional battalions of troops for the war effort.[46]

The most eventful part of Heath's service during this period was in June 1780, when General Washington ordered him to report to Providence, Rhode Island, in order to manage the reception of the incoming French fleet. This naval force was carrying the French army units intended to aid the Continental Army in their war effort against the British. Heath's charge was to assist the French military commander, the Comte de Rochambeau, with the necessary logistics for getting the French force landed and ready for battle. Due to the great strategic value of this alliance, Heath's assignment was of the utmost importance. After the fleet arrived in Newport on July

11, Heath and Rochambeau quickly developed a close friendship that lasted for the duration of the war. The French landing soon attracted the attention of the British, and Heath spent several weeks preparing for a possible enemy attack.[47] Although the attack did not materialize, his ability to develop a strong rapport with Rochambeau played a vital role in strengthening the Franco-American military alliance.

Following Maj. Gen. Benedict Arnold's treason at West Point, Heath assumed command of that important garrison in mid–October 1780. He remained in the Hudson Highlands region for the rest of the war, monitoring enemy activity in New York and helping to prevent British marauding in the region. He also lobbied the governors of New England states for supplies desperately needed by the Continental Army, another service vital to the war effort. The following year, General Washington placed Heath in command of the army's entire northern wing, while he moved forces south for the eventual campaign against the British at Yorktown.[48]

By most accounts, Heath did an exemplary job in that role, earning the gratitude of many throughout the region. On October 22, 1781, the Corporation of Albany issued him a formal vote of thanks for his efforts in defending the northern frontiers of New York State against the British. Upon General Washington's return from the south in spring 1782, he also thanked Heath publicly "for the successful execution of the trust reposed in him" during Washington's absence.[49] Through his efforts in working with the French Army and leading the Continental Army's northern wing, Heath succeeded in at least partially rebuilding his reputation.

Yet, the incident at Fort Independence was not the only one to negatively impact Heath's reputation. It took one more beating toward the end of the war, due to a highly publicized dispute with Maj. Gen. Alexander McDougall. A New York native with a fiery temper and large ego, McDougall had proven to be a highly controversial commander within the Continental Army. During the war's later phases, McDougall and Heath were both stationed in the Hudson Highlands region and had a mutual disdain for one another. McDougall considered Heath to be pompous and incompetent, while Heath considered McDougall to be too unrefined and radical. However, as long as General Washington was based in the region, they played down their animosity toward one another.[50]

Open conflict finally arose between the commanders when General Washington left in summer 1781 to initiate the Yorktown Campaign. Heath and McDougall argued over who had superiority in command in the Hudson Highlands sector; angry letters flew in both directions.[51] Although Heath was technically the highest ranking commander in General Washington's absence, McDougall refused to acknowledge it and often issued contradictory orders.[52] The feud came to a boiling point when McDougall launched a bitter, public attack on Heath's character. After Heath ordered McDougall's arrest, both wrote to Washington to argue their cases. What followed was a highly embarrassing six-month episode for the Continental Army, with McDougall using every tactic possible to delay his trial while trying to rally support for his cause. He also did his best to publicize the controversy and maximize Heath's humiliation. The trial finally took place in August 1782, with McDougall found guilty of only one of the seven charges: pulling down two buildings and moving them to West Point without the knowledge of the commanding general (Heath). McDougall's punishment consisted of only a simple reprimand issued with extreme reluctance by General Washington.[53]

The awkward incident was highly embarrassing and problematic for all parties concerned, especially Maj. Gen. Robert Howe of North Carolina. Howe, who was friendly with both Heath and McDougall, had the unenviable task of presiding over the court-martial. Placed in a no-win situation, Howe's friendship with Heath was ruined as a result of the verdict, which left Heath feeling angry and betrayed.[54] Following the trial, Heath served in administrative roles until the war's end, returning home to Roxbury for good in July 1783.[55] He took particular pride in being the last general of the day while on camp duty. That responsibility had brought him full circle from serving as the first general officer on the field at the outset of the Revolution in 1775. Upon Heath's departure, he was given a private note from General Washington (see Chapter 9) thanking him for his long service and reaffirming their friendship. Heath was so moved by the letter that he considered it a "patent of nobility superior to any that a monarch ever issued," surpassing "all of the eagles and ribbons in the world."[56]

Life Following the War

Following his service in the Continental Army, Heath stayed in public life. In 1784 he helped to establish the Roxbury Artillery, an elite militia unit commanded by Heath's son-in-law, which saw service during Shay's Rebellion. A few years later, Heath was also appointed a major general in the Massachusetts Militia. As an avowed Federalist, he served in 1788 as a member of the Massachusetts state convention that ratified the U.S. Constitution.[57] By the early 1790s, Heath entered electoral politics, serving as a state senator from 1791 to 1792.[58] During this period, Heath's growing concern about the potential taxing power of the central government made him drift toward Jeffersonianism, and he quickly became a leader of the Democratic-Republican Party in his native state. Highly ambitious for statewide office, Heath was a frequent candidate for governor and lieutenant governor throughout the 1790s and early 1800s.[59] In 1798, he ran for Congress in the 8th Massachusetts district, losing to Federalist Harrison Gray Otis, who garnered 55.9 percent of the vote.[60] One factor that most likely contributed to Heath's lack of electoral success was the Federalist Party's dominance in Massachusetts during that time.

Nevertheless, Heath finally obtained a statewide electoral victory in 1806 by winning election for lieutenant governor.[61] Surprisingly, Heath declined the honor and politely refused to serve, citing his advancing age. At the time, speculation was rampant that the real reason centered on Heath's refusal to serve with Federalist Governor Caleb Strong. However, Heath told friends privately that he was actually disgusted at the highly corrupt nature of that particular election and did not want to hold elected office under those circumstances.[62] Instead, he retired from electoral politics and continued his service as a probate court judge; a position he had held since 1792.[63] By this point in his life, Heath's corpulence forced him to conduct his judicial duties traveling on a chaise accompanied by his son William Jr. on horseback. Known for his Republican simplicity, Heath often traveled to Sunday church services with his ox-team. This was an obvious jab at more aristocratic neighbors who sported showy and stylish carriages.[64] Despite Heath's anti-aristocratic sentiments, his pompous nature prompted many associates to refer to him as the "Duke of Roxbury," a nickname first coined by his brother officers during the Revolution.[65] The nickname also suitably described his influential status in postwar Massachusetts. In his later years, Heath enjoyed spending time on his farm and corresponding with Revolutionary War-era luminaries such as George Washington, John Adams, Thomas Jefferson, and James Madison.

Although Heath had a productive postwar career, his advancing age finally took its toll. One of his last public acts was to oppose the War of 1812, which he felt was an unwise endeavor, even though it was conducted by the Jeffersonian President James Madison.[66] When Heath died on January 24, 1814, just shy of turning 77, he was the last survivor of the Continental Army's major generals.[67] Although he had his challenges and setbacks, he led an eventful life which brought him into contact with some of American history's greatest figures, including many of the country's Founding Fathers. Heath also lived long enough to see the establishment and development of a nation he had worked so hard to create.

William Heath as a postwar civilian.

Ultimately, General Heath's legacy is not as a great battlefield commander. His skills as a military leader laid elsewhere. Instead, Heath should be honored as an effective army administrator and military diplomat who was steadfast in his loyalty to the Revolutionary cause. While it did not earn him everlasting fame, his behind the scenes work in lobbying for troops and supplies, solidifying Franco-American military relations, and supervising the Convention Army all played a valuable role in securing the United States' victory against the British. The nation was fortunate to have him as a public servant, and we are equally fortunate to have this unique first-person account of his Revolutionary War journey.

CHAPTER 1

1775

Maj. Gen. William Heath descended from an ancient family in Roxbury, near Boston, in Massachusetts, and is of the fifth generation of the family[1] who have inherited the same real estate (taken up in a state of nature) not large, but fertile, and pleasantly situated. He was born on March 2, 1737, and was brought up a farmer, of which profession he is yet passionately fond. He is of middling stature, light complexion, very corpulent, and bald-headed, which led the French officers who served in America very frequently to compare him to the Marquess of Granby.[2] From his childhood he was remarkably fond of military exercises, which passion grew up with him, and as he arrived at years of maturity led him to procure, and attentively to study, every military treatise in the English language that was obtainable. This, with a strong memory, rendered him fully acquainted with the theory of war in all its branches and duties, from the private soldier to the Commander in Chief.

Through the inactive state of the militia company to which he belonged, in the spring of the year 1765, he went over to Boston, and entered a member of the Ancient and Honorable Artillery Company.[3] This immediately recommended him to the notice of the Colonel of the first regiment of militia in the county of Suffolk, who sent for him, and importuned him to take command of his own company; to which Mr. Heath was reluctant; apprehensive that his youth, and stepping over those who had a better claim, by former office in the company, to the command of it, might produce an uneasiness. He was, however, commissioned by Gov. Bernard[4]; and his apprehensions of uneasiness proved to be groundless.

In the Ancient and Honorable Artillery Company, he was chosen, and served, first as Lieutenant, and afterwards as Captain. In the first regiment of militia of Suffolk, he became the military favorite of Gov. Bernard, who publicly declared, that he would not only make him Colonel of the regiment, but, if it were in his power, a General Officer also.

Lt. Gen. John Manners, Marquess of Granby. French Army officers noted that Heath bore a remarkable resemblance to him.

As the dispute between Great Britain and her American Colonies put on a more serious aspect, our Captain did not hesitate, for a moment, to declare his sentiments in favor of the rights and liberties of his fellow-country men. This alarmed Gov. Bernard's apprehensions, but did not alter his open conduct towards our Captain; though he privately intimated, that if he should promote him, he might injure the cause of his royal master. It was afterwards intimated to our Captain, that if he was not advanced to the command of the regiment, he might rest assured, that his feelings would never (during Gov. Bernard's administration) be hurt by any other officer being promoted over him; which was verified; Gov. Bernard leaving the province with this regiment unorganized.

Capt. Heath, convinced that the cloud was rapidly gathering, and would assuredly burst over America, in the beginning of the year 1770 commenced his addresses to the public, under the signature of *A Military Countryman*, and which were occasionally continued until hostilities commenced. In them he urged the importance of military discipline, and skill in the use of arms, as the only means, under Heaven, that could save the country from falling prey to any daring invader.

Gov. Hutchinson[5] succeeded Gov. Bernard. He organized the first regiment in Suffolk; and, as might be expected, our Captain had a respite from command. When it was recommended to the *people* of Massachusetts, to choose officers themselves to command them, our Captain was unanimously chosen to take the command of the first company in the town of Roxbury (his old and favorite company), and on the meeting of the Captains and subalterns of the first regiment of militia in Suffolk, he was chosen Colonel.

The people of Massachusetts, having determined to support their rights and liberties at every hazard (finding that such was the sense of the people of their sister Colonies) after the dissolution of their General Court, elected a Provincial Congress. This Congress appointed a Committee of Safety (of whom our Colonel was one), vested with executive powers; and another committee, called the Committee of Supplies. The latter were to purchase military stores, provisions, etc. and deposit them in such places as the former should direct. Both committees entered on the duties of their respective functions. The Provincial Congress voted a sum of money for the purpose of procuring military stores and provisions; and a quantity of both were collected, and stored in the town of Concord.

The militia, and the corps of minutemen, as they were called (the latter composed of the young and active) were furnished with officers of their own choosing. The greatest attention was exhibited by the officers, which was as cheerfully seconded by the citizen soldiers, to acquire a knowledge of military duty. In the month of February, 1775, the Provincial Congress passed the following resolutions:

In Provincial Congress, *Cambridge*, February 9, 1775, Resolved, That the Hon. Jedidiah Preble, Esq.[6]; Hon. Artemas Ward, Esq.; Col. Seth Pomeroy; Col. John Thomas, and Col. William Heath, be, and they hereby are, appointed General Officers, whose business and duty it shall be, with such and so many of the militia of this province as shall be assembled by order of the Committee of Safety, effectually to oppose and resist such attempt or attempts as shall be made for carrying into execution an act of the British Parliament, entitled, "An Act for the better regulation of the Government of the Province of Massachusetts Bay in New England"—or who shall attempt the carrying into execution, by force, another act of the British Parliament, entitled, "An Act for the more impartial administration of justice, in cases of persons questioned for any act done by them in the execution of the law, or for the suppression of riots and tumults in the Province of Massachusetts Bay"—so long as the said militia shall be retained by the Committee of Safety, and no longer. And the said General Officers shall, while in the said service, command, lead and conduct, in such opposition, in the order in which they are above named; any order of any former Congress varying herefrom, notwithstanding.

In Provincial Congress, Cambridge, February 15, 1775, Resolved, that the Hon. John Whitcomb, Esq.,[7] be added to the General Officers.
A true extract from the minutes,

(Signed) BENJ. LINCOLN, Sec'y.

In the month of March following, the Provincial Congress appointed a committee to make a minute inquiry into the state of the operations of the British army. On March 20, the committee reported, that the British army then consisted of about 2850 men, distributed as follows: On Boston common, about 1700 on Fort-Hill, 400; on Boston Neck, 340; in barracks at the Castle, 330; quartered in King Street, 80;— that they were erecting works on Boston Neck, on both sides of the way, well-constructed and well executed; the works were in forwardness, and then mounted with ten brass and two iron cannon; that the old fortification, at the entrance of the town, was repaired, and rendered much stronger by the addition of timber and earth to the parapet; that ten pieces of iron cannon were mounted on the old platforms; that a block-house brought from Governor's Island, was erecting on the south side of the Neck, between the old fortification and the new works advanced on the Neck.

On April 18, our General had been sitting with the Committee of Safety, at Menotomy[8] in Cambridge; and on his return home, soon after he left the committee, and about sun-setting, he met eight or nine British officers on horseback, with their swords and pistols, riding up the road towards Lexington. The time of day, and distance from Boston, excited suspicion of some design. They indeed were out reconnoitering and getting intelligence, but were not molested.

On April 19, at day-break, our General was awoke, called from his bed, and informed that a detachment of the British army were out; that they had crossed from Boston to Phipps' farm, in boats, and gone towards Concord, as was supposed, with intent to destroy the public stores. They probably had notice that the committees had met the preceding day at Wetherby's tavern, at Menotomy; for, when they came opposite to the house, they halted. Several of the gentlemen slept there during the night. Among them were Col. Orne,[9] Col. Lee,[10] and Mr. Gerry. One of them awoke, and informed the others that a body of the British were before the house. They immediately made their escape, without time to dress themselves, at the back door, receiving some injury from obstacles in the way, in their undressed state. They made their way into the fields. The country was immediately alarmed, and the minutemen and militia turned out with great spirit. Near Lexington meetinghouse the British found the militia of that town drawn up by the road. Towards these they advanced, ordered them to disperse, huzzaed, and fired upon them; when several were killed and wounded, and the rest dispersed. This was the first shedding of blood in the American war.

This company continuing to stand so near to the road, after they had certain notice of the advancing of the British in force, was but a too much braving of danger;

for they were sure to meet with insult, or injury, which they could not repel. Bravery, when called to action, should always take the strong ground on the basis of reason.

The British proceeded on to Concord, where they destroyed a part of the stores, while others were saved by the vigilance, activity, or policy of the inhabitants. In the latter, a Capt. Wheeler[11] practiced with such address, as to save a considerable quantity of flour, although exposed to the *critical examination* of a British officer. The British had sent a party to the North Bridge, while they were destroying the stores in the town. A body of militia, who had retreated beyond the bridge, and collected in this quarter, now marched up resolutely to the bridge. The British officer, finding their firmness, ordered his men to fire, which they did, and two men of the militia were killed. The fire was briskly returned; some were killed and wounded of the enemy, and an officer taken prisoner. The British party retreated with precipitation to their main body, and the whole soon commenced their retreat towards Boston; the militia galling them on all sides. This detachment, under the command of Col. Smith,[12] must have been worn down, and the whole of them killed, or taken prisoners, had it not been for the reinforcement sent out to them, under the command of Lord Percy,[13] with two field-pieces, who joined them in the lower part of the town of Lexington.

Our General, in the morning, proceeded to the Committee of Safety. From the committee, he took a cross road to Watertown, the British being in possession of the Lexington road. At Watertown, finding some militia who had not marched, but applied for orders, he sent them down to Cambridge, with directions to take up the planks, barricade the south end of the bridge, and there to take post; that, in case the British should, on their return, take that road to Boston, their retreat might be impeded. He then pushed to join the militia, taking a cross road towards Lexington, in which he was joined by Dr. Joseph Warren (afterwards a Major-General), who kept with him.

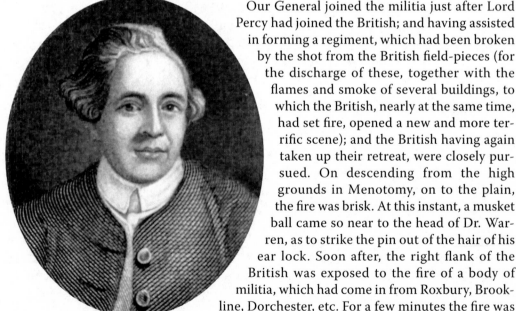

Our General joined the militia just after Lord Percy had joined the British; and having assisted in forming a regiment, which had been broken by the shot from the British field-pieces (for the discharge of these, together with the flames and smoke of several buildings, to which the British, nearly at the same time, had set fire, opened a new and more terrific scene); and the British having again taken up their retreat, were closely pursued. On descending from the high grounds in Menotomy, on to the plain, the fire was brisk. At this instant, a musket ball came so near to the head of Dr. Warren, as to strike the pin out of the hair of his ear lock. Soon after, the right flank of the British was exposed to the fire of a body of militia, which had come in from Roxbury, Brookline, Dorchester, etc. For a few minutes the fire was brisk on both sides; and the British had here recourse to their field-pieces again;

Dr. Joseph Warren.

but they were now more familiar than before. Here the militia was so close on the rear of the British that Dr. Downer,[14] an active and enterprising man, came to single combat with a British soldier, whom he killed with his bayonet.

Not far from this place, several of the militia (among whom was Isaac Gardner, Esq. of Brookline, a valuable citizen) imprudently posted themselves behind some dry casks, at Watson's Corner, and near to the road, unsuspicious of the enemy's flank-guard, which came behind them, and killed every one of them dead on the spot. The militia continued to hang on the rear of the British, until they reached Bunker's Hill in Charlestown; and it had become so dusk, as to render the flashes of the muskets very visible. At this instant, an officer on horseback came up from the Medford road, and inquired the circumstances of the enemy; adding, that about 700 men were close behind, on their way from Salem to join the militia. Had these arrived a few minutes sooner, the left flank of the British must have been greatly exposed, and suffered considerably; perhaps their retreat would have been cut off. As soon as the British gained Bunker's Hill, they immediately formed in a line opposite to the Neck; when our General judged it expedient to order the militia, who were now at the common, to halt and give over the pursuit, as any further attempt upon the enemy, in that position, would have been futile.

Our General immediately assembled the officers around him, at the foot of Prospect Hill, and ordered a guard to be formed, and posted near that place, sentinels to be planted down to the Neck and patrols to be vigilant in moving during the night; and an immediate report to him, in case the enemy made any movements. The militia were then ordered to march to the town of Cambridge; where, below the town, the whole were ordered to lie on their arms.

About midnight there was an alarm that the enemy was coming up the river. It proved to be only an armed schooner, probably sent to make discovery. She got aground, and continued so until the next tide; and if there had been a single field-piece with the militia, she might have been taken. The marsh was too deep to approach sufficiently near to do any execution with small arms; and the first day's hostilities of the ever memorable American war, was, on their part, without a single piece of cannon in the field! Gen. Whitcomb was in this day's battle.

On the morning of April 20, our General ordered Capt. John Battle of Dedham, with his company of militia, to pass over the ground which had been the scene of action the preceding day, and to bury such of the slain as he should find unburied. The grounds around Cambridge were immediately reconnoitered, and alarm-posts assigned to the several corps; and in case the British should come out in superior force, and drive the militia from the town, they were ordered to rally and form on the high grounds towards Watertown.

How to feed the assembled and assembling militia, was now the great object. All the eatables in the town of Cambridge, which could be spared, were collected for breakfast, and the college kitchen and utensils procured for cooking. Some carcasses of beef and pork, prepared for the Boston market on the 18th, at Little Cambridge, were sent for, and obtained; and a large quantity of ship-bread at Roxbury, said to belong to the British Navy, was taken for the militia. These were the first provisions that were obtained.

At 11 o'clock a.m. our General appointed Mr. Joseph Ward,[15] a gentleman of abilities, his Aide-de-camp and Secretary (afterwards Muster-Master-General of the

The Battle of Lexington, April 19, 1775 (Library of Congress).

army) who entered on the duties of his new office. This was the first appointment of the kind in the American army. Before noon, a letter was received from the Committee of Supplies at Concord, expressing their joy at the event of the preceding day, with assurances that every exertion in their power should be put in exercise, to forward supplies to the militia in arms. In the afternoon, Gen. Ward arrived at Cambridge, who, being senior in the order of appointment, took the command accordingly.

In the battle on April 19, the British were said to have 65 killed, 180 wounded, and 28 made prisoners; in all, 273. Of the militia, 50 were killed, and 34 wounded; in all, 84. It might have been expected, that in a retreat of so many miles, the British loss would have been greater; but it is to be remembered, that as they kept the road, the fences (a large proportion of which are stone walls) covered their flanks almost up to the height of their shoulders. It will also be observed, that the wounded of the militia did not bear the common proportion with the killed, and is an evidence that the British did not choose to encumber themselves with prisoners, either wounded or not, as the marks left at Watson's Corners, and on the height above Menotomy meeting-house evinced. Nor was the dashing in of many windows, the firing of musket-balls into the houses, in some of which there were only women and children, or the soldiers' leaving their ranks, and going into the houses to plunder (in consequence of which a number lost their lives) marks of humanity or discipline. Their whole force on this enterprise, including the reinforcement, was from 1500 to 2000 of their best troops.

Gen. Ward was now the Commander in Chief of the assembled army, and exercised the immediate command on the Cambridge side; while Gen. Thomas had the immediate command on the Roxbury side. A few days after this, the Cambridge camp being very numerous, and the Roxbury camp judged to be weak, the British having gone over from Charlestown to Boston, Gen. Ward ordered our General, with three or four regiments, to march from Cambridge, and reinforce Gen. Thomas; and he continued in the Roxbury camp until after the arrival of Gen. Washington, in the month of July.

In the month of May, the Provincial Congress passed resolutions for raising 24 regiments, to serve during the remainder of the year. The General Officers were each to have a regiment. As the new regiments began to recruit, the militia went home, and the camps became very weak; that at Roxbury did not exceed 1000 men. Had the British sallied at that time, there would have been but few to oppose them on that side. However, the army soon became strong, it being reinforced by the arrival of Gen. Putnam from Connecticut, Gen. Sullivan from New Hampshire, and Gen. Greene from Rhode Island; each with a respectable body of troops; and, in the month of June, it was determined to take possession of the heights of Charlestown. Preparations were made for the purpose; and on May 16th, at night, a strong detachment from the American army marched on, and broke ground on *Breed's Hill*, in front of Bunker's Hill. The latter ought to have been taken possession of at the same time, but it was somehow omitted.

By the morning of May 17, the troops had a redoubt and line on its left flank in good forwardness, when they were discovered by the British. The *Lively*[16] man-of-war first began to cannonade the Americans; she was soon seconded by other ships, floating batteries, and some heavy cannon on Cop's Hill, on the Boston side, which the Americans bore with a good degree of firmness, and continued at their work. The British army in Boston were greatly alarmed at this near approach, and immediately resolved on an attack, before the works could be completed. A detachment was formed for the purpose, consisting of ten companies of Grenadiers, ten of Light Infantry, and the 5th, 38th, 43rd, and 52nd regiments, and a corps of artillery under the command of Maj. Gen. Howe, and Brig. Gen. Pigot. In the afternoon they landed on Charlestown Point without opposition, where they were afterwards reinforced by the 47th regiment, and first battalion of marines.

The regiments in Cambridge camp were ordered down to support the detachment at Charlestown, and to occupy other posts thought to be essential, and contiguous thereto. The British began their attack with a severe fire of artillery, and advanced in a slow and regular pace. The Americans who had marched on to the aid of the detachment, consisting of the New Hampshire, Massachusetts and Connecticut troops, hastily formed a line of defense, composed of rails and other materials found nearest at hand. This line extended down towards the low ground on the left, and was nobly defended. The Americans reserved their fire until the British came very near, when they gave it to great effect; it staggered, and even broke them, but they rallied, and returning to the charge again and again, drove the Americans from the lines on the left of the redoubt, and had nearly surrounded it, when the Americans rushed out of the redoubt, their ammunition being expended, and made their retreat, even through a part of the British forces. About this time Maj. Gen. Warren, who had been but a few days before commissioned, and was then on the hill as a spectator only, was killed. A number of the Americans were killed in retreating from Breed's Hill to Bunker Hill, and some in passing off over the Neck. Perhaps there never was a better-fought battle than this, all things considered; and too much praise can never be bestowed on the conduct of Col. William Prescott,[17] who, notwithstanding anything that may have been said, was the proper commanding officer at the redoubt, and nobly acted his part as such, during the whole action.

Just before the action began, Gen. Putnam came to the redoubt, and told Col. Prescott that the entrenching tools must be sent off, or they would be lost; the Colonel replied, that if he sent any of the men away with the tools, not one of them would return; to this the General answered, they shall every man return. A large party was then sent off with the tools, and not one of them returned; in this instance the Colonel was the best judge of human nature. In the time of action, Col. Prescott observing that the brave Gen. Warren was near the works, he immediately stepped up to him, and asked him if he had any orders to give him. The General replied that he had none, that he exercised no command there—"the command," said the General, "is yours."

While many officers and soldiers gallantly distinguished themselves in this action, others were blamed, and some were brought to trial by court-martial. This was a sore battle to the British, who did not forget it during several campaigns, nor until a tide of successes in their favor had removed it from their minds. Their whole force on this day, which was in action, was supposed to be about 2000, and their whole loss, in killed and wounded, was said to be upwards of 1000, of whom 226 were killed, and of these 19 were commissioned officers, including one Lieutenant-Colonel, two Majors, and seven Captains. Another account stated their killed and wounded to be 753 privates, 202 sergeants and corporals, and 92 commissioned officers; in the whole, 1047. The loss of the Americans, in killed, wounded, and prisoners, about 450.[18]

The Battle of Bunker Hill, June 17, 1775 (Library of Congress).

At the time the British made their attack, the houses in Charlestown were set on fire, and burnt most furiously, which increased the horrors of the scene. At the same time a furious cannonade and throwing of shells took place at the lines on Boston Neck, against Roxbury, with intent to burn that town; but although several shells fell among the houses, and some carcasses near them, and balls went through some, no other damage was sustained than the loss of one man killed by a shot driving a stone from a wall against him.

On June 15, Congress appointed GEORGE WASHINGTON Commander-in-Chief; and on the 17th Artemas Ward, first Major-General; Charles Lee, second Major-General; Horatio Gates, Adjutant-General, with the rank of Brigadier-General; and on the 19th, Philip Schuyler, third Major-General; and Israel Putnam, fourth Major-General; and on June 22, Seth Pomeroy, first Brigadier-General; Richard Montgomery, second; David Wooster, third; William Heath, fourth; Joseph Spencer, fifth; John Thomas, sixth; John Sullivan, seventh; Nathanael Greene, eighth[19]; and made provision for raising an army for the defense of the United Colonies. Before these appointments were made known at camp, on the 21st of June, our General received from the Provincial Congress a commission of Major-General. Generals Ward, Thomas, and Warren had before received their commissions, the latter just before he was slain. Gen. Pomeroy declining an acceptance of the commission from Congress, that Honorable Body, on the 19th of July, resolved that Gen. Thomas be appointed first Brigadier-General in the army of the United Colonies, in the room of Gen. Pomeroy, who never acted under the commission sent to him, and that Gen. Thomas's commission bear the same date that Gen. Pomeroy's did; indeed this was the rank to which Gen. Thomas was entitled by former standing. Congress now also appointed Joseph Trumbull to be Commissary-General of stores and provisions, for the army, but left the appointment of a Quarter-Master-General, and some other officers, to Gen. Washington, who appointed the able and very active Col. Thomas Mifflin, Quarter-Master-General, who did himself much honor, and his country service, in this important department.

Immediately after the Battle of Bunker Hill, the Americans began to erect works on Prospect Hill, a very commanding height above Charlestown common, and at several other places. Several works were also constructed at Roxbury, and the British confined to Boston and Charlestown, within the Neck. The works now going on, both on the Cambridge and Roxbury side, were considerable, and there was a great want of engineers. Col. Gridley[20] was chief Engineer, and was aided by his son. But the strength of body, activity and genius of the Americans capable of constructing with surprising dispatch any works in which they were guided, called for many instructors in this department. Lt. Col. Rufus Putnam,[21] of Col. David Brewer's[22] regiment, was very serviceable in this line, on the Roxbury side; a was also Capt. Josiah Waters of Boston, and Capt. Baldwin[23] of Brookfield (afterwards Colonel of Artificers) and others on the Cambridge side, and Capt. Henry Knox, who had been an officer in the Boston Grenadier Company (and who was afterwards at the head of the American artillery, to the close of the war) occasionally lent his aid. His military genius and acquaintance with our General led him to be importunate with Capt. Knox to join the army: not did he need persuasion to join in the cause of his country. His removal out of Boston, and the then state of his domestic concerns, required some previous arrangement; as soon as this was affected, he joined the army.

June 24—About noon, a heavy cannonade and throwing of shells from the lines on Boston Neck into Roxbury—but no damage done. Two American soldiers attempting to set fire to Brown's barn, on Boston Neck, were killed by the British. The same evening two heavy cannon were brought to the work on the hill above Roxbury workhouse.

June 25—At night, an attempt was made to burn the buildings on Boston Neck; a firing took place between the parties, but the object was not affected.

June 26—A party of British, about daybreak, advanced and fired on the American sentinels near the George tavern. The picket turned out—the British retreated.

July 1—A platform in the work above Roxbury workhouse being laid, a 24-pounder was mounted and discharged twice at the British lines; the second shot grazed the parapet and struck on the parade, and occasioned some confusion: There was more or less firing of cannon on both sides, daily: All the works were pushed with the utmost diligence.

July 2—About two o'clock, p.m. Gen. Washington, attended by several officers, arrived at the camp in Cambridge. On the morning of this day, the British cannonaded briskly from their lines on Boston Neck against Roxbury, and threw some shells; a carcass set fire to the house of Mr. Williams, the tinman, which was burnt down; by the activity of the troops, the flames were prevented from spreading further, although they had to work in the face of a constant and heavy fire from the enemy.

July 5—Gen. Washington, accompanied by Maj. Gen. Lee, visited the Roxbury camp, works, etc.

July 8—A little after two o'clock in the morning, a number of volunteers, under the command of Majors Tupper and Crane,[24] attacked the British advance guard at Brown's house, on Boston Neck, and routed them, took a halbert,[25] a musket, and two bayonets, and burnt the two houses; the store and barn escaped the flames; a scattering fire at the outpost continued for some time; a floating battery was brought up into the bay, and moored so as to cover the right flank of the British works on the Neck.

July 11—In the morning, a party of Americans drove back the British advance guard, and burnt Brown's store. The same night a detachment went on to Long-Island, and brought off the stock, etc. The next day in the forenoon, Col. Greaton with 136 men, went on to Long Island, and burnt the barns; the flames communicated to the house, and all were consumed. An armed schooner and several barges put off after the Americans, and some of the ships of war near the island, cannonaded them. The detachment made their way for the shore, and narrowly escaped being taken. One man on the shore who came to the assistance of the detachment, was killed: it was supposed that several of the British were killed and wounded. The same day six transports, appearing to be full of men, arrived in Boston harbor.

July 13—A heavy cannonade from the British, at the American workmen but no damage done. Gen. Washington visited the camp. The men were employed on the works going on upon the strong rocky hill (Col. Williams's) to the south-west of those above Roxbury workhouse. This was one of the strongest works that were erected.

July 14—The British fired several cannon, and a Connecticut soldier was killed in the street, near the George tavern. The shot entered his body, drove it some distance, and lodged in him, in a remarkable manner.

July 18—Five transport ships arrived in Boston harbor. Fresh provisions were very scarce and dear, in Boston—mutton and veal, 2s. per pound; fresh beef and pork a pistareen,[26] salt pork sixpence.

July 20—A day of public fasting—no fatigue—all still and quiet.

July 21—Maj. Vose[27] returned from Nantasket. The detachment under his command brought off 1000 bushels of barley, all the hay, etc. went to Light-House Island; took away the lamps, oil, some gun-powder, the boats, etc. and burnt the wooden parts of the light-house. An armed schooner and several boats with men, engaged the detachment; of the Americans, two were wounded.

July 22—A general order came out for forming the army into divisions and brigades.

July 25—Maj. Gen. Ward removed from Cambridge, and took the immediate command of the troops at Roxbury.

July 29—The British formed a bomb battery, at Bunker's-Hill, and advanced their advance guard.

July 30—In the morning there was a skirmish at Charlestown Neck, between the riflemen and some British troops. Two of the latter were taken prisoners, and several were killed. Of the riflemen, one was killed. The same day, the British advanced over the Neck, and threw up a slight work to cover their guard.

July 31—A little before one o'clock, a.m. a British floating-battery came up the river, within 300 yards of Sewall's Point, and fired a number of shot at the American works, on both sides of the river. At the same time the British, on Boston Neck, sallied towards Roxbury; drove in the American sentinels, set fire to the George tavern, and returned to their works. The same morning, Major Tupper, with 300 Americans, went to Light-House Island, attacked a British guard of 33 marines, killed a subaltern officer and several soldiers, took 23 prisoners, several refugees, and burnt all the buildings on the island, with the loss of one American soldier. There was a firing, during the day, from the British at Charlestown, at intervals. Two Americans were killed; an officer, and several British soldiers, were supposed to have been killed. The Americans took several muskets.

August 2—There was a considerable firing between the advanced parties, and the Americans burnt a barn, near Charlestown Neck, in which the British had some hay. A British officer was wounded, and carried within their lines.

August 4—A ship of war came up above the ferry, at Charlestown, and there took a station.

August 6—In the afternoon, a party of the British, in two barges, covered by a floating battery, burnt the house on the other side of Penny Ferry.

August 11—One of the ships which had been stationed above the ferry, went down.

August 15—There was a smart cannonade on the Roxbury side. There was more or less firing every day; but little damage done.

August 17—A shot from the British lines on Boston Neck, struck among the main guard, at Roxbury, and damaged two muskets in a very remarkable manner; but did no other harm. The same day six or seven tons of powder arrived from the southward.

August 18—Several shells were thrown into Roxbury; but did no damage.

August 26—The Americans broke ground on Plowed Hill, in front of Bunker's Hill, without molestation.

August 27—There was a brisk cannonade from the British on Bunker's Hill, the ship, and floating batteries, at the Americans on Plowed Hill. Adjutant Mumford of Col. Varnum's[28] Rhode-Island regiment and a soldier, belonging to Col. Hitchcock's[29] regiment, were killed, and a rifleman lost a leg.

August 28—In the night the camp was alarmed, and some of the troops turned out, but nothing ensued. The fire continued against Plowed Hill; one American was killed and several wounded.

August 29, 30, and 31—The British continued their cannonade and bombardment of Plowed Hill. One shell fell within the works; but no damage was done.

September 1—The preceding night there was an excessive hot cannonade and bombardment from the British works, on Boston Neck, against the works at Roxbury. Two Americans were killed, and several wounded.

September 2—The British threw up a slight work on Boston Neck, advanced of their lines, to cover their guard. Cannonading and throwing of shells, on this day, both against Roxbury and Plowed Hill. Two shells fell into the works on the latter, but did no harm.

September 5—A sergeant, belonging to the 64th British regiment, and a seaman, were taken prisoners at Noddle's Island. The heavy rains, about this time, did some damage to the American works. Preparations were made for sending a detachment to Canada.

September 6—The Americans advanced some works towards Boston Neck, without molestation.

September 9—Two riflemen deserted to the British. A number of British soldiers, at different times, had come over to the Americans.

September 10—A strong work at Lamb's Dam, in Roxbury, was completed, and mounted with four 18-pounders. The same day, a shot from the British destroyed three muskets at Roxbury.

September 11—A boat, with six or seven British soldiers, was driven on shore at Dorchester. They were taken prisoners and sent in.

September 13—A detachment, under the command of Col. Arnold, marched for Canada. They were to take a north eastern route, up the Kennebec River,[30] and down the river Chaudière.[31] Generals Schuyler and Montgomery were making their way into Canada, with a considerable force, by way of the lakes. They had advanced as far as Fort St. John's; but, finding that this fort would make considerable resistance, they fell back. Schuyler returned to Albany, to hold a treaty with the Indians; and Montgomery waited for the arrival of his artillery, that he might reduce the forts.

Sometime before this, Col. Ethan Allen, of the New Hampshire Grants (since Vermont) with a number of volunteers, took possession of Ticonderoga. The artillery, secured by Allen, were an acquisition to the Americans; and Colonel Knox went up the next winter, and selected and brought forward a number of pieces to the camp before Boston. The garrison of this place, which was commanded by a Captain apprehending no danger, was negligent and remiss in duty. Allen was acquainted at the place, and now, as is said, requested a part of the garrison to aid him, in transporting some goods. Nearly half the garrison was granted him. These were plentifully served with liquor; and, in the night, Allen entered the fort, and demanded a delivery of it. The commandant asking by what authority he required him to surrender, Allen replied—"I demand it in the name of the great Jehovah and the Continental Congress."

He also took possession of Crown Point; and, before Montgomery was ready to proceed against the Forts Chambly and St. John's, Allen determined to surprise Montreal. For this purpose, he marched across, with a body of militia; but he was met, before he got to the town, by what force the British could collect there, who attacked and defeated Allen, taking him, and a number of his party, prisoners. He was put in irons, and sent in a man-of-war to England. His narrative was long since published.

September 18—Several seamen deserted from the British—they brought off three boats. The same day, a cannon shot, from the lines on Boston Neck, went through the guard house at Roxbury. A splinter wounded the Captain of the guard.

September 21—The cannonade, which continued more or less every day, was more brisk at some workmen, between Plowed Hill and Prospect Hill. Two Americans were wounded.

September 23—A brisk cannonade and bombardment on the works at Roxbury 108 cannon and mortars were discharged, but no damage done.

September 29—500,000 dollars in Continental bills, were brought to Head-Quarters, from Philadelphia. Several deserters from the British, about this time.

October 3 and 4—General Officers in council, on the supposed treachery of Dr. Church,[32] who was taken into close custody, and afterward kept in confinement.

October 6—A brisk cannonade at Roxbury. An American lost an arm. An 18-pound shot went through the gate-way, at the British lines, as their guard was marching out.

October 8—The British did some mischief at Bristol, in Rhode Island. The report of the cannon were heard at camp.

October 17—Two American floating-batteries were rowed down the river; several shot were discharged towards the British. A nine-pounder burst, and five or six men were wounded; one of which died soon after.

October 22—Intelligence was received, that some British ships had entered the harbor of Casco Bay, and burnt a part of the town of Falmouth.

November 4—Intelligence was received, that the British fort at Chambly, on the lake, had surrendered to the Americans. The artillery and military stores in this fort were truly an acquisition. The privateers fitted out by the Americans, about this time, began to send in a few prizes.

November 9—At the top of high water, the tide being very full, some British light infantry, in boats, came over from Boston, and landed on Lechmere's Point. The sentinels on the point came off; the alarm was given; and several hundred Americans forded over the causeway, in the face of the British, the water at least two feet deep. The British, seeing the spirit of the Americans, although they were very advantageously posted, made a precipitate retreat to their boats. Three or four Americans were wounded, one mortally. The British ship and floating batteries kept up a brisk fire; but to little purpose.

November 11—The King of England's Proclamation for suppressing rebellion (as he called it) made its appearance. It was taken on board a vessel from Ireland, which was captured by an American cruiser. It was reported that the British had received a reinforcement.

November 14—Intelligence was received of the capitulation of the British garrison of Port St. John's on the lake. Montgomery was now proceeding rapidly into Canada. His troops took possession of Montreal on the 13th.

November 16—Several deserters came in, and two soldiers were taken prisoners.

November 22—A strong detachment from the army, under the command of Maj. Gen. Putnam, broke ground on Cobble Hill, without annoyance. The fatigue men worked until near break of day, when the whole came off.

November 23—At night, our General, with a detachment of similar strength to that of the preceding night, were ordered to Cobble Hill, to complete the works. A sally from the British was expected, and Col. Bridge[33] with his regiment was ordered to the foot of the hill, and to patrol towards the bay and Neck, constantly, during the night. The picket at Prospect Hill was also ordered to be in readiness to succour the troops at the works, if they were attacked; and Col. Bond's[34] regiment also lay on their arms; but the British did not move. Two of the British sentinels came off in the night to the detachment; the whole came off at day-break; and other troops were ordered on the works, in the day time, now in good forwardness, and defensible.

November 25—An additional ship came up and took station at the ferry. Upon a few shot being fired, by the American advance sentinels, the British drums on Bunker's Hill beat to arms, which were followed by the Americans. At this time the British were erecting several bomb-batteries at Boston to annoy the Americans. Col. Enos, who was of Col. Arnold's detachment, from the army destined to cross the woods by a north-eastern route into Canada, having proceeded a very considerable distance, Arnold's sick returning back, and his own men growing sickly, returned with his part of the detachment. This lessened the expectation of success to the American army in Canada.

November 30—Intelligence was received from Cape Ann, that a vessel from England, laden with warlike stores, had been taken and brought into that place. There was on board one 13 inch brass mortar, 2000 stand of arms, 100,000 flints, 32 tons of leaden ball, etc. A fortunate capture for the Americans!

December 2—The brass 13-inch mortar, and sundry military stores, taken in the ordnance prize, were brought to camp.

December 5—Intelligence was received, that Col. Arnold had made his way safely into Canada.

December 12—A causeway was begun over the marsh, to Lechmere's Point. Two 18-pounders were brought from Roxbury, and mounted at Cobble Hill.

December 13—An express arrived from Marblehead, with advice that three British men-of-war were standing for that harbor. Col. Glover's[35] regiment, with Capt. Foster's[36] company of artillery, and a company of riflemen, were ordered to march to Marblehead with all expedition.

December 14, 15, and 16—Approaches were carried briskly on to Lechmere's Point, and nearly to the top of the hill.

December 17—The morning was foggy. A detachment of 300 men, under the direction of Gen. Putnam, broke ground on the top of the hill, on Lechmere's Point, at a distance of not more than half a mile from the ship. Between twelve and one o'clock, the fog cleared away, and the ship began to cannonade the Americans, with round and grape shot, and some shells were thrown from West-Boston. One soldier was wounded, and the party driven from the works. Several cannon were fired from Cobble Hill, at the ship; one shot was supposed to have struck her.

December 18—Our General was ordered, with 300 men, to prosecute the work begun on Lechmere's Point. It was expected that this would have been a bloody day, and Dr. Downer, one of the surgeons, was ordered down with the detachment, with his instruments, etc. to assist the wounded. Fortunately for the detachment, Capt. Smith of the artillery, had, in the morning, discharged an 18-pounder from Cobble Hill at the ship, which induced her to weigh anchor, and run below the ferry-way.

When our General arrived nearly at the summit of the hill, lie halted the detachment, and went forward himself and took a view of the state of the works, which in some places were but just begun; in others were carried halfway up. He then ordered the front company to move up the hill, ground their arms, and move into a part of the works assigned to them—and so on through the whole, to prevent confusion in entering the works, and thereby increasing an object to the British gunners. As soon as the men were placed in the works, two sentinels were posted to watch the British batteries, with orders, on discovering the discharge of cannon, to call out, *a shot!* The men in the works were ordered to be steady; on the signal of a shot, to settle down and remain so, until the shot had struck; or if a shell, until it had burst; then to rise and prosecute the work—no man to step out of his place. In a very short time, a shot was cried by the sentinels. It proved to be a shell, which fell and burst within a few feet of a part of the workmen, throwing the dirt among them, and a piece of the shell hitting a soldier's hat.

On the second discharge the men fell as before; when, on rising, two or three heavy cannon-shot struck in the face of the work; the British having discharged the cannon in such time after the mortar, as that the shot might take effect just as the men arose after the bursting of the shell: but in this they did not succeed; the men being ordered to keep down until both had struck. Finding this deception to fail, a shell was broke in the air, directly over the party, at 60 or 70 feet high. This also had as little effect upon the Americans. The fire continued until the afternoon, when it ceased: and it was afterwards learnt, that the commanding-officer of the British artillery, who stood and observed the effect of their fire upon the Americans, went to their General and informed him that from his own observation, their fire had no other effect than to inure[37] the Americans to danger, and advised its discontinuance. In the afternoon, Gen. Washington and several other General Officers came on to the Point. Towards night, the detachment were ordered to move out of the works by companies, as they went in; take up their arms, move under the hill, and form the detachment; from whence it was marched to Cambridge, attended by their surgeon, who had been in waiting all the day, but had no occasion to draw his instruments from their case, or a bandage or dressing from his box.

December 19—The prosecution of the work on Lechmere's Point was continued. The British cannonaded and bombarded the new detachment; but to no effect. The same took place on the 20th. On this day, a 13-inch shell was thrown almost up to No. 2. It was probably thrown, either at the works before mentioned, or at the colleges. It did not burst. Nearly five pounds of powder was taken out of the shell.

December 22—The British threw one shell, and fired two shot, from Bunker's Hill in Charlestown, at the works on Lechmere's Point. The cannonade, etc. continued, on the 23rd and 24th; but to no effect.

December 28—A strong detachment from Winter Hill marched, in the night, to surprise the British outposts in Charlestown. They passed on the south side of Cobble Hill, and were to cross the cove on the ice. When they came to the channel, it was found to be open. A soldier slipping down on the ice, his piece accidentally went off, which caused an alarm, and the detachment returned.

December 31—Intelligence was received, that there had been an action[38] at Norfolk in Virginia, between Dunmore's[39] army and the Virginians, to the advantage of the latter. Fifty of the regular troops were said to have been killed and wounded; among the former was Capt. Fordyce, of the 14th British regiment, an active and good officer. The Virginians had not a man killed. Dunmore's force was supposed to be about 500.

Chapter 2

1776

January 1, 1776, presented a great change in the American army. The officers and men of the new regiments were joining their respective corps; those of the old regiments were going home by hundreds and by thousands. The best arms, such as were fit for service, were detained from the soldiers who were going home; they were to be paid for; but it created much uneasiness. Such a change, in the very teeth of an enemy, is a most delicate maneuver; but the British did not attempt to take any advantage of it.

January 8—It having been thought expedient to deprive the British of the houses in Charlestown, below Bunker's Hill, a detachment was ordered for the purpose. One hundred men from the First Brigade, and a like number from Frye's[1] Brigade, with Captains Williams, Gould and Wyman[2]; Lieutenants Foster, Shaw, Patterson and Trafton, and Ensign Cheeney[3]; the whole under the command of Major Knowlton,[4] aided by Brigade-Majors Henly and Cary.[5] The detachment marched between eight and nine o'clock in the evening, and the object was affected without the loss of a man. Several British soldiers were taken prisoners. The garrison of Bunker Hill works commenced a brisk fire down the hill, towards the houses; but no damage was sustained. There had been a number of deserters from the British, since those heretofore mentioned.

January 17—Intelligence was received, that on the 31 of December, at three o'clock, a.m., General Montgomery made an attempt to carry Quebec by assault. Col. Arnold had entered the lower city, and Gen. Montgomery was ascending the barriers at the other end, when he was killed by a musket-ball, as was his Aide-de-camp. A number of those who had entered the lower city, were killed or taken prisoners, and the enterprise defeated. No account of the American loss was at this time reported. Great address and gallantry were exhibited on this expedition. The Americans ascending Kennebec River, crossing the height of land, and descending into Canada, was an arduous undertaking. Montgomery was fired with a noble ardor. He had been successful hitherto, and the reduction of the city of Quebec would have been the finishing stroke. With this he hoped to close the year. To reduce the city by siege would require a long time (if not relieved) nor had he a train of artillery for the purpose.

With this day would expire the time of service of many of his troops. He therefore resolved to attempt to carry the place by assault. Two real attacks were to be made on the lower city, at the opposite ends; one guided by himself, the other by Arnold; and there were to be two false attacks made on the upper city, to divide and distract the enemy. Everything was well arranged. Arnold forced his way in, was wounded, and carried away—his party fighting on. Montgomery passed along a very narrow defile, next to the bank, to a barrier obstinately defended; and here he fell—here was an end to his attack. The other party fought on; but these being now the only enemy to oppose, the British turned their whole force to that quarter. They could not well retreat: the whole were killed, wounded, or taken prisoners. There was here barely a prospect of success, unless fortune should prove more favorable to merit than she is wont to do. Nothing more could be done on the score of gallantry. How far the attempt was a prudent one, is another question. It is a military maxim, that "fortune may fail us, but a prudent conduct never will." At the same time, some of the most brilliant victories have been obtained by a daring stroke.

January 18—Col. Knox, of the artillery, came to camp. He brought from Ticonderoga a fine train of artillery, which had been taken from the British, both cannon and mortars, and which were ordered to be stopped at Framingham.

January 22—Several Indians came to camp from the west-ward. Intelligence was received from Canada, that the blockade of Quebec was continued, notwithstanding the rebuff on the morning of the 31 of December.

February 1—A number of British soldiers from Bunker's Hill, went to pulling down the tide-mill at Charlestown. A cannon was discharged at them from Cobble Hill, which dispersed them for a short time, but they returned again.

February 5—Three cows were feeding near the British outpost at Charlestown Neck.[6] A party of the British came out, got above them, drove them to the Neck, and killed them. This brought on a brisk firing at the outposts, and some cannon were discharged from Bunker's Hill. It was supposed that the British had one man killed, and one wounded.

February 8—At night, a party of Americans, from Winter Hill, went down and burnt the old tide-mill in Charlestown.

February 14—In the morning, a party of British troops from the Castle, and another from Boston, crossed over to Dorchester Neck,[7] with intent to surprise the American guard, which they came well-nigh effecting; the guard but just escaping them. There was but one musket fired, on the side of the Americans. An old inhabitant and his son were taken prisoners. The British burnt the houses on the point, and then returned.

February 15—Intelligence was received from Canada, that some of the British garrison of Quebec, having made a sally,[8] in order to get fuel, they were driven back, with the loss of twelve killed, and fifteen wounded. The heights round Boston, except those at Dorchester, having been taken possession of, it was now determined that these also should be occupied; and great previous preparation was made for the purpose. It was imagined that so near an approach to the British would induce them to make a sally, to dislodge the Americans. It was therefore deliberated in Council, that, in case the British should come forth, a strong detachment of Americans, from the Cambridge camp, in boats, should proceed down the river, and land at the bottom of the common, in Boston.

To this our General made a most pointed opposition; alleging, that it would most assuredly produce only defeat and disgrace to the American army; that the British General must be supposed to be a master of his profession; that as such, he would first provide for the defense of the town, in every part, which was the great deposit of all his stores; that when this was done, if his troops would afford a redundancy, sufficient for a sally, he might attempt it; but it was to be remembered that, at any rate, the town would be defended; that it was impossible for troops, armed and disciplined as the Americans then were, to be pushed down in boats, at least one mile and a half, open to the fire of all the British batteries on the west side of the town, and to their whole park of artillery, which might be drawn to the bottom of the common long before the Americans could reach it, and be flanked also by the works on the Neck; that under such a tremendous fire, the troops could not effect a landing; and that he would never give his vote for it. It was however carried, that the attempt should be made.

February 18—It being Lord's Day, after the public service, a proclamation from the General Assembly of Massachusetts, for the reformation of manners, was read to the first division by the Rev. Mr. Leonard.[9]

February 21—A picket of 60 men was ordered to Lechmere's Point[10]; and Col. Sargent's[11] regiment at Inman's farm was ordered to be in readiness to support them, in case they should be attacked by the British; as some grounds for suspecting it had been discovered.

February 23—Ensign Lyman,[12] of Huntington's[13] regiment, with a small party, took a corporal and two men, who were sentinels at Brown's chimneys, on Boston Neck, without firing a gun. These prisoners reported that the heavy cannon were removed from Bunker's Hill, and put on board ship.

February 25—Some heavy cannon were mounted on the works at Lechmere's Point. The same day the British were busily employed in erecting a work, a little to the north of the powder magazine in Boston.

February 29—The British threw some shells to Lechmere's Point.

March 1—Several mortars were sent over to Roxbury, and great preparations were made to annoy the enemy. Bundles of screwed hay were brought from Chelsea, to be used in the works.

March 2—At night, a cannonade and bombardment began at the American works, on Cobble Hill and Lechmere's Point on the Cambridge side, and at Lamb's Dam on the Roxbury side, against the British works; and a number of shells were thrown into Boston. The British returned the fire, and threw out a number of shells; one of which, of 13 inches, reached Prospect Hill. One of the American mortars of 13 inches, and two of 10 inches, were burst. They were not properly bedded, as the ground was hard frozen.

March 4—There was an almost incessant roar of cannon and mortars during the night, on both sides. The Americans took possession of Dorchester heights, and nearly completed their works on both the hills by morning. Perhaps there never was so much work done in so short a space of time. The adjoining orchards were cut down to make the abattis[14]; and a very curious and novel mode of defense was added to these works. The hills on which they were erected were steep, and clear of trees and bushes. Rows of barrels, filled with earth, were placed around the works. They presented only the appearance of strengthening the works; but the real design was, in case the enemy made an attack, to have rolled them down the hill. They would have descended with such increasing velocity, as must have thrown the assailants into the utmost confusion, and have killed and wounded great numbers.

This project was suggested by Mr. William Davis, merchant, of Boston, to our General, who immediately communicated it to the Commander in Chief, who highly approved of it, as did all the other officers: But the credit of it is justly due to Mr.

Davis, and to him the writer gives it. As the regiments at Roxbury were parading, in the after noon of this day, to march to Dorchester, a shot, from the British lines on Boston Neck, carried away a thigh of Lt. John Mayo, of Learned's[15] regiment: he soon died. One man was killed by a shell at Lechmere's Point, in the night.

March 5—The British, it was expected, would attempt to dislodge the Americans from Dorchester heights. Signals had been prepared at Roxbury meeting-house to mark the moment. The detachment at Cambridge (designed to push into Boston in the boats) was paraded, not far from No. 2, where it remained a good part of the day. But kind Heaven, which more than once saved the Americans when they would have destroyed themselves, did not allow the signals to be made. About 3500 of the British troops, it was said, had been sent down to the Castle, with the intent to have made an attack on the Americans; but about midnight the wind blew almost a hurricane from the south; many windows were forced in, sheds and fences blown down, and some vessels drove on shore; and no attempt was made on the works. Some were ready to blame our General, for the sentiments which he expressed against the going into Boston, as was proposed, in the boats, and attributed it to the want of firmness: But the opinion of every military man, since that time, whether American, French, or British, who have taken a view of the land and water which was to have been the scene of action, with the concomitant circumstances (as far as we have heard) hath been coincident; and those who may in future review them, will for themselves determine whether the independence of spirit and sentiment of our General, expressed on the occasion, merited *applause* or *censure*: For himself, he has been frequently heard to say that he *gloried in them.*

March 7—Capt. Erving made his escape out of Boston. He reported, that the British were preparing to leave the town; that they were putting their cannon, mortars, shot, shells, etc. on board the store ships; that some of the shot and shells, sent into the town by the Americans, had been well directed.

March 9—The Americans at Dorchester Neck opened a battery to the northeast of Bird's Hill, near the water, with the intent to annoy the British shipping. This night a strong detachment went down to open a work on Nook Hill in Dorchester, still nearer to Boston. Some of the men imprudently kindled a fire behind the hill, previous to the hour for breaking of ground. The enemy discovered the light of the fire; and there was, during the evening and night, a continual roar of cannon and mortars, from the Castle and lines on Boston Neck, south end of that town; as well as from the Americans at Roxbury, Cobble Hill, and Lechmere's Point, at Cambridge. The second shot from the British at the old fortification, south end of the town of Boston, killed four Americans, who were standing around the fire before mentioned, at Nook Hill; one of whom was Dr. Dow, of Connecticut. Another man was killed at the point next to the Castle. This suspended the work for the night, during which more than 800 shot were fired.

March 10—The cannonade continued. The British were putting their cannon, military stores, and baggage, on board the store-ships and transports. This evening two pieces of cannon, and two small mortars, were carried on to Noddle's Island, to disturb the British shipping; but the enemy being quiet at their different works, they were not molested from that quarter.

March 11—In the evening there was a brisk cannonade from the British, at the south end of Boston, and the lines on the Neck.

March 12—A Mr. Woodward came out from Boston. He reported that the British were making the greatest preparations to leave the town; that a number of gun-carriages, ammunition wagons, etc. had been broken to pieces, and thrown off the wharves; that some furniture had been destroyed, and that many dry goods had been seized, etc.

March 13—Six regiments of the American army, viz.[16] Greaton's, Stark's, Paterson's, Bond's, Webb's,[17] and the rifle regiment, were put under orders to march for New York; of these our General was to take the command. A detachment of artillery was also ordered to march with this brigade.

March 15—a fire broke out in the Paterson barracks at Cambridge, which consumed six rooms, destroyed some musket-cartridges, etc. This day the rifle regiment commenced their march for New York.

March 17—In the morning the British evacuated Boston; their rear guard with some marks of precipitation. A number of cannon were left spiked, and two large marine mortars, which they in vain attempted to burst. The garrison at Bunker's Hill practiced some deception to cover their retreat. They fixed some images, representing men, in the places of their sentinels, with muskets placed on their shoulders, etc. Their immovable position led to the discovery of the deception, and a detachment of the Americans marched in and took possession. The troops on the Roxbury side, moved over the Neck and took possession of Boston; as did others from Cambridge, in boats. On the Americans entering the town, the inhabitants discovered joy inexpressible. The town had been much injured in its buildings, and some individuals had been plundered. Some British stores were left. The British army went on board their transports below the Castle. A number of American adherents to them, and the British cause, went away with the army.

March 18—The brigade destined for New York, marched from the vicinity of Boston.

March 19—The British blew up Castle William,[18] and burnt some of the barracks.

March 20—The British cannonaded, from the Castle, the Americans on Dorchester Neck. The same morning our General left Roxbury for New York. He reached Mendon, from whence, on the same evening, he observed the light in the air of the finishing stroke of burning the barracks, etc. at the Castle. The British destroyed the gun-carriages, and knocked the trunnions[19] off the cannon, and left them spiked. The cannon were afterwards drilled free, and mounted on a new construction, in stocks, placed on carriages, and were thereby rendered serviceable.

March 22—Our General reached Norwich in Connecticut. The troops marched with great expedition; but by the badness of the roads, the frost then coming out of the ground, the baggage wagons moved heavily. The transports, destined for the troops, were fitting for sea.

March 26—They fell down to New London.

March 27—The troops were marched to that place, where they embarked, and came to sail about noon.

March 30—They arrived at Turtle Bay, disembarked, and marched into the city at noon. The transports fell down to the city wharves, and landed the baggage, etc. Gen. Thompson[20] and Lord Stirling, with some New York and New Jersey troops, were in the city; and works were constructing in and around the city, on Long Island, and at Horn's Hook; the command of the whole devolved on our General. The *Asia,*

British man-of-war, then lay off in the harbor, with the *Lady Gage*, of 20 guns; but on the arrival of the brigade, the Asia moved further down, just out of shot. Our General put a stop to the intercourse between the inhabitants and the ships, which had, until then, been kept up.

April 2—Major DeHart,[21] of the Jersey troops, with 200 men, about midnight, made a descent on a small island in the harbor, which the British had begun to fortify; burnt a building or two, took two muskets, some entrenching tools, and came off. The *Asia* fired several cannon, but did no harm.

April 3—Maj. Gen. Putnam arrived at New York, to whom the command fell. About this time, a vessel arrived from France, with a large quantity of gunpowder.

April 7—A barge from one of the ships going near Staten Island, was fired upon by the Americans: two men were killed, the barge and eight men taken. The British cannonaded the shore for some time, and one American was wounded.

April 9—Intelligence was received that Commodore Hopkins[22] had fallen in with the British frigate *Glasgow*, a bomb brig, and two tenders, and after a smart engagement took the brig and two tenders. The *Glasgow* made off.

April 10—Gen. Sullivan's brigade arrived from the eastward.

April 12—There were eighteen pieces of brass cannon in the American park, at New York, which were viewed with no small degree of pride and wonder.

April 13—In the forenoon, Gen. Washington arrived in the city, attended by Gen. Gates and several other officers.

April 14—The British men-of-war were all out of the bay. The *Asia* fell below the Narrows; the *Phenix* and others went out to sea.

April 15—Four American regiments, viz. Poor's,[23] Paterson's, Greaton's, and Bond's, were ordered for Canada; Gen. Thompson was to command them. Gen. Thomas[24] had been, sometime before, sent from Boston to command in Canada.

April 17—Gen. Greene's brigade arrived at New York, as did a part of Spencer's. Mrs. Washington arrived the same day in the city.

April 21—The regiments destined for Canada, sailed for Albany.

April 26—Six more regiments were ordered for Canada, viz. two from the Pennsylvania line, two from the New Jersey, and two from the New Hampshire.

April 27—Our General, having been inoculated with the small-pox, went to Montresor's Island,[25] where he went through the operation of that distemper.

May 8—An express arrived from Boston, with an account that a number of British transports had arrived in Nantasket Road, with troops on board. All the American regiments were ordered to hold themselves in readiness, to march at a moment's notice. Several soldiers were taken down with the smallpox, and some of them died.

May 28—Our General having recovered from the smallpox, which had been pretty severe, returned to the city, and took the command of his brigade; and was the next day General of the day.

May 31—A large ship and two tenders arrived at the Narrows. A great number of works were now constructing, and in good forwardness. A strong work was raised at Paulus Hook, on the Jersey side of the Hudson.

June 4—A French vessel, with West-India goods, arrived in the harbor.

June 7—Intelligence was received that two Philadelphia privateers had taken two rich Jamaicamen, laden with sugars, etc. and some plate on board.

June 9—Unfavorable news was received from Canada. The smallpox, which was raging in the American army, in that quarter, had carried off Gen. Thomas; and that Col. Bedel[26] and Major Sherburne,[27] with the detachments under their command, were taken prisoners, at or near a place called The Cedars. The army in New York was now growing sickly; and there was not a sufficiency of hospital room, or of medicines.

June 14—Congress gave intimations, that General Howe, with the British army under his command, might soon be expected at New York. Some persons, suspected of treacherous designs, were seized and confined.

June 15—Some intelligence, more favorable than the former, was received from Canada. The Canadians were friendly. Gen. Sullivan, who was now in that quarter, having gone from New York, with the reinforcement heretofore mentioned, was fortifying; the enemy were advancing; but Gen. Thompson was sent out to oppose them. This, however, proved ineffectual; Thompson was defeated and taken prisoner. A number of Scotch troops,[28] with Col. Campbell,[29] had been made prisoners, near Boston harbor.

June 18—The Pennsylvania regiments, commanded by Colonels Shee and Magaw,[30] were arriving in the city; they had the appearance of fine troops. The day before, Gen. Wooster[31] arrived from Canada.

June 20—Gen. Gates, who was made a Major-General, was to proceed immediately to Canada, where he was to take command.

June 22—A plot was discovered in the city; it was to have burst on the Commander in Chief, and others. The mayor of the city was taken into custody as was a gunsmith, and some of the General's own guard, who were foreigners, were said to be in the plot. The same day, more particulars were received from Boston; that the troops at Boston had driven the King's ships from the Lower Harbor, and taken several transports, with Scotch soldiers on board.

June 25—Two deserters came in, from the *Liverpool* man-of-war. They reported, that the fleet from Halifax, with Gen. Howe's army, were hourly expected to arrive in New York. Every exertion was now in exercise, to complete the works, and to obstruct the river. The latter was near Port Washington, and prosecuted by sinking a number of large hulks, and frames called *chevaux-de-frise*, composed of large and long timbers framed together, with points elevated, to pierce and stop the way of vessels meeting of them. These were boxed at the bottom, to contain a vast weight of stones, which were put into them, and with which they sunk. A line of these, and hulks, was formed across the river; some of them sunk very well; others, rather irregular; and some of the hulks, which were strapped together with large timbers, separated in going down. A passage was left open for vessels to pass through; and the British, as it was proved afterwards, found the means of knowing where it was, and of passing through it.

June 27—Intelligence was received, that Gen. Burgoyne had arrived in Canada, with a strong reinforcement. The militia were called in, to reinforce the army at New York.

June 28—One Thomas Hickey, a private soldier in the General's guard, was executed. He was found guilty of mutiny, sedition, and the worst of practices, as it was expressed. The same day, the British fleet arrived at Sandy Hook.

June 29—The transports were coming in, during the whole day. At evening, nearly 100 sail had arrived. Col. Durkee's[32] regiment was ordered over to Paulus Hook. The General Officers were in council.

June 30—Mrs. Washington left the city.

July 2—Between 10 and 11 o'clock a.m. four British men-of-war, and several tenders, came through the Narrows, and anchored near the watering-place on Staten Island. In the afternoon, they cannonaded towards the island. A little before sunsetting, about 40 sail of transports came up to the ships of war. The Americans lay on their arms during the night.

July 3—The British troops landed on Staten Island. A part of the stock had been taken off. The inhabitants, who were about 350 men, were supposed to be generally opposed to the revolution.

July 9—At evening roll-call, the declaration of the Congress, declaring the United Colonies FREE, SOVEREIGN, AND INDEPENDENT STATES, was published at the head of the respective brigades, in camp, and received with loud huzzas.

July 12—Two British ships of war, the *Phenix* and *Rose*, and three tenders, at about four o'clock, p.m. taking advantage of the tide and a fresh breeze, came up from the fleet, and passed the city up the Hudson. A brisk cannonade took place from Red Hook, Governor's Island, Paulus Hook, and all the batteries on the North River side. The ships were several times struck by the shot, but received no material damage. The ships returned the fire, as they passed the batteries; and the encampment of our General's brigade (the right flank of which being Col. Shepard's[33] regiment) was on the bank of the river. The tents were struck, and dropped on the ground, before the ships came a-breast of them. Several shots fell on the encampment, and one entered the embrasure of a small redoubt, on the flank of the encampment, and struck in the banquette on the opposite side of the redoubt, between the legs of two soldiers, but did no damage. Several American artillerists were killed and wounded, by the bursting of some of our own cannon. The ships ran nearly up to Tappan Bay, and came to anchor.

July 14—A British officer came up with a flag, with a letter to Gen. Washington; but the letter not being properly addressed, it was not received. The same day a flag was sent by Lord Howe to Amboy, with sundry letters, directed to the chief magistrates of several of the Colonies, and a declaration, offering the King's pardon to such Colonies, towns, or boroughs, as should submit to His Majesty's laws, etc. Lord and Gen. Howe were Commissioners appointed to receive submissions.

July 16—Another flag came up from Lord Howe, with a letter directed to George Washington, Esq. etc., etc., etc. which was likewise rejected, for the want of proper direction.

July 17—In the morning, one or two of the British ships sailed out through the Narrows; and it was conjectured that a number sailed out during the night. The British ships which had sailed up the Hudson, had moved higher up. The Connecticut light-horse, which had come out to reinforce the army, were returning home.

July 20—A flag from Gen. Howe, with Adj. Gen. Patterson,[34] came up with a message to Gen. Washington, respecting the recent capitulation in Canada, and insinuating that Gen. Howe was desirous, if possible, to bring about an accommodation. The same day, news was received from South Carolina, that the British, in attempting Sullivan's Island, with their ships and a large body of troops, said to be from 1300 to 2000, were defeated by the Americans; one frigate burnt and blown up, several others

Opposite: **Gen. Sir William Howe, KB (Library of Congress).**

damaged, and 172 men killed and wounded. On the side of the Americans, 10 were said to be killed, and 22 wounded.

July 21—A man dressed in woman's clothes, was taken up, in attempting to get to the British fleet: he was committed to prison. The same day, Gen. Sullivan arrived from Canada. About noon, a number of cannon and small arms were heard towards Elizabeth-Town.

July 25—A row-galley or two arrived from Connecticut; and fire-ships, rafts, etc. were preparing with great expedition.

July 26—The British ships up the river fell some distance lower down.

July 27—A regiment of militia, under the command of Col. Holman,[35] arrived from Massachusetts.

July 28—Two row-galleys moved up the Hudson.

July 29—Col. Sargent's regiment of Continental troops arrived at Horn's Hook,[36] from Boston, and Col. Hutchinson's from the same place. Several British ships arrived and joined the fleet.

July 31—Intelligence was received, that Dunmore, with his fleet, had got nearly 200 miles up Potomac River in Virginia; that he had burnt one house, and was within about 30 miles of Gen. Washington's seat.

August 1—About 30 sail of British ships arrived at the Hook. Three or four more row-gallies went up the Hudson. In bringing the hulks, chevaux-de-frise, etc. round from the East River, to the Hudson, a sloop sunk, not far from the Grand Battery.

August 2—Glover's regiment arrived from the eastward.

August 3—About noon there was a brisk cannonade up the Hudson, between the American row-gallies and the British ships: the former had two men killed; two mortally, and 12 slightly wounded. The British loss was not known.

August 7—There were some movements among the British fleet: the men-of-war appeared to be formed in line. Two deserters came in, who reported that an attack on the Americans was intended soon.

August 8—A row-galley and two fire-sloops went up the river. It was intended to attempt burning the British ships in Tappan Bay. The American army was now very sickly; four soldiers were buried on this day, from our General's brigade only. About, and a little after this time, the army was more sickly than at any other period. The newspapers at Philadelphia and Boston rated the army at 70,000 strong, and in high spirits, and that they would soon clear the enemy from America. This was not a little mortifying to Gen. Washington, who had the evidence that the army did not exceed 40,000, officers included; and a large portion of these were levies and militia, called out for short periods, and unacquainted with a camp life. Hence the number of sick amounted to near 10,000; nor was it possible to find proper hospitals or proper necessaries for them. In almost every barn, stable, shed, and even under the fences and bushes, were the sick to be seen, whose countenances were but an index of the dejection of spirit, and the distress they endured.

August 9—It was learnt that the British were preparing for an attack, and were putting their heavy artillery, etc. on board ship. In reconnoitering the position of New York, long before this time, all were agreed, that the upper end of the island, and above Kingsbridge, must be secured, or there could be no security to an army on the island; but there was borne difference in opinion as to the place. A commanding height, near Morris's house, some distance below the bridge, within the island, was thought by some, among whom was Gen. Putnam, a position which, if properly fortified, would be almost impregnable. While others, among whom was our General, and his brother Gen. Greene, who were generally in sentiment, insisted that there could be no security on the island, although the post before mentioned was made as strong as Gibraltar, if the heights above the bridge were left unfortified, as the enemy might at any time, in an hour or two, possess themselves of those heights above the bridge, and completely entrap the army; and each declared positively, that he would not rest easy or satisfied, until those grounds were taken possession of. Fort Washington was begun on the hill first mentioned, and the works were pushed as fast as possible; and it was determined to erect another fort above the bridge, which was also begun, and called Independence. Every exertion was now in exercise to complete the works in and about the city, some of which were strong. Indeed, immense labor had been bestowed on the works at the city, on Long Island, at Horn's Hook, near Hell Gate, and at Paulus Hook on the Jersey side, opposite the city, on Governor's Island, etc.

Maj. Gen. Israel Putnam (Library of Congress).

August 11—Our General received a communication from Congress, dated the 9th, appointing him a Major-General in the army of the United States of America. Generals Spencer, Sullivan, and Greene received, at the same time, commissions of the same tenor.

August 12—In the afternoon, 30 or 40 British vessels came through the Narrows, and joined the fleet.

August 13—A number more of ships, some of them very large, came in and joined the fleet: the ships up the river fell a little lower down.

August 14—Our General rode to Horn's Hook and Kingsbridge. The person who had the direction of the fire-vessels requested him to be a spectator on the bank of the river, of an attempt, intended to be made on that night, to burn the ships. Attended by Gen. Clinton, and several other officers, they waited on the bank until about mid night; but no attempt on the ships was made, and they returned disappointed.

August 16—Our General was again requested to be a spectator on the bank of the river, the approaching night, with the most positive assurances that he should not be again disappointed: he accordingly went, attended as on the preceding time, and took a proper position on the bank. The night was pretty dark; they soon found that the gallies and fire-vessels were silently moving up with the tide. After some time, and almost immediately after the sentinels on board the British ships had passed the word "*all is well*," two of the fire-vessels flashed into a blaze; the one, close on the side of the *Phenix*, the other grappling one of the tenders. To appearance, the flames were against the side of the *Phenix*; and there was much confusion on board. A number of cannon were discharged into the fire-vessel, in order to sink her. A number of seamen ascended, and got out on the yardarm, supposed to clear away some grapplings. The fire-vessel was alongside, as was judged, near ten minutes, when the *Phenix* either cut, or slipped her cable, let fall her fore-topsail, wore round, and stood up the river, being immediately veiled from the spectators by the darkness of the night.

The tender burnt down to the water's edge, and was towed to the shore by the Americans; out of which was taken, one iron six-pounder, two three-pounders, one two-pounder, ten swivels, a caboose, some gun-barrels, cutlasses, grapplings, chains, etc. The *Rose*, and the two other tenders, remained at their moorings; but it was said that one of the tenders was deserted by her crew, for a time. Several of our gallies were said to have been inactive; otherwise, a very considerable advantage would have been reaped. The Americans sustained no loss or injury, save one man, who, in communicating fire to one of the vessels, got considerably burnt in the face, hands, etc.

August 17—The Commander in Chief having ordered our General to take the command of the troops and posts, at the north end of the island, and above Kingsbridge, within which command fell the Forts Washington and Independence, and a number of other works, he took the command accordingly.

August 18—Very early in the morning, the wind being pretty fresh, and it being very rainy, the ships and tenders which were up the river got under sail and ran down, keeping as close under the east bank as they could, in passing our works. They were, however, briskly cannonaded at Fort Washington and the works below: were several times struck, but received no material damage. They joined their fleet near Staten Island.

August 19—It was made pretty certain, that the British were upon the point of making an attack somewhere. By an express, which our General received from Gen. Washington, at half past two o'clock, a.m. of the 22nd, he was pleased to communicate, that, by intelligence which he had received, the enemy had intentions of making attacks on Long Island, up the North River, upon Bergen Point, Elizabeth-Town Point, Amboy, etc. Perhaps so many places were mentioned, in order to divide the force of, and distract the Americans. On this morning, however, they landed, near Gravesend Bay, on Long Island, about 8000 men; Col. Hand,[37] with his rifle corps, retreating moderately before them, and destroying some wheat which would fall into their hands. The British advanced as far as Flatbush, where they halted. Six American regiments were sent over, as a reinforcement. Gen. Sullivan had the command on the island.

August 24—There were some skirmishes on Long Island; but nothing very material.

August 25—A number of the enemy's ships fell down towards the Narrows; it was supposed, with intent to land more troops on Long Island.

August 26—In the morning, a brisk cannonade on Long Island, for some time. The British had thrown up some works, at Flatbush, from which they fired at the Americans.

August 27—Early in the morning, two ships and a brig came to anchor a little above Frog Point. Our General immediately detached Col. Graham[38] with his regiment, to prevent their landing to plunder or burn. Before he arrived, several barges full of men landed on New City Island, and killed a number of cattle. Two companies of the regiment, immediately on their arrival, ferried over to the island. The enemy carried off one man and 14 cattle the remainder of the cattle were secured.

On the same day there was a most bloody battle on Long Island,[39] between the Americans and the British. The British, by a long circuitous march in the night of the 26th with a part of their army, found the left of the Americans not so well secured as it ought to have been; and they had an opportunity to reach ground which gave them great advantage, while it equally exposed the Americans in the strong grounds towards Flatbush. There was here also another circumstance of ground, which now proved very disadvantageous to the Americans. There was a considerable marsh, into which a creek ran, and on which there was a mill, known by the name of McGowan's. At the mill there was a pass way over; but unluckily, when some of the Americans had retreated by this mill (for they were soon routed by the British, who formed an attack almost in a semi-circle) it was set on fire. This would have been a politic step, had all the Americans on the other side, in that quarter, previously passed; but those still beyond the creek were now driven to almost desperate circumstances: they could not pass at the head of the creek , for the British column, which made the circuitous movement, were in possession of the ground on the left; consequently many were here killed or taken prisoners, and numbers perishing in attempting to get over the creek, some of them sticking in the mud. Those who escaped retreated to the American works. The British sustained a considerable loss in killed and wounded, and a subaltern and 23 men were taken prisoners; but the American loss was far greater in killed, wounded, and prisoners. Among the latter were Gen. Sullivan and Lord Stirling. Several field-pieces were also lost. At evening, the British army encamped in front of the Americans.

On the morning of August 28, there was a skirmish between the Americans and die British which terminated rather in favor of the former. The same night, the British began to open works, at the distance of about 600 yards from the American works on the left. Gen. Washington wrote to our General, to send down to the city all the boats that could be spared, from Kingsbridge and Fort Washington; intimating, that he might possibly find it necessary, at night, to throw over more troops to Long Island. This order was immediately complied with, and the boats sent down; while the real intention of their use was fully understood.

August 29—The ships on the East River fell down to Hunt's Point. On the same night, the Americans evacuated Long Island, bringing off their military stores, provisions, etc. Some heavy cannon were left. In this retreat from the island, and which was well conducted, an instance of discipline and of true fortitude was exhibited by the American guards and pickets. In order that the British should not get knowledge of the withdraw of the Americans, until their main body had embarked in the boats and pushed off from the shore (which was a matter of the highest importance to their safety) the guards were ordered to continue at their respective posts, with sentinels alert, as if nothing extraordinary was taking place, until the troops had embarked: they were then to come off, march briskly to the ferry, and embark themselves. But somehow or other, the guards came off, and had got well toward the landing place, when they were ordered to face about, march back, and re-occupy their former posts; which they instantly obeyed, and continued at them, until called off to cross the ferry. Whoever has seen troops in a similar situation, or duly contemplates the human heart in such trials, will know how to appreciate the conduct of these brave men, on this occasion.

August 31—In the forenoon, the British appeared at Newtown, where they pitched a number of tents. Governor's Island was evacuated the preceding night by the Americans. It was now evident that the next object of the enemy would be to get the city; and it was equally so, that they would land somewhere on the island without it. This night, several of the regiments of Gen. Mifflin's brigade, of our General's division, lay on the hills towards New York; and Gen. Clinton's brigade on their arms. The same evening, Hand's, Shee's, Magaw's, Broadhead's, and Miles'[40] battalions, joined our General's division. Some of these corps had suffered greatly, in the action on Long Island.

September 1—The British appeared to be encamped in several places on Long Island. They had run in a ship between Nutten Island and Red Hook.

September 2—They ran a ship past the city up the East River: she was several times struck by the shot of a 12-pounder, which was drawn to the river's bank. Major Crane of the artillery was wounded in the foot, by a cannon shot from this ship. It was now a question, whether to defend the city, or evacuate it, and occupy the strong grounds above. Every exertion had been made to render the works both numerous and strong; and immense labor and expense had been bestowed on them; and it was now determined that the city should be obstinately defended.

September 4—Gen. Washington came up, and dined at our General's quarters. The same day, a detachment of the artillery, with one 24-pounder, three 12-pounders, three three-pounders, and a howitzer, joined the division. The enemy were plundering cattle on Long Island, now fully in their possession.

September 5—Our General ordered a chain of videttes[41] and sentinels to be formed at Morrisania, Hunt's and Frog's Point, etc. The British were pressing a great number of teams on Long Island their headquarters were at Bedford.

September 7—The militia on Long Island were ordered to muster, to raise recruits for the King. The General Officers of the American army were in council, at headquarters in New York. The British were now erecting a work, nearly opposite to ours at Horn's Hook, and the distance not great.

September 8—The British opened their battery against Horn's Hook Fort. The fire was briskly returned. The Americans had one man killed, and two wounded.

September 9—In the morning there was a brisk cannonade on both sides. At Horn's Hook, the American artillery was so well plied that the British ceased firing. The British were said to be encamped in three divisions; one at Newtown, which was headquarters, one at Flushing, and one at Jamaica.

September 10—The British landed a number of troops on Montresor's Island.

September 11—The British continued to cannonade and bombard our fort at Horn's Hook, and to land more troops on Montresor's Island.

September 12—The cannonade continued against our fort at Horn's Hook, and the British were moving their troops to wards the East River. This day, Col. Ward's regiment of Connecticut troops removed from Burditt's Ferry, and joined our General's division. The General Officers were in council. A former resolution to defend the city was rescinded, with three dissentients.

September 13—Four British ships, one of which was a two-decker, ran by the city up the East River. The cannonade and bombardment at Horn's Hook continued. This evening, Col. Chester,[42] with five regiments, joined our General's division.

September 14—The British sent three or four ships up the North River, as far as Greenwich. The cannon and stores were removing from New York, during the night.

September 15—About noon, the British landed at Kepp's Bay.[43] They met with but small resistance, and pushed towards the city, of which they took possession in the afternoon. They availed themselves of some cannon and stores; but their booty was not very great. Here the Americans, we are sorry to say, did not behave well; and here it was, as fame hath said, that Gen. Washington threw his hat on the ground, and exclaimed, "Are these the men with which I am to defend America?"

But several things may have weight here; the wounds received on Long Island were yet bleeding; and the officers, if not the men, knew that the city was not to be defended. Maj. Chapman[44] was killed, and Brig. Maj. Wyllys[45] was taken prisoner. A few others were killed, wounded, and taken prisoners. The Americans retreated up the island; and some few, who could not get out of the city that way, escaped in boats over to Paulus Hook, across the river. The house in the fort at Horn's Hook, was set on fire by a shell, and burnt down. The fort was afterwards abandoned.

September 16—A little before noon, a smart skirmish happened on the heights west of Haarlem Plain, and south of Morris's house, between a party of Hessian Jägers, British Light-Infantry and Highlanders, and the American rifle men and some other troops, which ended in favor of the latter. The troops fought well on both sides, and gave great proof of their marksmanship. The Americans had several officers killed and wounded; among the former, Lt. Col. Knowlton, of the Connecticut line, and Capt. Gleason,[46] of Nixon's Massachusetts regiment, two excellent officers; and Maj. Leitch,[47] of one of the southern regiments, a brave officer, was among the latter. This skirmish might have brought on a general action; for both armies were then within supporting distance of the troops which were engaged.

It now became an object of high importance to calculate, if possible, where the British would make their next attempt; and here the General Officers were divided in opinion. A part of them imagined that the British would first endeavor to make themselves masters of the whole of New York Island, and that, therefore, the reduction of Fort Washington and its dependencies would be their object. Others supposed, that they would make a landing either at Morrisania, Hunt's or Frog's Point, which eventually would produce as certain a reduction of the works on the island, with very little loss to the British. It was therefore determined in council, to guard against both; and for this purpose, 10,000 men were to be retained on the island, at and near Fort Washington. Our General's division was to be augmented to 10,000 men, and a floating bridge was to be thrown across Haarlem Creek, that these two bodies might communicate with and support each other, as circumstances might require; and Maj. Gen. Greene was to command the flying camp on the Jersey side of the Hudson, which was to consist of 5000. The different arrangements took place accordingly.

September 17—The remains of Lt. Col. Knowlton were interred with military honors. The same day, a troop of militia light-horse arrived from Connecticut; others, and many of the militia were on their way to join the army.

September 18—Gen. Parsons'[48] and Scott's[49] brigades, and the brigade commanded by Col. Dudley Sargent, joined our General's division; and Shee's, Magaw's, Haslet's,[50] Atlee's,[51] and Broadhead's battalions were ordered away. The British army encamped between the American army and the city. A picket from our General's division, of 450 men, constantly mounted, by relief, at Morrisania; from which a chain of sentinels, within half gunshot of each other, were planted, from the one side of the shore to the other, and near the water passage, between Morrisania and Montresor's Island, which in some places is very narrow. The sentinels on the American side were ordered not to presume to fire at those of the British, unless the latter began; but the British were so fond of beginning, that there was frequently a firing between them. This having been the case one day, and a British officer walking along the bank, on the Montresor's side, an American sentinel, who had been exchanging some shots with a British sentinel, seeing the officer, and concluding him to be better game, gave him a shot, and wounded him. He was carried up to the house on the island. An officer, with a flag, soon came down to the creek, and called for the American officer of the picket, and informed him, that if the American sentinels fired any more, the commanding officer on the island would cannonade Col. Morris's[52] house, in which the officers of the picket quartered.

The American officer immediately sent up to our General, to know what answer should be returned. He was directed to inform the British officer, that the American sentinels had always been instructed not to fire on sentinels, unless they were first fired upon, and then to return the fire; that such would be their conduct: as to the cannonading of Col. Morris's house, they might act their pleasure. The firing ceased for some time; but a raw Scotch sentinel having been planted one day, he very soon after discharged his piece at an American sentinel, nearest to him, which was immediately returned; upon which a British officer came down, and called to the American officers, observing that he thought there was to be no firing between the sentinels. He was answered, that their own began; upon which he replied, "He shall then pay for it." The sentinel was directly after relieved, and there was no firing between the sentinels, at that place, anymore; and they were so civil to each other, on their posts, that one day, at a part of the creek where it was practicable, the British sentinel asked the American, who was nearly opposite to him, if he could give him a chew of tobacco: the latter, having in his pocket a piece of a thick twisted roll, pent it across the creek, to the British sentinel, who, after taking off his bite, sent the remainder back again.

September 20—The Commander in Chief, Maj. Gen. Putnam, and some other officers, came up to our General's division, and rode round the camp, which, by the return, given in on the next day, consisted of 8771; but of these there was 1294 sick present, and 1108 sick absent.

September 21—Between one and two o'clock, the light of a great fire was discovered to the southward, which proved to be at New York; when a considerable part of the city was consumed.

September 22—Two seamen, belonging to *La Brune*, a British ship of war, which lay near Montresor's Island, deserted, and came to our General's quarters; and informed him, upon examination, that the British had then but a few men on the island, stating the number; that the piece of cannon, which had been put on the island, was taken back again, on board *La Brune*; that there were a number of officers at the house, in which there was a considerable quantity of baggage deposited, etc. Our General supposed that these troops might be easily taken; and, having called the General Officers of his division together, took their opinion, who all coincided with him in sentiment. He then communicated his intention to the Commander in Chief, who gave it his approbation.

Two hundred and forty men were destined for this enterprise: the command was given to Lt. Col. Michael Jackson, of the Massachusetts line, with Majors Logan[53] and 172_____, whose name cannot be recollected, of the New York troops. They were to embark on board three flat-boats, covered by a fourth with a detachment of artillery, with a light three-pounder, in case it should be found necessary in retreating from the island. The mode of attack was settled, and every circumstance secured, to promise success. They were to fall down Haarlem Creek with the ebb. The time was so calculated, that the young flood was to be so much made, at the break of day, as to cover the flats at the island, sufficiently for the boats to float. Matters being thus settled, our General ordered the two sailors to be brought in: he then told them that in consequence of their information, an enterprise against the British troops on Montresor's Island was to take place that night; that he had ordered them to be kept in safe custody until the next morning, when, if their declarations respecting the state of the British on the island proved to be true, he would give them a passport to the back country, whither they wished to go; but, in case their information was false, he would order them hanged immediately, as spies; that he gave them the opportunity, if they had made a wrong statement to him, then to correct it. They both answered, with perfect composure, that they would cheerfully submit to the condition.

Major Thomas Henly was now one of our General's Aides-de-camp. He importuned that he might go with the detachment. He was refused, and told that he had no business there; that he could exercise no command. He grew quite impatient, returned again to the General's room, and addressed him: "Pray, Sir, consent to my going with the party—let me have the pleasure of introducing the prisoners to you tomorrow." All his friends present advised him not to go. The General finally consented. The troops, at the hour assigned, embarked. Our General informed them, that he, with others, would be spectators of the scene, from a certain point near Haarlem Creek. Notice had been given to the guards and pickets on the York Island side, not to bail the party as they went down.

Unfortunately, the lower sentinel had not been so instructed. He was nearly opposite to the point where our General was to be; and just at the instant when he arrived, had challenged the boats, and ordered them to come to the shore. From the boats they answered, "Low! We are friends." The challenge was repeated. The answer was, "We tell you we are friends—hold your tongue." A bounce into the water was heard; and instantly Maj. Henly came wading to the shore, stepped up to our General, caught him by the hand, and said, "Sir, will it do?" Our General, holding him by the hand, replied, "I see nothing to the contrary;" to which Henly concluded by saying, "Then it shall do." He waded back to his boat, and got in. The sentinel called again: "If you don't come to the shore, I tell you I'll fire." A voice from some one in the boats, was, "Pull away!" The boats went on and the sentinel fired his piece. The boats reached the island almost at the moment intended, just as the glimmer of dawn was discoverable. The three field-officers were in the first boat. Their intention, on the moment of landing, was, for the two seconds in command to spring, the one to the right, and the other to the left, and lead on the troops from the other two boats, which were to land on each side of the first boat.

The field officers landed, and the men from their boat. The enemy's guard charged them, but were instantly driven back. The men in the other two boats, instead of landing, lay upon their oars. The British, seeing this, returned warmly to the charge. The Americans, finding themselves thus deserted, returned to their boat; but not until Lt. Col. Jackson received a musket-ball in his leg, and Maj. Henly, as he was getting into the boat, one through his heart, which put an instant end to his life. The boats joined the others, and they all returned, having, in the whole, about 14 killed, wounded and missing; Maj. Henly deeply regretted. Had only one of the other boats landed her men, the success would have been very probable; but the two would have insured an execution of the whole plan, in the opinion of all concerned. The delinquents in the other boats were arrested, and tried by court-martial, and one of the Captains cashiered.[54]

September 23—The British got possession of the works at Paulus Hook. The Americans had previously taken off all the cannon and stores. On the afternoon of the 24th, the remains of Maj. Henly were interred by the side of Lt. Col. Knowlton, on New York Island, with military honors.

September 25—The militia, which had come out from the western parts of the State of Connecticut, were discharged.

September 26—The General Officers were in council with a committee of Congress, sent to make inquiry into the condition of the army, and agree upon the necessary augmentation.

September 27—The Council set again. The same day, Maj. Gen. Sullivan, who had for some time been a prisoner with the British, came to headquarters. The American prisoners which were taken in Canada, were sent round by water, and landed at Bergen Point, New Jersey, where they were set at liberty. Gen. Thompson was among them.

September 28—Seven recruits for Maj. Rogers's[55] corps, raising for British service, were taken, going to Long Island, and sent in.

September 29—There was an unusual movement of boats from Long Island to Montresor's Island, and an attack was soon expected.

September 30—The moving over of boats to Montresor's Island continued. The same day, a frigate went through Dell Gate, and came to anchor about 10 o'clock, a.m. near *La Brune*. At 12 o'clock, she came to sail, and stood to the eastward. Just at evening another ship came up; and the next morning, October 1, was at anchor in the channel, between Haarlem and Baman's[56] or Eldridge's Island.

October 3—The Brigadier-Generals of our General's division were in council, and several new works were laid out; among others, a redoubt on the hill above Williams's Bridge. Our General, in reconnoitering his position, accompanied by Col. Hand, below the camp of the rifle corps, being apprehensive that the British might land on Frog's Neck, took a view of the causeway between West-Chester and the point. Upon the creek, which runs between these two, is a tide-mill and a plank bridge: at the mill, at the west end of the causeway (the side of the American army) was at this time a range of cord-wood, as advantageously situated to cover a party to defend the pass, as if constructed for the very purpose. After taking a full view, our General directed Col. Hand, immediately upon his return to his camp, to fix upon one of the best subaltern officers, and 25 picked men of his corps, and assign them to this pass, as their alarm-post at all times; and, in case the enemy made a landing on Frog's Neck, to direct this officer immediately to take up the planks of the bridge; to have every thing in readiness to set the mill on fire; but not to do it, unless the fire of the riflemen should appear insufficient to check the advance of the enemy on to the causeway; to assign another party to the head of the creek; to reinforce both, in case the enemy landed; and that he should be supported. Col. Hand made his arrangements accordingly.

October 4—The brig and tenders in the East River came down, and cast anchor near *La Brune* frigate; and the *Roebuck* and *Phenix* sailed up the North River, and joined the other ships which lay at anchor there.

October 5—There were some movements among the British; and a party appeared to be very busy at work, a little be low Haarlem. The same night, the Americans left the heights of Bergen. They were upwards of 2000 strong. They retreated as far back as Burditt's Ferry.

October 6—Orders were given for throwing up a new work on Haarlem Creek, below the wood at Morrisania.

October 7—Gen. Lincoln came to camp. He had come from Massachusetts with a body of militia. This was the first of his joining the main army. The same day the British were putting over horses from Horn's Hook to Long Island, and fixing their pontoons.

October 9—Early in the morning, three ships, two of 40 guns, and one frigate, with two or three tenders, stood up the North River. They were briskly cannonaded from Fort Washington and Fort Constitution. They however passed our works and the chevaux-de-frise; the American galleys, small craft, and two large ships standing on before them. The two ships were ran on shore near Phillips's[57] mills, and two of the galleys near Dobbs' Ferry. The enemy took possession of the two galleys, and got them off. A boat landed a number of men, who plundered a store, stove the casks, and then set the store on fire, and left it. The Americans soon extinguished the fire.

Our General ordered Col. Sargent, with 500 infantry, 40 light-horse, Capt. Horton[58] of the artillery, with two 12-pounders, and Capt. Crafts[59] with a howitzer, to march immediately, with all possible expedition, to Dobbs' Ferry. The enemy took a schooner loaded with rum, sugar, wine, etc. and sunk a sloop, which had on board the machine, invented by, and under the direction of, a Mr. Bushnell,[60] intended to blow up the British ships. This machine was worked under water. It conveyed a magazine of powder, which was to be fixed under the keel of a ship, then freed from the machine, and left with clock-work going, which was to produce fire when the machine had got out of the way. Mr. Bushnell had great confidence of its success, and had made several experiments which seemed to give him countenance; but its fate was truly a contrast to its design.

Our General's division was formed in line, with its advance, reserve, flank-guards, and artillery, all in order of battle, when they were moved down over the different grounds, which it was supposed might be the scene of action. Some of this ground was very broken, and there were many fences. These afforded frequent opportunities for the troops to break off and form; for the pioneers to open avenues, etc. and for the whole to become acquainted with every part of the ground, and the best choice of it, if suddenly called to action.

October 10—One of the ships which was ran aground, was got off by the Americans. Col. Sargent returned, having left 180 men to watch the motions of the British up the river.

October 11—There was a considerable movement among the British boats below. This afternoon, Gen. Washington's pleasure-boat, coming down the river with a fresh breeze, and a topsail hoisted, was supposed, by the artillerists at Mount Washington to be one of the British tenders running down. A 12-pounder was discharged at her, which was so exactly pointed as unfortunately to kill three Americans, who were much lamented. The same day, several of Gen. Lincoln's regiments arrived, two of which were posted on the North River.

October 12—Early in the morning, 80 or 90 British boats, full of men, stood up the sound, from Montresor's Island, Long Island, etc. The troops landed at Frog's Neck, and their advance pushed towards the causeway and bridge, at West Chester mill. Col. Hand's riflemen took up the planks of the bridge, as had been directed, and commenced a firing with their rifles. The British moved towards the head of the creek, but found here also the Americans in possession of the pass. Our General immediately (as he had assured Col. Hand he would do) ordered Col. Prescott, the hero of Bunker Hill, with his regiment, and Capt. Lt. Bryant of the artillery, with a three-pounder, to reinforce the riflemen at West Chester causeway; and Col. Graham of the New York line, with his regiment, and Lt. Jackson of the artillery, with a six-pounder, to reinforce at the head of the creek; all of which was promptly done, to the check and disappointment of the enemy. The British encamped on the Neck. The riflemen and Jägers kept up a scattering popping at each other across the marsh; and the Americans on their side, and the British on the other, threw up a work at the end of the causeway. Capt. Bryant, now and then, when there was an object, saluted the British with a field-piece. In the afternoon, 40 or 50 sail of vessels passed up, and came to anchor off Frog's Point. The same evening, Gen. McDougall's[61] brigade joined our General's division.

October 13—The brigade formerly under the command of our General, when he was Brigadier, joined his division. The division now became very strong. The General Officers of the army were this day in council, at our General's quarters.

October 14—Our General, with the Generals under his command, reconnoitered the enemy at Frog's Neck; afterwards, the General Officers of the army reconnoitered the various grounds. The same day, Maj. Gen. Lee was ordered to the command of the troops above Kingsbridge, now become the largest part of the American army. But Gen. Washington had desired him not to exercise the command for a day or two, until he could make himself acquainted with the post, its circumstances, and arrangements of duty. A great number of sloops, boats, etc. were passing the Sound eastward, just at dusk probably conveying ammunition, provisions, etc. to the troops at Frog's Point.

October 15—Five sailors came off from La Brune. They informed, that there was a large body of the British on Frog's Point, and that an attack might soon be expected. The scattering fire across the marsh continued, and now and then a man was killed.

October 16—Two works were discovered on Frog's Neck, nearly finished. The General Officers of the army rode to reconnoiter the ground at Pell's Neck, etc. and it was determined that the position of the American army should be immediately changed; the left flank to be extended more northerly, to prevent its being turned by the British.

October 17—Wadsworth's[62] and Fellows's[63] brigades came to Kingsbridge. The British shipping, etc. continued moving eastward.

October 18—The regiment at West Chester causeway had been relieved by another. The officer on command there, this morning, sent up an express to our General, informing him that the British were opening an embrasure in their work at the

end of the cause way, and that he apprehended they intended, under a cannonade
from this, to attempt to pass. Our General
ordered one of his aides to gallop his horse
to the officer commanding the brigade,
near Valentine's, the nearest to West
Chester, and order him to form his brigade
instantly. Arriving, himself, by the time
the brigade was formed, he ordered the
officer to march, with the utmost expedition, to the head of the causeway, to reinforce the troops there; himself moving on
with them. When the troops had advanced
to about half the way between the head of
the creek and the post at the head of the
causeway, another express met him,
informing him that the whole British army
were in motion, and seemed to be moving
to wards the pass at the head of the creek.

Upon this, the brigade was ordered
to halt, the whole to prime and load, and
the rear regiment to file off by the left, and
march briskly to reinforce the Americans
at the pass, at the head of the creek. At

Maj. Gen. Alexander McDougall.

this instant, Gen. Washington came up, and having inquired of our General the state
of things, ordered him to return immediately, and have his division formed ready for
action, and to take such a position as might appear best calculated to oppose the
enemy, should they attempt to land another body of troops on Morrisania, which he
thought not improbable. Our General immediately obeyed the order. The wind was
now fresh at southwest. The British crossed to the other side of Frog's Neck, embarked
onboard their boats, crossed over the cove, landed on Pell's Neck, and moved briskly
upwards. Three or four of the American regiments advanced towards them, and took
a good position behind a stone fence. When the British had advanced sufficiently
near, they gave them a pretty close fire, which checked them, and even obliged them
to fall back; but being immediately supported, they returned vigorously to the charge.
The action was sharp, for a short time; but the Americans were soon obliged to give
way to superior force. Shepard's, Read's, Baldwin's and Glover's[64] regiments, had the
principal share in this action. The Americans had between 30 and 40 men killed and
wounded; among the latter, Col. Shepard, in the throat, not mortally, although the
ball came well nigh effecting instant death. The loss of the British was not known,
but must have been considerable. They advanced almost to New Rochelle, and halted.
The American army extended its left.

A number of boats went down towards New York. It now became necessary,
immediately to quit the position in the neighborhood of Kingsbridge, the British
being in the rear of the left of our army; and it is not a little unaccountable that they
did not attempt to stretch them selves across to the Hudson, which might have been
done with great ease. They only moved higher up, on the other side of the little rivulet

Bronx, which was generally fordable. The White Plains were fixed upon for the next position of the American army. A strong garrison was to be left at Fort Washington, and our General was to leave one of his regiments, to garrison Fort Independence.

October 21—At about four o'clock p.m. our General's division moved from above Kingsbridge, having, besides their light field-pieces, two heavy iron 12-pounders. About eight o'clock in the evening, they passed Gen. Lincoln's quarters on Valentine's Hill, where the Commander in Chief was to spend the night. Our General waited upon him, to know if he had any particular commands for him. The Commander in Chief only advised to send forward one of his regiments, to occupy the road coming from Ward's Bridge, nearly to whose farm the British had now advanced; lest, apprised of his moving, they should annoy his right flank, which, if it had been day-light, would have been open to their view: But before the column reached this cross road, it was learnt that Col. Jonathan Brewer's[65] regiment of artificers, who were pretty strong, and well armed, were to pass the night at the entrance of the road, leading to the bridge before mentioned. The division reached Chatterton's Hill, to the south of White Plains, at four o'clock in the morning of the 22nd, having marched all night.

The instant our General ascended the hill, he noticed, to appearance, many flashes, resembling the flash of the pan of a musket, on the other side of the lot; on which he immediately ordered a Captain, with a party, to discover what it was; who returned, that he could not make discovery of any thing. These were indeed the flashes of discharged muskets at some distance; the height of ground having decoyed the appearance of the distance. Lord Stirling, who was before in this vicinity with his brigade, had formed an enterprise against Maj. Rogers's corps. The old Indian hunter in the late French war, who had now engaged in the British service, with his corps, now lay on the out-post of the British army, near Mamaroneck. The enterprise was conducted with good address; and if the Americans had known exactly how Rogers' corps lay, they would probably have killed or taken the whole. As it was, 36 prisoners, 60 muskets, and some other articles were taken. The Major, conformably to his former general conduct, escaped with the rest of his corps. This was a pretty affair; and if the writer could recollect the name of the commanding officer, with pride and pleasure he would insert it.[66] He belonged to one of the southern lines of the army; and the whole of the party were southern troops.

The same day, our General moved his division, and took post on the high strong ground, to the north of the courthouse. Gen. Sullivan's division reached the Plains in the course of the succeeding night. In the position of White Plains, our General's division was on the left of the line. On his left was a deep hollow, through which ran a small brook, which came from a mill-pond a little above. On the east side of this hollow was a very commanding ground, which would enfilade the division. The top of this high ground was covered with wood. To this hill he ordered Col. Malcolm,[67] with his regiment of New York troops, and Lt. Fenno[68] of the artillery, with a field-piece, directing them to take post in the skirt of the wood, at the south brow of the hill. The ground, from our General's left to the right, descended gradually a very considerable distance, and then gradually ascended up to the plain, and still on to the right, to more commanding ground. On this was the American army formed, the line running nearly from northeast to southwest. There were some strong works thrown up on the plain, across the road, and still to the right of it. Chatterton's Hill was a little advanced of the line, and separated from it by the little rivulet Bronx. A body of the Americans were posted on this hill. Headquarters were on the plain, near the crossroads. Our General's division had only slight works for musketry.

October 23—A cannonade was heard towards the Hudson. The same evening, Col. Tyler's, Huntington's, and Throop's[69] regiments, of General Parson's brigade, and of our General's division, moved, and took post at the head of King-street, near Eye Pond. Gen. Lee's division had not yet got up to the army.

October 24—At five o'clock, a.m. a firing of small arms was heard to the southward. It was a skirmish between 200 men of Gen. Lee's division, and 250 Hessians 10 of the latter were killed, and two taken prisoners. The British continued moving up, but with great caution, their rear scarcely advancing, when they came to encamp again, much further than where the advance had moved from they advanced in two columns.

October 25—Eight American regiments were ordered to be ready to march in the approaching night. Gen. Putnam was to command them; and they were intended to make an attack on the enemy's advance, if it should appear to be practicable. The same morning, one 12-pounder at Dobbs' Ferry drove the British man-of-war off that place from her station.

October 26—Gen. Lee's division joined the army. In ascending some of the hills on the road, this division, encumbered with many wagons, was obliged to halt, and double the teams, in open view of the British, and at no considerable distance, who did not attempt to disturb them; which, had they done, the loss of the cannon, wagons, etc. could not have been avoided. The troops would have bent their march unencumbered towards the Hudson; but the wagon, etc. must have been left. Two or three British soldiers and a Hessian were taken prisoners, and sent in.

October 27—In the forenoon, a heavy cannonade was heard to wards Fort Washington. Thirteen Hessians and two or three British soldiers were sent in on this day. From the American camp to the west-south-west, there appeared to be a very commanding height, worthy of attention. The Commander in Chief ordered the General Officers who were off duty, to attend him to reconnoiter this ground, on this morning. When arrived at the ground, although very commanding, it did not appear so much so as other grounds to the north, and almost parallel with the left of the army, as it was then formed.

"Yonder," says Maj. Gen. Lee, pointing to the grounds just mentioned, "is the ground we ought to occupy." "Let us go and view it," replied the Commander in Chief. When on the way, a light horseman came up in full gallop, his horse almost out of breath, and addressed Gen. Washington, "The British are on the camp, Sir." The General observed, "Gentlemen, we have now other business than reconnoitering," putting his horse in full gallop for the camp, and followed by the other officers. When arrived at headquarters, the Adjutant-General (Reed)[70] who had remained at camp, informed the Commander in Chief that the guards had been all beat in, and the whole American army were now at their respective posts, in order of battle. The Commander in Chief turned round to the officers, and only said, "Gentlemen, you will repair to your respective posts, and do the best you can." Our General, on arriving at his own division, found them all in the lines; and, from the height of his post, found that the first attack was directed against the Americans on Chatterton's Hill.

The little river Bronx, which ran between the American right and this hill, after running round its north side, turned and ran down on the east and southeast. The

British advanced in two columns. At this instant, the cannonade was brisk on both sides; directed by the British across the hollow and Bronx, against the Americans on the hill, and by them returned. Almost at the same instant, the right column, composed of British troops, preceded by about 20 light-horse in full gallop, and brandishing their swords, appeared on the road leading to the court-house, and now directly in the front of our General's division. The light-horse leaped the fence of a wheat-field, at the foot of the hill, on which Col. Malcolm's regiment was posted; of which the light-horse were not aware, until a shot from Lt. Fenno's fieldpiece gave them notice, by striking in the midst of them, and a horseman pitching from his horse. They then wheeled short about, galloped out of the field as fast as they came in, rode behind a little hill in the road, and faced about; the tops of their caps only being visible to our General, where he stood. The column came no further up the road, but wheeled to the left by platoons, as they came up; and passing through a bar, or gateway, directed their head towards the troops on Chatterton's Hill, now engaged. When the head of the column had got nearly across the lot, their front got out of sight; nor could the extent of their rear be now discovered.

The sun shone bright, their arms glittered, and perhaps troops never were shown to more advantage than these now appeared. The whole now halted; and for a few minutes, the men all sat down in the same order in which they stood, no one appearing to move out of his place. The cannonade continued brisk across the Bronx. A part of the left column, composed of British and Hessians, forded the river, and marched along under the cover of the hill, until they had gained sufficient ground to the left of the Americans; when, by facing to the left, their column became a line, parallel with the Americans. When they briskly ascended the hill, the first column resumed a quick march. As the troops which were advancing to the attack ascended the hill, the cannonade on the side of the British ceased; as their own men became exposed to their fire, if continued. The fire of small-arms was now very heavy, and without any distinction of sounds. This led some American officers, who were looking on, to observe that the British were worsted, as their cannon had ceased firing; but a few minutes evinced that the Americans were giving way. They moved off the hill in a great body, neither running nor observing the best order. The British ascended the hill very slowly; and when arrived at its summit, formed and dressed their line, without the least attempt to pursue the Americans. The loss on the side of the Americans was inconsiderable; that of the British was not then known. The British having got possession of this hill, it gave them a vast advantage of the American lines, almost down to the center.

October 29—The British began to throw up some small works on the hill, of which they had got possession. The Americans were drawing back; and a position was to be taken on the high strong grounds, before in the rear of a part of the army. The left of our General's division was not to move; but the remainder of his division, and all the other divisions of the army, were to fall back and form nearly east and west. About this time, Col. Lasher,[71] who belonged to our General's division (and who had been left with his regiment to garrison Fort Independence, near Kingsbridge) sent an express, who passed the enemy in the night, to know what he should do, the regiment growing weak and sickly. Our General applied to the Commander in Chief, to know his pleasure, who directed that the Colonel should give notice to Col. Magaw, who commanded at Fort Washington, that he might take away the cannon, stores, etc. and that Col. Lasher, after destroying the barracks, huts, etc. should join the army, which he soon affected. This day, three prisoners were sent in; and the Americans were throwing up some strong works on the high grounds.

October 30—The British remained upon the ground they had taken.

October 31—The British continued as before, throwing up a work, etc. At night, the Americans evacuated their works on the plain, near late headquarters, setting fire to several barns, and one house, which contained forage, and some stores that could not be removed.

November 1—In the morning, the British advanced with a number of field-pieces, to the north of the road, near late headquarters (a heavy column appearing behind on the hill, ready to move forward) and commenced a furious cannonade on our General's division, which was nobly returned by Capt. Lt. Bryant and Lt. Jackson,[72] of the artillery. Our General's first anxiety was for Col. Malcolm's regiment on the hill, to the east of the hollow on the left, lest the enemy should push a column into the hollow, and cut the regiment off from the division. He therefore ordered Maj. Keith,[73] one of his aides, to gallop over, and order Col. Malcolm to come off immediately, with Lt. Fenno's artillery: But, upon a more critical view of the ground in the hollow (at the head of which there was a stone wall, well situated to cover a body of troops to throw a heavy fire directly down it, while an oblique fire could be thrown in on both sides) he ordered Maj. Pollard,[74] his other aide, to gallop after Keith, and countermand the first order, and direct the Colonel to remain at his post, and he should be supported.

A strong regiment was ordered to the head of the hollow, to occupy the wall. The cannonade was brisk on both sides, through which the two Aides-de-camp passed, in going and returning. At this instant, Gen. Washington rode up to the hill. His first question to our General was, "How is your division?" He was answered, "They are all in order." "Have you," said the Commander in Chief, "any troops on the hill over the hollow?" He was answered, "Malcolm's regiment is there." "If you do not call them off immediately," says the General, "you may lose them, if the enemy pushes a column up the hollow." He was answered, that even in that case, their retreat should be made safe; that a strong regiment was posted at the bead of the hollow, behind the wall; that this regiment, with the oblique fire of the division, would so check the enemy, as to allow Malcolm to make a safe retreat. The Commander in Chief concluded by saying, "Take care that you do not lose them." The artillery of the division was so well directed as to throw the British artillerymen several times into confusion; and finding that they could not here make any impression, drew back their pieces, the column not advancing.

The British artillery now made a circuitous movement, and came down toward the American right. Here, unknown to them, were some 12-pounders; upon the discharge of which they made off with their field-pieces as fast as their horses could draw them. A shot from the American cannon at this place took off the head of a Hessian artilleryman. They also left one of the artillery horses dead on the field. What other loss they sustained was not known. Of our General's division, one man only, belonging to Col. Pawling's[75] regiment of New York troops, was killed. The British made no other attempt on the Americans, while they remained at White Plains. The two armies lay looking at each other, and within long cannon shot. In the nighttime, the British lighted up a vast number of fires, the weather growing pretty cold. These fires, some on the level ground, some at the foot of the hills, and at all distances to their brows, some of which were lofty, seemed to the eye to mix with the stars, and to be of different magnitudes. The American side, doubtless, exhibited to them a similar appearance. On this day, our General ordered three redoubts, with a line in front, to be thrown up on the summit of his post, so constructed that the whole of them could make a defense, and support each other at the same time, if attacked. These, to the enemy, in whose view they fully were, must have appeared very formidable, although they were designed principally for defense against small-arms; and perhaps works were never raised quicker. There were the stocks of a large cornfield at the spot: the pulling these up in hills, took up a large lump of earth with each. The roots of the stalks and earth on them, placed in the face of the works, answered the purpose of sods, or fascines: the tops being placed inwards, as the loose earth was thrown upon them, became as so many ties to the work, which was carried up with a dispatch scarcely conceivable.

The British, as they say, had meditated an attack on the Americans, which was only prevented by the wetness of the night. Be this as it may, our General had ordered his division, at evening roll-call, to be at their alarm-posts (which they every morning manned, whilst at the place) half an hour sooner than usual. He had then no other reason for doing this than the near position of the enemy, and the probability that they would soon make an attack. But the Commander in Chief must have made some other discovery; for, after our General was in bed, Col. Cary,[76] who was one of the Aides-de-camp of General Washington, came to the door of his marquee, and calling to him, informed him that the whole army were to be at their alarm-posts, the next morning, half an hour sooner than usual, and that he was to govern himself accordingly. Our General replied, that he had fortunately given such orders to his division, at evening roll call. He therefore neither got up himself, nor disturbed any other of his division.

November 3—The sentinels reported that, during the preceding night, they heard the rumbling of carriages to the south-eastward; and it was apprehended that the British were changing their position.

November 5—The British sentinels were withdrawn from their advanced posts. It was apprehended that they meant a movement. The American army was immediately ordered under arms. At two o'clock, p.m. the enemy appeared, formed on Chatterton's Hill, and on several hills to the westward of it. Several reconnoitering parties, who were sent out, reported that the enemy were withdrawing. About 12 o'clock, this night, a party of the Americans wantonly set fire to the courthouse, Dr. Graham's house, and several other private houses, which stood between the two armies.[77] This gave great disgust to the whole American army, and drew from the Commander in Chief the following paragraph, in his orders of the 6th: "It is with the utmost astonishment and abhorrence, the General is informed, that some base and cowardly wretches have, last night, set fire to the courthouse, and other buildings which the enemy left. The army may rely upon it, that they shall be brought to justice, and meet with the punishment they deserve." The British were moving down towards Dobbs' Ferry. A detachment from the American army was sent out in the morning to harass their rear, but could not come up with them.

November 7—Several deserters came in from the enemy: they reported that they were moving towards New York. The reconnoitering parties discovered them encamped near Dobbs' Ferry. They were foraging grain and hay, and driving in the cattle. Two store-ships had run up past Fort Washington.

November 8—The enemy continued encamped at and below Dobbs' Ferry. A new disposition of the American army was now to take place. The southern troops were to cross over into the Jersies. Gen. Lee, with his own, Spencer's, and Sullivan's divisions, were to remain, to secure and bring off the stores; and were then to follow into the Jersies. Our General was ordered to march with his division to Peek's Kill.

November 9—The division moved from near White Plains, and the same night halted at North-Castle.

November 10—In the afternoon, the division reached Peek's Kill. Gen. Washington arrived at the same place at about sunset. It was this day learnt, that Gen. Carleton's army in Canada, after pushing the Americans in that quarter from post to post, until they arrived at Ticonderoga, just made their appearance before that place, and then retired towards Quebec.

November 11—The Commander in Chief directed our General to attend him in taking a view of Fort Montgomery, and the other works up the river. Lord Stirling, Generals James and George Clinton, Gen. Mifflin and others were of the company. They went as far up the river as Constitution Island, which is opposite to West Point, the latter of which was not then taken possession of; but the glance of the eye at it, without going on shore, evinced that this post was not to be neglected. There was a small work and a block-house on Constitution Island. Fort Montgomery[78] was in considerable forwardness.

November 12—The Commander in Chief directed our General to ride early in the morning with him, to reconnoiter the grounds at the Gorge of the Highlands; and, on his return, gave him the command of the troops and posts in the Highlands, on both sides of the river, with written instructions to secure and fortify them with all possible expedition, making a distribution of his troops to the different posts; and, at about 10 o'clock, a.m. Gen. Washington crossed over the river into the Jersies.

November 13—Our General made a disposition of the troops under his command, to their several destinations. Col. Huntington's and Tyler's regiments, to the west side of the Hudson, to Sidnum's Bridge on Ramapo River, to cover the passes into the Highlands, on that side: Prescott's, Ward's and Wyllys's regiments, of Parsons's brigade (as were the other two regiments) to the south entrance of the Highlands, beyond Robinson's Bridge: Gen. George Clinton's brigade, to the heights above Peek's Kill Landing: Gen. Scott's brigade, with the three regiments of Gen. Parsons's brigade: Gen. James Clinton, with the troops under his command, were at the forts up the river. The British moved down, near to Kingsbridge.

November 16—The British made their attack on Fort Washington. General Knyphausen, with a heavy column of Hessians, advanced by Kingsbridge. They were discovered by the Americans, from the high grounds north of Fort Washington, as the day broke; and cannonaded from the field-pieces, placed at this advanced post. The Hessian column divided into two; the right ascending the strong broken ground towards Spuyten Duyvil Creek; the left nearer to the road, towards the Gorge. The first obtained the ground without much difficulty; but the Americans made a most noble opposition against the latter, and, for a considerable time, kept them from ascending the hill, making a terrible slaughter among them; but the great superiority of the assailants, with an unabating firmness, finally prevailed: their loss was greater here than at any other place.

Meanwhile, the British crossed Haarlem Creek, in two different places, charged, and finally routed the Americans on that side, and possessed themselves of the strong post on Laurel Hill, on the other side of the road from Fort Washington, and not very distant from it; Lord Percy at the same time advancing, with the troops under his command on the island, towards the fort on that side. The Americans, now generally driven from their out works, retired to the fort, which was crowded full. A single shell, now dropping among them, must have made dreadful havoc. Gen. Washington was now a spectator of this distressing scene, from the high bank at Fort Lee, on the opposite side of the Hudson; and having a wish to communicate something to Col. Magaw, the commanding officer at Fort Washington, Capt. Gooch[79] of Boston, a brave and daring man, offered to be the bearer of it. He ran down to the river, jumped into a small boat, pushed over the river, landed under the bank, ran up to the fort and delivered the message—came out, ran and jumped over the broken ground, dodging the Hessians, some of whom struck at him with their pieces, and others attempted to thrust him with their bayonets—escaping through them, he got to his boat, and returned to Fort Lee. The British had summoned Col. Magaw to surrender, and were preparing their batteries to play on the fort, when Col. Magaw thought it best to surrender the post, which he did accordingly, between two and three thousand men becoming prisoners.

The loss in killed and wounded, on the American side was inconsiderable; but the loss in prisoners was a serious blow indeed. The prisoners were marched to New York; where, being crowded in prisons and sugar-houses (many of them being militia from the Jersey flying-camp, who had been sent over to reinforce the garrison, and were unused to a soldier's life, much less to the poisonous stagnant air of a crowded prison), they fell sick, and daily died, in a most shocking manner. It was common, on a morning, for the car-men to come and take away the bodies for burial, *by loads!*— O ye officers of the provost! To whatever nation or people you belong, when the unfortunate of your fellow-men are thus committed to your charge, clothe yourselves with humanity, and soothe distress as far as in your power; for by this, you will secure a better reward than your present wages. And you who have the honor to command armies, when your victories have filled provosts and prisons, think it not beneath you to visit the prisons, that with your own eyes you may see the state of your prisoners: for such visits, the great Captain of your Salvation hath said, shall be considered as made to Himself; while it also gives you a name among men closely allied to that of the conqueror. The truly brave are always humane. Elated with the easy reduction of Fort Washington, the British determined to cross into the Jersies, and attack Gen. Washington on that side.

November 18—Lord Cornwallis, with a strong body of the British forces, landed at Closter Landing, on the Jersey side, above Fort Lee, the garrison of which were obliged to leave that post; and some cannon, stores and provisions, which could not be removed, fell into the hands of the enemy.

November 20—Just at evening, an express, which our General had sent down to Gen. Washington before he had any knowledge of what had happened, returned with a most alarming account of what he had seen with his own eyes, viz. that the Americans were rapidly retreating, and the British as rapidly pursuing. The Adjutant-General (Reed) wished to write to General Lee; but he had neither pen, ink, or paper with him. The light-horseman had a rough piece of wrapping-paper in his pocket, and the Adjutant-General had an old pencil. Bringing these two together, he wrote to Gen. Lee, "Dear General, we are flying from the British, I pray—" and the pencil broke. He then told the light-horseman to carry the paper to Gen. Lee, and tell him that he was verbally ordered to add, after *I pray*, "you to push and join us." The light-horseman, when he arrived at our General's, was both fatigued and wet. He requested that one of his brother horsemen might proceed to Gen. Lee; but he was told that no other could discharge the duty enjoined on him by the Adjutant-General, and that Gen. Lee might wish to make many inquiries of him. He was therefore refreshed and pushed on. Gen. Lee, instead of moving his division, or any part of it, wrote our General, by the returning express, the following letter.

> CAMP, Nov. 21st, 1776.
>
> DEAR GENERAL,
>
> I have just received a recommendation, not a positive order, from the General, to move the corps under my command to the other side of the river. This recommendation was, I imagine, on the presumption that I had already moved nearer to Peek's Kill. There is no possibility of crossing over Dobbs' Ferry, or at any place lower than King's Ferry, which to us would be such an immense round, that we could never answer any purpose. I must therefore desire and request, that you will order 2000 of your corps, under a Brigadier-General, to cross the river opposite the General, and wait his further orders. As soon as we have finished a necessary job, I will replace this number from hence, which job will, I believe, be finished tomorrow.
>
> I am, dear General, yours,
> (Signed) CHARLES LEE.
>
> Gen. HEATH.

Upon receiving this letter from Gen. Lee (for our General did not receive the least hint from Gen. Washington, to move any part of the troops under his command, by the express who brought the order to Lee) he took up his instructions from Gen. Washington, to see if he might dare to make any detachment; upon which he wrote Gen. Lee the following answer to his letter.

> PEEK'S KILL, Nov. 21st, 1776,
> 10 o'clock at night.
>
> DEAR GENERAL,
>
> I am now to acknowledge the receipt of your favors, of this date, the former of which I had answered early in the evening. With respect to the latter, upon having recourse to my instructions, I find they are such as not to admit of moving any part of the troops from the posts assigned to me, unless it be by

Maj. Gen. Charles Lee (Library of Congress).

express orders from his Excellency, or to support you, in case you are attacked. My instructions, among other things, are as follow:

Your division, with such troops as are now at Forts Montgomery, Independence and Constitution, are to be under your command, and remain in this quarter, for the security of the above posts, and the passes through the Highlands, from this place, and the one on the west side of Hudson's River. Unnecessary it is for me to say anything to evince the importance of securing the land and water communication through these passes, or to prove the indispensable necessity of using every exertion in your power, to have such works erected for the defense of them, as your own judgment, assisted by that of your Brigadiers and Engineer, may show the expediency of.

You will not only keep in view the importance of securing these passes, but the necessity of doing it without delay: Not only from the probability of the enemy's attempting to seize them, but from the advanced season, which will not admit of any spade-work, after the frost (which may daily be expected) sets in. Lose not a moment, therefore, in choosing the grounds on the east and west side of the river, on which your intended works are to be erected. Let your men designed for each post be speedily allotted, etc.

After Instructions so positive and pressing, you will readily agree that it would be very improper, in me, to order any of the troops from posts to which they are so expressly assigned, and from business which in his Excellency's view is so very important. Add to this, their present disposition is such, that to collect any thing near the number you mention, would occasion as great delay, and cause many of them to march nearly as far, as if sent immediately from your quarter.

I am, dear General, with esteem,
Yours respectfully, Gen. LEE.

(Signed) W. HEATH.

This did not seem to satisfy Gen. Lee, who wrote our General the following:

CAMP, Nov. 23rd, 1776.

SIR,

By your mode of reasoning, the General's instructions are so binding, that not a tittle must be broke through for the salvation of the General and the army. I have ordered Glover's brigade to march up towards Peek's Kill, to put the passage of the Highlands out of danger; but I intend to take 2000 from your division with me into the Jersies; so I must desire that you will have that number in readiness by the day after tomorrow, when I shall be with you early in the forenoon;

And am, Sir,

Your most obedient servant,
(Signed) CHARLES LEE.

Maj. Gen. HEATH.

To which our General returned the following answer:

PEEK'S KILL, Nov. 24th, 1776.

SIR,

Be my mode of reasoning as it may, I conceive it to be my duty to obey my instructions, especially those which are positive and poignant, and that to deviate from them even in extreme cases, would be an error; though perhaps an error on the right side. I can assure you, Sir, that I have the salvation of the General and army so much at heart, that the least recommendation from him, to march my division, or any part of them, over the river, should have been I instantly obeyed, without waiting for a positive order. My conduct must be approved or censured, as I adhere to, or depart from, my orders;

and, as it is my duty, I shall strictly abide by them, until they are countermanded in such manner, as will justify a deviation from them, to him who instructed me, and to the world. I shall be happy in being honored with your company tomorrow;

And am, with respect and esteem,

Your humble and obedient servant,

(Signed) W. HEATH.

Gen. LEE.

After the foregoing was sent off, our General reflected for a moment, that as circumstances alter cases, Gen. Washington being now pressed, and the army with him but feeble, he might possibly wish for some aid from his division. He therefore sat down and wrote him a short letter, stating in what manner he had disposed of the troops under his command, and wishing to know his pleasure whether any part of them should join him; enclosing copies of the letters he had received from Gen. Lee, and of his answers. The express was directed to make the utmost dispatch out and returning, which he effected on the 26th (several days before Gen. Lee got up to Peek's Kill) bringing with him the following letter from Secretary Harrison:

NEWARK, Nov. 25th, 1776.

DEAR GENERAL,

I am directed by His Excellency to acknowledge his receipt of your letter of yesterday, and to inform you, the disposition of the troops, mentioned in your former letter, has his approbation. In respect to the troops intended to come to this quarter, his Excellency never meant that they should be from your division. He has wrote Gen. Lee, since, so fully and explicitly upon the subject, that any misapprehensions he may have been under at first, must now be done away. He will most probably have reached Peek's Kill before now, with his division, and be pushing to join us. No new event has taken place.

I am, Sir, very respectfully,

Your most obedient servant,

(Signed) R. H. HARRISON.

Maj. Gen. HEATH.

November 21—A heavy cannonade was heard towards Amboy.

November 22—Col. Tupper, who was down near Tappan, got up to King's Ferry. He brought off the two 12-pounders which were at Dobbs' Ferry, and a quantity of provisions. The same evening, our General ordered the Washington galley to take station at King's Ferry.

November 24—Our General gave orders for Clinton's and Scott's brigades to hold themselves in readiness to march to the Jersey side.

November 25—Scott's brigade was ordered over to Haverstraw, and Col. Tyler's regiment, then at Ramapo River, to march down to Tappan, to secure and bring off the provisions, which were at that place.

November 27—Capt. Treadwell,[80] of the artillery, with a three-pounder, was ordered to move over the river, and join Gen. Scott's brigade. It was learnt that many of the inhabitants of New Jersey, especially in the neighborhood of Hackensack, were swearing allegiance to King George, taking letters of protection, etc.

November 28—Mr. Livingston came from Congress, to advise with our General on measures to obstruct the river. The same day, Capt. Harrod brought off from Tappan a considerable quantity of pearl-ash, bees-wax, oil, etc.

November 29—Two of the regiments of Gen. Clinton's brigade were ordered to move to Fort Constitution, in order to attempt the forming of obstructions in the river near Polipins[81] Island.

November 30—Just before dinner, Gen. Sullivan arrived at our General's quarters; and in the afternoon Gen. Lee arrived. He called at the door; when our General waiting upon him, requested him to alight, he asked if he could have a cup of tea, and was answered that he should have a good one. Upon coming into the house, before he sat down, he wished to speak in private, which being instantly granted, he told our General that, in a military view, or, to use his own words exactly, "In *point of law*, you are right; but in point of policy, I think you are wrong. I am going into the Jersies for the salvation of America; I wish to take with me a larger force than I now have, and request you to order 2000 of your men to march with me." Our General answered, that he could not spare that number. He was then asked to order 1000; to which he replied, that the business might as well be brought to a point at once—that not a single man should march from the post by his order.

Gen. Lee replied, that he would then order them himself. He was answered that there was a wide difference between the two; that Gen. Lee was acknowledged by our General to be his senior; but, as he had received positive written instructions from him who was superior to both, he would not *himself* break those orders. If Gen. Lee was disposed to counteract them, its being done by him could not be imputed to any other person; and that he knew the Commander in Chief did not intend any of the troops should be removed from that post having expressed it not only in his instructions, but also in a letter just received from him. On the letter being shown to Gen. Lee, he observed, "The Commander in Chief is now at a distance and does not know what is necessary here so well as I do"—asked if he might be favored with the return-book of the division. Major Huntington,[82] the Deputy-Adjutant General, was directed to hand it.

Gen. Lee ran his eye over it, and said, "I will take Prescott's and Wyllys's regiments" and turning to Major Huntington, said, "You will order those two regiments to march early tomorrow morning to join me." Our General, turning to the Major, said, "Issue such orders at your peril!" and then turning to Gen. Lee addressed him: "Sir, if you come to this post, and mean to issue orders here, which will break those positive ones which I have received, I pray you to do it completely yourself, and through your own Deputy Adjutant-General, who is present, and not draw me, or any of my family, in as partners in the guilt." Gen. Lee replied, "It is right. Col. Scammell,[83] do you issue the order;" which he did, and Huntington communicated it to the regiments, who were now posted at the gorge of the mountains, near Robinson's Bridge, afterwards called the Continental Village.

Matters carried thus far, our General turned to Gen. Lee again: "Sir, I have one more request to make, and that is, that you will be pleased to give me a certificate, that you *exercise command* at this post, and do order from it Prescott's and Wyllys's regiments." Lee replied, "I do not know that I will comply with your request." Gen. Clinton, who was present, observed, "Gen. Lee, you cannot refuse a request so reasonable." Upon which Gen. Lee wrote as follows:

PEEK'S KILL, Dec. 1st, 1776.

For the satisfaction of Gen. Heath, and at his request, I do certify, that I am commanding officer, at this present writing, in this post, and that I have, in that capacity, ordered Prescott's and Wyllys's regiments to march.

(Signed) CHARLES LEE, Maj. Gen.

Gen. Lee, stepping out on the piazza, observed to an officer, "Gen. Heath is right." Early the next morning, the regiments moved from their cantonment towards Peek's Kill; but before they had reached it, Gen. Lee, now ready to pass into the Jersies, rode up to our General's door, and calling him, observed, "Upon further consideration, I have concluded not take the two regiments with me—you may order them to return to their former post."

This conduct of General Lee's appeared not a little extraordinary, and one is almost at a loss to account for it. He had been a soldier from his youth, had a perfect knowledge of service in all its branches, but was rather obstinate in his temper, and could scarcely brook being crossed in anything in the line of his profession. Gen. Lee took with him into the Jersies some as good troops as any in the service; but many of them were so destitute of shoes, that the blood left on the rugged frozen ground, in many places, marked the route they had taken; and a considerable number, unable to march, were left at Peek's Kill. The time of service for which Gen. Scott's brigade was engaged to serve, expired, when the whole, except about 50, went home, notwithstanding the generous encouragement offered them by their State (New York) if they would continue one month longer.

December 2 and 3—Gen. Lee's troops were passing the ferry. Gen. Carleton having returned into Canada, a number of Gen. Gates' s regiments were now moving to reinforce Gen. Washington their van as far as Morristown—the enemy as far as Brunswick.

December 6—Intelligence was received, that on the 4th, about sunset, 70 sail of ships of war and transports passed in the Sound towards New England. Our General immediately sent expresses to General Washington, Gov. Trumbull, Mr. Bowdoin,[84] at Boston, the Convention of New York, etc.

December 7—Three regiments, viz. Greaton's, Bond's, and Porter's,[85] arrived off the landing from Albany, on their way to Gen. Washington. Matters now looked serious in Jersey. The British were extending themselves in all directions, and the inhabitants obliged to become passive, if not worse. Gen. Gates had ordered the troops, moving from the northward, to rendezvous at Goshen.

December 8—Our General wrote Gen. Lee, that the troops were moving on from the northward, and as Gen. Gates had not yet overtaken them, some of the commanding-officers appeared to wish for orders how to proceed. Gen. Washington, it was said, was as far as Trenton—Lee, the preceding night, as far as Pompton. A flag schooner came up from New York, to obtain leave for some families to go in. A Parson Inglis[86] was on board. Orders were given to treat the flag with politeness, and at the same time with proper precaution; and the business was laid before the Convention of the State. The same day, Gen. Clinton, with two British and two Hessian brigades, with a squadron of ships under the command of Sir Peter Parker, took possession of Rhode Island, without the loss of a man; the Americans quitting the island without making any opposition. Rhode Island was a great acquisition to the British, for quarters, forage, and a safe harbor; but lessened their ability for other more important operations in the field.

December 9—our General received orders from the Commander in Chief, to move over the Hudson, with Parsons's brigade, and to move on so as to give protection to the country, and vigor to the cause in Jersey.

December 10—A little after noon, Parsons's brigade marched down to King's Ferry; the greatest alertness having been discovered by both officers and men on the occasion.

December 11—About eleven o'clock, a.m. our General left Peek's Kill, and proceeded for the Jersies; on crossing King's Ferry, gave orders for the flag to be detained from returning until further orders. The troops crossed the ferry, and marched as far as Col. Hay's[87] at Haverstraw. Huntington's and Tyler's regiments were ordered to advance from Ramapo Bridge to Paramus. Our General received a letter from Gen. Lee, in answer to the one he wrote on the 8th from Peek's Kill, as follows:

> CHATHAM, Dec. 9th, 1776.
>
> DEAR GENERAL,
>
>   I am very much obliged to you for your welcome tidings; and have only to beg that you will direct the regiments you speak of, to march without loss of time to Morristown. I sent an express to you last night, from the General, ordering your division over the river, which I confess, for my own part, I am heartily sorry for; as I think we shall be strong enough without you, and New England, with your district, will be too bare of troops. I am in hopes here to re-conquer (if I may so express myself) the Jersies. It was really in the hands of the enemy before my arrival. Adieu, dear Sir,
>
> Maj. Gen. HEATH
>
> (Signed) CHARLES LEE.

The foregoing letter appears very different from the former ones.

December 12—Early in the morning, the troops took up their line of march from Haverstraw, and before sun-set reached Tappan.

December 13—Sent out a reconnoitering party towards Hackensack, to get intelligence, etc. This day Gen. Lee was taken prisoner, near Chatham, by a party of light-horse, commanded by Col. Harcourt.[88] Lee took quarters at a small distance from his troops: an inhabitant gave notice of it to Col. Harcourt, who was out reconnoitering near that neighborhood, and who had the address to take and carry him off.

December 14—Our General held up every appearance of moving to Paramus, and sent off his baggage under escort to that place; and between 11 and 12 o'clock, marched briskly for Hackensack, having sent orders for Huntington's and Tyler's regiments to move from Paramus at the same time. Buskirk's regiment was at Hackensack Bridge the preceding day, where they did duty, and it was expected they were still at the same place. To surprise and take them was the object; but it was found that Buskirk's[89] men had moved the preceding day to Bergen, in order to draw new arms. The town was completely surprised, not having an idea that any but British troops were near them. One British soldier and 20 or 30 of their adherents, were taken, a number of arms, etc. and at the wharf, several vessels loaded with hay, etc. on the point of sailing for New York.

A brig had come to sail in the morning, and run some distance down the river, and came to anchor. An officer with a party was sent down to take her, and bring her up; but the wind was so strong ahead that it could not be affected. The officer was then directed to destroy the vessel, as she had a large quantity of forage on board, destined for New York; but it was said, there were some valuable articles on board, which might be taken out and brought up in the boats. The orders were varied accordingly, with directions, that in case the enemy advanced before the business was completed, to set the brig on fire. The boats brought up one load; but on returning to the brig, they discovered a body of the enemy advancing, when the brig was abandoned without being set on fire. The enemy immediately took possession of her. Among the articles taken out, was a large chest of plate. This was conveyed to Peek's Kill, and delivered to the Deputy Quarter-Master-General; and when the British afterwards destroyed the public stores at that place, the chest of plate was removed by the Quarter-Master into Connecticut; where afterwards Gen. Parsons, in behalf of the officers and soldiers of the division, filed a libel in the Maritime Court, and the officer who boarded the vessel filed one in his own behalf.

On trial, the Court adjudged the plate to the latter, although he boarded the vessel in obedience to express orders. About 100 barrels of flour, which had been abandoned by the Americans when they retreated before Lord Cornwallis, were recovered and sent off; and about 100 arms were also secured, with a quantity of rum, gin, etc. In the evening, as two or three American officers were walking along the street, a gentleman, who was an inhabitant, came up to them, and expressed his joy on the arrival of the troops (supposing they were British.) The officers immediately conducted him to our General, and on entering the room informed him, that they came to introduce a friend who had joined them in the street, and who was able to give some important information. Our General expressed a high satisfaction, and wished to know what information he could give. He replied that he heard there was a large body of rebels collecting up above them. He was asked if in case these rebels should advance, any assistance could be afforded by the people of the town, and whether they could be depended upon?

He answered there were a considerable number, and that they might be depended upon. He was asked, whether there was not a number in the town who were in favor of the rebels? He answered, that there was; but that they had seized and sent off the principal ones among them, and that now the others dared not show themselves. The joke was thus going on, when Col. Prescott, who stood near him, holding his hat in his hand, in which there was a red cockade (at that time a mark of the distinction of rank) the gentleman fixed his eye upon it, and his countenance immediately fell. He was then told that those whom he termed rebels were now in possession of the place, and had now received his information. He was ordered into custody.

December 15—All the wagons in the vicinity were collected, and the flour and other stores moved off to Paramus. Reconnoitering parties were sent out to a distance, to observe the motions of the enemy.

December 16—The effects were generally removed, and about noon the reconnoitering parties reported that the enemy were advancing on both sides of the place. They were soon after discovered by the guard at Acquackanonk Bridge. A little before sunset, the troops left the town. A strong rear-guard was ordered to remain on the high ground back of the town, until after dark, to light up a number of fires, and then to move on after the troops. Just before the division left the town, Gen. George Clinton, attended by some light-horse, joined the division.

December 17—Reconnoitering parties were sent out on all the roads.

December 18—Intelligence was received, that some of the Jersey militia had had a skirmish with a body of British troops under Gen. Leslie, near Springfield. Both parties retired. Of the militia, several were killed and wounded. The Contention of New York, greatly alarmed at the removal of our General with the continental troops from the important passes of the Highlands, sent a request to Gen. Washington, desiring that they might be ordered back again. To insure dispatch, they offered the express extra pay. The Commander in Chief was pleased to grant their request, and ordered our General to return to Peek's Kill, and re-occupy his former positions. Our General, having received certain information that Buskirk's regiment was at or near Bergen Woods, it was determined to strike them. For this purpose, on the evening of the 19th about eight o'clock, Gen. Parsons, with 250 continental troops, and Gen. Clinton, with a like number of the militia of New York, marched from Paramus church, and a covering party of 300 men was ordered to Tappan. About one o'clock the next morning the detachment reached Bergen, and completely surprised the enemy's guard, making 22 men prisoners. The regiment was alarmed, and a pretty brisk skirmish ensued. The enemy were collecting, and it was judged best for the detachment to come off, having been so far victorious.

December 20—About one o'clock, p.m. the detachment returned to Paramus, having, in the short interval of time, marched (out and returning) upwards of 40 miles. They brought back with them, besides their prisoners, 16 new fire-locks, six horses, and one wagon; having sustained the loss of one man. The enemy were supposed to have had several killed.

December 21—Orders were given for the troops to be ready to march early the next morning. The gentleman who was taken into custody at Hackensack, chagrined almost to death, had been spending his time, like April, in weeping and lowering; and much intercession having been made for his release, our General told him that in case he would faithfully perform a piece of secret service allotted to him, he should be released. This he performed with punctuality, and consequently was set at liberty.

December 22—The troops marched from Paramus round by the side of Kakaat, to Clark's-Town,[90] which they reached about sunset.

December 23—The troops took up their line of march, crossed the Hudson, and arrived at Peek's Kill.

December 24—Gave permission for the flag to return to New York, having on board the families of Mr. Inglis, Moore, etc.

December 25—It was learnt that a body of Hessian troops had not long before moved to the upper end of York Island. The militia of the State of New York were this day beginning to come in.

December 26—A severe snowstorm. Some of the militia from Massachusetts had reached Danbury.

December 29—Intelligence was received from Providence, that a most valuable prize, taken by the ship *Alfred*, had arrived safe at New Bedford, in Massachusetts.

December 30—Col. Chester, of Connecticut, arrived at Peek's Kill, from Gen. Washington's camp, with the agreeable news, that on the preceding Thursday morning, being the 26th, Gen. Washington, at the head of about 3000 men, crossed the Delaware, and attacked the enemy at Trenton, being about 1600 Hessians; and in about 35 minutes entirely defeated them. One Colonel, two Lieutenant-Colonels, three Majors, four Captains, eight Lieutenants, 12 Ensigns, one Judge Advocate, two Surgeon's Mates, 92 Sergeants, 20 Drummers, nine Musicians, 25 Officers' servants, and 740 rank and file were taken prisoners, besides the killed and wounded. Six pieces of brass cannon, 12 drums, four standards, 1200 small-arms, six wagons, a number of swords, caps, etc. were the trophies of victory. The same day, Colonel Sparhawk's[91] regiment of militia arrived from Massachusetts.

December 31—Information was given, that a company of 60 disaffected inhabitants were on their way to join the enemy. Parties were sent out to intercept them.

Chapter 3

1777

January 1—By a letter from Gen. Washington, it appeared that the enemy were retreating towards Amboy. Generals Mifflin and Ewing,[1] and Col. Cadwalader[2] had crossed the Delaware, and Gen. Washington was about to follow them, and pursue the enemy.

January 2—Several infamous disaffected persons were taken and sent in. The same day, Gen. Washington being at Trenton, Gen. Howe advanced to attack him; a cannonade ensued: Gen. Washington retired to the other side of the Mill Creek; and, as soon as it was dark, ordering a great number of fires to be lighted up, to deceive the enemy, stole a march, and at nine o'clock next morning attacked three regiments of the enemy who were posted at Princeton, routed them, driving them from two small redoubts. The enemy lost, in killed, wounded and taken prisoners about 500. The American loss was inconsiderable, except in the brave Gen. Mercer, of Virginia, who fell in this action, greatly regretted. In this maneuver and action Gen. Washington exhibited the most consummate generalship, and the British were struck with consternation. *Ambuscade, surprise,* and *stratagem* are said to constitute the sublime part of the art of war, and that he who possesses the greatest resource in these, will eventually pluck the laurel from the brow of his opponent. The stratagems of war are almost infinite, but all have the same object, namely, to deceive to hold up an appearance of something which is not intended, while under this mask some important object is secured; and be a General never so brave, if he be unskilled in the arts and stratagems of war, he is really to be pitied; for his bravery will but serve to lead him into those wily snares which are laid for him.

January 3—Thirty-seven recruits going to Rogers,[3] taken the preceding night, were brought in; and our General ordered out Capt. Graham[4] at 12 o'clock at night, to intercept another gang.

January 4—Gen. Lincoln arrived from Massachusetts; he had come on with a body of militia.

January 5—It was learnt that on the 1st inst.[5] Gen. Putnam took a large quantity of baggage, provisions, etc. at Bordentown; and on the 3rd, Gen. Washington's army came up with the rear of the enemy, at or near Rocky Hill, when a brisk action ensued, and the enemy were defeated, with the loss of between 50 and 60 killed, and upwards of 100 taken prisoners, together with 6 pieces of cannon, and all their baggage: the Americans had six men killed. The same day Col. Sparhawk's regiment of militia, from Massachusetts, with two field-pieces, marched for King's Ferry, on their way to the Jerseys.

January 7—Our General received the following letter from Gen. Washington:

PLUCKEMIN, Jan. 5th, 1777.

SIR,

We have made a successful attack upon Princeton. General Howe advanced upon Trenton; we evacuated the town, and lay at the other side of the Mill Creek until dark; then stole a march, and attacked Princeton about 9 o'clock in the morning. There were three regiments quartered there. The killed, wounded, and prisoners taken, amounted to about 500. The enemy are in great consternation; and as the present affords us a favorable opportunity to drive them out of the Jersies, it has been determined in Council, that you should move down towards New York with a considerable force, as if you had a design upon the city; that being an object of great importance, the enemy will be reduced to the necessity of withdrawing a considerable part of their force from the Jersies, if not the whole to secure the city. I shall draw the force on this side the North River together at Morristown, where I shall watch the motions of the enemy, and avail myself of every circumstance.

You will retain 4000 of the militia coming on from the New England Governments for the expedition. You will act with great precaution, but avail yourself of every favorable opportunity of attacking the enemy, when you can do it to advantage. Gen. Lincoln must cross the North River, and come on with the remainder of the militia to Morristown. Leave a sufficient guard at the Highlands. You will also have as many boats collected together, or in such a manner as you may always avail yourself of them, if it should be found expedient for your troops or any part of them to cross the North River, at Dobbs' Ferry, or any other of the landings.

I am, etc.
(Signed) GEO. WASHINGTON.

Gen. HEATH.

Preparations for the before mentioned movement were immediately put in train. The militia and volunteers were coming in.

January 8—Gen. Parsons went down to King-street.

January 9—The remainder of Col. Sparhawk's and Col. Whitney's[6] regiments passed over the river, to join Gen. Washington.

January 10—Col. Frost's regiment marched to North Castle, and Gen. Scott's militia to White Plains.

January 11—A number of British officers, taken at Princeton, passed Peek's Kill, on their way to Connecticut. The same day it was learnt, that on the 8th, Gen. Maxwell, with the Jersey militia, and some continental troops, routed the enemy at Elizabeth-Town, where he took 50 Highlanders, a schooner loaded with baggage, and fell in with a party of 30 Waldeckers,[7] whom he also took prisoners.

January 12—Gen. Moulton[8] from Massachusetts, and Col. Gilman[9] from New Hampshire, came to camp. A number of British prisoners, taken in the Jersies, passed Peek's Kill, on their way to Connecticut.

January 13—Our General moved to the southward, and reached North-Castle just before sunset, where he found part of four regiments had arrived, and Gen. Scott's militia of New York had moved down to Wright's Mills.

January 14—Our General moved to King-street to Mr. Clap's—about 3000 militia had arrived, and Gen. Lincoln's division marched to Tarrytown on this day. The Commander in Chief in another letter had intimated that Gen. Lincoln, instead of moving on to join him, should stay on the east side of the Hudson, and join in the expedition.

January 15—The Connecticut volunteers marched from Kingstreet to New Rochelle, and Gen. Scott's brigade to Stephen Ward's. Plenty of provisions were arriving. A deserter came in from the enemy, and gave an account of their situation and numbers.

January 17—At night the three divisions began to move towards Kingsbridge: Gen. Lincoln's from Tarrytown, on the Albany road; Generals Wooster and Parsons's from New Rochelle and East-Chester, and Gen. Scott's in the center from below White Plains. The several distances and rate of marching were so well calculated, that, on the 18th, just before sunrise, the three divisions, although so far apart, arrived at the outposts of the enemy almost at the same instant. Gen. Lincoln's on the heights above Col. Van Cortlandt's[10]; Wooster's at Williams's; and Scott's on the back of Valentine's. Our General, who moved with the center division, knew that Valentine's house was the quarters of one of the guards; he did not know but it might be defended: as he approached it, he ordered Capt. Lt. Bryant to advance a field-piece to the advance-guard, and if there was any opposition from the house, to cannonade it immediately. He then ordered 250 men from the head of the column (as it was moving on) to incline to the right, and by a double step to push into the hollow between the house and the fort, to cut off the guard who were at the house, in case they should run towards the latter.

At this instant, two light-horsemen who had been sent out by the enemy as the day broke to reconnoiter the vicinity came unexpectedly at the descent of a hill, plump upon the head of Wooster's column. They attempted to turn about, but before it could be fully affected, a field-piece was discharged at them; one of them was pitched from his horse and taken prisoner, the other galloped back to the fort, hollowing as he passed, "The rebels! The rebels!" This set all the outguards and pickets running to the fort, leaving in some places their arms, blankets, tools, provisions, etc. behind them. Those who fled from Valentine's and the Negro Fort were fired at as they ran, but none were killed: one, who could not run so fast as the rest, was taken prisoner. Ten muskets were taken at Valentine's house. The guard above Van Cortlandt's was as completely surprised as the others, where Gen. Lincoln took about 40 arms, some blankets, etc. etc. The left and center divisions moved into the hollow, between Valentine's house and the fort, from whence our General immediately sent a summons to the commanding officer of the fort to surrender. The Commandant of the fort, and a considerable part of the garrison, being Hessians, the summons held out to these generous terms. The answer, which was verbal, was a refusal to surrender.

A detachment with two field-pieces

Gen. George Washington (Library of Congress).

was ordered to move to the south of the fort, to a hill above Haarlem Creek, not far from the New Bridge. When the detachment arrived at this place, a battalion of Hessians appeared drawn up on the side of the hill just within Kingsbridge, and back of Hyatt's tavern. Our General ordered the artillery to cannonade them immediately. The first shot just cleared the right of the battalion, nearly a platoon settling down as the shot passed them, which entered the bank close behind them. The second shot passed about the center of the battalion, when to the amount of a grand division settled down, which was evidence that they would not stand much longer. One of the pieces was ordered to be drawn lower down the hill; on which the battalion quitted their ground, and marched off as fast as they could without running, to get behind the redoubt and hill at the bridge, receiving one shot more as they were turning round the point. It was not suspected that the enemy had any cannon in the redoubt within the bridge, but they now began to cannonade the artillery-men who had descended the hill, who had to draw up their piece as fast as possible, which they effected without any loss, but received three or four shot quite among them, before they could reach the top of the hill. This success at the out-posts flew through the country, and was soon magnified to a reduction of the fort, and capture of the garrison. It reached Gen. Washington long before the official account, and he had communicated the report to Congress; hence a double disappointment, when the true state of facts was received.

January 19—The enemy cannonaded from the fort, and killed one American, as the guards were relieving at the Negro Fort. It was determined to make an attempt to cut off the battalion within Kingsbridge, early the next morning, by passing a strong detachment over Spuyten Duyvil Creek on the ice, which, however, was not now very strong, but the weather was cold. One thousand were detached for the purpose; but the weather having grown warm in the night, the ice was judged, by the unanimous opinion of all the General Officers on the ground, to be too hazardous on the morning of the 20th to venture the attempt. On this day there was a cannonade on both sides, and the enemy on the island side were thrown into much confusion. Our General observing that when the enemy within the island were cannonaded across Haarlem Creek, they sheltered themselves behind the little hill near the bridge, next to Spuyten Duyvil Creek, on this afternoon he rode round on to Tibbett's Hill, which was in its rear, and found that a field-piece drawn up on that side would leave the enemy no hiding-place.

January 21—A cannonade on both sides. In the afternoon a field-piece was hauled up to Tibbett's Hill, and the enemy were cannonaded both in front and rear: they were thrown into the utmost confusion: some secured themselves in their redoubt, others under the banks: some lay flat on the ground, and some betook themselves to the cellars; so that in a short time there was no object for the gunners. The weather had now grown very moderate.

January 22—There was a pretty smart skirmish with the enemy near the fore. This day our General ordered a number or chandellers,[11] two fascines,[12] etc. to be made; and having nothing but light field-pieces with him, in order to keep up an appearance of a serious design on the fort, he sent to North-Castle, where was a field brass 24-pounder and some howitzers, to bring forward the former and one of the latter.

January 23—A smart skirmish took place just before dusk, in the broken ground near the south side of the fort; an Ensign and one man belonging to the New York militia were killed, and five wounded; the loss of the enemy unknown, as it was close under the fort.

January 24—Excessive stormy. Gen. Lincoln's division, who were in huts in the woods, back of Col. Van Cortlandt's, were obliged to quit their ground, and move back into the houses where they could find them; some of them as far as Dobbs' Ferry; with the loss of a great many cartridges, from the badness of the boxes. The fall of rain was so great as to cause a great fresh in the Bronx, the water running over the bridge by Williams's.

January 25—Early in the morning, the enemy made a sally towards Delancey's Mills,[13] where they surprised and routed the guard, wounding several, but not killing or taking any of them; and a regiment near that place quitted their quarters. Emboldened by this success, about 10 o'clock, a.m. they made a powerful sally towards Valentine's, instantly driving the guards and pickets from the Negro Fort and Valentine's house; pushing on with great impetuosity, keeping up a brisk fire, the balls passing at Williams's house sufficiently strong to do execution. The retreating guards threw themselves into the old redoubt on the north side of the road, to the west of the bridge; on which the enemy lined a strong stonewall, a few rods distant to the southwest. Two regiments of the militia being at this instant formed in the road near Williams's, and the horses in the limbers of the field-pieces, our General ordered Capt. Bryant to ford over the bridge with his piece, and the militia to follow and cover the artillery. When Capt. Bryant had ascended almost to the top of the hill, to prevent his horses being shot he unlimbered, and the men took the drag-ropes; but the ascent of the hill was such that they were obliged to drag the piece almost with in pistol-shot, before the ground would admit the piece to be so depressed as to bear on the enemy. The moment this was affected, a round shot opened a breach in the wall, four or five feet wide; a second shot in less than a minute opened another, when the enemy fled back to the fort with the greatest precipitation. Of the Americans, two were killed and a number wounded.

January 27—The brass 24-pounder and howitzer were brought up, and ordered to open upon the fort; on the third discharge of the former, she sprang her carriage; nor were there any *live* shells for the howitzer, there being none at North-Castle; nor was a regular cannonade or bombardment of the fort ever contemplated. Every attempt was now made, by feint and otherwise, to draw the enemy out of the fort. A detachment was sent down to Morrisania, to light up a great number of fires in the night, to induce the enemy to suppose that a body of Americans were collecting at that place, with a design to cross on to New York Island, at or near Haarlem; and to heighten this, several large boats were sent for, and brought forward on carriages. The British guard on Montresor's Island were so much alarmed at this as to set the buildings on fire, and flee to New York. A brigade of the British were said to have moved towards Fort Washington; and orders had been sent to Rhode Island, for a detachment to be sent from thence.

January 29—There was the appearance of a severe snow storm coming on, when all the General Officers on the ground, viz. besides our General, Lincoln, Wooster, Scott and Ten Broeck,[14] were unanimously of the opinion that the troops ought to move back before the storm came on, to places where they could be covered from the inclemency of the weather, as there was no artillery to batter the fort. And from first to last they were unanimously opposed to any idea of an assault or storm of the fort with the militia, the principal object being now to secure and bring off or destroy the forage, which could be as well done where the troops could have covering, as to harass them in the open fields by multiplying guards, or their being constantly exposed in the scattered houses to be surprised and cut off. For these several reasons, the troops were ordered as soon as it grew dark to move back, Gen. Lincoln's division to Dobbs' Ferry and Tarrytown, Gen. Wooster's to New Rochelle, and Gen. Scott's to White Plains; the guards to remain at their posts and alert, until the troops were all moved off, and then to form rear guards on the several roads, following the troops to whom they respectively belonged; all of which was performed in good order, in a very heavy fall of snow.

January 30—The storm cleared up, when 15 ships, one brig, two schooners, and two sloops came to, between Hart[15] and City Islands; they were from the eastward, and were supposed to have troops on board. The troops on this expedition, as it was called, were in a very hazardous situation, and had continued in it from the morning of the 18th, to the evening of the 29th; they were entirely a body of militia, except a few artillery-men. So apprehensive of this being a critical situation was the Commander in Chief, in the year 1780, when Gen. Sir Henry Clinton menaced the French army at Rhode Island, and had embarked his troops on board transports for the purpose of proceeding to that place, and Gen. Washington had determined to move down towards Kingsbridge to induce Sir Henry to give up his design by menacing New York, our General being then at Rhode Island with the French army, Gen. Washington wrote him on the 31st of July from Robinson's House in the Highlands among other things, "You know the critical situation in which this army will be in a position below." This was undoubtedly a very just observation; but if the Commander in Chief, with the whole American army in 1780, well armed and highly disciplined, should so justly judge at the distance of 30 miles from the spot, what shall we say of those brave militia men who continued in the position itself, for more than *ten days* in the midst of winter? Whenever an enterprise is to be attempted in the teeth of an enemy, it should be a *dash* and away.

January 31—A cordon of troops was ordered to be formed, to extend from Dobbs' Ferry to Mamaroneck.

February 1—Foraging now being the object, a large number of teams were sent out towards Mamaroneck, and upwards of 80 loads of forage were brought off. Twelve more ships, four of which were of 40 guns, came down the Sound the preceding day.

February 2—Col. Humphrey,[16] of New York, arrived with a regiment of militia from Albany county, to continue in service six weeks.

February 3—There was another grand forage.

February 6—A strong detachment under the command of Col. Enos[17] was sent toward Fort Independence, to attempt to surprise some of the enemy's out-posts, but nothing could be effected. The smallpox was now making its appearance in the neighborhood.

February 8—There was a grand forage to the lower parts of Westchester County. A row-galley and a sloop were coming up the North River. The covering party to the foragers on this day was nearly 1000 strong, and large quantities of forage were brought off.

February 10—Our General rode to Peek's Kill, where he arrived a little after dark. Gen. Lincoln's troops were on their march to join Gen. Washington. Our General had obtained leave of the Commander in Chief, to make a short visit to New England, under an injunction to return very early.

February 12—About 10 o'clock, he left Peek's Kill, and arrived at his house in Roxbury on the 19th, about sunset.

March 14—Our General set out from Roxbury, on his way back to the army; but before he had got to Watertown, an express overtook him, with orders from Gen. Washington, for him to take command of the Eastern Department; Gen. Ward having applied for leave to resign the command, meaning to retire from the service: he therefore turned back, and rode into Boston. This year, 1777, formed an important era in the annals of America. Congress had determined to make great exertions to drive the British troops from America; for this purpose, they had ordered 88 battalions to be raised in the United States, 15 of which fell to the share of Massachusetts. Besides the foregoing 88 battalions, they also ordered the raising of 16 others, called the additional battalions; and of these, three were raising in Massachusetts, viz. Jackson's, Lee's and Henley's; besides Armand's[18] Legion, Artificers, etc.

The arming, equipping and sending on the recruits furnishing the Recruiting Officers with bounty monies and the forwarding on immense quantities of all kinds of military stores (for Massachusetts might now be called the great magazine of military stores of the Union, partly on account of her own resources, managed by the indefatigable industry of her Board of War) and the arrivals of public stores here and at Portsmouth, called for the utmost diligence and exertion of the commanding General. The Commander in Chief had given directions for the troops to be forwarded on, with all possible dispatch, to Ticonderoga.

March 20—Maj. Gen. Ward resigned the command of the Eastern Department to our General, who took the command accordingly.

March 23—A detachment of British troops, consisting as was said of about 500 men, destroyed the American stores at Peek's Kill; they met with but very little opposition: here our General lost a part of his baggage, which was left when he came away for Boston, in February. Monsieur De Borre,[19] a French General, came to Boston: he had been engaged by our Ministers in France, to enter the American service, etc.

March 27—Our General received orders from the Commander in Chief to make an alteration in the destination of the Massachusetts regiments, sending eight of the regiments to Peek's Kill, and seven to Ticonderoga.

March 31—Our General took a view of the state of the works at Dorchester, etc.

April 3—Capt. Sumner, of Greaton's regiment, marched a detachment of his regiment for Peek's Kill.

April 4—A part of Col. Shepard's regiment marched for Peek's Kill.

April 7—Our General took a view of the barracks at Prospect Hill, preparatory to the putting of the recruits under inoculation with the smallpox.

April 9—About 120 men of Paterson's regiment marched for Peek's Kill.

April 11—A part of Nixon's regiment marched for Peek's Kill; on the 12th, 160 men of Bailey's for Ticonderoga; and on the 13th, 200 of Wesson's[20] for the latter place. The same day, began to inoculate the recruits at Prospect Hill.

April 15—Col. Jackson's Independent Company marched to do duty at Providence; and a company of Col. Crane's artillery for the main army.

April 16—Two hundred men of Col. Wigglesworth's[21] regiment marched for Peek's Kill. The same evening, our General received orders from Gen. Washington to send the troops to Peek's Kill, by the route of Kinderhook. The same day, 10 tons of powder arrived at Boston, from Portsmouth (N. H.) A second division of recruits for Bailey's[22] regiment marched for Ticonderoga, as did a division from Col. Bradford's for the same place.

April 20—A large letter-of -marque ship arrived at Boston from Nantes in France, with a valuable cargo on private account.

April 23—An express from Portsmouth brought an account of the arrival at that place of the French ship *Amphitrite*, having on board 52 brass field-pieces, completely mounted, with apparatus; 6132 muskets; 120 barrels of powder, and many other articles.

April 24—A second division of Col. Crane's[23] artillery marched for the army.

April 28—A division of Wesson's regiment marched for Ticonderoga.

April 29—An express arrived from Gov. Trumbull, giving an account that the enemy had landed a body of men near Fairfield, and that a number of ships were standing up Hudson's River. This body of the enemy consisted of about 2000; they landed on the 25th at Fairfield, and pushed for Danbury, where the Americans had magazines of stores, which the British burnt and destroyed. Generals Wooster and Arnold were in that part of Connecticut; they assembled the militia of the vicinity, and at tacked the British on their return; and there were several very sharp skirmishes, at and near Ridgefield, in one of which the brave Gen. Wooster fell; and Gen. Arnold having his horse shot down under him, by a soldier who was very near him, and who was following up his shot with his bayonet charged, Arnold caught one of his pistols from the holsters on the slain horse, and instantly shot the soldier dead on the spot. The loss was considerable on both sides, in killed and wounded: the British say theirs did not exceed 172, killed, wounded and missing. The loss to the Americans in stores, etc. was considerable, and could but illy be spared at that time.

May 5—Col. Jackson's Independent Company returned from doing duty at Providence.

May 14—Gen. Du Coudray,[24] an experienced French artillery officer, engaged by our Commissioners in France to act at the head of the American artillery, arrived at Boston: on viewing, from Beacon Hill, the situation of Boston, and the American works around the town, he made a laugh at the British leaving the town when under no greater danger; adding that the force which they had might have defended the place against an army of 50,000 men. A valuable prize, loaded with dry goods, was sent into Newbury port.

May 21—The Continental frigates, and a fleet of private ships of war, sailed on a cruise, with a fair wind.

May 28—Intelligence was received, that a detachment of Americans, under the command of Col. Meigs,[25] of Connecticut, had passed the Sound on the 23rd to Long Island, and crossed to Sag Harbor, where they destroyed and burnt a number of vessels at the wharf, and every thing on shore, and brought off 80 or 90 prisoners. This enterprise was conducted with much address and great expedition.

May 29—A prize brig was sent in, laden with salt, cordage, etc. She was from Topsham in England. No reinforcement for the army in America had sailed the last of March.

June 8—Two prizes were sent in; one laden with coals, the other with dry goods.

June 9—A 50-gun ship of the enemy, and two frigates were cruising in our bay.

June 14—A prize taken by Commodore Manley,[26] laden with duck, cordage, etc. and two brigs from Bilbao, arrived safe.

July 1—Intelligence was received, that Gen. Howe evacuated Brunswick[27] on the 18th of the preceding month; he had before advanced as far as Somerset court-house, and had thrown up a number of works, which he abandoned; the American light troops harassed his rear. This day, four of the enemy's cruisers came so near in, as to be discovered from Nantasket.

July 4—The anniversary of the Independence of the United States was celebrated with proper demonstrations of joy.

July 6—An express arrived from Peek's Kill, with intelligence from Gen. Washington, intimating that on the morning of the 1st inst. the enemy's fleet, which lay at Amboy sailed round that town; and that the troops who lay encamped opposite to the town, struck their tents and marched off. The enemy were also advancing on the Lake with their fleet towards Ticonderoga. A detachment of soldiers for Col. M. Jackson's regiment marched for the northern army.

July 7—Capt. Clouston[28] arrived from France with powder, arms, etc. for the State; he had also made a successful cruise.

July 11—Intelligence was received, that the Americans evacuated Ticonderoga on the 6th, at night; a great many stores, etc. were lost. The British no sooner arrived before Ticonderoga, than they were discovered on Mount Hope: this steep and rugged hill was thought to be inaccessible by the Americans, at least with artillery; and therefore, notwithstanding its nearness to the works, and overlooking of them in part, it was not taken possession of; but they should have recollected what had been said by the late King of Prussia, as to such positions that "where a goat can go, a man may go; and where a man can go, artillery may be drawn up."[29] The British were no sooner seen on this hill, where the wily Phillips[30] of the artillery is said to have ascended, than they saw an additional reason for quitting the post. This was a sore and heavy loss to the Americans; but in the issue proved a more certain and earlier overthrow of all Burgoyne's army: yet so exasperated were the people at the time, that had the commanding General, St. Clair,[31] been immediately brought to trial, he would have stood but a poor chance: he was afterwards tried and acquitted with honor. The British took possession of the works, and pushed on rapidly after the Americans, taking and destroying every thing that fell in their way. Brig. Gen. Fraser, with the light troops, pursued with great ardor, and on the 7th came up with a body of the Americans, commanded by the brave Col. Francis,[32] of Massachusetts. A warm action ensued; the Americans were worsted; the Colonel was slain, and many other officers and soldiers killed, wounded and taken prisoners. This flew through the country like a shock of electricity, and roused the people to noble exertions. Gen. St. Clair joined Gen. Schuyler at Fort Edward after a fatiguing retreat.

On the 10th, a most conspicuous piece of gallantry was exhibited at Rhode Island. Maj. Gen. Prescott having command of the British troops at that place, Col. Barton[33] of Providence formed a resolution to surprise and take him; he accordingly proceeded to the island with a party of chosen men in two boats with muffled oars, taking with him a negro man whose hard head was nearly as efficacious as a beetle, to burst a door; and on this night with great address evading the British water-guards, passed down the west side of the island, and landed near a hollow ground, and instantly pushed for the house of a Mr. Overing,[34] where the General was quartered. The sentinel at the door was seized, the house entered and demand made whether the General was there; and finding that he was, and the apartment, the door was burst open and the General and his aide-de-camp seized, and told they must go off instantly. The General asked if he might put on his clothes. The Colonel answered, "very few, and very quick, Sir." The Colonel returned to his boats, and repassed the water-guards, which the General had much confidence would have released him; for on passing the last, he observed to the Colonel, "Sir, I did not think it possible you could escape the vigilance of the water-guards." This was a brilliant affair; and Congress duly rewarded Col. Barton for his distinguished address and gallantry.

July 13—An express arrived from Gen. Washington, with information that the British were preparing their transports for the embarkation of their troops from Staten Island, were fixing berths for the light-horse, etc. but their destination could not be developed. They had pushed into the Jersies, as if designing to march to Philadelphia, and then turned back, as has been mentioned, from Amboy, and were now preparing to embark; and we shall anon see more of their maneuvers and deceptions.

July 16—A number of Americans, who had left the northern army when it retreated, as is generally the case on similar occasions, came to Boston; they were immediately taken up and confined, to be sent back again: the best method in like cases.

July 19—At evening an express passed through Boston, on his way to Philadelphia, with dispatches, which had been brought to Portsmouth (N.H.) by a vessel in 42 days' passage from France. It was said that there was great probability of an immediate war between France and England.

July 21—By intelligence from Peek's Kill it was learnt, that on the preceding Wednesday 10 pieces of cannon were shipped for Albany; that a division of the American army was opposite to Fishkill; and that Gen. Washington was moving towards King's Ferry with the main army, said to be 20,000 strong, with near 800 wagons, and having a number of flat-bottomed boats on carriages, etc.

July 26—Count Pulaski, a Polish nobleman, came to Boston, and dined at headquarters.

August 1—Information was sent from Cape Ann, that a fleet of vessels, said to be near 100, had been seen from the high lands, standing to the northward. This caused some alarm: the guards at the magazines, etc. were doubled.

August 4—Intelligence was received that Gen. Washington was moving with the main army towards Philadelphia, and had detached Gen. Glover with his brigade to join the northern army. An account was received that there had been a skirmish on Wood Creek, between a party of the Americans and the enemy, to the advantage of the former.

August 6—Intelligence was received that the American northern army had fallen back to Saratoga. About this time, a party of the enemy landed on Boston Neck (so called) in Rhode Island: they were driven off without doing much damage. The same day intelligence was received, that on the 23rd of the preceding month the British fleet sailed from Sandy Hook, and had arrived off the Capes of Delaware.

August 8—Intelligence was received, that the British fleet sailed out of the Capes of Delaware on the 31st ult. standing to the eastward. This induced Gen. Washington to retrograde the main American army towards the North River.

August 11—There was a report that the northern army had fallen back to Still-water. One sixth part of the militia in a number of counties of Massachusetts were ordered to be detached and marched immediately to reinforce the northern army.

August 14—Intelligence was received that the British fleet had returned again to the Capes of Delaware. Col. Johnson and St. Leger[35] were advancing with a body of the enemy towards Fort Schuyler, on the Mohawk River. About this time, a Miss McCrea,[36] said to be a beautiful young lady, and in all the innocence of youth, her father warmly engaged on the side of the British, and she on the very point of marriage with a British officer, on some dispute between two Indians, as to which of them she of right belonged as a captive, was most inhumanly massacred! The act was probably as abhorrent to the British as to the Americans; but they ought not to have engaged the savages in their cause, as they might well have known their ungovernable temper, and disposition for blood; for this was not the only instance—a British officer sending his waiter to a spring for some cool water, in a few minutes an Indian came in, with the scalp of the waiter smoking in his hand.

St. Leger having gone up the Mohawk to reduce Fort Schuyler, Gen. Burgoyne determined to send out another strong detachment on his left, towards Bennington. The command of this detachment was given to Lt. Col. Baum,[37] a Hessian; and Col. Breymann,[38] with another detachment, was ordered to cover and support Baum. These were met by the brave Gen. Stark, who gave them a complete overthrow. On the morning of the 16th, 32 officers and near 700 men were taken prisoners, with four light field-pieces, nearly 1000 arms, a quantity of baggage, etc. The Americans were said to have had about 25 men killed: the loss of the enemy in killed was judged to be near 200. Fort Schuyler was closely besieged by St. Leger; and the brave Col. Herkimer,[39] with the Tryon county militia, was marching to its relief. St. Leger learning his advance, drew off a large part of his besieging troops, to meet and give him battle, before he got near the fort: the battle was obstinate, and the militia behaved with great bravery, but were at length defeated; their brave Colonel and many of the militia were slain: it was said that the action lasted five or six hours.

Matters now appearing more serious in this quarter, Gen. Arnold marched with a sufficient detachment to raise the siege. As soon as St. Leger learnt his approach, he sent off some Indians, as if friends, to meet Arnold and inform him that St. Leger had received a strong reinforcement, and advise Arnold to halt and wait for a rein-forcement himself then abandoned the siege with precipitation, leaving his tents standing, his baggage, artillery, etc. behind him. Thus were both Burgoyne's wings effectually clipped.

September 1—Intelligence was received, that after much maneuvering, Howe's fleet came to anchor in Chesapeake Bay, on the 21st ult. consisting of near 200 sail, and it was expected that he would soon land his troops. The 24th, Gen. Washington's army was on full march to meet Howe and then within five miles of Philadelphia. A valuable cargo arrived safe from Spain; among other articles, a large number of shoes, hose, blankets, shirts, cordage, duck, etc.

September 2—Intelligence was received, that Gen. Howe's army had landed at the Head of Elk.[40] A detachment from Gen. Sullivan's division a little before this time made an excursion on to Staten Island, and brought off several hundred prisoners, and a large quantity of baggage. The American loss was said to be about 60, including officers.

September 5—Four hundred and one prisoners, taken near Bennington by Gen. Stark, were escorted to Boston; they consisted of British, Brunswick and Canadian troops.

September 9—Capt. Haraden[41] arrived at Boston in a Connecticut State ship of 20 guns: he brought in with him a Jamaica packet, which he took during his cruise. It was said the packet had a large sum in specie on board; and a Mr. Shirley and family, on their passage to England. The last accounts stated both Gen. Washington's and the northern army to be near the enemy; and important news might be momently expected.

September 19—Col. Lee's[42] regiment moved into Boston.

September 20—The disagreeable news was received, that on the 11th inst. a severe action took place between Gen. Washington's and Howe's armies, near the Brandywine, which ended rather in favor of the latter, who remained masters of the field. The British here, as in several other instances, had recourse to stratagem: they held out the appearance of an intention of forcing their way at Chad's Ford, which Gen. Knyphausen menaced with a heavy column of Hessians; while the British column, by a long circuitous march, reached the forks of the river, and there secured a safe passage. Gen. Washington was pretty early apprised of this movement, and immediately took measures for strengthening his right, by ordering some troops from his left. After the action had become pretty warm on the right, and the British had got the advantage, Knyphausen passed Chad's Ford; and although the troops who were still on the left behaved well, they were by no means sufficient to resist the heavy column of Hessians. It is said that after the Hessian Grenadiers had crossed the Ford, they halted at the foot of the hill, below the Americans, under a warm fire, and with great deliberation changed their hats for their heavy brass caps, which they carried by a loop on a button at the hip, and then ascended the hill, from which the Americans were obliged to retire. Here the brave Capt. Bryant, of the artillery, who had before several times distinguished himself under the eye of our General, received a musket-ball in the bottom of his belly; a brother officer carried him off the field, but he died of the wound.

Gen. Washington, seconded by his officers, did everything in their power to check the British; and a part of the American army took a position which probably saved the army from a total defeat. Perhaps the American army were, more or less, more generally engaged in this action than in any other during the war. The American loss was considerable in killed and wounded, and a number of pieces of brass field artillery were lost. The British also suffered pretty severely in killed and wounded. The next night, Gen. Grey[43] made, with much secrecy, an attack[44] on a body of Americans, under the command of Gen. Wayne: the bayonet was chiefly made use of, and it proved but too efficacious against the Americans, who suffered considerable loss, in killed and wounded. Gen. Washington retreated first to Philadelphia, and then left the city. The British army a few days afterwards advanced to Germantown, and on the 27th a detachment of their army took possession of Philadelphia.

September 23—Gen. Washington's orders for sending forward Colonels Lee, Henley and Jackson's regiments, were received by our General.

September 24—Several prizes were sent in by a privateer brig belonging to Col. Sears.

September 25—Intelligence was received, that on Friday, the 19th instant, there was a warm and bloody action[45] between Gen. Gates's and Burgoyne's advanced troops, which lasted until dark. The troops behaved with the greatest bravery on both sides. Col. Morgan's light corps, and eleven other American regiments were more or less engaged. Of the Americans, two Lieutenant-Colonels, Coburn and Adams,[46] three Captains, three Subalterns, and 56 noncommissioned officers and privates were killed, and 248 wounded. The loss of the enemy was very considerable, and much greater than that of the Americans. On the 18th, the day preceding the foregoing battle, Col. Brown[47] made an excursion in the enemy's rear to Lake George; made 293 of the enemy prisoners: retook 100 Americans: he also took near 100 bateaux,[48] several large gun-boats, an armed sloop, etc. —took possession of the French lines (so called) at Ticonderoga, and summoned Fort Independence to surrender.

September 27—Col. Crafts' regiment of State artillery marched out of Boston, with four light field-pieces and an eight-inch howitzer, towards Providence, on a secret expedition, as it was called.

September 29—Intelligence was received, that several valuable prizes had been sent into Dartmouth.

October 2—Intelligence was received, that on the 16th, Gen. Du Coudray was drowned in the Schuylkill; he rode into the ferry-boat at one end, but was not able to command his horse, who went out at the other end of the boat, plunging into the river. This officer, as before mentioned, was engaged to come to America to take command of the artillery; but whatever may have been his talents, the artillery was so well commanded that the placing a foreign officer over them, in such a manner, and whose rank would also have soared above many other officers in the line, would most certainly have produced a convulsion in the army, had it been persisted in. This circumstance prevented the danger. The same day Col. Lee's regiment marched for the main army.

October 6—Col. H. Jackson's regiment encamped on Boston common, and the next day, about noon, marched out of town for the army; the regiment, although small, made a good appearance. About the same time that the regiment marched out of town, upwards of 100 British and Canadian prisoners, taken near Lake George, by Col. Brown, marched in.

October 8—It was learnt that a body of the enemy, said to be about 3000, were moving from New York towards Peek's Kill. Gen. Washington, after he left Philadelphia, encamped near a place called Skippack Creek, about 16 miles from Germantown.

October 13—At three o'clock a.m. an express arrived from Gen. Gates's army, with an account that on Tuesday, the 7th inst. a smart action[49] took place between the right of Gen. Burgoyne's army and the American left, when the enemy were repulsed, drove back to their works, and then forced from them. Three Field-Officers, six Captains, 10 Subalterns, one Quarter-Master-General, and 190 privates were taken prisoners, besides 300 taken in the hospital eight pieces of brass cannon, two twelve and six six-pounders, three ammunition wagons, 300 tents, 200 barrels of flour, and a large quantity of baggage were trophies of the victory. One hundred of the enemy lay dead on the ground. The American loss, although not exactly known, was said not to be more than 30 killed and 100 wounded; among the latter, Generals Arnold and Lincoln, both in the leg, the former but slightly; it was problematical whether the latter was wounded by a British or American soldier. Gen. Fraser,[50] an enterprising officer of the British, was mortally wounded, and died of his wounds.

October 15—Intelligence was received, that a body of the British from New York, in about 30 transports, had proceeded up the Hudson; they had made several landings below and at Peek's Kill: on Monday, the 6th, they crossed over, landed on the west side of the river, and marched along the hills towards Fort Montgomery and its dependencies: this fort was tolerably situated on the bank of the Hudson, to annoy shipping going up the river; and the works were pretty good on that side, but were not so, nor fully completed on the back side; and the right flank was commanded by higher ground on the south, and near the fort, on the other side of Pooplop's[51] Creek, the mouth of which was near to the south side of the fort; on this higher ground, and near to the small deep pond, a strong redoubt, called Clinton, was erected; it was equally essential that this redoubt should be taken, as a reduction of the fort: the British therefore moved against this redoubt, while another column, by a more circuitous movement, fell in the rear of Fort Montgomery; they were met in the defiles, where the skirmishes were sharp; but they continued to advance to the redoubt, which was nobly defended, and before which they sustained very considerable loss (a number of their slain were afterwards drawn out of the pond, where they had been thrown for concealment) but soon carried it, and afterwards Fort Montgomery.

The garrison principally made their escape in the dusk of the evening; among them were Gov. Clinton and his brother, who was a Brigadier General also: they made their escape in a very hazardous manner, and the latter was wounded. After the reduction of Fort Montgomery, the Americans evacuated Fort Constitution and the block-house on Constitution Island, opposite to West Point (the latter was not yet fortified); and two new frigates, *Congress* and *Montgomery*, which lay in the river, were set on fire by the Americans and burnt. The enemy afterwards proceeded up the river, and burnt Esopus[52]; their object was if possible to form a junction with Burgoyne, or open a water communication to Albany; and spies passed between them.

October 16—Two or three of the enemy's cruisers appeared in the bay, but a few leagues from the Light. While the British army lay encamped at Germantown, Gen. Washington resolved to attack them. This was a brave design; and the success of the first onset, at about three o'clock, a.m. of the 4th inst. after the Americans had marched all the night, was equal to the design; for the British, where the attack was first made, were almost instantly pushed from their ground, and were falling back panic struck on their other troops, when Lt. Col. Musgrave[53] had the presence of mind to throw several companies into a strong stone house.[54] Houses at all times, and especially those of stone and brick, under a judicious conduct, admit of a good defense; and at this time probably proved the means of the Americans losing an advantage, which no one can tell how far it might have been pushed. When an enemy is routed, and panic-struck are flying before the assailants, the best, if not the only way is to follow them, if the ground will permit of it, close at their heels, taking care not to fall into ambuscades. Thus the panic of fear continues to multiply; but if the pursuers stop, and especially if those who were flying hear a firing behind them, but not upon them, they conclude that their own troops in turn have gotten an advantage, or at least are holding their pursuers at bay. This immediately recovers them from their panic; they will next return to the charge, and will be more likely to make an obstinate resistance than before they were at first routed; while their return to the charge will greatly damp those who before considered themselves almost in the grasp of victory.

Hence what took place at Germantown was no wonder. The fogginess of the morning was unfortunate for the Americans: but the British taking possession of the stone house, and defending it, was the most unfortunate circumstance. The loss on both sides was considerable; on the side of the Americans, Brig. Gen. Nash,[55] and on the side of the British Brig. Gen. Agnew,[56] were among the slain; but though this attempt was not crowned with victory, it caused the British to have a more reverential opinion of Gen. Washington, whom they now found dare to attack their whole army, even in a chosen position of their own. Perhaps is was best that the action closed as it did; had the Americans made their way far into the long street of that town, probably many other houses would have been occupied in the same way. The burying-yard, with a strong wall, was lined with troops by the enemy; and the position in which their army lay was calculated for their wings closing in to much advantage; at any rate, the battle must have been very bloody, and situation and circumstances were in favor of the British. After the British were in possession of Philadelphia, they had much to do in order to get possession of the Delaware, and remove the obstructions which had been formed in it. There were also several works to be reduced; among others, a fort on Mud-Island, and a pretty strong work at Red Bank.

October 22—Highly important and most interesting intelligence was received, that on the 17th inst. Gen. Burgoyne and his whole army surrendered, under Convention. They were to be marched to the neighborhood of Boston, and from thence sent to England. Upon receipt of this news, the cannon on Fort Hill were discharged, and joy was seated on every brow.

October 23—At one o'clock, p.m. the cannon on Fort Hill and on the heights of Dorchester were discharged, and also on board the ships in the harbor. In the evening, our General's quarters[57] (the house of the late Hon. Mr. Russell) was beautifully illuminated. The following is the number of troops which surrendered to Maj. Gen. Gates, and the state of Gen. Burgoyne's army after he left Canada:

Under the Convention

British,	2,442
Foreign,	2,198
Canadians, etc. sent back to Canada,	1,100
Staff,	12
	5,752

Prisoners taken at different times,	400
Sick and wounded,	528
Deserters,	300
Lost at Bennington,	1,120
Killed since the 17th of September,	600
Killed and taken at Ticonderoga,	413
	Total, **9,113**

The brass ordnance taken were as follows: two 24-pounders; four 12-pounders; 18 six-pounders; four three-pounders; two eight-inch mortars; five howitzers; total, 35, exclusive of those taken at Bennington.

Thus were the British totally disappointed in this quarter. The troops intended to form a junction on the Hudson were as high up as Poughkeepsie; and Gen. Burgoyne informed our General after he arrived at Boston, that on the evening after he had proposed to Gen. Gates to surrender, in case he could obtain honorable terms,

The surrender of British forces at Saratoga, October 1777 (Library of Congress).

which were to be settled the next day, a spy came in from the troops down the river, stating how far they had got up and what steps were next to be taken; on which he (Gen. Burgoyne) assembled his officers more generally than usual in councils, and stated to them the circumstances and situation of both armies, and whether, consistently with fair principles of honor they could break off the negotiation for an honorable Convention, or not; when it was the unanimous opinion of every officer present that they could not. But in a situation like this at that moment, danger at hand is more powerful on the mind than the hope of relief at a distance. The troops who were up the river returned down.

The capture of Gen. Burgoyne and his whole army, who were now on their way to Boston, opened a new, important and delicate field for our General. This army, in which there were many officers of military erudition and some of refined and courtly manners, who had a high opinion of national honor and prowess, and who, in consequence of the Convention which they had formed, had their spirits by no means depressed, as those who are compelled to surrender at discretion, were sure to lay a heavy task on his shoulders. As soon as he was notified that these troops were coming under his direction, he set him self in earnest to prepare for their reception. The barracks at Prospect and Winter Hills were directed to be put instantly in order. The Council was applied to, to aid in the procurement of quarters from the citizens for the officers; nor was this an easy task. The families of the citizens generally wanting the room in their respective houses, rendered it difficult to obtain so many quarters as were necessary for so great number, and extended the limits of the parole very considerably. The Council were disposed to do everything in their power, and gave orders accordingly whenever they were necessary. A heavy duty was also falling on the Quarter-Master's department, as it respected quarters, and also fuel, the latter of which had been rendered scarce in the vicinity by the American army having been here in 1775; and the enemy's cruisers prevented its being brought from the eastern country.

But by the exertions of Col. Chase, who was Deputy-Quarter-Master-General, and the assistants and conductors in this department, and of Col. Davis, who was Deputy-Barrack-Master, and who, in the procurement of fuel, was indefatigable, a comfortable supply was obtained. Before the arrival of the troops at Cambridge, our General had digested and drafted a parole, and several articles for the government of the troops in quarters; these he had drawn in as an article in the parole; and the honor of the officers in this way was pledged for their observance of the articles, which rendered the government of them much easier; being thus bound to govern themselves with propriety, or infringe their paroles; knowing that many things in minutiae would be to settle, which would be tedious in an epistolary way. As soon as General Burgoyne had arrived at Cambridge, our General sent over one of his Aides-de-camp to invite Gen. Burgoyne to dine with him the next day, bringing with him his two Major-Generals, Phillips and Reidesel. An elegant dinner was prepared, and many other gentlemen invited, among whom were Generals Glover of Massachusetts, and Whipple[58] of New Hampshire, who were at the capture and had commanded the escort, etc. from Saratoga to Cambridge.

November 8—Our General sent one of his aides to accompany Gen. Burgoyne and the other officers into Boston by the way of Roxbury; they arrived some time before dinner, as was intended, that business might be considered. The parole was shown to them, and the articles for their government in quarters, with which they were well pleased. But here a discovery was first made of something which they wished to retain while in our country, and which our General would never for a moment allow; General Phillips turning to our General, observed, "Sir, you well know the disposition of soldiers, and that they will more or less in all armies commit some disorders; suppose you should delegate to Gen. Burgoyne the power of seeing your orders executed." Our General replied that he knew the disposition of soldiers, and also the necessity of order and discipline; that he was not only willing, but expected that Gen. Burgoyne, and every other officer, would exert them selves to keep order; that for this purpose among themselves, and for the internal order and obedience, he might command and punish as might appear to be necessary; but in no case to attempt capital punishment. But as to the exercise of his own command, and enforcement of his own orders when necessary, this was a jurisdiction which Gen. Burgoyne must not expect to exercise while here. Gen. Burgoyne smiled, and Gen. Phillips turned it off by saying, "I only meant it for your easement, Sir."

Before dinner was done, so great was the curiosity of the citizens of both sexes, and of all ages and descriptions, to get a peep at Gen. Burgoyne, that the streets were filled, the doors, windows, the tops of the houses and fences crowded. Gen. Burgoyne had asked our General if he would indulge him to go out of town by the way of Charlestown, which was instantly granted. When he was ready to depart, our General told him that he should accompany him to the ferry; and a procession was formed, the American gentlemen mixing with the British. The streets were so crowded, that it was difficult getting along; but not a word or a gesture that was disrespectful. When arrived opposite to the Province-House, General Burgoyne turned round to the other Generals, and observed, "There is the former residence of the Governor;" when some person on the side of the street, and in a tone fully to be heard, added, *"and on the other side is the riding school,"* alluding to the Old South Meeting-House having been put to that use in 1775: but the General, who must have heard it, made no reply, but soon after observed, "Sir, I am astonished at the civility of your people; for were you walking the streets of London in my situation, you would not escape insult." When arrived at the ferry-ways, the crowd were down to the water's edge; but when the boat put off, there was not the least indecency, or wry countenance discovered—O my dear countrymen! How did this your dignified conduct at that moment charm my very soul! Such conduct flows from a greatness of mind, that goes to conquer a world. Col. Keith was appointed Deputy- Adjutant-General, and Major Swasey[59] Town Major.

November 14—The Council were still deliberating on the subject of quarters, and determined to do every thing in their power; but some individuals were refractory.

November 19—Gen. Hancock arrived in town, and was saluted by the discharge of the cannon of the Fort, Park, etc.

November 22—Intelligence was received of the repulse of the enemy before the redoubt at Red Bank, on the 22nd ult. This redoubt or fort had a garrison by no means sufficient properly to man the whole work. The commanding officer had therefore wisely lessened it, by running a parapet with a ditch across the area of the fort, but had left the work entire in its largest extent. A body of chosen troops were sent to reduce this work, under the command of the Hessian Col. Donop,[60] a brave and good officer. In order if possible to get some idea of the work, he sent his summons for the fort to surrender by a very capable adjutant; but the Commandant of the fort took care to have him stopped without the work, and where he had no opportunity to see more than the ditch and parapet on that side. The commanding officer refusing to surrender, an assault was made; the assailants at the head of the column bringing in their hands a sufficient number of short fascines to fill the ditch where they meant to pass, which was well done, and the parapet was mounted; but to their disappointment and surprise, they now found there was another ditch and parapet to pass, and in the face of a dreadful fire too, which made great slaughter; a number of them, however, advanced into the second ditch, and began to remove the frizes on the berme; but these were generally killed in the ditch, and such as were not killed or wounded obliged to quit the outer work.

Their loss in killed and wounded was great; among the latter Col. Donop mortally; he was taken after the action near the fort, and brought in. An Ensign had made his way over the second ditch, had got on to the frizes, and lay close against the base of the parapet until the action was over, and then got up and surrendered, observing that he thought his position the only safe one; for had he attempted to put his head above the parapet, he knew his brains would have been instantly blown out; or if he had attempted to re-cross the ditch, he should have been shot in the back. Besides this severe check, the British met with considerable opposition and loss at other places, before they got full and peaceable possession of the river; particularly at Mud Island. They lost the *Augusta* man-of-war, and suffered other naval damage.

Gen. Washington being now considerably reinforced with a part of the northern conquering army, advanced to White Marsh, about 14 miles from Philadelphia, where he encamped in a strong and well chosen position. Gen. Howe, apprehensive that this movement indicated a design upon Philadelphia, determined to move out, and either invite Gen. Washington to a general action, or, if he found him vulnerable, to attack him in his own position. Accordingly, on the evening of the 4th of December, he marched with the British army, and on the next morning took post on Chestnut Hill, in front of the American right. Gen. Washington, knowing the goodness of his position, wisely continued in it; nor dare Gen. Howe attack him. The latter then changed his ground to a new position, opposite to the American left and center, but neither dare he attack either of these. Several skirmishes took place, as is usual in such cases; in one of which Brig. Gen. Irvine[61] on the American side was wounded. After several days spent in this way, Howe was obliged to return without affecting any thing, to the no small injury of his army, who had suffered much from the inclemency of the season. Indeed nothing is more destructive to an army than winter campaigns. After this, Gen. Washington moved the American army to Valley Forge, on the Schuylkill, about 16 miles from Philadelphia, where he took a position as wisely chosen as the other, and where the army erected huts for the winter. We now return to take up our chain of events.

November 23—A French ship, with dry goods from France, by the way of St. Pierre, arrived at Boston. Gen. Burgoyne had not yet signed the parole; he pretended to delay until their quarters were fully furnished, although he had every assurance that it should be done as fast as circumstances would possibly admit. On this day, therefore, our General wrote him the following letter.

HEADQUARTERS, BOSTON, Nov. 23rd, 1777.

SIR,

Two weeks have now elapsed since I had fully expected that the officers would have signed their paroles. They have, during this time, been enjoying in a great measure the liberty of the limits intended to be assigned to them, without pledging their honor by parole; which is not only contrary to the established custom of nations, but contrary to the eleventh article of the Convention. Whatever objections might at first be made to giving the parole must now be done away, by the fullest evidence that proper quarters shall be provided, and which in a very considerable degree is already done. I must, therefore, in the most explicit terms, insist that the officers who wish and expect to be permitted on parole, agreeably to the Convention, do sign it tomorrow. This is so reasonable, that I expect there will be no further hesitancy; and I still assure your Excellency, that no endeavors of mine shall be wanting to fulfill the Convention, and to treat the officers with politeness and generosity.

I am, etc.
(Signed) WILLIAM HEATH.

November 25—Gen. Burgoyne and the other officers of the Convention signed their parole. Congress before this, viz. on the 8th instant, passed the following resolve:

In Congress, Nov. 8th, 1777.

Resolved, That Maj. Gen. Heath be directed forthwith to cause to be taken down the name and rank of every commissioned officer, and the name, former place of abode and occupation, size, age, and description of every non- commissioned officer and private soldier, and all other persons comprehended in the Convention made between Lt. Gen. Burgoyne and Maj. Gen. Gates, on the 16th day of October, 1777, and transmit an authentic copy thereof to the Board of War, in order that if any officer or soldier, or other person as above mentioned, of the said army, shall hereafter be found in arms against these States in North America, during the present contest, he may be convicted of the offence, and suffer the punishment in such case inflicted by the law of nations.

That Maj. Gen. Heath be directed to take the parole in writing of the officers, according to the Convention, and transmit authenticated copies of such paroles to the Board of War.

Extract from the Minutes,
(Signed) CHARLES THOMSON, Sec'y.

Upon the foregoing being communicated to Gen. Burgoyne, and he called upon to have the said descriptive lists made out accordingly, he wrote our General the following letter:

CAMBRIDGE, Nov. 20th, 1777.

SIR,

I received a paper, dated headquarters, Boston, Nov. 20th, purporting to be

Gen. John Burgoyne.

founded upon express orders from the Honorable Continental Congress, which paper I return as inadmissible, because extending to matters in which the Congress have no right of interference. A list of the names and rank of every commissioned officer, and the numbers of the non-commissioned officers and soldiers, may be necessary to you, Sir, for the purpose of fulfilling the Convention, in quartering officers, and the regular delivery of provisions, fuel, etc. Such lists shall be prepared at your request; but before any other lists can be granted, I must be assured of the purposes for which they are intended, and the word order must neither be mentioned or implied.

I have the honor to be, etc.
(Signed) J. BURGOYNE, Lt. Gen.

To Maj. Gen. HEATH.

To the foregoing, our General wrote an answer as follows:

HEADQUARTERS, BOSTON, Nov. 21st, 1777.

SIR,

Yours of yesterday is before me; and although you might at first imagine that the Hon. Continental Congress have no right of interference in matters of the Convention, yet I conclude upon further reflection you must be convinced, that as that body are the Representatives of that people who are to reap the advantages or disadvantages of the Convention, and as all continental officers are acting by virtue of their authority, and under their direction, they assuredly have a right of interference, and to give such orders to their officers as they may think proper, for the full completion of the Convention, and for the safety and good of the people.

The paragraph of my orders of the 20th inst. respecting the troops of the Convention is founded in reason and justice, being designed only to ascertain the officers and soldiers who were comprehended in the Convention, that in case any of them (contrary to their faith and honor) should hereafter be found in arms against these States, in North America, during the present contest, they may be convicted of the offence, and suffer the punishment in such case inflicted by the law of nations. I must therefore insist that you furnish me with proper lists of names and descriptions, for the purpose before mentioned, as soon as may be.

The other lists of the names and rank of the commissioned officers, and number of non-commissioned officers and soldiers, so essentially necessary for the several purposes of regularity with Quarter-Masters and Commissaries (and which should be frequently renewed, as circumstances may vary) should long ere this have been exhibited. Some days since, I directed my Deputy-Adjutant-General to call for them; and I expect they will be sent in without delay, for the purposes above mentioned. I shall at all times endeavor to found my orders on the principles of honor, reason and justice, and not to infringe those delicate principles in others; but my orders for the purposes of order and regularity, must be obeyed by every man placed under my direction; and fully determined I am, that offenders shall not pass with impunity.

I am, etc.
(Signed) W. HEATH, Maj. Gen.

Lt. Gen. BURGOYNE.

November 23—Gen. Burgoyne wrote an answer to the foregoing. But he now acknowledged a further extent of the supreme power, than in his former letter; but still at least obliquely denied the right of their interference with the Convention troops, who were under express stipulations until they quitted the country, and that no new conditions could be imposed upon them; and asserting that no such requisitions were laid upon the American prisoners in Canada; and concluding, that if it could be found that such had been required by the British in any case, he would submit to it. About this time, an officer who had been a prisoner in Canada returned to Boston on parole, and gave information that he and others had complied with similar injunctions before they came away; upon this being communicated to Gen. Burgoyne, he found that he had got to the end of his tether of evasion; he did not attempt to dispute more, but observed that he supposed if it was done any time before the troops departed, it would answer the purpose. Our General found that nothing could be done by force, for were he to attempt of himself to have the lists taken, everything might be evaded except the size and complexion. He therefore laid the matter before Congress, with the copies of what had passed. Congress took the matter into consideration, and President Laurens wrote our General an approbation of his conduct, and not to push the matter, as Congress would take a more extensive view of the business; concluding his letter, "I have in conclusion to assure you, Sir, that Congress repose the utmost confidence in your address and abilities for conducting with propriety this important business, in which, on one side, the faith and honor of these infant States are to be preserved, and on the other, the magnanimity and resolution of Congress to be exemplified."

December—Congress had received some intimations that an application would be made to them for leave for the troops of the Convention to embark at some other place than Boston; they therefore on the 1st of December passed a resolution that no other place than that stipulated in the Convention, viz. Boston, should be admitted. A few days after, Gen. Burgoyne applied, as was suspected, but to no purpose. Congress also passed resolutions that all the assistance of provisions and other necessaries furnished to the troops of the Convention should be paid for in specie, or replaced in quantity or quality.

CHAPTER 4

1778

January 1778—Gen. Burgoyne had now got himself into a very serious entanglement; he had not only refused, and then delayed to give descriptive lists of the troops of the Convention, but some time before, viz. in the month of November, had written a letter to Gen. Gates, complaining that the troops had not been furnished with quarters as they had a right to expect, and among other things a paragraph as follows:

> While I state to you, Sir, this very unexpected treatment, I entirely acquit Maj. Gen. Heath and every gentleman of the military department of any inattention to the public faith engaged in the Convention. They do what they can; but while the Supreme Powers of the State are unable or unwilling to enforce their authority, and the inhabitants want the hospitality, or indeed the common civilization to assist us without it, the public faith is broke, and we are the immediate sufferers.

This was unreasonable, both as it respected the civil power and the people; for the former did everything in their power, unless they had turned the citizens out of their houses to have let the Convention officers in, which was not to be expected; nor could it be supposed that the citizens would turn their families themselves into the streets. But Congress considered the conduct of Gen. Burgoyne, and these and other of his expressions on the occasion, as calling for serious consideration.

They therefore investigated the whole in all its latitudes; and the President of Congress wrote to our General that as it was a matter of high importance, and required deep deliberation, it would probably occupy some days, before the resolutions would be completed. But that, in case the fleet arrived before the papers were sent to him, to forbid the embarkation. Gen. Burgoyne had received intimations that a fleet of transports were about to come round for the troops, and that the *Juno* frigate was to wear a flag for his particular accommodation. This he mentioned to our General, and wished to know if the frigate might come up into the harbor. Our General had no apprehensions of any danger from a frigate entering the harbor, but apprehended that some people might think that he was not sufficiently vigilant, in case he allowed it. He therefore told Gen. Burgoyne that the frigate could not come up into the harbor, and hinted to him the taking of one of the most convenient transports in the fleet for the purpose; and he might do as he pleased when he got off. This touched Gen. Burgoyne exceedingly, who wrote a letter to our General, in which was the following paragraph:

> As to your allotment of a *convenient transport* for my passage, if it was from yourself, I am to thank you Sir, for a sort of insult which the most haughty man of office would

be ashamed of, in any other country. However, as I am determined every transaction concerning this Convention shall be notorious, and beyond the powers of subterfuge to explain away, I have directed the frigate together with the transports to come round, and it will then be for you, Sir, to prohibit the entry of Boston harbor to any ships bearing a flag of truce, and declaring they are sent for the express purpose of conveying to Great Britain any part of the troops of the Convention.

(Signed) J. BURGOYNE.

Maj. Gen. HEATH.

To which our General wrote the following answer:

HEADQUARTERS, BOSTON, Jan. 5th, 1778.

SIR,

Your Excellency's favor of yesterday came duly to hand; and I must confess I was not a little surprised at some expressions in it. As by the Convention, transports only are stipulated to receive the troops, I submit to you, Sir, whether a hint (if you were even sure that it came from myself) that you should take a convenient one, rather than introduce a frigate, which is neither expressed or implied in the Convention, merits those epithets which you are pleased to bestow on me.

I have every aimed to treat you with politeness; and the plighted faith and honor of my country require me to pay strict attention to the Convention on their part: of course, when transports arrive to receive the troops, they will enter the harbor; and if you can find by the Convention that a frigate is to enter for the particular reception of yourself, she will not be prohibited. But if it is rather uncommon for ships of war to bear flags of truce, and if consenting to it in the present case should appear to be rather an act of politeness and generosity than otherwise, I leave you to your own reflections whether you have made choice of the most happy expressions to obtain it.

(Signed) W. HEATH.

Lt. Gen. BURGOYNE.

Gen. Burgoyne somehow communicated to Viscount Howe[1] the subject of the frigate, who wrote Gen. Burgoyne the following letter some time after, but before the transports came round.

Eagle,[2] RHODE ISLAND, Feb. 3rd, 1778.

SIR,

I am much concerned to find by your letter I had the honor to receive from you, on the return of Capt. Piper, that you have suffered so greatly in your health. But I hope that a speedy removal to a milder climate will contribute to your effectual recovery. The transports have only been delayed to take the precautions necessary for their safe passage at this season of the year. As it is not to be expected that the frigate ordered for your reception, though carrying a flag of truce, and restricted from every act of hostility in consequence, whilst attending this service, should be admitted within the port of Boston, the commander, Capt. Jacobs, will be to land a letter under the same sanction, for giving you notice of his arrival off the entrance of the port. He will wait to be favored in your answer with notice of the time you may expect to embark, on which occasion I trust you will find every facility that your impaired state of health may require.

(Signed) HOWE.

Thus did the Admiral's opinion perfectly coincide with that of our General. But Congress had passed a resolution, on the 8th day of January, upon principles clearly expressed in a report of a committee upon which the resolution was founded:

That the embarkation of Lt. Gen. Burgoyne, and the troops under his command, be suspended, till a distinct and explicit ratification of the Convention of Saratoga shall be properly notified by the Court of Great Britain to Congress.

Our General's correspondence with Gen. Burgoyne, respecting the frigate, etc. was transmitted to Congress, and the President soon after wrote him: "The House appeared to be pleased with your conduct in every respect relative to that officer."

Gen. Burgoyne applied to Congress for leave to go to Europe himself; but Congress did not then think proper to grant his request. Although this denial must have been very painful to the General, he did not express himself, or write anything in the least improper. He observed to our General, that he was sorry; for that not only his health urged his departure, but that every day he was detained here, gave his enemies at home an opportunity for piercing the wound of his reputation the deeper.

But Col. Kingston was not so prudent as the General: a packet of letters, which Gen. Burgoyne wished to send to Gen. Howe, was sent to our General for inspection; among these was one from Col. Kingston to Lord Harcourt, in which, after observing that fortune had not shown them the smooth side of her face, yet they thought their misfortunes honorable, proceeded, that he (Gen. Burgoyne) was not well, but "you know his firmness. But I think the insincerity of France, bigotry of Spain, or the vindictive Portuguese, situated as he is, would not have sought for means unnecessarily to detain him." This insult to the authority of the country induced our General to detain this letter, and he notified Gen. Burgoyne of it, adding, that while it was his wish to gratify the officers as much as possible in writing to their friends, he expected they would be cautious and prudent in their manner of expression. When the American Deputy-Adjutant-General gave the letter from our General to Gen. Burgoyne, and he had read it, he observed: "I told Col. Kingston that Gen. Heath would not let that letter pass." He should have done more—forbid his making the attempt.

Another serious matter took place about this time: Col. Henley,[3] who had the immediate command at Cambridge, a brave and good officer, but warm and quick in his natural temper, having ordered some prisoners who were under guard turned out, that he might examine them, one of them treated him, as he judged, with much insolence; upon which he pricked him with a sword, or bayonet. Gen. Burgoyne immediately presented a complaint against Col. Henley, charging him with barbarous and wanton conduct, and intentional murder, as appears in the following letter :

CAMBRIDGE, Jan. 9th, 1778.

SIR,

A report has been made to me of a disturbance that happened at the barracks on Wednesday afternoon, for which I am much concerned; and though the provocations from your people, which originally occasioned it, were of the most atrocious nature, I was willing the offender on our part should be properly punished. But Col. Henley, not content with that, made prisoners of eighteen innocent men, and sent them on board a guard-ship, as alleged by your order. It is not only a duty to my situation to demand the immediate discharge of these men, together with a satisfactory apology; but I also mean it as an attention to you, Sir, that I give you an immediate opportunity to disavow so unjustifiable a proceeding as committing men to the worst of prisons upon vague report, caprice and passion.

Insults and provocations, at which the most placid dispositions would revolt, are daily given to the officers and soldiers of this army. Regular, decent complaints are received by your officers, sometimes with haughtiness, sometimes with derision, but always without redress. These evils flow, Sir, from the general tenor of language and conduct held by Col. Henley, which encourages his inferiors, and seems calculated to excite the most bloody purposes.

For want of sufficient information, and not bringing myself to believe it possible that facts as related by common report could be true, I have hitherto declined taking public notice of this man; but upon positive grounds I now and hereby formally accuse Col. Henley of behavior heinously criminal as an officer, and unbecoming a man; of the most indecent, violent, vindictive severity against unarmed men, and of intentional murder. I demand prompt and satisfactory justice, and will not doubt your readiness to give it. Whenever you will inform me that a proper tribunal is appointed, I will take care that undeniable evidence shall be produced to support these charges.

I am, etc.

(Signed) J. BURGOYNE.

To which our General returned the following answer:

HEADQUARTERS, BOSTON, Jan. 10th, 1778.

SIR,

Yours of yesterday's date, I received the last evening. What provocations you allude to, as having been offered by my troops, I am at a loss to determine. The insults and abuses which they have received, I will venture to say, unless I have been most grossly misinformed, are unparalleled; and whether you are willing or unwilling, Sir, offenders shall no longer pass with impunity. If it can be made to appear that any of those soldiers sent to the guard-ship by my orders, are innocent, they shall be released from their confinement: but with respect to such as have been guilty of violating my standing orders of the garrison, instead of disavowing or making any apology for the confinement of such, be assured that I do most explicitly avow it.

And as I have before observed to your Excellency in a former letter, of which you may be assured, I shall at all times endeavor to found my orders on the principles of honor, reason and justice, and not to infringe those delicate principles in others: so also be assured, Sir, that such my orders shall be obeyed by every officer and soldier placed under my direction; and such as have the hardiness to transgress them, shall abide the consequences. I have been informed of late, that some have hinted that such of your troops as break my orders, ought to be tried and punished by your orders. Even the mention of such a thing, I conceive to be (to use your own words in a late letter, with a little variation) a sort of insult that a man of military erudition in any country would be ashamed of, as being repugnant to every idea of military discipline; and from my opinion of your military knowledge, I cannot admit that you ever hinted it.

To convince you that it is my fixed determination to inquire into all abuses, whether committed by my own troops, or those of the Convention, whilst they remain within my department, I have ordered Col. Henley under arrest, and appointed a Court of Inquiry, whereof Brig. Gen. Glover is President, to examine into the grounds of your complaint, on Wednesday next, at 10 o'clock, a.m. at Cambridge; and if any complaints have heretofore passed un-redressed it is because they have not been laid before me. You hinted to me when I had the pleasure of seeing you last at Cambridge, that one of my officers had been enticing some of the troops of the Convention to enter our service. I then informed you, that if you would send the complaint, I would immediately bring the officer to trial. You promised to do it, but I have not yet received it. I now call upon you to exhibit that charge, or any other that you have to make against any officer under my command, for practices of that kind, or any other; being with yourself fully determined that all my conduct respecting the Convention shall be notorious, and beyond the powers of subterfuge to explain away.

Complaints of most enormous abuses have lately been made to me; one, of the conduct of a number of officers on the evening or night of the 25th of December, at Bradish's Tavern; others, of prisoners being rescued from the guards—sentinels abused and insulted on their posts—passes counterfeited, and others filled up in the most affrontive manner; and of late, several highway robberies committed in the environs of the garrison—one the last evening, in which a gentleman was robbed of between seven and 800 dollars, and a watch. The robberies I do not charge to your people, as it is unknown who were the perpetrators; but there are several reasons to suspect it. All these, Sir, tend not only to exasperate the troops, but to enrage the inhabitants of the country, who view such abuses as insufferable. I therefore call upon you to exert your endeavors to suppress all abuses, as far as in your power.

(Signed) I am, etc.
W. Heath
Lt. Gen. BURGOYNE.

Col. Henley was ordered under arrest, and Col. Lee to take command at Cambridge; and the general order of the 10th of January announced:

Lt. Gen. Burgoyne having entered a complaint against Col. Henley, charging him with gross misconduct while in command at Cambridge; the honor of the United States, and the justice due to an officer of Col. Henley's character, demand a public inquiry: for which purpose a Court of Inquiry is to sit at Cambridge on Wednesday next, at 10 o'clock in the morning, at such place as the President shall appoint.

Brigadier-General GLOVER—President.
Col. M. Jackson, Col. Nixon, Col. H. Jackson—Members.

All persons concerned, to attend the Court.

Gen. Burgoyne found fault, that a Court of Inquiry only was appointed, and not a Court-Martial. He was answered, that this was frequently the case; that it did not preclude the latter; and where an officer of rank, and in particular one who had the immediate command was the object, this previous step was both justifiable and proper. The Court of Inquiry met, and gave in their opinion; and in the general orders of January 18, the following was announced:

The Court, whereof Brig. Gen. Glover was President, appointed by the orders of the 10th inst. to inquire into the grounds of a complaint exhibited by Lt. Gen. Burgoyne again Col. Henley, late commanding officer of the American troops at Cambridge—after mature consideration are of opinion, that from the evidence offered on the side of Gen. Burgoyne against Col. Henley, it will be most for the honor of Col. Henley, as well as for the satisfaction of all concerned, that the judgment of a Court-Martial should be taken on his conduct, during his command at Cambridge. The General, approving the opinion of the Court, orders that a special general Court-Martial sit on Tuesday next, at 10 o'clock, a.m. at the courthouse in Cambridge, for the trial of Col. David Henley, late commanding officer at that post, accused by Lt. Gen. Burgoyne of a general tenor of language and conduct heinously criminal as an officer, and unbecoming a man; of the most indecent, violent, vindictive severity against unarmed men, and of intentional murder.

Brigadier-General GLOVER—President.
Col. Wesson, Col. M. Jackson, Col. Lee, Col. H. Jackson, Lt. Col. Colman,
Lt. Col. Badlam, Lt. Col. Popkin, Maj. Curtis, Capt. Langdon, Capt. Sewall,
Capt. Hastings, Capt. Randall—Members[4]
Lt. Col. Tudor is desired to act as Judge Advocate. All evidences and persons concerned, to attend the Court.

The Court met, and adjourned several times, through a long, particular, and tedious trial. Gen. Burgoyne attended, and in a very engaged and eloquent manner said everything which he judged proper; which, although novel in Courts-Martial, was yet permitted. The general orders of the 27th of February announced as follows:

> Col. David Henley, late commanding officer of the post at Cambridge, tried at the special general Court-Martial, whereof Brig. Gen. Glover was President, accused by Lt. Gen. Burgoyne of a general tenor of language and conduct heinously criminal as an officer, and unbecoming a man; of the most indecent, violent, vindictive severity against unarmed men, and of intentional murder.
>
> The Court, after mature consideration, are of opinion that the charge against Col. Henley is not supported, and that he be discharged from his arrest. The General approves the opinion of the Court; thanks them for their unwearied endeavors to investigate the truth; and orders Col. Henley to resume his command at Cambridge immediately. The General thinks it to be his duty on this occasion to observe, that although the conduct of Lt. Gen. Burgoyne (as prosecutor against Col. Henley) in the course of the foregoing trial, in his several speeches and pleas, may be warranted by some precedents in British Courts-Martial, yet as it is altogether novel in the proceedings of any general Court-Martial in the army of the United States of America, whose rules and articles of war direct that the Judge-Advocate-General shall prosecute in the name of the United States; and as a different practice tends to render Courts- Martial both tedious and expensive he does protest against this instance being drawn into precedent in future.

February 7—A British soldier at Cambridge stabbed one of the American guard.

February 18—Intelligence was received from Gov. Cooke[5] that three frigates and twenty-three sail of transports sailed from Newport, on Sunday the 15th instant, standing to the northeast. Our General received a letter from the President of Congress, in which he observed, "I had the honor of receiving, by Mr. Closki, the 5th instant, your favor of the 10th ult. including a late correspondence with Lt. Gen. Burgoyne; these were immediately reported to Congress, and transmitted to the Board of War, from whence a report has not yet ascended; therefore I have no particular commands relative to your said dispatch. I may, however, with propriety and pleasure intimate, that your conduct towards the British General and his dependents receives the continued approbation of Congress, if I may be permitted to make this conclusion from the general sentiments of the Members."

February 23—Just before noon, Gen. Lincoln arrived in Boston from Albany; his leg was recovering fast, but he was still very lame, and was conveyed from place to place on a move-able bed, with handles, which was fixed on the runners of his sleigh, with a canopy and curtains, and was convenient also to remove into the house, etc. In this was blended ingenuity and convenience.

February 28—Intelligence was received that the British transports, destined to take away the troops of the Convention, had arrived at Holmes' s Hole; and the next day, March 1, that they had arrived at Cape Harbor, Province-Town, Cape Cod. But Gen. Burgoyne was not now to depart.

March 7—General Lincoln left Boston for Hingham; our General accompanied him as far as Milton.

March 8—A cartel arrived from Cape Cod, with the following letter to Gen. Burgoyne:

Juno, CAPE COD HARBOR, 4th March, 1778.

SIR,

I take the earliest opportunity, by Lt. Carter, in the *Haarlem* cartel, to inform you of the arrival of the transports under my charge, and that I am appointed by the Viscount Howe, to receive you and your suit on board the

Juno, under my command, for your conveyance to England, when you shall be at liberty to embark separately, or together with the troops, as you will let me know in return to be your intention. And I am to acquaint you that I will move the *Juno* to Nantasket Road, for facilitating your embarkation, if you will please to inform me of your having negotiated an agreement to such effect, upon faith duly pledged, that no insult shall be offered in the meantime to any of the ships of war, or other ships and vessels, appointed for fulfilling the purpose of the Convention, and distinguished by flags of truce, in testimony of the restriction they are under from committing any acts of hostility.

You are otherwise to take your passage in the *Haarlem*, in order to your being received on board the *Juno*, in Cape Cod Harbor. Enclosed is a list of the transports, with their tonnage, that you may be able to settle the proper arrangement of the troops destined for Europe; for every thing else I refer you to our meeting on board the *Juno*, where I have a number of private letters for you, Gen. Phillips, and Col. Kingston, and a large box of letters for the army.

I am, etc.

(Signed) HUGH DALRYMPLE.

Lt. Gen. BURGOYNE.

Gen. Burgoyne having written an answer to Capt. Dalrymple, and submitted it for inspection, requested our General to send it down by the cartel; which he did under the following cover:

HEADQUARTERS, BOSTON, March 10th, 1778.

SIR,

Enclosed are sundry letters from Lt. Gen. Burgoyne, by which you will learn his present situation. Although I wish on every occasion to extend the utmost generosity to the gentlemen of the army, yet to allow letters to pass unopened would be betraying the trust reposed in me. Therefore any idea of granting such an indulgence cannot be admitted. If any advantage in the economy of expense to the government of Great Britain may be derived from landing any surplus of provisions from the fleet, for the use of the troops of the Convention, I have not the least objection to it; but wish you would ascertain the matter as soon as possible. I rest assured that whilst your vessels enjoy perfect security under the sanction of their flags, not the least molestation or inconvenience will happen to any of our vessels or inhabitants. I do myself the pleasure to send down to the flag a turkey, sent here by Gen. Burgoyne.

I am, etc.

(Signed) W. HEATH.

Capt. DALRYMPLE.

Many people having grown jealous that the troops of the Convention had collected and secreted arms in the barracks, they could not be quieted until the matter was ascertained; and on the 18th, our General ordered a strict search to be made, when nothing was found but the officer's fusees,[6] to which by the Convention they had a right. A *wag*,[7] coming from the barracks, was asked if anything was found; he answered, "Yes—in one of the rooms a large brass mortar." This spread, and was alarming to be sure. The fact was, that in one of the rooms there was a large bell-metal pestle and mortar, for family use. Jealousy, like the other passions, although a virtue in itself, may exceed its bounds; and when it does, "trifles, light as air, to jealous minds are strong as proofs of holy writ." Capt. Dalrymple wrote to Gen. Burgoyne again, on the 15th, and proposed to put the spare provisions on board one of the flags, and send them up to Boston harbor. But on the 23rd, Capt. Braithwait of the *Centurion* wrote the General that he had arrived with orders from Viscount Howe for the men-of-war and transports with the provisions on board them to return to Rhode Island, which they did accordingly.

March 12—Intelligence was received that a 40-gun ship had arrived at New London laden with clothing for the United States.

March 18—A detachment of Col. Henley's regiment marched out of Boston for the army.

March 19—Gen. Burgoyne having again applied to Congress for leave to go to England himself, they now gave him liberty. This was joyous to the General, and he wrote our General that he had assured himself that there would be nothing thrown in the way on his part, and wished for his passports. The President of Congress, in his letter to our General, by the same express, informed him that it was late in the evening when the resolve, granting Gen. Burgoyne leave to depart, passed, and nothing was said respecting the settlement of the accounts before his departure; but that it was fully his opinion that the former resolve should be strictly observed; for Congress had before resolved, that neither he nor the troops of the Convention should depart, before the accounts were settled and paid.

Our General, therefore, told Gen. Burgoyne that this must first be done and that then he should meet with no delay: on this he hesitated, and then asked how the accounts were to be settled? He was answered—Strictly conformable to the resolves of Congress. He then asked if Congress could be serious in their resolution, requiring in specie the same sum which they had expended in paper money. Our General replied that he supposed that honorable body were serious in all their resolutions. He then replied that this was unjust, for the odds was double; and appealed to our General to say whether he thought it just himself: Our General answered, that as an executive officer, it was not for him to judge or determine whether the orders of his superiors were just or not. General Burgoyne replied that was true. He was then told, that if he did not choose to pay for the supplies, the act allowed him to replace them, in quality and quantity; and this seemed to remove his objections.

After further discussion the two Generals pledged their faith and sacred honor to each other, in which they both had the fullest confidence, that Gen. Burgoyne should proceed to Rhode Island, accompanied by such officers as our General might think proper to send, to whom Gen. Burgoyne should pay in specie the amount of supplies furnished in the Quarter-Master's department; and that he should forward in vessels bearing flags, provisions of the different species they had received, within a certain number of days stipulated; that no advantage should be taken by delay occasioned by stress of weather; that a box of gold, as a pledge for any deficiencies in the provisions, should be deposited with our General, the balance of which, after the full settlement of the accounts, to be paid to the senior officer of the troops of the Convention.

April 2—Gen. Burgoyne came into Boston, and dined at headquarters; and before he took leave of our General, observed, "I know your situation, Sir, and the difficulty of obtaining many foreign necessaries you may want or wish. If you will give me a memorandum, on my arrival in England I will with great pleasure forward them to you." Our General thanked him for his politeness, but was careful not to mention any, choosing rather to suffer with his fellow-countrymen the necessities of the times, than to avail himself of so exclusive a favor.

April 5—Between 11 and 12 o'clock General Burgoyne left Cambridge for Rhode Island, accompanied by Colonel Pollard and Samuel Barrett, Esq.

April 8—The *Raleigh* frigate, it was learnt, had arrived at Portsmouth, N.H. A part of the Convention troops were ordered to be removed to Rutland, in the county of Worcester, and temporary barracks were erected for the purpose.

April 15—A division of the Convention troops marched for Rutland under escort of a detachment of militia, commanded by Major Read. Our General received a letter from the President of Congress, dated the 4th instant, in which he observed, "Yesterday I had the honor of presenting to Congress your favors of the 21st and 24th of March; and, although I have received no particular commands relative to their several contents, I am warranted by the general voice of Members to intimate, that you have received the applause of the House for your determination respecting the adjustment of accounts with General Burgoyne."

April 18—Mr. Barrett returned from Rhode Island, accompanied by a British Commissary, Major Morrison, who was sent on by Gen. Pigot,[8] to negotiate a plan for the future supply of the troops of the Convention.

April 19—About two o'clock p.m. a wagon arrived from Rhode Island with a large sum of money, received in discharge of the accounts, and for the troops of the Convention. The same day, Mr. Deane[9] arrived from France, with the highly important intelligence that the Court of France had acknowledged the Independency of the United States of America, and a treaty of alliance was concluded.

April 22—Five sail of victuallers[10] arrived in the lower harbor from Rhode Island, with provisions, for a replace of those supplied the troops of the Convention.

April 28—The British handbill for quieting America, as it was called, was received at Boston. It was forwarded from Connecticut, where it had been sent by Governor Tryon[11]—Governor Trumbull[12] had made a most magnanimous reply.

April 30—A valuable prize was sent into Boston, laden with dry goods, teas, flour, etc.

May 4—Several French ships had arrived with goods and stores from France for the United States.

May 5—The French frigate *Nymphe*, Capt. Senneville, arrived in Boston harbor, and sailed out again on the 16th.

May 23—Certain intelligence was received, that the French Ambassador left England about the 20th of the preceding March, and that the English Ambassador had returned to England.

May 30—The British made an excursion to Tiverton and Little Compton, and did some damage. Our General concluded with Gen. Pigot a system for the future supply of the troops of the Convention, by sending provisions from Rhode Island. This mode tended to the increase of provisions in the States, and the easier supply of our own troops. The plan was submitted to Congress, who were pleased to honor it with their approbation, which they expressed in the following resolution:

In CONGRESS, May 22, 1778.

Resolved, That Congress approve of Maj. Gen. Heath's conduct relative to the proposals made by Maj. Gen. Pigot, for supplying with provisions the troops who surrendered prisoners under the Convention of Saratoga. That the President be directed to inform Maj. Gen. Heath, that Congress expect that all assistance afforded to the enemy, in unloading, storing, or transporting provisions for the support of the Convention prisoners, be paid for in solid coin, agreeably to the spirit of their resolution of the 19th of December last.

The Convention troops complained exceedingly of this discrimination in payment, because it was notorious that there was a considerable difference between paper money and specie; indeed, at first view, it seems scarcely reconcilable on the principles of justice and equity; but when the grounds on which the resolve of the 19th of Dec. 1777 is predicated are considered, it seems to place the matters in a different light. It is expressed as follows:

In CONGRESS, Dec. 9, 1777.

Whereas Sir William Howe, Commander in Chief of His Britannic Majesty's forces, has required that provisions should be sent in, for the subsistence of the American prisoners in his possession, and for the purchase of such necessaries as they may stand in need of, and has prohibited the circulation of the money struck by the authority of these States, within such parts of the country as are at present subjected to his power, whereby great difficulties have occurred in relieving the distresses of the American prisoners; and whereas large sums of continental bills of credit have been counterfeited and issued by the agents, emissaries and abettors of Sir W. Howe,

Resolved, That the accounts of all provisions and other necessaries, which already have been, or which hereafter may be supplied by the public to prisoners in the power of these States, shall be discharged by either receiving from the British Commissary of Prisoners, or any of his agents, provisions or other necessaries equal in quantity and kind to what have been supplied; or the amount thereof in gold or silver, at the rate of four shillings and sixpence sterling for every dollar of the currency of these States; and that all these accounts be liquidated and discharged, previous to the release of any prisoners to whom provisions or other necessaries shall have been supplied.

Extract from the Minutes.
(Signed) C. THOMSON.

Maj. Gen. William Phillips (National Archives).

By the foregoing it appears that the British were allowed to replace any and all the supplies which were furnished to them, and in that way might make all the savings in their power; and certainly they ought to be checked, if they attempted to destroy that currency on which the States had solely to rely for the prosecution of the war, which had been forced upon them by this same power.

June 17—A British officer was shot by an American sentinel on Prospect Hill, the officer attempting to pass, contrary to the standing orders. The sentinel was immediately relieved and put under guard, and as soon as the official account of the event was received by our General, he wrote the following letter to Gen. Phillips:

HEADQUARTERS, BOSTON, June 17th, 1778,
8 o'clock, p.m.

Sir,

I am at this moment informed than an officer of the Convention has been shot by one of our sentries. I have ordered the man into close confinement, and have directed the Town-Major to desire the Coroner of the county of Middlesex to summon a Jury of Inquiry to sit on the body; and I desire that it may not be removed until that step be taken. I can only say, Sir, that you may be assured that I will take every step in my power which honor and justice require. Your letters of this date were handed to me by the person who brought the disagreeable news of the officer's being shot. I will answer them tomorrow.

I am, Sir, your obedient servant,
(Signed) W. HEATH.

Maj. Gen. PHILLIPS

A few minutes after our General had sent his letter, he received the following from Gen. Phillips:

CAMBRIDGE, June 17th, 1778.

Murder and death has at length taken place. An officer, riding out from the barracks on Prospect Hill, has been shot by an American sentinel. I leave the horrors incident to that bloody disposition, which has joined itself to rebellion in these Colonies, to the feelings of all Europe. I do not ask for justice, for I believe every principle of it is fled from this Province. I demand liberty to send an officer to Gen. Sir Henry Clinton, by way of the headquarters of Gen. Washington, with my report of this murder.

(Signed) W. PHILLIPS, Maj. Gen.

Maj. Gen. HEATH.

The next morning our General wrote the following to Gen. Phillips:

HEADQUARTERS, BOSTON, June 18th, 1778.

SIR,

Immediately upon my receiving the disagreeable report, the last evening, that an officer of the Convention had been shot by an American sentinel, and that the sentinel was confined, I ordered him to be closely kept so, and the Coroner of the county of Middlesex to be certified, that a Jury of Inquiry might be summoned to sit on the body of the officer. Decency and the utmost attention, in any country, could not have done more. A few minutes after I had dispatched the officer with the foregoing orders, I received your letter, couched in such terms that I am at a loss what epithets to give it. Were it even certain that the shooting of the officer was an act of the most deliberate willful murder, why should you charge these free independent States with a bloody disposition and with rebellion, and this State in particular as void of every principle of justice?

Although I ever had and still have a personal regard for you, and wish in every respect to treat you with the utmost generosity yet that duty which I owe to the honor and dignity of the United States will not allow me to pass unnoticed such expressions as are contained in your letter; and I cannot put any other interpretation upon them, than that they are a violent infraction of your parole, most sacredly given. I do conceive it to be my duty, and I do hereby restrict you to the limits of your house, gardens and yard, and to the direct road from your quarters to the quarters of the troops of the Convention, on Prospect and Winter Hills; expecting from you a parole, for propriety of conduct within those limits; which if you refuse, I shall be under the necessity of ordering you to narrower limits, until I can obtain the pleasure of the Honorable the Congress, touching this matter, to whom I shall transmit your letter, and crave their directions.

As to your demand of liberty for an officer to proceed to Sir Henry Clinton with a *report of this murder* as you are pleased to express yourself, I have only to reply, that as soon as the Coroner has taken an inquisition, in which all the evidence respecting this unhappy affair will be contained, I shall transmit a copy thereof to Congress; and I shall have no objection to your sending a copy also to Sir Henry Clinton, by way of the head-quarters of His Excellency General Washington (if His Excellency should approve of it) together with any just and decent representations which you may think necessary to make on this occasion or any other, after I have examined such letters; but as to an officer's going to Sir Henry Clinton, it is altogether unnecessary—so you will please to excuse my refusal of it. I am, Sir, your obedient servant,

(Signed) W. HEATH, Major-General.

P. S. I shall not at this time comment on the indelicate manner in which your letter is addressed.

Maj. Gen. PHILLIPS

––––––

I, William Phillips, Major-General and senior officer of the troops under the restrictions of the Convention of Saratoga, do promise and engage, on my word and honor, and on the faith of a gentleman, to remain in the quarters now assigned to me in Cambridge, in the State of Massachusetts Bay, and at no time to exceed or pass the limits of the gardens and yards adjoining and belonging to said quarters, except in the road by the nearest and most direct route from my said quarters to Prospect and Winter Hills, and the limits of said hills within the chain of sentries—until it shall be permitted or ordered otherwise by the Continental General commanding in this State, His Excellency General Washington, or the Honorable Congress of the United States of America; and that I will not, directly or indirectly, give any intelligence to the enemies of the said United States, or either of them, or do or say anything in opposition to or in prejudice of the measures and proceedings of any Congress for the said States, during my continuance here as aforesaid, or until I am duly exchanged or discharged.

Given under my hand at Cambridge, this eighteenth day of June, 1778.

––––––

HEADQUARTERS, BOSTON, June 18th, 1778.

SIR,

You will immediately repair to Cambridge, and wait upon Maj. Gen. Phillips: present him the letter addressed to him. After he has read the letter, present the parole; if he signs it, well; if he refuses, you will please to inform him, that in consequence of the indecent, dishonorable, and highly insulting expressions in his letter of yesterday, against the honor and dignity of the Free, Sovereign, and Independent States of America, and in prejudice of the measures and proceedings of the Honorable the Congress— as it is my duty, so it is my express orders, that he, the said Maj. Gen. Phillips, be restricted to the limits of his house, yards and gardens, beyond which he is not to pass, until it be otherwise ordered; and that you immediately plant and continue by relief so many sentries as may be necessary to prevent his exceeding those limits.

You will give orders that the sentries so planted observe a strict decorum and soldier-like behavior, avoiding insult, and behaving with becoming dignity. After which, you will wait on the next senior officer, and acquaint him of Gen. Phillips being confined.

I am, Sir, your most obedient servant,
(Signed) W. HEATH, Maj. Gen.

Lt. Col. POLLARD, Dep. Adj. General.

The same day Gen. Phillips wrote our General as follows:

CAMBRIDGE, June 18th, 1778, 3 o'clock, p.m.

SIR,

Lt. Brown of the 21st regiment, who was shot yesterday by an American sentinel, died about midnight in the last night. I am informed some person, whom you have sent to examine the body, is now doing it; and, as I suppose every inspection of that sort will be over by tomorrow, I would propose to bury the corpse to-morrow evening. I am to desire to know if you have any objection, and whether you have any particular intentions relating to the body of the murdered officer. If it is to be allowed Christian burial, I would wish to deposit it in the vault appropriated for strangers, in the Protestant church at Cambridge.

In this case, I am to desire you will give the necessary permission for this purpose, and allow a sufficient number of men from the barracks to assist in carrying down the corpse from the barracks to the church. As I am totally ignorant to whom it may be necessary to apply for leave to open the church, it obliges me to give you this trouble; and I hope, if permission is granted, that it may be done so fully as will prevent the sanguinary people of this country from insulting and treating with indignity the dead body of the unfortunate officer, who, in their rage, revengeful tempers, and barbarity, they have put to death. I am, Sir,

Your most obedient and humble servant,
(Signed) W. PHILLIPS.

Maj. Gen. HEATH.

To this letter the following was returned:

HEADQUARTERS, BOSTON, June 19th, 1778.

SIR,

Yours of yesterday afternoon was handed me the last evening; I most sincerely regret the unfortunate death of Lt. Brown. As I apprehend the coroner has taken his inquisition, or will do it this morning—which is in conformity to the laws of the land in that case made and provided, for the sole purpose of investigating the truth of facts—you not only have my permission, but request, that every mark of respect may be paid to the corpse of the deceased; and you have my permission also for such a number of non-commissioned officers and privates to attend, as may be necessary to bear the corpse from the funeral house to the place of interment.

I do not know under whose direction the church at Cambridge now is; but I have given orders to Maj. Hopkins and the Town-Major to afford every kind of assistance in their power, and to inquire who has the direction, and to obtain permission. I have also given orders that decency be exhibited by our troops during the time of procession of interment, which the solemnity of so mournful an occasion points out as the duty of rational beings; and from the universal respectful behavior of the people of this country on such occasions, you may be sure that not the least insult will be offered.

I am, Sir, your most obedient servant,
(Signed) W. HEATH.

Maj. Gen. PHILLIPS.

June 19—Gen. Phillips wrote another letter, as follows:

CAMBRIDGE, June 19th, 1778.

SIR,

I shall not animadvert upon, nor answer any part of your letter of yesterday, except what relates to your meaning to restrict me to my house, garden and yards, and to the direct road from my quarters to the quarters of the troops of the Convention on Prospect and Winter Hills, and requiring my signing a new parole for my propriety of conduct within those limits. When by the treaty of Convention of Saratoga the officers were to be admitted on parole, it was clearly intended that a liberal interpretation was to be given of that agreement; and, to use your own words, generous limits were to be granted. I will not deny that the limits have been sufficient.

I apprehend, Sir, that under no sense or explanation of the treaty, the officers were to be denied intercourse with the soldiers indeed, there is an article particularly on that point; and by restricting me to my quarters, allowing me only the passage to the barracks by the direct road, you would have certainly have restricted me as you have done several other officers, from whom you have taken the benefit of their parole, allowing for the distinction of my rank, having obtained a quarter instead of a barrack: it seemed therefore a very extraordinary proposal made to me that I should sign a parole under a restriction which deprived me of any advantage arising from my giving one, according to the article on that subject in the treaty of Convention of Saratoga; and on this consideration I refused it.

You have, Sir, made me a prisoner in my quarters, under a guard, and I am perfectly at ease about it—shall bear it, Sir, and any other violence of power which may happen to me, with more patience than you may suppose. I am very regardless about insults and injuries done me personally—I feel only, and then severely, when any are offered to the troops I command. But, Sir, you attempt at much more than restricting my person; for in a paper sent me this day, being your instructions to Lt. Col. Pollard, dated June 18, 1778, you direct him, after he has planted sentinels around my quarters, that he is 'to wait on the next senior officer, and acquaint him of General Phillips being confined.' I am to inform you, Sir, that, bearing the King's commission, I shall consider myself senior officer of the troops of the Convention; and every officer of them will obey my orders as far as their present situation will allow.

You may confine my person, but you cannot have power to take from me my military place, nor my connection with the Convention troops—it is too extravagant an idea to suppose you capable of; so little can it be in the power of an individual to deprive me of the commission I hold, that were these Colonies really acknowledged Independent and Sovereign States, it would not be in the power of their government to deprive an officer of another nation of his military commission, how far so-ever they might stretch and extend their power over his person. But, Sir, I must be allowed to declare, that until the Colonies are acknowledged by Great Britain to be Independent Sovereign States, I cannot view them in any other light than that in which they are considered by Great Britain. As you will not allow me to send an officer to Sir Henry Clinton, I must request to take advantage of your express for sending my report and representations to him; and I will beg to know when I must send you my letters.

I am, Sir,
Your most obedient, humble servant,
(Signed) W. PHILLIPS.

Maj. Gen. HEATH

To which the following answer was returned the next day:

HEADQUARTERS, BOSTON, June 20th, 1778.

SIR,

Another of your favors of yesterday was handed to me this morning. You may be assured that the reason of my restricting you to your quarters, the day before yesterday, was personally no agreeable service. Duty to the honor and dignity of my country made it indispensably necessary. Apprehending that so great a restriction from your former limits as I pointed out, might be construed by you a dissolution of your parole, I thought it necessary and also reasonable that you should give a new one. I wished that you might retain your quarters, and at the same time have a free intercourse with the troops who are quartered at a distance from you; this distance is so considerable that a parole is necessary. I acknowledge that by the Convention, you are to be admitted on parole, and this parole is for propriety of conduct under such admittance; but that parole being forfeited, by misconduct, ceases to be, and confinement in proportion to the offence, no breach of the Convention, but fully justifiable upon every principle of reason and justice.

It was never in my idea to take away your commission, or dissolve your connection with the troops of the Convention; but, while under confinement, your power of acting might with propriety be suspended, so far as respected the transacting of public business between myself and you; but personal regard has prevented my going that length, any further than to notify the next officer of your confinement. I do not insist that you, as an officer in the British army, are obliged to view the Free, Independent and Sovereign States of America in any other light than they are acknowledged by the government whose service you are in. But, under your present situation and circumstances, I do insist that you shall not openly insult the honor and dignity of these States with impunity.

I am, Sir,
Your obedient servant,
(Signed) W. HEATH, Major-General.

Maj. Gen. PHILLIPS.

_____

Middlesex, Mass.

An inquest taken at Cambridge, within the said County of Middlesex, on the 18th of June, A.D. 1778, before Joel Smith, one of the Coroners for the county aforesaid, upon view of the body of Lt. Richard Brown, one of the British officers (Charlestown, in the county aforesaid) then and there being dead, by oaths of William Howe, Benjamin Lock, John Brown, Ebenezer Steadman, Samuel Manning, Nathaniel Austin, Joseph Read, Jr., James Hill, Thomas Barret, Benjamin Barker, Aaron Hill, Isaac Bradish, James Munro, Joseph Johnson, good and lawful men of Cambridge aforesaid, who being charged and sworn to inquire for the sake of the government and people of the Massachusetts Bay, when, and by what means, and how the said Richard Brown came to his death—upon their oath do say, that the said Richard Brown was shot with a fire-arm by the sentinel in Charlestown, near Prospect Hill, between the hours of five and six p.m. on the 17th day of June, A.D. 1778, in attempting to pass the sentinel with two women, after being properly challenged by said sentinel and so came to death.

JOEL SMITH, Coroner.

Nathaniel Austin, James Munro, Joseph Read, Jr., Joseph Johnson, James Hill, William Howe, Thomas Barret, Benjamin Lock, Benjamin Barker, John Brown, Aaron Hill, Ebenezer Steadman, Isaac Bradish, Samuel Manning,

CAMBRIDGE, June 18, 1778.

Extract of a letter from Maj. Gen. HEATH to the President of Congress, dated Headquarters, Boston, June 19th, 1778:

> Since my last, of the 9th instant, I have received the honor of yours of the 23rd, by Capt. Nevers. The day before yesterday, one of our sentinels, posted at the foot of Prospect Hill, shot a Lt. Richard Brown, of the troops of the Convention, for not stopping when repeatedly challenged, as he was riding out of the lines with two women. The orders given to the sentinels being not to allow any officer without side-arms, or non-commissioned officer, private soldier, woman or child, without a written passport, to pass the chain of sentries. Immediately upon my receiving the report of the officer's being shot, and that the sentinel was confined, I gave orders for his being kept so, and notice to be given to the coroner of the County of Middlesex, that a Jury of Inquest might sit on the body for the investigation of the truth of facts; at the same time I wrote to Maj. Gen. Phillips—I do myself the honor to enclose copy thereof, No. 1; a few minutes after, I received a paper from him, No. 2; the next morning I again wrote him, No. 3; and a parole, No. 4; and gave Col. Pollard written orders for the delivery thereof, No. 5. Gen. Phillips refusing to sign the parole, Col. Pollard, in obedience to my orders, restricted him to the limits therein mentioned, and planted three sentinels around the house and gardens; in which state matters now remain.

In CONGRESS, July 7th, 1778.

Resolved, That Congress approve of Maj. Gen. Heath's conduct respecting Maj. Gen. Phillips, consequent upon the death of Lt. Richard Brown, of the troops of the Convention.

Extract from the Minutes.

CHARLES THOMSON, Secretary.

The whole of the foregoing correspondence was published by order of Congress; and our General was informed that it was left for him to conduct towards the British General, as to the continuance of his arrest, as he might judge the honor of the United States required. Gen. Phillips continuing to exhibit the same temper, or it rather growing upon him, he was continued in his arrest until the troops of the Convention were ordered to be removed to Charlottesville in Virginia. It has before been observed, that the officers had certain articles prescribed to them, for their government in quarters, and that these were drawn into the parole, and subscribed by them.

If any abuses took place, a Court of Inquiry was directed to investigate the complaints, and report to our General; thus giving the accused officers an opportunity to exculpate their conduct, if it was in their power; and no officer could wish more than our General to treat them with generosity and indulgence, as far as was compatible with good order and discipline. But notwithstanding the fairness of this mode of procedure, Gen. Phillips forbid the officers appearing before any Court so appointed; and on the 18th ult. Mr. Bibby, the Deputy-Adjutant-General to the troops of the Convention, came into a Court of Inquiry and declared the following, which, in order to have the whole together, we now retrospect.

> Maj. Gen. Phillips will not permit any officer under his command to be brought before a Court of Inquiry of the American troops, for the purpose of scrutinizing their conduct; but if any complaints are lodged against any British officers, and Maj. Gen. Heath shall desire their conduct to be inquired into, Maj. Gen. Phillips will give such orders as are customary in such cases among the British troops.

By order of Maj. Gen. Phillips:
(Signed) THOS. BIBBY, Dep. Adj. Gen.

MONDAY, May 18th, 1778.

The same day, Gen. Phillips sent a letter to our General, expressive of the same sentiments; to which the following answer was sent to him.

HEADQUARTERS, BOSTON, May 19th, 1778.

SIR,

Your favor of yesterday came to hand the last evening; and, I must confess, contained matter novel and surprising to me. What ideas of a co-partnership in command you have entertained, I cannot tell. From the beginning, I have found a disposition in the senior officer of the Convention to assume the right and authority of trying and punishing offenders for breaches of my orders. This I ever have and ever shall view in no other light than that of insult. As such, I represented it to His Excellency Lt. Gen. Burgoyne, whose good sense and thorough knowledge of discipline led him, in a letter to me of the 13th Jan. to yield the matter in the following words: 'I do not mean to deny that you have a right to take justice into your own hands.' Indeed it is a subject concerning which, having heretofore said and wrote very fully, I shall not at this time dwell long upon. As to agreement or co-partnership in command, it is absurd.

In military command there must be one supreme head; at present, the Honorable Congress have honored me with the command of this department, and I imagined that no officer within its limits would dare dispute it. My orders, as I have repeatedly heretofore declared, shall ever be founded on the principles of honor, reason, and justice, and not to infringe those delicate principles in others; so I again declare that such my orders shall not be broken or disputed, by any officer or soldier placed under my direction, with impunity. The matter of command is no hidden mystery; the usage and customs of nations are known. The celebrated Vattel,[13] Pufendorf[14] and Grotius,[15] with whose writings I dare say you are acquainted, elegantly explain how an army that submits to another, whether the conditions are more or less honorary to themselves, are to conduct whilst they remain within the limits of the victors' camp, or jurisdiction of their country. But I shall not spend time to reason on a subject which would reflect dishonor on myself to allow even to be disputed. Therefore, to sum up all in a few words—that, as I am determined to treat the troops of the Convention with strict justice and generosity, so I am determined that all offenders against my standing orders of the garrison shall be brought to proper punishment; that I will not allow the senior officer of those troops to try or punish for any offence against my orders; and, that the truth may at all times be properly investigated, I shall, from time to time, when occasion requires, appoint Courts of Inquiry for that purpose; and such as presume to dispute or counteract them, I shall duly notice.

I am, etc.
(Signed) W. HEATH, Major-General.

Maj. Gen. PHILLIPS

Gen. Phillips finding that he could not get any thing by assault, he next tried his skill in attempting to sap, with the policy of friendship; he therefore wrote another letter of the same date, under the name of "Private."

MONDAY, May 18th, 1778.

Sir,

I have, this morning, written to you a letter upon public matters. I will now assure you, that I am sorry that my earnest desire of preserving a communication of intelligence between you and I, does not meet your consent; and I will lament that you will attend to the sudden reports you receive, so fully, and act upon them, without that good-humored attention to me, which I had hoped and have endeavored should subsist between us. You and I are nearly of an age—I will not dispute understandings with you; but I certainly am an older soldier, and must necessarily know the customs of armies. Allow me to assure you, that the manner with which things are taken up sometimes deviates from military rule. It is a fixed custom to go from the head, downwards; and, when an Ensign offends against order, the *General* does not condescend to altercate with *him*, but sends his orders, his desire, or his opinion, to the commanding officers; and, in your sending messages to young officers, it injures your own consequence, and certainly hurts mine.

Believe me, that I am strict against any breach of orders, and will never suffer it to pass un-censured. I allow, the two officers have behaved ill, and I will punish them; but the getting the countersign was an effect of good humor and simplicity in an American soldier. Let me once more request of you to recollect your own situation, and it will put mine in a clear view to you. Whenever you have reports against any of our troops, let me know them, and I will give instant attention to them; but you will, I am sure, immediately feel that sending a threat to two officers, that you would send them on board a prisonship, and never informing me wherefore, was not strictly conformable to good humor or good discipline. I am, with a very hearty desire of preserving harmony and order, and with much personal regard,

Yours, etc.
(Signed) W. PHILLIPS.

Maj. Gen. HEATH.

To which the following answer was returned:

HEADQUARTERS, BOSTON, May 19th, 1778.

SIR,

Having, in my other letter of this date, answered yours of yesterday, I now reply to your favor of the same date, which you are pleased to style "private." I can assure you, Sir, that no person living wishes to act with good humor more than I do; or would take more pains to cultivate harmony and a good understanding. But in the present case, you must not expect that I shall allow myself, either by frowns or flatteries, to give up the dignity of command reposed in me. I wish, I am determined, to extend every act of generosity towards the officers of the Convention which is compatible with the safety and honor of my country. I shall not take up matters suddenly, or proceed rashly, unless circumstances shall render it unavoidably necessary; and although you may be possessed of a greater share of under standing than I am, and an older soldier—yet I have endeavored to acquire a knowledge of my duty, and the customs of armies and nations. I am not conscious of any deviations from those rules or customs in general adopted by them.

The General who commands is undoubtedly the fountain of power, and all orders should descend from him through the proper officers, until they are communicated to the lowest order of the army; and that commander who disputes with, or threatens young officers, undoubtedly lessens his consequence, and will soon become contemptible in the eyes of an army. Nothing of this was in the late transactions, that I know of: having received a report of the conduct of the two officers, I ordered them to be confined to their quarters, and appointed a Court of Inquiry to examine into the grounds of the complaint, that I might have a clear understanding of the affair, and order accordingly. In all cases where you or the troops of the Convention are immediately concerned in the orders, I have always directed that you should be served with a copy. As to any threatenings being sent to the two officers, of confining them on board a guard-ship, I know nothing of it.

The main difficulty seems to arise from your apprehension, that you are to try and punish all offenders against my orders. Here, Sir, notwithstanding your knowledge and age in soldiery, you much mistake, and cannot support those your pretensions by any rule or authority, civil or military. The moment you piled your arms, and marched off the ground, you became subject to the standing orders of the victor; and in every jurisdiction through which you marched or where you remain, are subject to all the orders and laws of the place; and such as violate them are obnoxious to punishment. The law and custom of nations explicitly tell us who are to try and punish: and although I do not in the least doubt your ready disposition to inquire into, and even to punish offenders against my orders yet when you attempt it, it is such an indignity offered to my authority, that you may be assured it ever will raise my resentment; and if it did not, I am confident that your self (at least hereafter) and all military men would despise me for my insensibility.

In a word, Sir, cultivate those principles of obedience to orders among the officers in your situation, recommended and inculcated by the custom and usage of nations, and dictated by reason and you may depend, that I shall exert myself to make your situation as agreeable as possible; and you may be also assured, that I never shall require that of the troops of the Convention which, in the opinion of the just and wise in any country, shall reflect dishonor on them. With the strongest desire to cultivate and maintain harmony, and to treat you with respect, and with much personal regard,

I am, etc.

(Signed) W. HEATH.

Maj. Gen. PHILLIPS.

The same feelings which had great weight in the beginning of the war, continued for some time, namely, that Great Britain was one of the greatest and most powerful nations in the world, in arts, and arms; while the Americans were yet their Colonies, young, weak, and but barely civilized, ignorant of the world, and especially so of arts and of arms. Hence we see it so frequently breaking out (until experience had taught them a different opinion). There was frequently, as in the atmosphere, placid intervals; but whenever any cross wind happened to blow (and there is no season or circumstances without them) then instantly appeared those ideas of self-superiority and contempt for the Americans, which was the true cause of many uncomfortable hours. Mankind have the same passions; the difference lies in some riding with a double curb, while others give the reins.

This Convention business was a heavy task for our General, and the whole subject would form an entertaining volume of itself; we are now circumscribed by our limits, and have only given a small specimen for mankind to form an opinion for themselves. In all the letters or conversation which was had on the occasion, we find scarcely a reflection cast by our General on the British nation, the cause in which they were engaged, or against any who were fortunate or unfortunate; but a uniform desire to make those placed under his orders as comfortable as circumstances would admit; at the same time an unshaken determination, a perseverant watchfulness, with decent language, to defend the cause and honor of his own country, by arguments supported by the customs and maxims of the civilized world. The hundreds of letters on file are all proofs of this; and in many instances it was politely acknowledged. The two following letters of different dates, are some of the specimens—Major Harnage[16] had his lady with him.

CAMBRIDGE, October 30th, 1778.

SIR,

   With great pleasure I acknowledge the favor of your obliging letter; and Mrs. Harnage joins me, with Capt. Hawker, in returning to you our sincere thanks for your kind
representation of us, and solicitation in our favor, to the Honorable Congress. With
your leave, we shall with patience wait the result; and, let the Congress determine in
what manner they please, our obligations to you, Sir, will be ever acknowledged.
Believe me, Sir, with respect,

Your obliged and humble servant,
HENRY HARNAGE.

Maj. Gen. HEATH.

————

CAMBRIDGE, June 10th, 1779.

SIR,

   Being this moment informed that you are about to quit Boston, I must beg leave,
previous to your departure, to trouble you with these our acknowledgments, for the
civility and attention you have been pleased to show us; and to assure you that Mrs.
Harnage, Capt. Hawker and myself shall ever retain a due sense of all favors, by which
you have kindly endeavored to alleviate, and make easy the restraints and disagreeable
circumstances that unavoidably attend our present situation. We hope you will mention us to the gentleman who is to succeed to the command in the Eastern Department.

   Wishing you all personal happiness, I remain with respect, Sir, your most

obedient and
Obliged humble servant,
HENRY HARNAGE.

The Hon. Maj. Gen. HEATH

June 29—A Spanish xebeck[17] and a French cutter arrived at Boston, with dispatches from their respective Courts, which were forwarded to Congress.

   June 30—Certain intelligence was received, that the British had left Philadelphia.

   July 9—Intelligence was received, that a warm action happened on the 28th ult.
between Gen. Washington's and Gen. Clinton's armies, near Monmouth courthouse,
in the Jersies. Gen. Clinton, having taken the resolution to move from Philadelphia
to New York, through the Jersies, commenced his movements accordingly, encumbered with an immense train of stores and baggage, which occupied some miles in
length; and these are the greatest encumbrance to a General on a march of danger,
from an attack of his opponent, to which he can be exposed. Gen. Washington was
no sooner apprised of this intention and movement of the British General, than he
made his arrangements accordingly, crossed the Delaware, and pushed detached corps
forward to obstruct the advance, gall the flanks, and fall on the rear of the enemy,
while he moved on with the body of his army. By the 27th, Gen. Clinton had got on
as far as Monmouth, and Gen. Washington's detached troops were on his flanks, and
close on his rear. Here the British General took a wise resolution, to make a stand
with a part of his best troops, while he pushed on his baggage through the difficult
defiles, under the careful and experienced hands of Gen. Knyphausen.

General Washington acting with equal skill and equal bravery, made every arrangement which the moment called for. On the morning of the 28th, he ordered Maj. Gen. Lee to attack the enemy's rear, himself moving on briskly to support him; but to his surprise, as he advanced on, he met Lee's troops retreating and the enemy impetuously pursuing. Here was Gen. Washington seen in all his splendor; for this critical situation is the orb in which he shines the brightest. He rallied the retreating troops; he inspired them by precept and by example; and the misfortune of the morning was considerably retrieved. The Americans fought bravely, and so did the British. After hard fighting, in a most intense hot day, when scores died of the heat, and drinking too freely of cold water when they could find it, both armies remained on the ground.

The Americans determined to recommence the action early on the next morning; but Gen. Clinton, finding that his baggage had struggled pretty well through the defiles, and had got tolerably well advanced, took the advantage of the cool of the night to slip off, unperceived by the Americans, and got to ground where he was safe. Some sharp words took place between Gen. Washington and Maj. Gen. Lee, as the one advanced and the other retreated, which issued in the arrest, trial, and suspension of the latter. Gen. Washington reported to Congress, that the Americans buried of the British four officers and 245 privates; among the former, the Hon. Col. Monckton (who was a brave and experienced officer) and that there were a few prisoners. The American loss; killed, one Lt. Colonel, one Major, three Captains, two Lieutenants, one Sergeant, 52 rank and file—wounded, two Colonels, eight Captains, four First-Lieutenants, two Second-Lieutenants, one Ensign, one Adjutant, eight Sergeants, one Drummer, 120 rank and file; missing, five Sergeants, 126 rank and file; of the artillery, one First Lieutenant, seven Matrosses,[18] and one Bombardier were killed—one Captain, one Sergeant, one Corporal, one Gunner, and 10 Matrosses wounded—one Matross missing—six horses killed, and two wounded.

Both Generals undoubtedly have much credit for their conduct in this action. Gen. Clinton's object being to reach New York with his baggage, etc. obtained this victory, with the loss which he sustained. Gen. Washington's conduct was well calculated for victory on his side; and how far he would have succeeded, had it not been for the misfortune of the morning, none can tell. This misfortune began by exposing the American advanced troops, in line, on the side of the field where they were cannonaded by the British, who at the same time wisely exposed only their artillery to that of the Americans. It is to be remembered, that men may be led on to action in the face of a cannonade, before which they will not *stand*; the point of decision is in the mind; while advancing, although galled by the fire of their opponents, the dead and wounded are left behind them as they fall, and the troops feel an ardor for arriving in a few minutes at a point where they can use their own arms, to retaliate for the injury they sustain.

But when men are placed open to the fire of the artillery of their enemy, at such a distance as to prevent the use of their own arms in their defense, the dead and wounded fall and lie among them, or are drawn away, and every groan they make is heard. The troops soon conceive that they are placed as marks to be shot at; while the greater policy of the enemy keeps their column or line out of the rake of their cannon; the mind gives way and retreat will be inevitable. This was experienced in this instance, and the fairest hopes of a noble on set in a few minutes blasted; and these were some of the best troops in the army too. It was here that the firm Col.

Wesson had his back peeled of its muscles, almost from shoulder to shoulder, by a cannon-ball. The confidence of the troops could not be fully recovered, until they saw the presence of their beloved General.

July 18—Intelligence was received that the Count D'Estaing had arrived, with the fleet under his command, off the Capes of Delaware. The fleet consisted of 12 sail of the line, and four frigates. Off the coast of Virginia, they took a privateer, fitted out of New York, of 26—guns a ship, bound from New Providence to London—re-captured a French snow,[19] laden with dry goods, and drove a British ship of war on shore.

July 19—Intelligence was received, that about 2000 men, said to be invalids, had arrived at Rhode Island from New York.

July 21—Intelligence was received, that a body of refugees and Indians had destroyed the town of Wyoming, on the Susquehanna, and butchered many of the inhabitants. The same day, it was learnt, that Gen. Washington had crossed Hudson's River with the main army, except Gen. Wayne's brigade—that Count D'Estaing had appeared off Sandy Hook—that the inhabitants of New York were in great consternation, and that the Marquis de Lafayette, with Glover's and Varnum's brigades, were on their march for Providence. The British were very busy in fortifying Rhode Island.

July 25 and 26—Sent for Providence 43,000 flints, five tons hard bread, a quantity of dry fish, etc. and sent a large number of the large flat-bottomed boats to Weymouth; they were to be conveyed, taking advantage of the river, to the vicinity of Rhode Island. Half of Col. Crafts' regiment of State artillery were ordered to Tiverton; the other half of the regiment of artillery, and a draft from the militia, to the number of 3000 men, including 1000 before ordered, were to march and reinforce Maj. Gen. Sullivan in the State of Rhode Island. On the 29th, at noon, the Count D'Estaing's squadron came to anchor off Point Judith, and at evening stretched a line from that Point to Seaconnet.

July 31—The regiment of State artillery, with six brass four-pounders and two brass howitzers, marched for Tiverton; and the next day the marine mortar was sent on, slung under two pair of stout cart-wheels. The British sloop of war *Kingfisher*, a row-galley and a sloop, stationed near Seaconnet, upon the approach of the French frigate were run on shore by their own crews, set on fire, and left to burn and blow up. Maj. Bumstead's[20] company of Boston artillery, with two brass field-pieces, and Lt. Dunnel,[21] with a detachment of the Continental artillery, with two field-pieces, marched for Rhode Island, and the militia and volunteers were on their march that way; and large quantities of military stores and provisions were going from hence.

August 10—Maj. Gen. Hancock,[22] with his suit, went for Rhode Island, to take the command of the militia. The same morning, Gen. Sullivan made a landing on the island without opposition. About the same time the Count D'Estaing, with his squadron, passed the British batteries at Newport, when there was a brisk cannonade on both sides. Many of the shot struck in the town, and the inhabitants were in much consternation, not knowing in what place they were safe. A shot entered the door of the house of Mrs. Mason, a widow lady, a little above the floor: as the family were passing from room to room not knowing where the next shot might strike, young Mr. Mason, passing through the entry, found the black man of the family sitting with his back against the shot-hole in the door; on being asked why he sat there, he answered, "Master, you never know two shot to go in the same place." Under this idea he was tranquil. Lord Howe's fleet appeared in the offing, consisting of eight sail of the line, and 12 frigates.

August 11—The Count came to sail, and stood out, and the British fleet stood off—the wind very fresh.

August 13—A most severe storm of wind and rain, which stripped many trees of their fruit, and tore others up by the roots, etc. The troops on Rhode Island, under the command of Gen. Sullivan, were on the 11th numbered 10,122, including officers, exclusive of some volunteers from New Hampshire, and other corps, arranged as follows:

Varnum's brigade, including officers,	1,037
Glover's,	1,131
Cornell's,	1,719
Greene's,	1,626
Lovells,	1,158
Titcomb's,	957
Livingston's advance,	659
West's reserve,	1,025
Artillery,	810
Total,	10,122

Jean Baptiste Charles Henri Hector, Comte d'Estaing.

These were encamped at and near Quaker-Hill. The storm destroyed a great number of cartridges, owing to the badness of the boxes. A fresh supply was sent on from Boston.

August 15—The army advanced, and in the afternoon arrived within two miles of the enemy, without the least opposition. Gen. Washington, with the main army, was at the White Plains, in the State of New York, said to be about 20,000 strong. Seventeen transports with troops from Gen. Howe's army at New York, sailed for Rhode Island; but finding the French squadron in the way, could not come to the place. On the evening of the 16th, Gen. Sullivan took possession of some high grounds which commanded the enemy's works on their right, and was not discovered until morning, when they began to cannonade the Americans, but did them no damage, which was continued the next day with out injury. On the night of the 17th, the covered way was nearly completed, and also two batteries of cannon. The enemy fired 300 or 400 shot, but did no other damage than slightly wounding two men.

August 19—The American works were advanced nearer to the enemy, and on the 20th, they had one man killed and two wounded by the enemy's cannon. In the afternoon the Count D'Estaing returned to Newport—his own ship, the *Languedoc*, was totally dismasted in the storm, and lost her rudder. In this situation, an English 50 gun ship of Lord Howe's squadron came across her, and got under her stern, where she did the *Languedoc* some small damage; but on wearing the *Langue-*

doc, so as to bring some of her heavy metal to bear, the Englishman bore away. The *Marseilles*, a 74, lost her foremast in the storm, and the *Cesar*, a 74, parted from the squadron.

August 22—In the afternoon, the *Cesar* came to anchor in the light-house channel (Boston lower harbor). After parting from the squadron in the storm, she fell in with a British 50 gun ship, with whom she was engaged for near three glasses,[23] and would have taken her, had not some other English ships hove in sight. The *Cesar* had 160 men killed and wounded, about 60 of which were of the former; and the Captain among the latter, who lost an arm. On his being brought up to Boston, our General immediately paid him a visit, and expressed to him his regret for the arm he had lost; to which the Captain replied, although very weak through the great loss of blood he had sustained—that he was ready to lose his other arm in the cause of the Americans. Remember this, ye Americans, in future times!

The same day, the enemy threw 200 or 300 shells at our troops on Rhode Island; two men only were wounded, and the fire briskly returned. The Count D'Estaing determined to come round with his squadron to Boston, and Gen. Sullivan must retreat to the north end of the island.

August 26—Maj. Gen. Hancock returned to Boston. The volunteers were coming home.

August 28—The Count D'Estaing, with his squadron, arrived in Nantasket Road, and the next day the Count came up to town.

August 29—there was a smart action between the British and Americans, towards the north end of Rhode Island, which terminated in favor of the latter. The most severe part of this action was at the hollow between Butts' Hill and Quaker-Hill, a ground situated for slaughter on both sides, rather than for decisive victory on either. Col. Jackson's regiment of Continental troops, and Gen. Lovell's[24] brigade of militia, are said to have distinguished themselves; and the artillery drove off two frigates that attempted to cover the enemy's flank. The Americans had about 60 men killed, and 180 wounded. The loss of the enemy unknown.

August 30—Gen. Sullivan left the island; and on the morning of the 31st, an express from Plymouth brought intelligence that 20 sail of topsail vessels were seen off that place the evening before—some of them very large ships. In consequence of this intelligence, our General, the President of the Council, Gen. Hancock, and others, went down the harbor, to confer with the Count D'Estaing.

September 1—the Count came up to town, with a number of his officers, and was to dine with our General. Just as the company were going to sit down, the signal guns announced the appearance of the fleet, and which were visible from the town (Mr. John Cutler having discovered them from the steeple of the Old South meeting-house) appearing to be about 20 sail, eight of which at least were two-deckers. The Count immediately put off for the squadron. Several of the islands next to the road had been fortified, and the squadron moored, in order to give a warm reception to the British, should they attempt to enter the road. A number of regiments of the militia of the vicinity were ordered to march immediately to the Castle, Dorchester Heights, Boston, Noddle's Island, etc. Several signal guns were heard in the bay the latter part of the night, and the next morning the fleet was out of sight. The militia which were coming in were countermanded. Admiral Byron's[25] squadron arrived a few days before, at Sandy Hook. The enemy made a descent on New Bedford, and did considerable damage: they also made a demand on the inhabitants of Martha's Vineyard, for a large number of cattle, sheep, etc.

September 9—An affray happened in Boston between some American and French sailors; two French officers in attempting to part them, were much wounded—one of them, a Major of the fleet, died of the wounds on the 15th. Brig. Gen. Specht,[26] the eldest Brigadier of the Hessian troops under the Convention, wrote a letter to our General, in which he informed him that, being advanced in age, he had but little taste for those pleasures and amusements which please the young and gay; but he had not lost his taste for sporting with his gun, and requested that he might do it within the limits of his parole. Nothing could be more pleasing to our General, than to gratify this brave veteran soldier; he therefore wrote him the following answer.

HEADQUARTERS, BOSTON, Sept. 10th, 1778.

SIR,

Your letter of the 9th inst. came to hand. The frequent informations which I have received of your civil and polite behavior, since you have been at Cambridge, and your taste for little diversion except shooting, leads me to grant you every indulgence which is compatible with my duty, and the honor and safety of my country. You therefore have my permission to go a-shooting within the limits assigned you, attended by one servant; and hope the amusement will equal your expectation.

I am, etc.
(Signed) W. HEATH.

Brig. Gen. SPECHT.

September 17—The General Assembly ordered 1200 men to be detached from the militia, and marched to Boston immediately; and on the 19th, ordered one-third part of their train-band to be immediately detached for the purpose of completing the works in and about the town of Boston—garrisoning the works, etc. Our General went on board the Count's ship, and with him to view the works on George's Island.

September 22—The Count D'Estaing, with the officers of his squadron, made a public appearance in town—were received by a Committee of both Houses of the General Assembly, at their landing—breakfasted at Gen. Hancock's—took punch and wine at Headquarters, at 12 o'clock; and then returned to the fleet, under a salute on leaving the town, and on passing the Castle. The grand army under Gen. Washington took a new position; one division under the immediate command of Gen. Putnam, at Fishkill; one under Gen. De Kalb, Frederickburg; and one under Gen. Gates, at Danbury.

September 24—The General Assembly countermanded their orders for calling out one-third part of their train-band, and ordered that they be held in readiness to march on the shortest notice, wherever occasion shall require.

September 25—The General Assembly made a public dinner for the Count D'Estaing, etc. etc. The next day, the Count D'Estaing, Marquis de Lafayette, and a number of other officers and gentlemen, dined with our General.

October 5—The British destroyed the salt-works and several stores, and did other damage, at Egg-Harbor; they also surprised a part of Pulaski's legion in that neighborhood, whom they handled very severely. The British pretended that they had heard that Pulaski had instructed his men not to give them quarter; they therefore anticipated retaliation. About the same time, Baylor's dragoons were surprised at

Tappan, and treated much in the same manner. Nocturnal enterprises, in which the bayonet is principally made use of, are generally uncommonly bloody. The *Languedoc*, the Count's ship, having been completely repaired, fell down to Nantasket Road, and joined the squadron.

October 6—Gen. du Portail, the Chief Engineer of the American army, came to Boston to survey the several works, in order to their being repaired or augmented, as might appear necessary; and fatigue parties were employed on the different works, and every thing put in the best posture of defense.

October 20—Our General, in company with the Count D'Estaing and others, went to Nantasket, to take a view of the works there, and to review a battalion of marines, who maneuvered well, and in every particular were well disciplined, owing to the unwearied attention of their Major, McDonald, a Scotchman, whose father was in the rebellion in England, and with this son fled to France for safety. Gen. Bougainville[27] had the command at Nantasket; he was also commander of one of the first ships in the fleet under the Count D'Estaing. The enemy left the Jersies, and prepared to embark a large body of troops. About 100 sail of shipping, including men-of-war, fell down to the Hook on the 17th of October. On the 19th and 20th, the fleet sailed from Sandy Hook; the first division consisted of upwards of 120 sail, of which 15 were of the line, and 10 or 12 frigates. This fleet went to the West Indies, with about 4000 troops. The second division, about 30 sail, of which two were of 50 guns, and 2 frigates. They stood to the eastward; there was but few troops on board the latter. Six brigades of the Continental army were on their march for Hartford, in Connecticut, to be ready to move this way, should the enemy appear in this quarter; and Maj. Gen. Gates was ordered to take the command in the Eastern Department.

November 4—In the morning the Count D'Estaing's squadron sailed from Nantasket Road.

November 6—Maj. Gen. Gates, with his lady, suite, etc. arrived at Boston. The *Somerset*, British man-of-war, of 64 guns, run ashore on Cape Cod, and was taken possession of by the militia, who sent the crew prisoners to Boston.

November 7—Maj. Gen. Gates took the command at Boston. In the next *Continental Journal*, printed by John Gill, the following made its appearance:

BOSTON, Nov. 12th.

On Thursday last, arrived in town, from Hartford, the Hon. Horatio Gates, Esq., Major General in the army of the United States, being appointed by Congress to the chief command in the Eastern District, in the room of the Hon. Maj. Gen. Heath. While we receive with the highest pleasure, a General justly celebrated for his personal virtues and martial achievements, we cannot but pay a due tribute of respect to one, whose accomplishments as a citizen, a gentleman, and an officer, have shown so conspicuously in the delicacy, propriety, and dignity of his private and public conduct, through the whole of his command in this department.

Tenacious of the civil rights of the community, and of the honor and safety of these Free, Sovereign and Independent States, so far as they were entrusted to his protection, in the most interesting and critical circumstances in which a General could possibly be placed, he has uniformly exhibited a prudence, animation, decision and firmness, which have done him honor, and fully justified the confidence reposed in him.

The cordial and most explicit approbation of the army, the inhabitants of this town, the army and navy of our illustrious ally, the Government of this State, His Excellency the Commander in Chief, and of Congress, added to the consciousness of his having discharged his trust with fidelity—must, in a great measure, have alleviated the fatigues incident to his arduous station, and compensated the loss of his health, so much impaired by an incessant attention to business. The very polite and affectionate terms in which he has taken leave of the department, in his last general orders, demand also our most grateful acknowledgements.

November 10 and 11—The Convention troops marched for Virginia. They were marched to Connecticut, and delivered to the orders of Gov. Trumbull; and were in like manner to be conveyed from State to State, each furnishing an escort, wagons, etc. until they reached Virginia. Gen. Sir Henry Clinton having refused to give passports to American vessels to bring to Boston provisions for the use of the Convention troops, or otherwise supplying of them, Congress on the 15th of October, passed a resolve that the troops of the Convention should be removed to Charlottesville in Virginia, and they were now moving accordingly.

November 24—It was learnt, that the brigades which marched from the American grand army to Hartford, marched back to Danbury. In this month, Col. Alden,[28] of one of the Massachusetts regiments, with his clerk, were surprised and killed by the Tories and Indians, at Cherry Valley, in the State of New York. The regiment defended the place, and repulsed the enemy. The American army went into winter quarters in the Jersies, at Danbury, Peek's Kill, etc. Capt. Hallet, on the 23rd, on George's Bank, latitude 41 40 north, in 18 fathoms water, discovered a mast 10 or 12 feet above water; upon a close examination, supposed it to be the top mast of a 74-gun ship of Admiral Byron's squadron, which foundered in the storm when the Somerset ran on shore.

December 19—It was learnt that the small armed vessels of the enemy did considerable damage to the inhabitants along the eastern coast of Massachusetts, by plundering, taking their coasting vessels, etc. A little before this time, Col. Joseph Ward,[29] Muster-Master-General, and Lt. Col. Bradford,[30] were taken by a gang of refugees, in the Jersies, and carried to New York.

December 27—Our General received letters from Admiral Gambier,[31] respecting the prisoners taken from the *Somerset* man-of-war, and proposing an immediate exchange; the letters couched in very polite terms.

December 28—A wagoner, his horse and four oxen were found frozen to death near the dyke, on Boston Neck; they perished in the severe cold storm on the preceding Saturday evening. A more particular account from Cherry Valley stated, that there were 32 persons killed, beside Col. Alden, and 10 rank and file belonging to the Continental army, and about 30 other persons taken prisoners; 32 houses, 31 barns, one grist-mill, fulling-mill, and blacksmith's shop, burnt. The enemy consisted of 200 refugees, and 443 Indians, commanded by Joseph Brandt, Walter Butler, and the Seneca Chief. In the late storm, the *General Arnold* privateer drove on shore near Plymouth, and bilged; 80 of the crew perished; the survivors were much frost bitten.

CHAPTER 5

1779

January 6—The Marquis de Lafayette, and Captain Raimondis, of the *Cesar*, French man-of-war, who was wounded and left at Boston, sailed for France in the *Alliance* frigate.

January 8—Capt. Mowatt,[1] with his fleet of picaroons,[2] were still infesting the eastern harbors; they had already captured about 60 sail of vessels, inward and outward bound, and burnt several houses, etc. Congress had passed a resolution for calling in the whole emission of Continental bills of May 20, 1777, and April 11, 1778, for which the possessors were to receive loan certificates, or new emission bills.

January 21—It was learnt, that the enemy had made an irruption into the State of Georgia, and were in possession of Sunbury. Their force, at first about 500, was said to have increased to upwards of 1000. The British ship which foundered on George's Bank, and whose masts were discovered by Capt. Hallet, was supposed to be the *Cornwall*, of 74 guns. It is said her whole crew were lost.

February 3—It was learnt, that the Count D'Estaing, on his arrival in the West Indies, made an attack on the British in the island of St. Lucia, but was defeated with considerable loss, after which he returned to Martinique.

February 9—It was learnt, that a number of Americans confined in Gosport[3] prison, in England, among whom was Dr. Downer[4] of Roxbury, made their escape in the preceding September by sapping with great address from the prison under the yard and fence, to the distance of 20 feet, daily concealing the earth which they dug, in the chimney of the prison.[5] This Dr. Downer is the person mentioned to have killed a British soldier in single combat, on the 19th of April, in the battle of Lexington.

February 11—Intelligence was received, that the British troops had made themselves masters of Savannah in Georgia.[6] Their light-infantry having stole a march upon the Americans, by a pass through a swamp, which was supposed impassable, and thereby defeated our army, under the command of General Robert Howe.[7] The American loss was said to be about 30 officers, and near 400 men, killed, wounded and taken prisoners. This event threw the whole State of Georgia into the hands of the British. The American General was accused of misconduct, and a longtime after brought to trial, and honorably acquitted. The British here practiced art, and force was obliged to yield to it. Their light infantry finding their way through the path in the swamp, bringing of them on the flank and in the rear of the Americans, where they were not expected, or not guarded against, proved their overthrow. A few shots on the flank or rear of an enemy, serves to disconcert them more than a heavy fire in the front. The point of decision here lies not in the force, but in the mind. A company of 50 men cannot fire more shots in the same given time on the flank, or in the rear, than they could in the front; but these few shots will have more effect on the minds of the enemy than the fire of a whole regiment in their front. The Americans were vastly inferior in numbers to the British, and must at any rate have been forced from the ground; but the British light infantry passing through the swamp was the first misfortune.

The Continental currency was now greatly depreciated. Provisions very scarce and dear, flour especially so, and many families in Boston almost destitute of this necessary article.

February 26—The following resolution of Congress was published in the Boston newspapers:

> In CONGRESS, October 8th, 1778.
>
> *Resolved*, That all limitations of prices of gold or silver be taken off.

February 27—It was learnt, that the Supreme Executive Council of the State of Pennsylvania had exhibited a number of charges against Maj. Gen. Arnold, while in command at Philadelphia.[8]

March 7—Intelligence was received that Gen. Tryon[9] had lately made an excursion to Horseneck, in Connecticut, where he burnt three small vessels, destroyed all the salt works, and one store; plundered the inhabitants of their clothing, etc. and carried off about 200 cattle and horses, and some small stock. The party consisted of about 600 light-horse, light-infantry, rangers, etc. The enemy got off with the loss of two men killed and 20 made prisoners; giving out that their party was the advance of a body of 3000 or 4000, they deceived the militia, and so escaped a severe drubbing.

March 11—It was learnt, that on the 25th ult. the British made an excursion from Staten Island, with intent to surprise General Maxwell,[10] who was stationed with his brigade at Elizabeth-Town, in the Jersies. They landed at the point a little before day-break and in such superior force as obliged the General to abandon the town, which he effected without loss. The enemy burnt the General's quarters, the barns, and a store or two, and then returned.

March 29—Intelligence was received, that General Washington had issued a proclamation offering a pardon to all deserters from the army of the United States, who should return to their duty by the first day of May following; and also called upon all absent officers to join their respective corps by that time. Maj. Gen. Sullivan was ordered from Providence to the main army, and Maj. Gen. Gates to the command at Providence. Capt. Mowatt again made his appearance on the eastern coast; he had landed some men, and burnt Mr. Shaw's house.

Intelligence was received, that the British had gained an advantage on the borders of Georgia, near Briar Creek. Col. Elbert,[11] with a number of others, were taken prisoners. Matters did not wear a favorable aspect in that quarter; but it was hoped that Gen. Lincoln, who had now got the command, would give a new complexion to things at the southward.

April 2—Maj. Gen. Gates left Boston for Providence; in consequence of which, the command again devolved on our General.

April 11—It was learnt, that a fleet of refugee cruisers made an attempt to land a number of men near Falmouth (Cape-Cod) but were repulsed by the militia. They next proceeded to Nantucket, where they plundered the inhabitants of goods and effects. Edward Winslow,[12] formerly of Marshfield, was said to be commander, with George Leonard,[13] and others.

April 16—The Continental frigates, *Warren*, *Ranger*, and *Queen of France*, had been very successful in a cruise, having taken seven or eight prizes going from New York to Georgia: they were now coming in; among them the *Jason*, of 20 guns and 150 men; and *Maria*, of 16 guns—four field and about 20 commissioned officers, were on board. A large number of accoutrements for dragoons, dry goods to the amount of £100,000, and it was said a sum in specie a large quantity of flour, etc. A great uneasiness prevailed in the army at Providence, on account of the scarcity of flour. Relief was sent on.

May 3—Capt. Fernald,[14] of New Hampshire, was unfortunately shot in the breast, as he was standing on Hancock's wharf, by a musket-ball discharged from the *Warren* frigate.

May 7—Intelligence was received that Col. Van Schaick,[15] of the New York line, with about 500 men, had lately made an excursion to Onondaga, surprised the castle, killed 12 Indians, and took 34 prisoners; destroyed their castle, cattle, provisions, etc. without the loss of a man.

May 11—Several vessels laden with rice, on account of the United States, arrived at Boston from the southward, which was a great relief to the troops. An embarkation of troops had sailed from New York, under the command of Gen. Mathew,[16] convoyed by the ships under the command of Sir George Collier.[17] They entered the Capes of Virginia, on the 8th. The 9th or 10th they took possession of a fort at the entrance of Elizabeth River, on the west side. They destroyed a number of vessels, stores, provisions, etc. and returned.

May 30—Sir Henry Clinton moved up the Hudson, with a large body of troops, covered by Sir George Collier's naval force, which had just returned from Virginia. The intention of Sir Henry Clinton was to seize the posts at King's Perry.

May 31—Gen. Vaughan, with the troops under his command, landed on the east side of the river, a few miles below Verplank's; and Gen. Sir Henry Clinton on the west side, a little below Stony-Point. They soon got possession of both the points, and immediately rendered them more defensible.

June 4—Our General received orders from Gen. Washington to join the main army. He had before ordered all the heavy cannon at Boston and Providence, belonging to the United States, to be sent on to Hudson's River; they were sent on, slung under two pair of stout cart-wheels each, and were a ponderous load. Our General received polite and affectionate addresses, on his leaving the department, from the officers of the line—staff department—the officers of the Boston regiment of militia, etc. On the 11th, he left Boston, accompanied by a large and respectable number of

Gen. Sir Henry Clinton, KB.

officers and citizens, in carriages and on horseback, as far as Watertown, where the gentlemen had ordered an elegant dinner to be provided. After having dined, he took his leave, amidst a shout of hearty wishes for his health and prosperity.

June 14—He reached Springfield—was met some distance out of town, by Col. Armand's dragoons, and the officers of the Springfield department; and, on entering the town, was received by the infantry of the legion, and a salute of cannon from the park. Here he quitted the extent of his late eastern command. He was escorted out of town by the officers of the several military departments, and Armand's dragoons.

June 21—He arrived at New Windsor; and on the 22nd, attended Gen. Washington to West Point.

June 23—Our General took the command of the troops on the east side of the Hudson, having in front all the out posts towards New York, on that side of the river. The British were now in possession of both the points at King's Ferry; and a number of transports had lain in the river for some time. The advanced posts of the Americans at this time, on this side, did not extend lower than Peek's Kill; and a picket mounted every night at the south foot of Sugar-Loaf Hill.

June 24—About 200 of the enemy's light horse[18] came up as far as Crom Pond— surprised two militia pickets killed and took prisoners about 30 men. About 130 light infantry of the enemy, at the same time, came out from Verplank's Point, made an excursion round, and then returned. On the morning of the 25th, the enemy's light horse, and about 1000 infantry, were at Pine's Bridge. Our General ordered 200 light infantry, under the command of Lt. Col. Grosvenor,[19] to march to Robinson's stores, near Lake Mahopac, to cover that quarter.

June 27—A deserter came in from Verplank's Point, who reported that the British army, except five or six regiments, were to leave the Points, and were then embarking. Soon after, upwards of 30 sail of transports were seen, standing down the river. The British had a sloop at anchor off Peek's Kill landing, and a ship off the Dunderberg.[20] Lest the enemy meant a deception, the Americans were ordered to lie on their arms, and a regiment extra was ordered to advance on the heights.

June 28—Three deserters, one a Hessian musician with his horn, came in from the enemy; they confirmed the testimony of the former deserter, that the body of the British army had left the Points.

June 29—Moylan's horse crossed the river, to reinforce the left; they were to be followed by Armand's legion. At evening a deserter came in from the enemy. A detachment from the British at Rhode Island arrived at New York.

Congress, by ballot, chose our General a Commissioner of the Board of War; which was communicated to him by a letter from His Excellency the President, which he received on the 30th, as follows:

PHILADELPHIA, June 24th, 1779.

SIR,

I have the pleasure of transmitting to you, enclosed, an extract from the minutes of Congress, of the 22nd ult. by which you will perceive that you are elected to the place of a Commissioner to the Board of War.

I have the honor to be, etc.

(Signed) JOHN JAY, President.

Maj. Gen. HEATH.

In CONGRESS, June 22nd, 1779.

Congress proceeded to the election of a Commissioner for the Board of War, and the ballots being taken, Maj. Gen. W. Heath was elected.

Extract from the Minutes.
(Signed) C. THOMSON, Secretary.

Although this appointment was, in its nature, very honorable, with a salary proportionate (4000 dollars per annum) and our General was informed that he would also retain his rank in the army, he absolutely declined an acceptance of it; expressing, in a letter to His Excellency the President, the high sense he entertained of the honor done him by the appointment; yet, that he chose rather to participate in the more active operations of the field.

July 1—Gen. Huntington's brigade moved down, and took post at the gorge of the mountains, near the Continental Village. A deserter came in from the enemy.

July 2—Col. Rufus Putnam reconnoitered the enemy's positions at Verplank's and Stony Points. At evening a deserter came in from the enemy. About 360 of the enemy's light horse and light infantry came out from Mile-Square, and attacked Col. Sheldon's[21] light horse, who were posted at Poundridge, about 90 in number. The superior force of the enemy obliged our horse, at first, to retreat, but, being reinforced by the militia, they in turn pursued the enemy. Our loss was one Corporal, one Trumpeter, and eight privates wounded; three Sergeants, one Corporal, and four privates missing; and 12 horses missing. The standard of the regiment being left in the house when the dragoons suddenly turned out, was lost. Of the enemy, one was killed, four taken prisoners, four horses taken, and one horse killed. The enemy set fire to and burnt the meetinghouse and Maj. Lockwood's house; they also burnt Mr. Hay's house, at Bedford.

July 5—An excessive hot day, with a thundershower; the lightning struck in the encampment of Col. Putnam's regiment, on Constitution Island, by which one man was killed; several received much hurt, and a large number were stunned. The enemy entered the Sound—landed, and took possession of New Haven plundered and insulted the inhabitants, and left the place.

July 7—The enemy landed at Fairfield, and burnt many houses, etc.

July 10—About six o'clock, p.m. our General received orders from Gen. Washington to march, with the two Connecticut brigades, by the way of Crom Pond, towards Bedford. The next morning, although rainy, the first brigade marched to the Village.

July 12—The storm ceasing, the tents (although as wet as water could make them) were struck, and the troops took up their line of march, reaching Amawalk about sun-setting. A report having been spread in the fore part of the day, that the enemy were at or near Pine's Bridge, our General ordered the baggage-wagons, under proper escort, to file off to the left and pursue a road running parallel with the one on which the column was moving, thereby keeping the column between the enemy and the wagons. Both arrived on the ground of encampment within a few minutes of each other. The troops lay on their arms, with out pitching their tents. The enemy continued their depredations at the Sound, and burnt some houses at Norwalk.

July 13—At five o'clock, a.m. the troops took up their line of march, and reached Ridgefield, where they halted for the night. The next morning, our General sent off all the tents and other baggage to Danbury, and took up his line of march towards

Stamford. When he ascended the high grounds in sight of the Sound, the enemy's fleet was observed under sail, standing off and on between Stamford and Long Island. About 12 o'clock, two deserters from Gen. Clinton's army came to our troops; they had left the British army two or three hours before, at which time the enemy were on the point of making a movement; the corps of guides and pioneers being then assembled at Gen. Clinton's quarters. This called for the exercise of discretion.

The troops on board the transports, with Gen. Tryon, if the whole should land, were far inferior to the force with our General; but the main British army, with Gen. Clinton, was by far superior to his. If the whole of the Americans had marched down to Stamford, Clinton, by five or six hours' forced marching, might have crossed his rear and have cut him off from a communication with the Highlands; he therefore resolved to march forward to the Cross Roads, one of which went directly to the British army, an other to Stamford, and in his rear to the Highlands. Here he took a position in order of battle, and detached Col. Starr's[22] and Meig's regiments, with one field-piece, to Stamford, whose approach towards the town, in open view, would prevent Tryon from landing; or, in case he did with superior force, the detachment might be surrounded. In this situation the troops remained until dusk, and then took a more advantageous position for the night, the whole lying on their arms, in order of battle. Early on the morning of the 15th, our General received information that the shipping had gone down towards New York; he therefore moved and took a strong position, between Ridgefield and Bedford, sending out patrols of horse and foot, on all the roads. This movement towards the Sound quieted the minds of the people, and saved Stamford and other towns from destruction.

While the attention of both the grand armies, and of the adjacent country, was turned towards the Sound, the Great WASHINGTON ordered General Wayne to strike at Stony Point with the light infantry, which lay not far distant from that post. This was done with great promptitude, the works being carried by assault, and the whole garrison made prisoners of war, with all the artillery, ammunition, stores, etc. This was a most brilliant affair. In advancing to the assault, the front of the American column led, with unloaded arms, relying solely on the use of the bayonet. As they approached the works, a soldier insisted on loading his piece—all was now a profound silence—the officer commanding the platoon ordered him to keep on; the soldier observed that he did not understand attacking with his piece unloaded; he was ordered not to stop, at his peril; he still persisted, and the officer instantly dispatched him. A circumstance like this shocks the feelings; but it must be considered how fatal the consequence would have been, if one single gun had been fired; scores would have lost their lives, and most probably defeat would have been consequent; and therefore this was the lesser evil.

On the morning of the 16th, signal guns were heard in the Sound, towards New York, at intervals, from two o'clock until daylight. Gen. Clinton's army moved to Mile-Square. Stony Point having been taken, with so much *eclat* to the American arms, Gen. Washington determined an attempt on Verplank's Point, on the east side of the Hudson and opposite to Stony Point: for this purpose Maj. Gen. Howe,[23] with two brigades and some 12-pounders on traveling carriages, was ordered to proceed by the way of Peek's Kill, throw a bridge over the creek, move on to the point, and open batteries against the enemy's works, while a cannonade and bombardment was kept up across the river from Stony Point.

July 17—At about 10 o'clock, a.m. our General, while out reconnoitering, received, by an express from Gen. Washington, orders to move as expeditiously as possible to Peek's Kill, where he would find Gen. Howe with two brigades. Our General was to take the command of the whole, and carry into effect the orders which had been given to Gen. Howe. Our General returned immediately to the troops, and at 12 o'clock began his march towards Peek's Kill marched until dusk 15 miles, when the troops halted and laid down to rest on the side of the road; the dragoons not unsaddling their horses. At three o'clock the next morning, the troops resumed their march, and in the afternoon our General received information from Gen. Howe, by express, that Gen. Clinton was on full march with his whole army towards Verplank's Point: an answer was returned, at what point the troops then were, and that they were marching as fast as the men could endure, and would continue so until they reached him.

When the troops had advanced a little to the westward of Drake's farm, Col. Moylan came up from Gen. Howe, with information that a part of Clinton's army were then above the New Bridge on Croton river, pushing for the point; and that he was retreating from the point as fast as possible. On this, our General ordered Gen. Huntington, with his brigade and two fieldpieces, to push forward as fast as the troops could march and keep in breath, and take a position on the high ground to the south of Peek's Kill, which commands the road to the point, and also that to the New Bridge, on Croton River; and ordered a regiment to file off to the right, and secure the pass over the hills between Drake's and Peek's Kill, and also ordered the flank-guard on the left to be reinforced, and to send out small flank-guards still further from its flank. The troops moving on with the utmost expedition to the ground which Gen. Huntington had been ordered forward to secure. Every moment that passed was expected to announce the commencement of an action between the advanced or flanking parties of the two armies, but it did not take place. At this moment, Gen. Washington, having learnt how matters stood, and that possibly Gen. Clinton might attempt to push into the Highlands, sent an express to our General, to move into the Highlands immediately, which was done just after dark, the troops passing the night on Bald Hill.

It was generally the opinion, that if our General had not been at hand to advance in the manner he did, that Gen. Clinton, by a forced march of his light troops, backed by his army, would have got in the rear of Gen. Howe before he could have possibly gained the road at Peek's Kill, and between his army and a sally from the garrison at Verplank's Point inevitably cut off the whole. Our troops at Stony Point cannonaded and bombarded the enemy's works at Verplank's during the whole day, and until near midnight. The post was then evacuated, and the *Washington* galley was blown up.

July 19—The troops moved from Bald Hill, Parson's brigade to Robinson's, Huntington's and Paterson's to Nelson's, Nixon's to the gorge of the mountains. On the morning of the 20th, the British army moved from their encampment, near the New Bridge, to Dobbs' Ferry. The shipping in Tappan Bay came to sail, and stood down the river. By a new disposition of the American army, on this day, our General was to command the left wing; it then consisted of two regiments of horse, and two divisions of infantry.

July 22—Two deserters came in from Verplank's Point; they reported that the garrison consisted of about 1000 men. This day about 40 sail of transports sailed up the Sound. The British army encamped near Dobbs' Ferry, their advanced picket at Jonathan Odle's, three miles below Tarrytown; from this encampment the enemy moved to Mile-Square, Valentine's Hill, etc. A deserter from Verplank's Point reported that the British had again taken possession of Stony Point, and were repairing the works, their force on both sides of the river being about 1500; and that they had got up the guns of our galley, which had been blown up.

July 25—The British having sent Col. McLean,[24] in the month of the preceding June, with six or seven hundred men, to establish a post at the mouth of Penobscot River, the Legislature of Massachusetts determined to dislodge them, and made arrangements for the purpose. The armament, with the troops, made their appearance on this day before the posts; the issue is detailed in a subsequent page.

July 26—Four deserters came in from the enemy; they reported that Stony Point was repairing with great expedition, and that Lord Cornwallis arrived at New York on the 24th.

July 28—Four deserters came in from the enemy. Capt. Hopkins, of the dragoons, took the Captain of the *Bellona* transport, a sergeant and corporal of the 64th British regiment, and two seamen, who had ventured too far on the shore near Sing-Sing.

July 29—Two deserters came in from the enemy.

July 30—Three deserters came in from Verplank's Point. This morning, Capt. Hopkins, of Moylan's[25] light dragoons, fell in with a party of the enemy, under Col. Emmerich,[26] near Young's tavern, and charged them vigorously; but the Colonel being supported by the Hessian Jägers, Capt. Hopkins was obliged to retreat: he brought off with him three prisoners and four horses, and killed six of the enemy on the spot, and wounded a number. Several prisoners which he had taken, were retaken by the enemy. Capt. Hopkins had one dragoon and two horses wounded. The British army were under marching orders for several days.

July 31—Three deserters came in from the enemy. A body of the enemy landed in the Jersies.

August 1—Capt. Hopkins gave notice that the British army had moved below Kingsbridge. Three deserters came in from the enemy.

August 2—Six deserters came in from the enemy. The British army encamped on York Island: Emmerich's and Bearmore's corps above Kingsbridge. The American army remained at their respective posts in the Highlands.

August 5—About 100 horse of Sheldon's, Moylan's and of the militia, and about 40 infantry of Glover's brigade, passed by Delancey's mills to the neighborhood of Morrisania, where they took 12 or 14 prisoners, some stock, etc. The enemy collected—a skirmish ensued, in which the enemy had a number of men killed and wounded; our loss, two killed, and two wounded. The British army, below the seven mile stone on York Island, were alarmed by a report that a French fleet were on the coast. Three deserters from Verplank's Point; they reported, that the garrison, except 400 men, were to remove to New York.

August 9—Four deserters from the point.

August 10—Two deserters from the enemy. There were some desertions from our army to the enemy.

August 14—Four prisoners, taken the 12th, near Sing-Sing, were sent up, and two deserters from the British 33rd regiment came in.

August 17—Three deserters from the enemy.

August 18—Seven deserters came in; the enemy were very strongly fortifying Laurel-Hill, on New York Island, nearly opposite to Fort Washington.

August 19—23 wagon-loads of forage were brought off from the vicinity of Peek's Kill, covered by 250 men, under the command of Lt. Col. Putnam. The galley and one of the enemy's gunboats fired a number of cannon-shot at the party, but did them no harm. The night before, Maj. Lee, with about 400 men, surprised and took the garrison at Paulus Hook.

August 20—Two deserters came in from the enemy.

August 21—Two deserters came in. At night, the enemy's guard-boats came as far up the river as Anthony's Nose, and fired several shot at the camp of our light infantry.

August 23—Three deserters came in from the enemy. The enemy burnt two houses belonging to the Lents, near Verplank's Point. Accounts were received that Gen. Sullivan had advanced into the Indian country, and taken two of their principal villages.

August 25—Admiral Arbuthnot arrived at New York, with about 200 sail of transports: between 2000 and 3000 troops arrived in the fleets, and a large sum of money was brought for the army. The Continental frigates were very successful at sea, and sent into Boston several rich sugar ships.

August 30—Three deserters came in from Verplank's Point; and a prisoner belonging to the 33rd regiment, taken by one of our patrolling parties, was sent up. About 15 sail of square-rigged vessels lay at anchor near King's Ferry. 1231 recruits, of the 2000 ordered by Massachusetts, to serve nine months, had already joined the army.

September 4—Three deserters from the enemy.

September 5—Two deserters came in. Preparations were making in New York for an embarkation of troops. The British army sickly, especially the newly arrived reinforcement.

September 6—The enemy made an excursion from Kingsbridge, towards Horseneck; on their return they carried off some cattle, sheep, poultry, etc. Accounts were received, that General Sullivan had obtained further advantages in the Indian country.

September 9—Two deserters came in from the enemy. Putrid fever and scurvy raged at New York, among the British troops. The American army remained in their former position: the Virginia line, near Ramapo, on the right; the light infantry, near Fort Montgomery; the Maryland line, on the left of the light infantry; Pennsylvania line and two brigades of Massachusetts, at West Point; North Carolina brigade, at Constitution Island; the Connecticut line, on the east side of the Hudson, between Nelson's and Robinson's; Nixon's brigade, at the gorge of the mountains, above the Continental Village; Glover's brigade, Moylan's, Sheldon's and Armand's horse, at Lower Salem. On the west side of the Hudson, besides Fort Clinton, at West Point, and Fort Putnam, on the height back of it, there were seven or eight redoubts, built and building. On the east side of the river, the north and middle redoubts, and a redoubt at the gorge of the mountains. Great expectations of the arrival of a French fleet on the American coast.

September 13—Four deserters came in from the enemy.

September 14—Just after reveille, our General received orders to put Nixon's brigade under marching orders, which was done immediately. Gen. Howe was ordered to move with Glover's to Pine's Bridge, Croton River, and Nixon's to join him.

September 15—A deserter came in from Verplank's Point. The day before, a party of the enemy's horse came out from Kingsbridge, with intent to surprise Lt. Col. White[27]; but by the desertion of one of the party, they were disappointed. The Count de la Luzerne,[28] the new French minister, arrived and dined at Gen. Washington's.

September 16—Nixon's brigade marched to form a junction with Glover's, and a picket of 150 men mounted at the Village. Four deserters came in from the enemy. Count Luzerne was highly pleased with the treatment he received in passing through the New England States. The 17th, he left headquarters, on his way to Philadelphia.

September 18—Gen. Howe was ordered to march back to Lower Salem, with Glover's and Nixon's brigades.

September 19—Two deserters came in from the enemy. Some appearances indicated an evacuation of Verplank's Point.

September 22—A deserter came in from Kingsbridge. Preparations for the embarkation of a large body of troops continued at New York.

September 29—Two deserters from the enemy, and one the day before.

September 30—The engineers, covered by a detachment of 300 men, reconnoitered the enemy's works at Verplank's; the enemy appeared to be much alarmed, and fired a number of cannon and small-arms at our party, and a reinforcement came over from Stony Point. At evening another deserter came in.

October 1—The American light infantry moved down near to Kakeat, and the North Carolina brigade from Constitution Island to New Windsor. One deserter from the enemy.

October 2—Two deserters came in from the enemy. Certain intelligence was received, that the Count D'Estaing had arrived at Georgia. The enemy at Verplank's Point opened a number of pits, about five feet deep, and four feet over, with a sharp stake in the middle, around the outside of the abatis. By the last accounts from Gen. Sullivan, he was at Tioga, on his return this way; he had destroyed a great number of Indian towns, and immense quantities of corn and other produce, and cut down many fruit trees.[29] It is a great pity the latter were not spared; they would have been very pleasing to the American settlers, who will one day, not far distant, fill that fertile country. A number of armed vessels, from the Connecticut ports on the Sound, cut out and brought off a number of the enemy's vessels from Huntington harbor, Long Island, and the Halifax brig was taken by an armed galley.

October 4—Five deserters came in from the enemy. Gen. Howe was ordered to take post again at Pine's Bridge.

October 5—The Sieur Gerard,[30] the late French Minister, came to camp, and dined at headquarters. Two days before, Lt. Gill,[31] of the dragoons, patrolling in East Chester, found a superior force in his rear, and no alternative but to surrender or cut his way through them; he chose the latter, and forced his way, when he found a body of infantry still behind the horse; these he also charged, and on his passing them, his horse was wounded and threw him, when he fell into the enemy's hands. Two of the Lieutenant's party, which consisted of 24, were killed, and one taken prisoner; the rest escaped safe to their regiments.

Congress about this time appointed the Hon. John Adams, a Plenipotentiary, *extra*, to repair to France to negotiate for a peace with Great Britain, when an opportunity occurred. The British fortified Governor's Island, in the harbor of New York, and appeared under great apprehensions of a visit from the French fleet under the Count D'Estaing. The troops and shipping at Rhode Island were ordered to New York.

October 7—One deserter from Verplank's Point. There was a cannonade between our infantry at Grassy Point and one of the enemy's guard-ships, when the latter was driven from her moorings.

October 8—The light infantry of Glover's brigade crossed the Hudson to join Gen. Wayne. The British had a number of ships ready to sink in the channel, in case a French fleet arrived, and attempted to enter the harbor of New York. The merchants in the city packing up their goods.

October 9—A fleet of transports passed the Sound towards Rhode Island. The General Officers of the American army resolved to address Congress, respecting themselves and the army.

October 11—There was a cannonade in the river between the American and British gunboats; but no damage was done. Sir Joseph Yorke,[32] the British Minister at the Hague, addressed their High Mightinesses on the 22nd of the preceding July, in such language as evinced the feelings of the British nation. One deserter from Verplank's Point.

October 12—Gen. Sir Henry Clinton and Col. Robinson came up to Verplank's Point, in the ship *Fanny*, and returned the next day; after which, the workmen at the point ceased working. The troops of the enemy sickly at the Points.

October 13—Two deserters came in.

October 14—Two prisoners of war were sent up, and four deserters came in. The British transports were collected near Turtle Bay, and their ships of war near the Narrows.

October 15—Seven deserters came in from Verplank's Point; they reported that the enemy were putting their baggage, sick, the women, etc. on board the transports.

October 16—14 prisoners, seamen taken by Capt. Hallett's[33] company of New York militia two days before, on the North River, near Teller's Point, were sent up, and one deserter came in. Just before sun-set, a galley and several of the enemy's gunboats came up the river as high as Fort Montgomery, and fired a number of shot at some of our boats, and at the troops on the west side of the river; the Americans discharged some muskets from the banks at the boats, and the latter returned down the river.

October 17—One deserter came in from the enemy.

October 19—One deserter from Verplank's Point.

October 21—Three deserters came in from Verplank's, and reported that the enemy were on the point of evacuating their works. The officer commanding the advance picket soon after sent information that the works appeared to be on fire, and the shipping standing down the river. Maj. Waldbridge,[34] who commanded the advance picket, immediately sent a detachment to take possession of the works. Several loaded shells left by the enemy, in places where the fire would come at them, burst, but did no harm. The enemy left one horse, a few old entrenching tools, and some other trifles at the point. The transports came to anchor off the mouth of Croton River; and information was received that the British grenadiers were on board the transports, in the river near Fort Washington, and the 7th and 33rd regiments in readiness to embark at a moment's notice. Our General, lest there might be an attempt made on Gen. Howe's division, ordered a detachment of 500 men and half the Village picket, under the command of Col. Bradley,[35] to march, and take post during the night, towards the New Bridge, on Croton River, to cover the right flank of Howe's division.

October 22—About noon, the enemy's transports came to sail with the ebb, and beat down against the wind, and were soon out of sight.

October 24—Col. Bradley's detachment returned to camp. The Colonel reported that he observed large quantities of forage and fruit in the fields between Verplank's Point and Croton River. To secure the forage, and cover the communication by King's Ferry, Gen. Washington ordered our General to move down and encamp at Peek's Kill.

October 27—The Connecticut line moved down and encamped on the high ground to the southward of Peek's Kill, and Maj. Gen. Howe's division was ordered up to form a junction. The day before, the enemy landed a body of troops, said to be some thousands strong, at Amboy, and advanced towards Brunswick. The light infantry, and the Virginia line, were ordered to move down that way. A man, who said he was a Lieutenant in the British service, and who produced a commission, came out, pretending that he had been ill-treated, etc.

The State of Massachusetts appeared to be determined to fill up their regiments, and offered 300 dollars bounty to those who would enlist, in addition to the Continental bounty, which was 200 dollars, making the whole bounty 500 dollars. This morning about 70 sail of vessels, many of them large ships, passed down the Sound, having the garrison of Rhode Island on board. When the enemy landed yesterday at South Amboy, 96 horse about the same time landed at Perth Amboy, and proceeded rapidly to Middlebrook—burnt Raritan meeting-house, Somerset court-house, and six boats, and returned through Spotswood to South Amboy. This party, on its retreat, was met by 13 of the militia, who fired upon them, killed one man and four horses, and took the commanding officer Lt. Simcoe, and one trooper, prisoners. By the capture of Simcoe, the inhabitants were freed of a very enterprising and troublesome officer.[36] The destruction of the boats was the object of this enterprise.

October 29—Gen. Howe's division formed a junction with the Connecticut line, and encamped with them. Strong fatigue parties were daily employed on the works evacuated by the enemy at Verplank's and Stony Points. Gen. Lincoln and the Count D'Estaing, by the last accounts from Georgia, had formed a junction, and were determined to attack the enemy.

October 31—Maj. Benschoten[37] arrived at camp, with a detachment of Lt. Col. Pawling's New York levies; they were ordered to garrison Stony Point.

November 1—Maj. Armstrong,[38] Aide-de-camp to Maj. Gen. Gates, called at camp, on his way to Congress, with official dispatches of the evacuation of Rhode Island, which took place on the night of the 26th ult. The British left large quantities of forage, fuel, etc. Brig. Gen. Stark had gone on to Rhode Island. A Hessian Lieutenant belonging to the Landgrave regiment, came out from the neighborhood of Fort Washington; he pretended to desire to enter the American service as a volunteer. A prisoner of war was also sent up from the advance guard.

November 2—Intelligence was received, that a body of Indians were advancing towards Fort Schuyler.

November 7—Two German Jägers, with their rifles, came to our camp. At night,

Col. Armand proceeded with his corps from near Tarrytown to the vicinity of Morrisania, to the house of Alderman Leggett, where he surprised and took Maj. Bearmore[39] and five other prisoners. The secrecy, precaution, gallantry and discipline exhibited by the Colonel and his corps on this occasion did them much honor. In the capture of Maj. Bearmore, the inhabitants of the adjacent country were relieved from the frequent excursions of a troublesome officer. The British augmented their troops on Staten Island.

November 9—In the morning an assault was made, which proved unsuccessful the Americans were repulsed and obliged to retreat; of the Americans, 170 were killed and wounded; among the former, Count Pulaski, a remarkably brave and enterprising officer, of Polish descent. The Count D'Estaing was wounded in the arm and leg. It was said, that of the French troops, 330 were killed and wounded. Gen. Lincoln retreated to Charleston. It being rendered certain that the Count D'Estaing would not come to the northward, the American main army was distributed to winter-quarters. Moylan's, Sheldon's, Baylor's, and Bedkins's dragoons to Connecticut—Poor's brigade to Danbury—the Massachusetts line to West Point, and the posts in the Highlands—the Virginia, Maryland, Pennsylvania, New Jersey, New York, and Connecticut lines, Hand's and Stark's mixed corps, back of the Scotch Plains, New Jersey—Lee's corps, and a detachment of infantry, towards Monmou—Maréchaussee,[40] with the main army.

November 11—Two deserters came in from Col. Wurmb's[41] Jägers.

November 13—Five prisoners taken by Lt. Oakley,[42] near Morrisania, were sent to camp. The enemy had a redoubt, called No. 8, on the east side of Haarlem Creek, nearly opposite to the fort on Laurel Hill, and under the fire of its cannon, for the security of their advanced troops on the Morrisania side.

November 16—Intelligence was received, that on the 23rd of September, Gen. Lincoln and the Count D'Estaing broke ground before the enemy's works, at Savannah, in Georgia; and on the 5th of October, batteries of 33 cannon and nine mortars were opened and continued firing with intervals, until the 8th, without the wished-for effect.

November 19—Four prisoners were sent up.

November 23—Maj. Gen. Gates and his family came to camp from Rhode Island.

November 25—The troops were moving to their different places of cantonment; many of the soldiers (as fine men as ever stood in shoes) were marched barefooted over the hard frozen ground, and with an astonishing patience. Remember these things, ye Americans, in future times!

November 28—The Commander in Chief gave our General the command of all the posts and troops on Hudson's River, which Gen. Washington very frequently called the key that locked the communication between the eastern and southern States; and of all the posts in the United States, was the most important. This was the second time that our General was designated to command them.

November 29—Three deserters came in from the galley in the river.

November 30—Early in the morning, Gen. Washington crossed the Hudson at King's Perry, into the Jersies. Maj. Gen. Gates was to proceed to Virginia—a sergeant, corporal, and three privates were carried off by one Joseph McKeel,[43] a sly, artful fellow, in the service of the enemy, and who conducted many recruits from the country to them.

Maj. Gen. Horatio Gates.

December 2—Col. Armand, with some of his corps, went down to Morrisania, and took a Capt. Cruger,[44] of Bearmore's corps, and two men, prisoners. At this time the troops were greatly distressed for bread and the horses for forage; the former occasioned by the want of water at the mills. All the horses, except such as were absolutely necessary for incumbent duties, were ordered out into the country. A man who pretended to be a prophet, came out from the enemy—he more probably was a spy.

December 16—Col. Pawlding's corps was ordered from Stony Point to Poughkeepsie, a great desertion having taken place in the corps. The Virginia line had marched to the southward the enemy at New York preparing for the embarkation of a large body of troops, said to be upwards of 10,000, under the immediate command of Gen. Sir Henry Clinton.

December 29—Three Hessian deserters came into our army; they reported that Gen. Mathew had command of all the posts and troops on the north end of York Island, above the bridge, etc. The long talked-of embarkation of troops at New York sailed on the 26th. The fleet was said to consist of near 200 sail. The enemy boasted that it was convoyed by nearly 20 ships of war; however, it was well known that they had very few ships of the line, and that they were under great apprehensions of falling in with a superior French force. They went to the southward.

December 30—Lt. Col. Newhall,[45] with 250 men properly officered, marched to do duty on the lines.

December 31—There was a great body of snow on the ground.

CHAPTER 6

1780

January 1—Early in the morning about 100 soldiers belonging to the Massachusetts regiments, who had enlisted at different periods subsequent to January, 1777, for three years, pretending that their time of service now expired (although many of them had months to serve, before their three years' service was completed) marched off with intent to go home: they were pursued and brought back: some of them were punished; the greater part of them pardoned. Some others, at other posts, conducted in the same manner, and were treated as the first mentioned. Those whose time of service was expired were all discharged with honor.

January 3—The snow had got to be about four feet deep on a level, and the troops were driven to great difficulties in keeping open the communications to the posts—obtaining provisions, fuel, forage, etc. and so intense and steady was the weather, that for more than twenty days there could not be discovered the least sign of the remission of the snow in any places the most open to the influences of the sun. The Hudson soon becoming passable on the ice, the troops were comfortably supplied with provisions; but many were in extreme want of clothing.

January 8—The light infantry belonging to the regiments in the Highlands, were joining their respective corps; the corps of light infantry being separated for the winter.

January 9—About dusk, the north redoubt was discovered to be on fire at the southwest corner, under the rampart, which was of timber; the fire was out of reach, and threatened the destruction of the whole redoubt. A detachment from West Point was ordered over to the assistance of the garrison of the redoubt; but so strongly dovetailed and strapped were the timbers of the rampart, that the fire for a time seemed to baffle every exertion to extinguish it. The ammunition and about 100 barrels of salted provisions in the magazine, were seasonably removed by the garrison; but the fire was not extinguished until about four o'clock in the morning of the 10th. All the officers and men distinguished themselves on this occasion; but the conduct of Col. Lyman,[1] Col. Sproat,[2] and Capt. Drew,[3] were conspicuous indeed, as was that of a Sergeant of the garrison of the redoubt, who, when all were on the point of quitting the redoubt, lest the magazine should take fire and blow up, instantly rushed into the magazine, and did not quit it until he had thrown out every cask of powder and box of ammunition deposited in it. If his name could be recollected, it should be inserted.

January 12—Artificers and fatigue-men were ordered to repair the redoubt. The weather continued intensely cold. A man belonging to the garrison of West Point was

131

frozen to death on his return from New Windsor to the point; and many soldiers were frost-bitten. Maj. Gen. Putnam, who had gone home on furlough about this time, received a paralytic stroke at Hartford in Connecticut, as he was on his return to the army.

January 17—The Hudson was so frozen, that travelers safely crossed the river on the ice at King's Ferry. A Hessian deserter came in. Two days before, viz. on the 15th, Maj. Gen. Lord Stirling made a descent on Staten Island, with a detachment, consisting of about 2500 infantry, and some artillery; a number of tents, arms, and some baggage, belonging to Col. Buskirk's regiment, was taken and brought off, with some liquors, etc. Some of the American soldiers deserted to the enemy, and 17 were taken prisoners.

January 19—Two deserters came in from the enemy, and reported the strength of the British at Fort Washington. The people crossed from New York to Long Island on the ice. About this time, a detachment from Col. Mead's[4] regiment of levies[5] at Horseneck, and a number of volunteers from Greenwich, the former under the command of Captain Keeler,[6] the latter under the command of Captain Lockwood,[7] the whole about 80, marched to Morrisania; and about one o'clock in the morning, made an attack on Col. Hatfield.[8] They first attacked the picket, killed three, and drove the rest into the Colonel's quarters. The Colonel and his men took to the chambers, and fired out at the windows and down stairs at those who had entered the house; it appeared difficult, if possible, to dislodge them, the house was instantly set on fire, by putting a straw bed into a closet, which compelled the enemy to jump out at the chamber windows, to avoid the flames. Colonel Hatfield, one Captain, one Lieutenant, one Quartermaster, and 11 privates, were taken prisoners and brought off. This was a pretty affair, but was a little tarnished on the return by some of the militia, who were fatigued, loitering on the road where they supposed there was no danger; but a party of horse pursuing, overtook, killed and captured several of them.

January 26—Between 11 and 12 o'clock at night, a fire broke out in the Quartermaster's barrack at West Point, which threatened the most serious and extensive damage. It had got to considerable height before it was discovered; the barrack was consequently consumed to ashes, notwithstanding every exertion of the garrison, which was numerous. Brig. Gen. Paterson,[9] who commanded the garrison, not only distinguished himself, but also exposed his person to the flames to save another building, which was fortunately effected. The loss by the fire was considerable, both to the public and to individuals. The night before, viz. the 25th, a detachment of the enemy, said to consist of 500 men, made an excursion to Staten Island, over the ice, to Elizabeth-Town, in the Jersies, and completely surprised the picket posted there, consisting of a Major and 100 men, properly officered; it was said that not a gun was fired, nor a man hurt. The enemy surrounded the houses, and took the troops asleep. He who suffers himself to be surprised, through the want of proper precaution, his character (says a great military writer) is irretrievable.

February 1—At two o'clock in the morning, the north redoubt was discovered to be on fire again in the top of the bomb-proof, between the sally-port and the door. Every exertion was made by the garrison of the redoubt, and detachments sent to their aid, to put out the fire, but it was so much out of reach, and spread among the joints of the large timbers, that it was not extinguished until about two o'clock on the morning of the 3rd. The redoubt received considerable damage, and would have been totally destroyed had it not been for the unwearied exertions of the troops, day and night, during the whole of the time: and much credit was due to Lt. Col. Vose, and the other officers who commanded. By a more accurate account of the loss at the Quartermaster's barrack at West Point, it appeared that six marques, 26 horsemen's tents, 80 common tents, 900 knapsacks, 250 narrow axes, and a number of other articles were burnt and destroyed.

On the morning of the 3rd, about nine o'clock, the enemy made an attack on Lt. Col. Thomson,[10] who commanded the troops on the lines; the Colonel's force consisted of 250 men, in five companies, properly officered; they were instructed to move between Croton River and the White Plains, Hudson's River and Bedford; never to remain long at any one place, that the enemy might not be able to learn of their manner of doing duty, or form a plan for striking them in any particular situation. The Colonel had for some days taken post himself at *Young's*, not far from the White Plains. Capt. Watson[11] with his company, was with the Lt. Colonel; Capt. Roberts,[12] and Capt. Stoddard,[13] with their companies, were on the right; Capt. Lt. Farley[14] and Capt. Cooper[15] on the left. The force of the enemy consisted of the four flank companies of the first and second British regiments of Guards—detachments from two Hessian battalions—some mounted Jägers and mounted refugees. The whole under the command of Col. Norton,[16] of the Guards. The roads were so filled with snow that the enemy advanced but slowly, and were obliged to leave their field-pieces behind them on the road. They were discovered at a distance by Mr. Campbell, one of our guides, who, from the goodness of his horse, reconnoitered them pretty near. He gave the Lieutenant-Colonel notice of their advancing, and that their force was considerable, and advised him to take a stronger position a little in his rear. But the Lieutenant-Colonel was very confident that the enemy were only a body of horse, and that he could easily disperse them, and would not quit his ground.

The enemy first attacked a small advance-guard, consisting of a Sergeant and eight men, who behaved well, and meant to reach the main body in season; but were prevented by the horse, and all taken prisoners. The enemy's horse soon appeared in sight of the Americans, and discharged their rifles at long shot, and waited the coming up of the infantry, when a warm action commenced; the enemy scattered, taking the advantage of the ground and trees in the orchard, and closing up on all sides. The three companies of the detachment, which had joined, fought well. After about 15 minutes' sharp conflict, our troops broke; some took into the house, and others made off; the enemy's horse rushing on at the same instant, and the whole shouting. At this time, the two flank companies came up, but finding how matters stood judged it best to retreat, Capt. Stoddard's company giving a fire or two at long shot, Capt. Cooper's, from their distance, not firing at all. Some who were engaged affected their escape, others were overtaken by the horse. The enemy collected what prisoners they could, set Mr. Young's house and buildings on fire, and returned. Of the Americans, 13 were killed dead on the spot, and Capt. Roberts, who was mortally wounded, lived but a few minutes. Seventeen others were wounded, several of whom died. Lt. Col. Thomson of Marshall's, Capt. Watson of Greaton's, Capt. Lieut. Farley of Wesson's, Lt. Burley[17] of Tupper's, Lt. Maynard[18] of Greaton's, Ensign Fowler[19] of Nixon's, Ensign Bradley[20] of Bigelow's, with 89 others, were taken prisoners. The enemy left three men dead on the field, and a Captain of grenadiers was wounded in the hip, and a Lieutenant of infantry in the thigh. The British, in their account of the action acknowledged that they had five men killed, and 18 wounded. Lt. Col. Badlam,[21] with the relief for the lines, was at the time of the action far advanced on his march, but not within reach of those engaged.

One Mayhew, a peddler, well known in Massachusetts, was of this detachment; he made off up the road, but finding the horse rushing on, he struck off into the snow, almost up to his hips. Two of the enemy's horse turned into his track after him; and, gaining fast upon him, he asked them if they would give him quarter; they replied, "Yes, you dog, we will quarter you." This was twice repeated; when Mayhew, finding them inflexible, determined to give them one shot before he was quartered; and, turning round, discharged his piece at the first horseman, who cried out "The rascal has broke my leg;" when both of them turned their horses round and went off, leaving Mayhew at liberty to tread back his path to the road, and come off.

February 7—A body of the enemy's horse, said to be about 300, and the 7th British regiment, came over from Long Island to West Chester on the ice. The troops in New York, about this time, drew four days' provisions, which they were directed to keep cooked, and the troops to be in readiness to move on the shortest notice, with arms and blankets only. A number of sleighs were collected, and some heavy cannon were drawn out; whether an attempt on Morristown or the Highlands was the object, was not known. Several deserters came in from the enemy, and in this month there were some desertions from the American southern regiments to the enemy. The enemy also made an excursion in the Jersies as far as Elizabethtown, and carried off great quantity of plunder.

February 19—Some small parties of the enemy were out towards the White Plains. Our General having obtained leave from the Commander in Chief, to make a visit to his friends in New-England, commenced his journey eastward on the 21st of February, and reached his house in Roxbury on the 29th. It appeared that the winter had been as severe, and the snow as deep, in the New England States, as in the Highlands of New York.

March 8—Our General addressed the Hon. Council of Massachusetts on the importance of the then moment for recruiting their battalions. By the master of a flag from Bermuda, information was received, that the fleet, in passing from New York to the southward, the preceding December, suffered considerably; and that an ordnance ship was lost.

March 9—A privateer ship of 18 guns, prize to the *Tartar* privateer, was sent into Boston.

March 13—The Committee of the General Court of Massachusetts were issuing notes for the depreciation of the pay of the troops of their line: these were sold at a very great discount.

March 20—A rich Jamaica ship, prize to the Continental frigate *Deane*, arrived safe in Boston harbor. The same day, there was a report that Sir Henry Clinton had arrived at South Carolina, with the British troops which sailed from New York in December. The Legislature of Massachusetts passed a resolution, granting a premium of £30 per man for each recruit that should be enlisted and pass muster for their line.

March 27—A Marblehead privateer, the *Aurora*, sent in a prize ship, with 1600 barrels of flour—1400 do. of beef and pork; and dry goods to the amount of £700 sterling.

April 1—News was received of a most obstinate engagement in Europe, between the French frigate, *Surveillant*, Capt. Conedic, of 36 guns, and the British frigate, *Quebec*, Capt Farmer, of the same force. The French frigate had 32 men killed, and 92 wounded. The *Quebec* blew up, and her whole crew, 300, except 40, were lost, either in action or in the explosion. This engagement did honor to the bravery of both nations.

The depreciation of the Continental money rapidly increased; many people withheld their merchandise and produce from sale, and the times were truly embarrassing. An embarkation of some thousands of Hessian troops took place at New York for Carolina. In the course of this month, the Maryland line of the army, and three companies of artillery, marched to the southward.

April 26—News was received that the British had got their shipping over the bar, at Charleston; that the Continental frigates in the harbor were hauled up, and their guns taken out and mounted on batteries: the garrison or Charleston numerous.

April 27—The privateers *Franklin* and *Jack* sent into Salem a large letter-of- marque ship, having on board 1000 barrels of pork and beef, 750 barrels of flour, 800 firkins of butter, and dry goods to the amount of £15,000; she was from London, bound to New York. During this month the enemy made two excursions to Paramus, where they killed and took a number of Americans; Maj. Byles,[22] of the Pennsylvania line, was mortally wounded, and died the next day. The enemy burnt Mr. Garret Hopper's houses and mills; the militia turned out spiritedly, repulsed and pursued the enemy. By accounts from Europe, the American cause was viewed in a very favorable light by the Courts in that part of the world.

The Marquis de Lafayette (Library of Congress).

April 28—The French frigate *Hermione*, Capt. Latouche,[23] arrived at Boston; in whom came the Marquis de Lafayette and suite, from France. The inhabitants of Boston exhibited the greatest demonstrations of joy on the occasion. The next morning the Marquis, Capt. Latouche, and other officers, made a visit to our General: the Marquis, the day before, on his landing at Hancock's Wharf, was received by a number of Continental officers, and escorted to his lodgings; after which he paid his respects to the Honorable Legislature, who were then in session; in the evening there were rejoicings.

May 2—The Marquis de Lafayette set out from Boston for the army. During the session of the Legislature of Massachusetts, they received an order from Congress, in favor of the State, for 2,000,000 dollars, to reimburse the State in part of the expense of the Penobscot expedition, which had greatly involved the State. The enemy having taken post at Penobscot, the Legislature of Massachusetts, without applying to Congress, determined to dislodge them; and, for this purpose, ordered a body of militia to be detached, under the command of Brig. Gen. Lovell; and, in addition to their own State vessels, procured a number of privateers, belonging to individuals. The expedition was attempted; the shipping arrived safe in Penobscot Bay; the troops, or a part of them, were debarked to attack the enemy, but they did not succeed in their attempt.

The armed vessels, instead of cruising off the harbor, where they could have had sea room, remained in the bay. The enemy sent a naval force to the relief of the post, which arrived and found the American shipping in the river, who immediately ran up as far as they could, where the whole were destroyed, and the militia and seamen left to find their way home through the woods. This was an unfortunate affair to Massachusetts, whose privateers, before, were numerous, able and active, and greatly annoyed the enemy; and, had it not been for this blow, would have been of great public benefit, by depriving the enemy of many of their provision vessels, and of increasing provisions in our own country. Congress, at first, seemed to decline bearing the expense, as they had never been consulted respecting the expedition; but they finally consented to a reimbursement. Congress ordered that 800 men, in the pay of the United States, should cover and protect the Eastern Country the ensuing summer.

May 12—The gentlemen of Boston gave a ball to the French and American officers.

May 14—The *Hermione* frigate, Capt. Latouche, sailed from Boston harbor on a cruise. A number of very valuable prizes, taken by the American cruisers, were sent into different ports.

May 19—The 19th exhibited a most extraordinary phenomenon.[24] The wind, in the morning, was southerly, a moderate breeze; the sun shone a little after it was up, but was soon clouded: there was some thunder and moderate showers. A little after 10 o'clock the clouds exhibited a yellowish cast, and every object seemed to present a brassy hue; it soon after began to grow dark, which gradually increased; between eleven and twelve it became necessary to light candles, to do household business. The darkness increased until near one o'clock, p.m. the inhabitants dining by candlelight. About one, the darkness began to decrease, and went off gradually, as it came on; between three and four, p.m. the usual light was restored. The evening, although the moon was at the full, was remarkably dark, and there was a sprinkling of rain— the people were in great consternation.

This phenomenon, in the opinion of our General, although he has no pretensions to astronomy, was produced by opposite winds forcing together a vast body of smoke and vapors (the air had been smoky for some days before) which, from the state of the atmosphere, as they accumulated, ascended, forming, from top to bottom, such a body, as to cause the darkness; and yet, so open were the particles, as to admit the sun's rays so far as to cause the brassy appearance: had the atmosphere been heavy, the vapors would probably have condensed, and rain, in torrents, would have ensued. Some observations made by our General, some years since the foregoing, on the darkness in Canada, and which, on the afternoon of the preceding day he noticed at Roxbury, and remarked thereon, afford strong collateral evidence that the foregoing opinion was not wholly unfounded.

As the learned and curious wish to ascertain, as far as possible, the true cause of the phenomenon, we throw in those rough materials which our observation at the time collected, that they may be shaped by those of greater skill, for the information and satisfaction of an enlightened public. Those called the dark days in Canada, were the 9th, 15th and 10th of October, 1785; but the greatest degree of darkness was on Sunday, the 16th, when the darkness was so great as to render the use of candles necessary in the churches and families; it is said to have been as dark as a dark night. On the 9th, at Roxbury, in Massachusetts, the wind was at southeast, and then at southwest; the day fair, cool and pleasant. The 15th, the prevailing wind was easterly; the day was cloudy and foggy; about two o'clock, p.m. it was uncommonly dark, and there was an opposite wind from the southwest. There were several hard claps of thunder at a distance, and a few drops of rain. Towards evening the sun was visible, but appeared very red, and the clouds exhibited a brassy complexion, so similar to the dark day in May 1780, as to be noticed and compared; in the evening the wind was southerly.

The 16th, which was the dark day in Canada, the wind, there at opposite points, N.E. and S.W. was at Roxbury S.W. The day was fair, warm and pleasant; from which it seems to be obvious, that the body of smoke and vapor, with which the atmosphere was fraught on the 15th, which pervaded a region which comprehended Canada and a part of New England, at least, was, by the strength of the southwest wind in the night, forced northward, and being still opposed by the northeast wind, pressing on the other side, produced the accumulation of smoke and vapor which occasioned the darkness, and if the northeast wind had prevailed against the south-west, the darkness would have probably been in New England.

May 21—Capt. Latouche returned from his cruise; he ran into Penobscot Bay, and cast anchor, firing several signal guns. Two British sloops of war, which were at anchor, upon the approach of the *Hermione* came to sail, and ran up the river. Capt. Latouche lay at anchor until he took a plan of the enemy's post. Our General intended to have commenced his journey for the army on Monday, the 29th of May; but on the afternoon of the preceding day, he received a letter from Gen. Washington, dated the 15th, in which His Excellency observed, "I have the pleasure to inform you, in strict confidence, that we have authentic advices of His Most Christian Majesty's determination to send a respectable armament of sea and land forces to operate on the continent, and that the period is not remote when we may expect their arrival." The Commander in Chief added that the seizing of Halifax was an object with the French; and our General was instructed to obtain, as soon as possible, the exact state of the British in that quarter, as to their works, garrisons, and troops; all of which was shortly after ascertained.

May 29—The *Hermione* fell down, in order to proceed on a cruise to the southward. The troops at West Point at this time were very short of provisions, and without rum. Congress and the Commander in Chief called upon the several States to complete their battalions of the army with all possible dispatch. The enemy at New York were under great apprehensions of a visit from the French, and were said to have prepared a number of hulks of different sizes to sink in the channel.

June 6—News was received that a French fleet had been seen at sea, in latitude 33, standing E. N. E. About this time, Capt. Latouche sent into Dartmouth a prize brig, having 1700 firkins of butter, 150 boxes of candles, and 150 boxes of soap on board. The Legislature of Massachusetts ordered a draft to be made from the militia to complete their Continental battalions. The drafts were to rendezvous at Springfield.

June 9—Our General received the following letter from the Commander in Chief:

HEADQUARTERS, MORRISTOWN, June 2nd, 1780

DEAR SIR,

It is expected that the fleet of our ally will, in the first instance, touch at Rhode Island for the purpose of landing their sick and supernumerary stores, and to meet the intelligence necessary to direct their operations. I have already sent forward Dr. Craik,[25] to take up proper houses for hospitals, and to make some previous arrangements in that department: but I apprehend the French General and Admiral will, upon their arrival, want the advice and assistance of a person of discretion and judgment, and acquainted with the country. I must request you to repair immediately to Providence, and, upon their arrival, present yourself to them, letting them know that they may command your services.

I would wish you to endeavor, in conjunction with the Governor, to establish a market between the fleet and army and country, and be careful that our allies are not imposed upon in the prices of articles which they may find necessary. This is a point recommended in the plan drawn up by the Ministry of France, and which policy and generosity directs should be strictly attended to.

(Signed) G. WASHINGTON.

Gen. HEATH.

About this time an engagement happened between the *Hermione* and a British man-of-war, which lasted near two glasses; it was a drawn battle. Capt. Latouche, and one of his Lieutenants were wounded; and it was said 13 men were killed and 39 wounded. Several of the wounded died soon after; among them, an officer.

June 15—At 11 o'clock, a.m. our General set out from his house, in Roxbury, for Providence, where he arrived the next day, at two o'clock, p.m., was met at Patucket Bridge by Deputy-Governor Bowen,[26] and a number of other gentlemen, who attended him into town. On Friday, the 2nd of June, the Continental frigate, *Trumbull*, James Nicholson commander, had an engagement with a British frigate of 36 guns, which lasted five hours. The *Trumbull* had all her masts wounded, eight men killed, and 31 wounded. The British frigate was supposed to have suffered much.

In this month a body of the enemy, under the command of Gen. Knyphausen, landed in the Jersies, and moved towards Springfield. Some skirmishing ensued; Col. Angell's[27] regiment suffered considerably. A number of men were killed on both sides. It was now fully-confirmed that the enemy's shipping passed Fort Moultrie, on Sullivan's Island, in South Carolina, on the 9th of April, with a fresh breeze, by which means they received but little damage: they came to anchor between Fort Johnson and Charleston, and just out of reach of the latter. Gen. Sir Henry Clinton had now advanced his approaches so far as to be erecting his batteries. The garrison made a good defense, but, on the 12th of May, were obliged to surrender. Of the Americans, one Colonel, one Aide-de-camp, six Captains, three Lieutenants, 10 Sergeants, and 68 rank and file, were killed; one Major, two Captains, five Lieutenants, 18 Sergeants, and 114 rank and file were wounded. Maj. Gen. Lincoln, with Brigadiers Moultrie, McIntosh, Woodford, Scott, Duportail and Hogan, with nine Colonels, 14 Lt. Colonels, 15 Majors, 84 Captains and Capt. Lieutenants, 84 Lieutenants, 32 Second Lieutenants and Ensigns, 209 non-commissioned officers, 140 drums and fifes, and

1977 rank and file, including sick and wounded, of the Continental troops, making in the whole, 2564, were taken prisoners.

Besides the foregoing, it was said that there were about 500 naval officers and seamen, 250 Charleston militia, and 500 country militia, also taken—the enemy pretended many more. About 20 American soldiers deserted to the enemy during the siege. Besides the artillery and stores which fell into the hands of the enemy (the former being 220 pieces from three- to 26-pounders) the Continental frigates *Providence*, *Boston*, *Ranger* and *Queen of France*, with four State gallies, and one French ship of war, were lost. It was supposed that about 500 American men, women and children, were killed during the siege. The enemy's loss in killed and wounded was considerable. The enemy broke ground before the town on the first of April at the distance of 800 yards from the American works. Before the surrender of the place, it was contemplated in Council of War, to embark the garrison, except about one regiment, on the shipping, in the night, and run up the river, and land them; thereby to save the army, leaving those in the town to make the best terms they could. The opinion for some time prevailed, but it was afterwards given up.

June 7—The British fleet left Charleston, said to consist of two ships of the line, two fifties, two forty-gun ships, six or seven frigates, and between 80 and 90 transports; near 2000 negroes were put on board the fleet. Lord Cornwallis, with about 2000 men, marched from Charleston towards North Carolina. A few days after the surrender of Charleston to the British troops, the grand arsenal, wherein was deposited all the arms, etc. taken from the Americans, took fire and blew up, by which it was said a number of men were killed and wounded. The loss of Charleston roused the country, and seemed to give a check to that spirit of avarice and speculation which had but too much prevailed in all places, and a determination, by every exertion to drive the enemy from the country, appeared to be catching from breast to breast. At Rhode Island, every preparation was making for the reception of the French fleet and army. The handsome college at Providence was given up for a hospital. The American privateers had been very successful, and many valuable prizes were sent in.

June 24—Monsieur Corny,[28] a French Commissary, arrived at Providence. About this time it was suspected that the enemy at New York had some intentions of an attempt on our posts in the Highlands; and some of their shipping were up the Hudson.

June 30—Capt. Latouche, in the *Hermione*, sailed from Newport harbor. The same day, the British frigate *Flora*, which was sunk in Newport harbor nearly two years before, was weighed; she had a quantity of provisions on board.

July 1—News was received that the enemy were again in motion in the Jersies.

July 2—News was received of the sailing of the French fleet, which left France on the 2nd of May. It was said in France, that if the fleet fell to the northward, it would visit Halifax; if to the southward, it would proceed to Rhode Island. A great uneasiness, at this time, prevailed in Ireland.

July 4—The anniversary of American Independence was celebrated at Providence, by a discharge of 13 cannon from the park. Governor Greene, Monsieur de Corny, and a number of other gentlemen, dined with our General. By the last accounts the main army was at Ramapo, in the Jersies. In the skirmish which happened some time before, near Springfield, the Americans had about 40 killed and wounded.

July 11—At one o'clock, a.m. our General received advice by express, that the

The landing of the French Army at Newport, Rhode Island, July 11, 1780 (Library of Congress).

fleet of our illustrious ally was seen off Newport, the evening before. Before sunrise an express was sent forward to Gen. Washington with the agreeable tidings, and our General immediately prepared to proceed to Newport, but the day being calm, the packet did not reach the town until 12 o'clock at night. Gen. Rochambeau had gone on shore in the evening. Early the next morning our General went on shore, and waited on the Count; from which moment the warmest friendship commenced between our General, the Count, and all the French officers. After breakfast, our General went on board the *Duc de Bourgogne* man-of-war, to pay his respects to the Chevalier de Ternay, who commanded the squadron, where the same friendship was commenced.

The fleet consisted of seven sail of the line, viz. the *Duc de Bourgogne*, of 80 guns; *le Neptune, le Conquerant* of 74; *le Jason, le Seville, le Ardent,* and *le Provence* of 64; and the *Fantasque* of 64; armed *en flûte*[29] with 40 guns as a hospital ship; two frigates and two bombs, with a number of transports, having on board about 5000 troops, besides the marines, the soldiers and sailors, something sickly. The joy in the town of Newport was great. At 11 o'clock, a.m. the Admiral saluted the town with 13 cannon, which was returned by the discharge of the same number. In the evening the town was beautifully illuminated, and fire works exhibited, to the great pleasure and satisfaction of our allies. The fleet, on its passage to America, fell in with five British ships of the line, who, after firing a few broadsides, bore away.

July 12—Our General dined with the Count de Rochambeau.

July 13—The Chevalier de Ternay, and the principal officers of the squadron, came on shore.

July 14—Count de Rochambeau, and the General Officers of the French army, dined with our General.

July 15—A number of the field officers of the French regiments dined with our General in the most happy fraternity.

July 18—Four sail of ships of war, two of them supposed to be of 40 or 50 guns, appeared in the offing; they were supposed to be British. The same day the Chevalier de Ternay, and the principal officers of the fleet, dined with our General. In the afternoon the remains of the officer who was some time before wounded on board the *Hermione* and died of those wounds, was interred with military honors. The missing transport of the fleet, with troops on board, arrived safe in Boston harbor, and the troops marched to Rhode Island.

July 19—Our General dined with the Count.

July 20—The frigates of the squadron came to sail in the morning; but the wind being ahead, they were obliged to come to anchor. Intelligence was received that Admiral Graves, with five or six sail of the line, arrived at Sandy Hook on the 13th.

July 21—In the afternoon, 15 or 16 sail of British ships of war appeared in the offing; more than one half of them were supposed to be ships of the line. At sunset, they appeared to be coming to under Block Island. The frigates, which attempted to get out in the morning, returned at evening. Apprehending that the British fleet might be cruising off, with a view to intercept the second division of the French fleet, which was expected soon to arrive, our General sent off expresses to headquarters, Boston and Hartford, advising of the British fleet being off Newport—that dispatch boats might be sent out to apprise the French, and point them to another port. Several works and batteries next to the harbor were mantled with cannon.

July 22—The British fleet were cruising off all the day, and rather nearer than they were the preceding day. Eighteen or nineteen sail were counted, eight or nine of which appeared to be of the line. The French squadron kept their former station in the harbor, and in the most perfect readiness for action. The army was in the same preparedness, and batteries so constructed as to afford a heavy cross-fire with the shipping, in the entrance of the harbor. All vessels and boats were forbid passing out of the harbor in the night.

July 23—The British were cruising off—early in the morning one of their frigates was near in. Col. Greene's regiment of Continental troops took post at Butt's Hill, Bristol and Rowland's Ferries. Fifty French soldiers from the army were sent on board each of the ships of the line. By accounts from West Point, it appeared that many recruits had joined and were joining the American army.

July 24—The British fleet continued off Newport. In the afternoon, 12 sail were at anchor to the east of Block Island and four frigates cruising between that Island and Point Judith. In the evening, the Marquis de Lafayette came to town, from headquarters.

July 25—Intelligence was received, that Sir Henry Clinton intended an attempt upon the French army, with 10,000 men; upon which 1500 of the militia of Rhode Island, and Brigadier Godfrey's[30] brigade of militia, of the county of Bristol, in Massachusetts, were called in to Tiverton; and the three months' men, who were destined to the main army, such of them as belonged to the counties of Suffolk, Essex, Plymouth, Worcester, Barnstable and Bristol, were ordered to march to Rhode Island.

July 26—A confirmation of the intention of Sir Henry Clinton against Newport was received from the neighborhood of New York. In consequence of which the whole militia of the State of Rhode Island was called in. Col. Tyler's, Col. Perry's, and Maj. Bullard's[31] militia regiments, in addition to Brigadier Godfrey's, from Massachusetts. Signals were fixed as far as Watch Hill, and everything put in train for the giving instant notice, both by day and night, in case the enemy should approach towards the place.

July 27—The wind being fresh at southwest, and the air hazy, the privateer ship *Washington*, Capt. Munroe, ran by the British fleet, and passed up the harbor. The stock on Conanicut Island was ordered to be taken off. Howland's Ferry was to be well secured on both sides.

July 30—Intelligence was received, that the enemy's shipping, which were in the Sound, and supposed to have taken in troops at Whitestone, had come to sail, and stood to the westward; on which, the militia who were coming in, except the three months' men, were permitted to return home. The militia had discovered great zeal and alertness on the occasion. About noon, the British ships that had been at anchor off Block Island, came to sail and stood out to sea. The same day a brig, with dispatches from France, passed up the harbor; she ran on one of the wrecks, and sunk immediately.

July 31—Our General received letters from Gen. Washington, Gen. Howe, Gen. Parsons, and Gov. Trumbull, intimating that the enemy intended an attack on Newport; that about 150 sail of vessels were in the Sound; that about 8000 troops were to be employed on the expedition; and that Gen. Sir Henry Clinton was to command in person; that 26 heavy cannon, some mortars, etc. were put on board. In consequence of this intelligence, the militia were again called in. The next day (August 1) our General received the following letter from Gen. Washington.

ROBINSON'S HOUSE, July 31st, 1780

DEAR SIR,

I arrived here last night; having met your favors of the 25th and 26th at Paramus, where the army then lay. Immediately upon hearing that the transports, with the troops, which had been some days on board, had sailed eastward, I put the army in motion again; they will cross the ferry today, and will be joined by the troops from hence. I propose moving as rapidly as possible down to wards Kingsbridge, which will either oblige the enemy to abandon their project against Rhode Island, or may afford us an opportunity of striking them to advantage in this quarter, if Sir Henry Clinton has carried with him the number of men reported (eight thousand) and with less than which, I think, he would scarcely risk an attempt upon Count Rochambeau, reinforced by the militia.

I entirely approve of the measures you have taken for calling in aid, and have the strongest hopes that if Sir Henry should venture upon an attack, that he will meet a reception very different from what he expects. You know the critical situation in which this army will be in a position below, and how much depends upon constant intelligence of the motions of the enemy. I shall direct relays of expresses the whole way, between this army and you, to convey intelligence in the most expeditious manner. The nearest express to you will be upon Tower Hill; and Gen. Greene advises that you should keep two whale-boats, to communicate with him, by South Ferry, so long as that passage shall be safe; and if that should be interrupted, by Bissell's Harbor.

(Signed) GEO. WASHINGTON.

P.S.—I wish the Count de Rochambeau had taken a position on the main.

G. W.

The militia came in with great spirit; they were formed into brigades, and every disposition made for instant and vigorous defense, at every point where it was supposed an attempt might be made. The batteries were strengthened, a very strong one erected on Rhode Island, and redoubts on Coaster's Island: the strong works on Butt's Hill pushed: avenues across the fields, by the shortest routes, were opened, from the encampment of the French army to those points where their instant presence was judged necessary; and such marks fixed, at small distances from each other as to prevent any mistake in the route, either by day or night; indeed, no one precaution was omitted, or probable advantage of ground or situation neglected. Had Sir Henry made the attempt which he menaced, he would undoubtedly have met a warm reception; but for some reason or other he gave up his design, and the militia were again sent home. Perhaps on no occasion did the militia discover more ardor, in pressing to the field, or more regularity when there, than at that time, which was everywhere testified by the inhabitants.

Our General had expressed a wish to the Commander in Chief to join the main army, that he might enjoy that command, to which he was at that time entitled, viz. the right wing; to which Gen. Washington, in a letter dated August 3rd replied: "As to your coming on to the army immediately, I shall leave it entirely to yourself to act in the affair as you please. Your command is, and will always be ready for you; however, if you find your presence where you are necessary, and that it will contribute to the accommodation of our allies, and to the cultivation of harmony (matters about which I am very anxious) it may possibly be more eligible for you to remain longer, as we shall not probably have any instant active operations. But, as I have already said, do in the matter as you like, and as circumstances may decide."

And in a subsequent letter some days after, he observed, "As to your wishes to join the army, as I observed before, your aid may be very material to the Count; and as we have no prospect of immediate active operations, I would rather wish you to remain with him longer. I thought it essential in the first instance that there should be an officer of rank sent to him; and a variety of reasons concurred to induce me to believe that you would answer the important objects I had in view, as well at least as any I could choose. I have not been disappointed in the least in my expectation, and the Count himself judges your continuing very essential, and expressed himself in the following manner upon the subject several days ago: *I shall keep with me if you think proper, Gen. Heath, whose ardor, spirit and activity are absolutely necessary to me.* For these several considerations, I wish you to reconcile yourself to remaining with him awhile, which will be more easy when you consider that you will be fully advertised whenever we are in a situation to attempt any thing offensive on a great scale, and will have your command."

The British ship-of-war, *Galatea*, appeared off Dartmouth. The British fleet went to Gardiner's Bay, excepting the frigates, which cruised off. The troops continued fortifying the island.

August 15—About this time the British fleet sailed from Gardiner's Bay to the eastward. About this time, Maj. Gen. Greene resigned the Quartermaster Generalship, and Col. Pickering was appointed to that office.

August 19—In the afternoon the British again appeared off the harbor of Newport. A few days before, the Continental frigate *Alliance* arrived at Boston, in five weeks and four days from France, and brought news that there had been a great mob[32] in England, headed by Lord George Gordon,[33] and that the prisons, etc. had been pulled down.

August 23—The privateer ship *Washington*, Capt. Talbot,[34] of 20 guns, came down the river, saluted the Commodore, and came to anchor.

August 24—The French army, joined by the Americans, fired salutes on account of its being St. Louis' day. The fleet fired on the next day. The enemy were preparing for an embarkation of troops at New York; their destination unknown. The evening of the 20th, three or four of the enemy's cruisers were off the harbor.

August 26—The British fleet, to the number of more than 20 sail, were in the Vineyard Sound.

August 29—A number of Indians from the northwestern tribes came to Newport to pay their respects to the General of the army of their father the King of France. They had a hearty welcome, a treat, and presents, and were much pleased. They were also invited by our General to a sumptuous treat. After dinner they performed their war dance before the officers of the armies, to the great satisfaction of those of the French, who had not seen the like before. The next day the French troops were under arms, maneuvered, and fired, in presence of the Indians, who were much pleased.

August 31—Information was received that Admiral Arbuthnot was near the Vineyard with nine sail of the line, eight other ships of war of different force, and two tenders; that he had made a demand of 11,000 Ib. of beef and mutton, to be delivered every other day, at five pence per Ib. The inhabitants remonstrating against furnishing so large a quantity, the Admiral assured them that in case they voluntarily delivered as much as their ability would allow, he would dispense with what might be wanting. The enemy continued their preparations for some grand enterprise, which could not be developed.

September 10—The British fleet were returned again to Gardiner's Bay, and their old station between Long Island and Block Island.

September 11—Intelligence was received that on the 16th ult. Maj. Gen. Gates was totally defeated by the British, at or near Camden, in South Carolina. The Maryland line suffered greatly, and Maj. Gen. Baron de Kalb was wounded, of which wounds he died.

September 14—Intelligence was received that Brig. Gen. Poor, of New Hampshire, died at camp on the 8th, of a putrid fever; and that Brig. Gen. Nixon had resigned his commission. Gen. Sir Henry Clinton was holding a body of troops, said to be about 6000, in readiness to embark at New York, said to be destined to the southward. The 17th, in the morning, the Continental regiment commanded by Colonel Greene, crossed over from the island to Greenwich, from whence they were to march to the main army.

September 21—Intelligence was received that Admiral Rodney arrived at Sandy Hook on the 13th, with ten sail of the line, and two frigates—that on the 15th, Commodore Drake, with four sail of the line, was detached from the Hook to join Admiral Arbuthnot near Gardiner's Island, and that these four ships joined on the 18th. This junction was intended to intercept 12 sail of the French men-of-war, which were to be expected to be coming from the West Indies to Rhode Island—that the 76th and 80th British regiments, one Hessian regiment, the Queen's Rangers, Fanning's corps, a part of the horse, and all the British grenadiers and light infantry, were ordered to embark immediately at New York—it was conjectured for Virginia. The disposition of the British troops at that time was said to be as follows: the 22nd, 76th British, 3 Hessian regiments, Robinson's corps, and some artillery in the city—Highland emigrants, at Brooklyn—a few invalids at Newtown—one regiment of Hessians at Jamaica—the 37th, 38th, and 43rd British, one Hessian regiment, one Jäger, one grenadier, and one light infantry from Jamaica to Flushing—about three regiments at Whitestone—Queen's Rangers, Oyster Bay—Fanning's regiment, the 3rd regiment of Delancey's, and the Jersey volunteers, Lloyd's Neck—Col. Abercrombie, with about 600 infantry, at Huntington—the 17th dragoons at Smithtown—about 1500 men from Haarlem to Kingsbridge. At this time, the Count de Rochambeau and Admiral de Ternay had an interview with Gen. Washington at Hartford.

September 22—Col. Greene's regiment was ordered to return from Greenwich to the island. The French army continued very busy in fortifying Rhode Island: some of their works were exceedingly strong, and mounted with heavy metal.

September 24—In the evening, Gen. Rochambeau and the Admiral returned to Rhode Island.

September 30—A French frigate arrived at Newport from the West Indies, but brought no news of consequence. The Count de Guichen,[35] instead of coming this way with the fleet from the West Indies, was going or gone for Europe.

While Washington was in interview with General Rochambeau at Hartford, Maj. Gen. Arnold, who had the immediate command of West Point, was playing a most traitorous game with the British, for the delivery of that important post into their hands which was communicated to our General by the Commander in Chief, in the following letter:

ROBINSON'S HOUSE, Sept. 26th, 1780

DEAR SIR,

   In the present situation of things, I think it necessary that you should join the army; and request that you will do it. You will come to headquarters yourself. The route through Litchfield will be the most eligible for you, on account of security; and you may direct your baggage to halt at Fish-Kill, for your further orders. I write to the Count de Rochambeau by this conveyance; and I trust that your coming away now, will not be attended with any material inconvenience to him.

   I cannot conclude without informing you of an event which has happened here, which will strike you with astonishment and indignation: Maj. Gen. Arnold has gone to the enemy. He had had an interview with Major André, Adjutant-General of the British army, and had put into his possession a state of the army of the garrison of this post, of the number of men considered as necessary for the defense of it; a return of the ordnance, and the disposition of the artillery corps, in case of an alarm. By a most providential interposition, Major André was taken in returning to New York, with all these papers in Gen. Arnold's handwriting; who, hearing of the matter, kept it to himself, left his quarters immediately, under pretext of going over to West Point, on Monday forenoon, about an hour before my arrival; then pushed down the river in the barge, which was not discovered till I had returned from West Point in the afternoon, and when I received the first information of Mr. André's capture. Measures were instantly taken to apprehend him; but, before the officers sent for the purpose could reach Verplank's Point he had passed it with a flag, and got on board the *Vulture* ship of war, which lay a few miles below. He knew of my approach, and that I was visiting, with the Marquis, the north and middle redoubts; and from this circumstance was so straightened in point of time, that I believe he carried with him but very few, if any, material papers; though he has very precise knowledge of the affairs of the post. The gentlemen of Gen. Arnold's family, I have the greatest reason to believe, were not privy in the least degree to the measure he was carrying on, or to his escape.

(Signed) G. WASHINGTON.

   Gen. Arnold's panic was so great when he found that the plot was discovered, that he called out for a horse, any horse that first came to hand, if it were a wagon-horse; upon the horse's being brought, the General mounted, and, instead of passing to the landing by the usual path, he rode down a steep bank, where it seemed impossible for a horse with a rider to get down, without being unhorsed.

   When Arnold had passed Verplank's Point, and had got under the guns of the *Vulture*, he told Corporal Larvey, who was coxswain of the barge, that he was going on board the ship, and that he should not return; that if he (Larvey) would stay with him, he should have a commission in the British service. To this, Larvey, who was a smart fellow, replied, that he would be d—d if he fought on both sides; the General replied, that he would send him on shore. Arnold then told the barge crew, that if any or all of them would stay with him, they should be treated well; but if they declined staying, they should be sent on shore. One or two stayed, the rest, with the coxswain, were sent on shore in the ship's boat; the barge was kept. Larvey, for his fidelity, was made a Sergeant. He thought he had merited more; that he ought to have had as much as Arnold promised him. He continued uneasy, until at his repeated request he was allowed to leave the army.

   Maj. André, on his return towards New York, fell in with three young men below the lines, John Paulding, David Williams, and Isaac Van Wert; they did not at first know that André was a British officer, and he was at a loss whether they were British, refugees, or staunch Americans. There was consequently a little finesse exhibited on both sides; but at length it was fully discovered who André was. He then attempted to bribe the young men, by offering them a large sum of money; but their fidelity was too great to be purchased. They brought him up, and delivered him to the Americans, where he was tried, sentenced, and hanged as a spy. The British General on the river endeavored to save his life, first by threats, and then by persuasions; but all was in vain. Maj. André's behavior, until the time of his execution, was becoming an officer and a gentleman; and such, in his last moments, as drew tears from many eyes. But it must be remembered that he who consents to become a spy, when he sets out, has by allusion a halter put round his neck, and that by the usage of armies, if he be taken, the other end of the halter is speedily made fast to a gallows.

Maj. Gen. Benedict Arnold (Library of Congress).

Congress, pleased with the conduct of John Paulding, David Williams, and Isaac Van Wart, passed a resolution on the 4th of October, directing that 200 dollars, in specie, should be annually paid them during life; and that a silver medal, descriptive of their fidelity, with the thanks of Congress, should be presented to each of them. The situation of the British army and other circumstances at the moment Andre was detected, were such as render it highly probable that if he had not been taken, the most serious consequences to the American cause would very soon have taken place.

October 1—The next day after our General received the letter from Gen. Washington, he took a most affectionate leave of the French officers, and left Newport, to prepare to go on to the army. His wagon-horses were out in the country at a distance; these were to be brought in, shod, etc. and other preparations to be made, which prevented his leaving Providence until the afternoon of the 9th, when he was attended out of town by a number of officers and other gentlemen. Before he left Providence, he bid Count Rochambeau another farewell, by letter, to which an answer was forwarded on after him, as follows:

NEWPORT, Oct. 12th, 1780

MY DEAR GENERAL,

I have received the letter that you have honored me with from Providence. I am extremely sensible of the marks of friendship that you give me, and likewise very grateful for all that your good heart has dictated to you upon the occasion of our present separation. I regret vastly your absence, my dear General, as well as all the army; and I shall never forget the zeal, the activity, and the intelligence with which you helped us in all our operations; and the French army will always be most grateful for it. I have the honor to be, with the most inviolable attachment, my dear General, your most obedient and humble servant,

(Signed) LE COUNT DE ROCHAMBEAU.

October 16—Our General reached West Point, where he met the following letter from Gen. Washington:

HEADQUARTERS, NEAR PASSAIC FALLS, Oct. 14th, 1780

DEAR SIR,

   In my letter of the 26th ult. by which I requested you to join the army, I desired that you would come yourself to headquarters: I am now to request that you will proceed to West Point, and take upon you the command of that post and its dependencies. Maj. Gen. Greene, who is at present there, will either communicate to you himself, or leave with Gen. McDougall to be transferred, the instructions he received respecting the post; to which you will be pleased to attend. If this should not find you at West Point, it is my wish that you should arrive there as soon as circumstances will possibly admit; and I hope there will be nothing to delay it.

(Signed) G. WASHINGTON.

Our General had scarcely entered on the command, before he received intelligence that the enemy were making an incursion upon the northern frontier of New York; upon which he immediately, without consulting the Commander in Chief, ordered Col. Gansevoort's regiment to their relief, and communicated what he had done to headquarters; to which he received the following answer:

Lt. Gen. Jean-Baptiste Donatien de Vimeur, Comte de Rochambeau.

HEADQUARTERS, PREAKNESS, Oct. 16th, 1780

DEAR SIR,

   I am favored with yours of yesterday, accompanied by a letter from His Excellency Governor Clinton, who gives me an account of the incursion upon the frontiers. I am happy that you detached Gansevoort's regiment immediately; you will be pleased to order either Weisenfeld's or Willet's, as you may judge proper, to follow, and take orders from the Governor or the commanding officer. This is all the force I think we ought to detach from the posts, until the views of the enemy are more fully ascertained. They put off the long-expected embarkation strangely. They had not sailed the 13th, and it was then said the expedition was delayed for some purpose. The number under orders, by estimate, are about 2000, or something upwards. If the militia should not have been discharged, when this reaches you, you will be pleased to detain about 500, to make up for the detachment you have sent up the river. I have received yours of the 13th, as I have done that enclosing the estimates, for which I am much obliged. You will be pleased to carry into execution what you proposed, respecting the posts at Stony and Verplank's Point.

(Signed) G. WASHINGTON.

This was followed by another, dated the 18th, in which the Commander in Chief observed, "I am glad to find, by your letter of the 17th, that you were arrived at West Point, and had taken the command of that important post." This was occasioned by our General's having been on the east side of the river a day or two, until the quarters on the point were quitted by Maj. Gen. Greene, who was ordered to the southward.

October 17—Intelligence was received, that the enemy had advanced to Fort George and Fort Ann, both of which had fallen into their hands; that after destroying the works, and burning about thirty houses, and as many barns, they had gone back; but it was apprehended that they would advance again.

October 19—Maj. Gen. Greene left West Point. The same day intelligence was received, that on the 16th the long talked-of embarkation of troops sailed from New York, supposed to be destined to the southward. The American troops at this time drove up the fat cattle which were near the lines, in consequence of a warrant from Gov. Clinton.

October 21—Intelligence was received that the enemy were meditating an excursion as far up as Crompond and its vicinity, to sweep off all the cattle. Our General immediately ordered Col. Hazen, with a detachment of 500 men, to move to Pine's Bridge, and Lt. Col. Jameson,[36] with 2nd light dragoons, to move from Bedford towards Col. Hazen. The detachment arrived at Pine's Bridge about 10 o'clock the same evening, and Col. Jameson with the dragoons at about two o'clock the next morning. The evening of the 23rd, Col. Hazen returned with the detachment; the enemy did not come out.

About this time the enemy received a small reinforcement at New York, from England, said to be 1500 or 2000. Two or three very valuable prizes, laden with rum, sugar, etc. were sent to Philadelphia, and news was received that upwards of 50 sail of British East and West Indiamen, outward bound, were taken by the combined fleets of France and Spain, near Cape Finisterre.

October 24—Intelligence was received that the enemy had laid waste a great part of the fertile country above Saratoga, and to the westward of Schenectady. The same night, 20 prisoners made their escape from the provost at Fish-Kill, by digging upwards of 20 feet under ground; parties were sent out after them in different directions, and some of them were retaken.

October 26—News was received that the militia, under Gen. Van Rensselaer, obtained a considerable advantage over the enemy at the northward, on the 19th inst, at the Fox Mills. The action lasted for some hours; the enemy left their baggage, prisoners, etc. Col. Brown[37] was killed in skirmishing with the enemy on the morning of the same day.

October 28—Official intelligence was received of a signal advantage gained by the Americans in North Carolina over a corps of fourteen hundred men, British troops, and new levies, commanded by Col. Ferguson. The militia of the neighboring country under Colonels Williams and Shelby and others having assembled to the number of 3000, detached 1600 men on horseback, to fall in with Ferguson's party on its march to Charlotte—they came up with them at a place called King's Mountain, advantageously posted and gave them a total defeat, in which Col. Ferguson, with 150 of his men were killed, 800 made prisoners, and 1500 stands of arms taken, with but inconsiderable loss, except, and greatly to be regretted, the brave Col. Williams, who was supposed to be mortally wounded. A second account stated the enemy's whole loss in killed, wounded and prisoners, at 1105; and that of the Americans in killed and wounded, 64.

October 29—Brig. Gen. James Clinton was ordered to Albany to take the command in that quarter.

October 30—Capt. Johnson, with a detachment consisting of 100 men, marched to do duty on the lines for the protection of the inhabitants against the enemy, and the cowboys (so called) a set of plundering thieves.

October 31—A ridiculous proclamation of the traitor Arnold made its appearance; he styled himself a Brigadier-General, and invited the officers and soldiers of the American army to join him, promising ample encouragement, etc. but it had no effect.

November 1—A severe storm of snow and rain. The brave soldiers who were but illy clad, and destitute of blankets, were in a shivering condition. The devastation committed by the enemy at the northward, was found to be very great; at least 200 dwellings and 150,000 bushels of wheat, with a proportion of other grain and forage, were supposed to have been destroyed; had not the pursuit after the enemy been very rapid, the devastations would have been much greater. The American army were at this time experiencing a great want of flour, which they bore with their usual patience.

November 4—Intelligence was received, that Maj. Carleton, after being reinforced with 500 men, was returning towards Skenesborough; it was supposed that his force had increased to about 1600, and further depredations on the frontiers were expected. The militia of the upper counties were again ordered out by Gov. Clinton. The same day, the new arrangement of the army was published. The encouragement to both officers and soldiers was generous.

November 5—The troops were again without bread. Intelligence was received that the enemy had landed a body of troops at Portsmouth, in Virginia, and that another embarkation was talked of at New York.

November 6th -News was received from Boston, that his Excellency John Hancock had been chosen Governor of the State of Massachusetts the first Governor under the new constitution. The same day intelligence was received from the northward, that the enemy had crossed Lake George the Thursday before, and advanced to Fort Edward, the small garrison of which abandoned the fort on the approach of the enemy, whose numbers were said to be about 800. The militia were out, and the 1st and 5th New York regiments were ordered to embark and sail for Albany immediately. They sailed early on the morning of the 9th. On the same day intelligence was received that the enemy had lately made an excursion to the upper parts of Connecticut river, and destroyed a number of houses at Royalton. The militia turned out with spirit, repulsed and pursued them; the enemy made off with precipitation, leaving their plunder, etc. behind them. Upwards of 2000 militia were assembled in that quarter.

The 2nd regiment of dragoons moved from Bedford to North Castle. The enemy published several letters in the New York papers, which were taken from the Fish-Kill post-rider not long before at Stratford; in particular, one from the general officers belonging to the New England States to their several Legislatures. A partial but not general exchange of prisoners took place about this time. Maj. Gen. Lincoln was exchanged for Maj. Gen. Phillips; General Thompson, and a number of American officers, who had long been prisoners, were also exchanged.

November 14—The great chain,[38] which was laid across the Hudson at West Point, was taken up for the winter; it was done under the direction of Colonel Gouvion,[39] Capt. Buchanan,[40] and Capt. Nevers, with a strong detachment of the garrison, and with skill and dexterity. This chain was as long as the width of the river between West Point and Constitution Island, where it was fixed to great blocks on each side, and under the fire of batteries on both sides of the river. The links of this chain were probably 12 inches wide, and 18 inches long; the iron about two inches square. This heavy chain was buoyed up by very large logs of perhaps 16 or more feet long, a little pointed at the ends, to lessen their opposition to the force of the water on flood and ebb. The logs were placed at short distances from each other, the chain carried over them, and made fast to each by staples, to prevent their shifting; and there were a number of anchors dropped at distances, with cables made fast to the chain, to give it a greater stability. The short bend of the river at this place was much in favor of the chain's proving effectual; for a vessel, coming up the river with the fairest wind and strongest way, must lose them on changing her course to turn the point; and before she could get under any considerable way again, even if the wind was fair, she would be on the chain, and at the same time under a heavy shower of shot and shells.

November 15—The 1st and 5th New York regiments returned from Albany, the enemy having returned to Canada, except about 400 men, chiefly British, who were encamped about 10 miles below Crown Point. Provisions were extremely scarce at Albany.

November 16—In the evening, a number of the boats were stove by the violence of the wind and storm. On the morning of the 18th, five large flat-bottomed boats, under the charge of a Subaltern and 25 picked watermen, were sent down the river to the slote above Dobbs' Ferry, where they were to be placed on carriages, and transported to a certain place, for an enterprise which was meditating against the enemy.

November 19—Five companies, of 50 men each, marched from West Point, for the purpose of impressing teams in the upper part of Westchester, and lower parts of Dutchess Counties, preparatory to the grand forage. The same day, the invalids of the Massachusetts and Connecticut lines, and a detachment of able-bodied men, the whole about 1000, arrived at West Point from the main army.

November 20—Three light field-pieces, with four ammunition tumbrels with ammunition for the artillery, and musket-cartridges, and also a quantity of hard bread, rum, etc. was sent down to Peek's Kill, for the use of the grand foragers.

November 21—The troops destined for the grand forage paraded between Nelson's Point and the church. Just before they marched, Chevalier Chastellux,[41] Major General in the French army, at Newport, and some other French officers arrived; the detachment defiled before them, and proceeded for the lines. The French officers were much pleased with the appearance of the troops.

Gen. Chastellux then accompanied our General over to the Point, and on landing was saluted by the discharge of 13 cannon; after dinner, he took a view of Forts Clinton,

Putnam, Wyllys, etc. At evening, Count Noailles,[42] Count Damas,[43] and Maj. du Plessis,[44] arrived at the Point. The next morning, about 9 o'clock, Gen. Chastellux and the other French officers, amidst a severe cold storm of rain, embarked on board the barge, and went down the river to King's Ferry, on their way to headquarters; on leaving West Point, they were again saluted by 13 cannon.

The evening of the 22nd, Brig. Gen. Stark arrived at Wright's Mills, and the wagons were collected at North Castle. This grand forage was to mask an enterprise which was to have been attempted by Gen. Washington, from the main army; although the foraging was in itself an important object. The enterprise, for some reasons, was not attempted, but the grand forage was very successful. Some of the light troops went as low down as East-Chester; and on the 27th, Gen. Stark returned with a large quantity of corn, some hay, cattle, etc.

The next day, the main army separated to move into winter quarters, and the light infantry corps was broken up for the winter, and the men ordered to join their respective regiments. The corps of light infantry was perhaps as fine a body of men as was ever formed. Maj. Gen. the Marquis de Lafayette had, with infinite pains and great expense, endeavored to render them respectable in their appearance as well as discipline, in which he was nobly seconded by the officers: it was a pity that the operations of the campaign did not afford an opportunity for the Marquis to signalize himself with this corps.

November 30—The New Jersey brigade left West Point, proceeding down on the west side of the Hudson, on their way to Pompton, where they took winter-quarters. In the afternoon, the four Massachusetts brigades arrived at West Point, and the two Connecticut brigades on the east side of the river, where the whole took winter-quarters. A few days before, viz. on the 23rd, Maj. Tallmadge, with a detachment from the 2nd regiment of dragoons, conducted with great address an enterprise against the enemy's fort, St. George, on Long Island. Fort St. George was stockaded, and encompassed a large spot of ground, a square redoubt, with a ditch and abatis. The enterprise succeeded completely. One half-pay Lieutenant-Colonel, one half-pay Captain, one Subaltern, and 50 rank and file, were made prisoners. The fort was destroyed and burnt. Two armed vessels burnt, and a large magazine of hay, said to be about 300 tons, was destroyed.

December 1—One of the largest scows at King's Ferry, in crossing, with several baggage wagons on board, sunk. The same day, our General began to discharge the six months' men, beginning with those who were the worst clothed and unfit for duty.

December 4—The three New York regiments sailed for Albany, where they were to take winter-quarters.

December 5—Marquis de Laval,[45] Count de Custine,[46] and Col. Fleury,[47] of the French army at Newport, arrived at West Point on a visit.

December 6—At evening his Excellency Gen. Washington, arrived at New Windsor, where he took winter-quarters. The same evening, accounts were received that there had been a terrible hurricane in the West Indies. On the evening of the 9th, Gen. Varnum and Col. Pickering arrived at West Point; at this time the troops were without bread, and very uneasy. The next day, 300 barrels of flour arrived. A little before noon, Gen. Washington visited West Point.

December 12—Intelligence was received from New York that another embarkation was to take place, and that Gen. Phillips and Gen. Arnold were to command.

Major Tallmadge received the thanks of Congress for his good conduct in taking Fort St. George.

December 17—An express from Major Maxwell[48] on the lines, brought up intelligence that the enemy at Morrisania, under Col. Delancey, were preparing for an enterprise. The Major was cautioned to be on his guard.

December 18—News was received that Monsieur de Sartines,[49] the primate of France had been removed—Mr. de Castries[50] appointed.

December 19—News was received that the Hon. Henry Laurens who was sent on a mission to Holland, had been taken by the British, carried into England, and closely confined. The British government talked of sending to America a large reinforcement for the next campaign.

December 20—Further intelligence having been received that Col. Delancey intended to visit our troops on the lines, in order to give him a proper reception, 150 men were ordered from the New Hampshire line to march to Crom Pond.

December 21—Intelligence was received that on the preceding Friday, the transports which had taken the troops on board at New York, fell down to the watering place. They were to be convoyed by one 50-gun ship and two frigates. On the night of the 9th, Major Huggeford,[51] of Delancey's corps, surprised and took prisoners Lt. Col. Wells, of a Connecticut State regiment, who was stationed near Horseneck, with one Captain, two Lieutenants, two Ensigns, and upwards of twenty privates.

December 23—Intelligence was received that Monsieur the Chevalier de Ternay, Admiral of the French squadron at Newport, had died there. The troops on the lines were reinforced with 50 men, and Lt. Col. Hull[52] was appointed to the command on the lines.

December 27—The Free and Accepted Masons of Washington Lodge celebrated the feast of St. John, at Starkean Hall, West Point.

December 30—Gen. Washington visited the Point, and, with a number of other officers, dined with our General. On the 25th inst. Major Humphreys, Aide-de-camp to the Commander in Chief, went towards New York on an enterprise; he was attended by Capt. Welles,[53] of the Connecticut line, Lt. Hart,[54] Ensign McCalpin, Mr. Buchanan, Mr. McGuyer, and twenty-four non-commissioned officers and privates, in one barge and two whale-boats. The wind was very fresh at northwest in the night, and the boats were forced past the city, and one of them almost down to Sandy Hook—one of the boats put in at Staten Island: at length the three went round to Brunswick, from whence the Major and all the others returned to the army on the 1st of January.

December 31—On the evening of the 29th, a party of the enemy from Delancey's corps, consisting of about 100 infantry and 50 horse, came up to North Castle, where, after a short halt, they proceeded towards Bedford New Purchase. Capt. Pritchard, who was ported at Bedford with a company of Continental troops, and some militia, immediately advanced towards them, attacked their van, who retreated, as did their main body. Capt. Pritchard[55] pursued them as far as Young's. It was said that one of the enemy was killed and several wounded, who were carried off in a wagon. Four oxen and between 30 and 40 sheep were retaken—eight or ten head of cattle were driven off; the Captain sustained no injury. This day the enemy were out again; Col. Hull immediately marched down with his whole force to meet them; by his vigilance they were prevented from doing any mischief, and on his advance, retired towards the saw-pits.

Chapter 7

1781

January 1—The Pennsylvania line mutinied almost to a man, seized the artillery, broke open the magazines of ammunition and provisions, took out what they judged necessary, and took up their line of march. The officers exerted themselves, both by threats and persuasion, to reduce them to order; but all was in vain. They were told that the enemy might take the advantage of their conduct, and come out—they answered, that if the enemy came out they would immediately put themselves under the command of their officers, and fight them; but that in any other case they would not be commanded. They took Gen. Wayne's horses out of his stable, and put them to draw the field-pieces. At night they encamped, posting out pickets, guards, and planting sentinels in a very regular manner. An alarm was given to the country by firing the beacons, etc. and the militia were assembling. The reasons given for the revolt were the intolerable sufferings of the army—the want of pay, of which 11 months was due—the want of clothing, many of the troops being almost naked—the want of provisions, and that many of them were held beyond the term of their enlistment. They directed their march towards Philadelphia, determined to demand redress of their grievances of Congress.

January 7—Maj. Gen. Knox was sent off by the Commander in Chief to the eastern States, to represent the alarming situation and sufferings of the army.

January 8—Major Throop, with 100 men, was sent towards Pompton, in the Jersies, to cover the public stores at Ringwood. In the afternoon, 169 barrels of flour arrived at the Point.

January 11—His Excellency the Commander in Chief came down to West Point, when a Council of War was held at our General's quarters, in which all the General Officers on the ground, and all the Colonels and commanding officers of the regiments sat, to consider what measures were necessary to be adopted, with respect to the Pennsylvania line. After the Council, by order of the Commander in Chief, our General issued orders for the forming of five battalions, by detachment from the several lines, to be held in the most perfect readiness to march on the shortest notice, with four days' provisions cooked. The mutineers remained on the heights of Princeton and two emissaries were sent out to them from the enemy, with offers, in writing, promising to redress their grievances by discharging them from their enlistments, paying all their arrearages of pay and depreciation, and exempting them from serving in the British army, if they should choose it. The mutineers nobly disdained these offers, and gave up the emissaries and their papers: they were tried, and hanged as spies; the one was an inhabitant of New Jersey, the other was a British Sergeant. Gen. Sir

Henry Clinton and Gen. Knyphausen were said to have been on Staten Island. The State appointed a Committee to inquire into the grounds of the complaints of the mutineers, and to redress such as appeared to have foundation: this brought the business to a close. A number of the soldiers were discharged, the rest returned to their duty.

Accounts were received from the southward, that the American army in that quarter were in a most miserable condition, on account of clothing and provisions, and that their sufferings were greater than those experienced by the main army. These sufferings of the army were rendered the keener, by the return of the officers and soldiers from furlough, who had been in the great sea port towns, where every necessary and luxury of life were enjoyed in the greatest abundance, many tables groaning under the pressure of the dainties with which they were covered. Their liquors were not only the best, but also of great variety. Such reports to men standing sentinel, as it were, in the jaws of death, ill clad, cold and hungry, with nothing but water oftentimes to drink, were trials almost too great for human nature to bear. The old Continental currency was fixed at 75 for one, at Philadelphia.

January 13—The Marquis de Lafayette and Count Deux-Ponts[1] visited West Point.

January 17—Intelligence was received that the troops which some time before sailed from New York, were in the Chesapeake, under the command of Gen. Arnold, and supposed to be on a plundering expedition. The enemy at New York removed the greater part of their shipping from the East River round into the North River.

January 18—Two hundred men, properly officered, marched down to the lines, under pretence of being a relief; 100 men of Hazen's regiment moved from Fishkill to the village, and a detachment of artillery from West Point. These were intended for an enterprise against the enemy.

January 19—150 men from the Connecticut line, and 200 from the New Hampshire line, were to move towards the lines; these, with those who marched from Hazen's the day before, were to form a covering party to the detachment under Lt. Col. Hull, who was to make an attempt on Delancey's corps.

January 21—A letter was received from Major Throop, at Ringwood, stating that the evening before the Jersey line, at Pompton, had revolted, and it was supposed would be joined by the other part of the line, who were at Chatham. Their intentions had not been developed.

January 22—His Excellency Gen. Washington, the Marquis de Lafayette, and a number of French gentlemen, visited the Point. The same day, 500 rank and tile, properly officered, from the Massachusetts, Connecticut and New Hampshire lines, were detached and ordered to march the next day under the command of Maj. Gen. Howe, to establish order and discipline in the Jersies.

January 23—The detachment marched from West Point for the Jersies. The battalion from thence was commanded by Col. Sprout. The troops on the east side of the river were to cross and join those from the Point, at King's Ferry: the detachment marched in high spirits.

January 24—In the morning about sunrise, a noise was heard in the air, resembling the firing of platoons, and there were various conjectures respecting it. Intelligence was received that Gen. Arnold had gone up James River, in Virginia, and had taken possession of Williamsburg, and was moving towards Richmond; that he met

Maj. Gen. Henry Knox.

with but little opposition, and would probably plunder large quantities of tobacco and other articles.

January 28—The detachment under the command of Lt. Col. Hull, returned from the enterprise against the enemy at Morrisania. The address and gallantry of the officers, the bravery and patience of the troops, exhibited on the occasion, did them much honor. Besides a number of the enemy who were killed, upwards of fifty were made prisoners; the pontoon bridge was cut away, the huts and forage were burnt, and a large number of cattle driven up. Of the detachment, one Ensign, one drummer, and ten rank and file, were killed; one Captain, one Sergeant, and eleven rank and file wounded; six rank and file were missing.

January 31—Maj. Gen. Howe returned with the detachment from the Jersies; order was established among the troops in that quarter: two of the ringleaders in the revolt were executed. It was learnt that considerable damage was done to the enemy's shipping at New York by the high gusts of wind, on the night of the 23rd. It was also said that a British 74 gun ship was dismantled off New London; another struck a reef, and a third went out to sea with one of her masts lost.

February 12—The Duke de Lauzun, Count Fersen[2] and Col. Sheldon,[3] of the French army, visited West Point.

February 13—Intelligence was received that on the 17th ultimo, an action[4] happened near Pee Dee, in Carolina, between a body of the enemy under Lt. Col. Tarleton, and a body of about 800 Americans, under the command of Gen. Morgan: the enemy were totally routed, and pursued upwards of 20 miles. Of the enemy, 10 officers and 100 rank and file were killed, and 200 wounded; 29 officers and 500 rank and file were taken prisoners, with two field-pieces, two standards, 800 muskets, 35 wagons, 70 Negroes, 100 dragoon horses, one traveling-forge, and all their music. The loss of the Americans was not more than 12 killed and 60 wounded.

February 14—General Warner[5] and Col. Ashley,[6] of Massachusetts arrived at West Point, to distribute to the soldiers of the Massachusetts line, engaged to serve during the war, 24 dollars in specie, each, as a generous gratuity from the State. The most sensible soldiers did not applaud this measure, as it did not assure to them the full payment of the wages due to them, while this boon increased the burden of debt on the State.

February 16—Count de St. Maime,[7] of the French army, visited West Point. The same day, orders were issued for augmenting the light companies of all the regiments at West Point, and its dependencies, to 50 rank and file each; they were to rendezvous, the 18th or 19th, at Peek's Kill.

February 17—The light companies were formed into battalions in the following order: the eight eldest companies of the Massachusetts line to form a battalion under the command of Col. Vose and Maj. Galvan; the two youngest companies of that line, and those of Connecticut and Rhode Island, to form a battalion, under the command of Col. Gimat[8] and Maj. Throop; those of the New Hampshire line, and Col. Hazen's regiment, and such others as might be joined to them, to form a battalion. This appointment of officers was declared to be intended not to affect the general plan of arranging the light infantry for the campaign. The preceding morning, the enemy made an excursion from Morrisania towards Bedford, took Lieutenants Carpenter, Wright and Peacock and five other inhabitants prisoners; burnt five houses, plundered and stript several other inhabitants, and returned. They were pursued by Capt. Pritchard, but could not be overtaken.

February 18—The light companies were inspected. It appeared that Admiral Arbuthnot's squadron was so much damaged in the storm on the 23rd ult. as to be rendered inferior to the French in these seas.

February 20—A detachment of artillery was ordered from the park to join the light infantry; the whole were to be commanded by the Marquis de Lafayette, and were to march to the southward. The same day, six of our guides, on a reconnoitering party towards King's Bridge, fell in with a reconnoitering party of Delancey's corps: the guides at tacked them and took five prisoners, all of whom were wounded.

February 24—The detachment doing duty on the lines was reduced to 50 rank and file, properly officered. Capt. Paul Jones, who arrived in the *Ariel*, at Philadelphia on the 17th, in eight weeks from L'Orient,[9] brought a large quantity of powder.

February 28—Intelligence was received that a considerable embarkation of troops was taking place at New York—the inhabitants and army in some consternation. It was said that a fleet of French merchantmen had arrived in the Chesapeake; but from appearances, there were good grounds to suspect that there was something more than merchant ships.

March 1—News was received that a part of the French squadron at Newport had sailed as far as the Chesapeake, where they took the *Romulus*, of 50 guns, and nine privateers and transports; four of the latter they destroyed, not having spare men to navigate them; but the remainder, with the *Romulus*, had safely arrived at Rhode Island.

March 2—In the morning, Gen. Washington set out from New Windsor for Rhode Island. By the last accounts from the southward, Lord Cornwallis was advancing rapidly, and Gen. Greene retreating moderately. His Lordship had destroyed his wagons, and disengaged himself of encumbrance as much as possible.

March 3—A Capt. Simmons, of Delancey's corps, was sent up to West Point; he asserted to be disaffected to the enemy on some pretences, and that he had resigned his commission, and deserted from them: he was sent to the Governor of the State.

March 5—Three prisoners were sent up; they were taken by a party of our guides within a small distance of the enemy's post, No. 8, near Morrisania.

March 6 and 7—Col. Van Shaick's regiment of the New York line arrived at West Point from Albany. The troops were at this time well supplied with provisions, but almost totally destitute of forage, and subjected to great fatigue in obtaining fuel, which part of the troops were obliged to bring on their backs, nearly a mile.

March 9—Intelligence was received, that the last embarkation of British troops sailed from New York the preceding Wednesday, said to be six regiments, making about 3000 men in the whole. The southern militia had been successful against the Cherokee Indians, and destroyed a number of their towns. The last advices from the southward stated that Lord Cornwallis had continued to push rapidly after Gen. Greene, who had crossed Dan River, and his Lordship had come up to it, and then began to retreat; on which Gen. Greene re-crossed the Dan, in order to pursue him, and that the militia were collecting. Gen. Arnold kept close at Portsmouth; Gen. Muhlenberg was near him, with a superior force, and the Marquis de la Fayette was as far as Elk on the 3rd with the light infantry.

March 11—A detachment of recruits from Massachusetts arrived. The same day, Capt. Pray[10] was ordered to take command of the Block-House at Dobbs' Ferry, the water-guards, etc. On the first of this month, the Confederation and perpetual Union of the Thirteen American States, from New Hampshire to Georgia, inclusive, was signed and ratified by all the Delegates in Congress.

On the evening of the 12th, intelligence was received from Capt. Pray, that at about two o'clock in the morning he was alarmed by the firing of guns, blowing of horns, etc., that the enemy were out on both sides of the river. In consequence of this, an express was sent off to Maj. Maxwell to be on his guard; and a detachment of 150 men was ordered to be in readiness to march early the next morning, if it should be necessary to cover him.

March 13—The intelligence of the enemy being out on both sides of the river, was confirmed; as to the west side of the river, the enemy came out from Paulus Hook about 200 strong, with two field-pieces, and had advanced within about three miles of the Block-House at Dobbs' Ferry. About noon a detachment of 150 men, under the command of Maj. Graham, with one field-piece, embarked on board a sloop, and with the gun-boat, having one six and one three-pounder, and a flat boat, fell down the river to King's Ferry, where they were ordered to debark and make a movement to Tappan, for the relief of the Block-House. The garrisons of the redoubts on the east side were doubled.

March 14—About noon, Maj. Graham returned; he had, with the detachment, embarked the preceding day, proceeded to King's Ferry, disembarked, marched to Haverstraw, where he met the militia returning; when he returned to the Ferry, re-embarked, and arrived at West Point about noon; having exhibited a spirit and expedition that did the detachment much honor. The enemy were completely defeated in their design by the militia, who early turned out, attacked, repulsed, and pursued them, until they retook all their plunder except two horses, and justly merited high commendation. The militia had one man wounded; the enemy were supposed to have had several killed and wounded. The same day, Brig. Gen. Hand was announced, in general orders, Adjutant-General of the army, in the room of Col. Scammell, who had discharged the duty of that office for some time, to great acceptation. Col. Scammell joined his regiment.

March 15—Intelligence was received that the enemy's fleet, which had sailed from New York the preceding week, returned on Sunday, having found that the French fleet were on the coast; their return occasioned some consternation at New York. The same day, news reached the army that Brig. Gen. Peleg Wadsworth, who commanded some militia levies in the eastern parts of Massachusetts, had been surprised and taken prisoner in the night by two British officers and some refugees, at a place called Camden.

March 16—It was learnt that the French fleet, with troops, sailed from Rhode Island on the 8th; and it was said that Admiral Arbuthnot, with the British fleet, came out of Gardiner's Bay on the 10th. The small pox at this time made its appearance in the vicinity of the army and several soldiers were taken down with that distemper. The enemy who were out a day or two before, on the east side of the Hudson, did no mischief. About this time a discovery was made that a number of persons at Stratford, Norwalk, etc. had been secretly associating to submit to the enemy if a favorable opportunity presented; and to supply them with provisions, furnish intelligence, etc.

March 19—Letters from Gen. Greene, of the 28th ult. at Highrock Ford, on Haw River, advised that Lord Cornwallis had retreated from Hillsborough, and that Gen. Pickens[11] and Col. Lee[12] had fallen in with Col. Hamilton's corps (rising of 200) and had killed and taken almost every individual of them; and that several other skirmishes had happened, but nothing decisive. Lord Cornwallis had erected the royal standard at Hillsborough and issued a vain proclamation, as usual. By accounts from New York, it appeared that the British had declared war against the Dutch, and had taken possession of St. Eustatia.

March 20—In the afternoon, Gen. Washington arrived at headquarters, at New Windsor, from the eastward.

March 21—Five prisoners of war were sent to West Point: they were taken by some of the light parties below the lines; a sixth who was taken was so badly wounded as to be left behind for the present.

March 22—Several resolutions of the State of Massachusetts in favor of the line of the army, and for the discharge of governmental securities, were received at West Point.

March 23—Intelligence was received that the British fleet which sailed from New York some time before, and had been chased back by the French fleet, sailed again on the preceding Wednesday for the southward. It was said that Sir Henry Clinton was on board, and that Gen. Knyphausen was to command in his absence—that the enemy were collecting a number of flat-boats in Spuyten Duyvil Creek, near Kingsbridge, and that 24 were then collected—that Arnold's corps was under orders to be in readiness to man the boats. Two spies were sent out of New York the same day the fleet sailed; they were to pass, by different routes, through the country to Canada.

March 24—A number of prisoners of war, who had been collected at West Point, were sent off under a guard of 60 men, commanded by Capt. Pope,[13] to Lancaster, in Pennsylvania.

March 28—The New Hampshire brigade were ordered to do duty on the lines; and the Rhode Island regiment to return to their quarters near Robinson's Mills.

March 29—News was received from Philadelphia that the French and English fleets had had an engagement off the Capes of Virginia, but that the issue was not known. The same day, intelligence was received from New York, that one of Admiral Arbuthnot's ships had returned to New York on Monday, and reported that there had been an engagement between the two fleets, and that it was a drawn battle.

March 31—A New York paper of the 28th was received, in which it was said that an engagement between the two fleets took place on the 16th, off the Capes of Virginia, in which several ships on both sides received considerable damage; and that the British had one Lieutenant, two midshipmen, and 40 seamen killed, and 80 wounded. The French account was not greatly different from that of the British, but did not mention the number of killed or wounded. A number of American soldiers who had not had the small pox, were collected and inoculated.

April 3—Intelligence was received, that a battle[14] had been fought between Gen. Greene's army and that of Lord Cornwallis. The action was bloody; and although his Lordship may be said to have gained the victory, as Gen. Greene retreated a mile from the field of battle, yet it was a dear bought victory. Gen. Greene having lost his horses, four pieces of cannon fell into the hands of the enemy. Some of the British corps, and in particular the Guards, suffered much. This day, Capt. Pray, of the water-guards, was reinforced with a whale-boat, a Subaltern, and 14 men.

April 4—Gen. Washington visited the Point. In the afternoon, two prisoners of war were sent up—they were of a party who had crossed Croton River and taken 16 head of cattle and four horses. On their return, near Dobbs' Ferry, they were overtaken by a party of the militia—the cattle etc. retaken, and two of the party made prisoners. About this time, the southern mail was carried off, between headquarters and the Jersies. The mail contained some letters of importance. The troops which had sailed from New York arrived safe in the Chesapeake.

April 7—Private intelligence was received, that four parties were to be sent out—one to take Gen. Washington, another the Governor of New Jersey, a third the Governor of New York, the object of the fourth not known. The same day, the gunboat was ordered to take a station opposite Fort Montgomery; additional guards to be mounted in the night time, and patrols to pass frequently.

April 8—The enemy's flat boats, which had been collected near Kingsbridge, were removed down into the East River.

April 9—Intelligence was received from the commanding officer on the lines, that the enemy were out towards White Plains, said to be about 90 horse and 50 foot.

April 10—The great chain was hauled from off the beach near the red house at West Point, and towed down to the blocks, in order to its being laid across the river—about 280 men were ordered on this duty.

April 11—The chain was properly fixed with great dexterity, and fortunately without any accident.

April 12—Our General visited the patients who were under inoculation with the small pox, when 500 were turned out and drawn up, all of whom were then under the operation, and in a fine way. The same day, intelligence was received that the enemy were preparing for another embarkation at New York, supposed for the southward.

April 14—A groom, belonging to Col. Gunning of the 82nd British regiment, came up; he deserted from his master with a very good saddle-horse, which he sold for 100 dollars in specie. Intelligence was received that the enemy had brought a large number of wagons across the Sound from Long Island for the purpose of making a grand forage; the covering party to consist of three or four hundred men, of different corps.

April 22—Two hundred and forty thousand dollars in new emission bills were brought to West Point, from Boston, for the troops of the Massachusetts line.

April 24—Monsieur Beville,[15] Quartermaster of the French army at Newport, arrived at headquarters, New Windsor; he came on to view the roads, and determine on the best route, should the French army move that way, and to fix on proper places for magazines, etc.

April 26—Gen. Washington visited West Point, with Monsieur Beville, etc. The next day, the latter set out on his return to Rhode Island, taking the lower road through Connecticut. Many of the soldiers who had gone through the small pox, joined their regiments the next day; of 500 who had been inoculated, four only had then died. At this time, provisions were growing very scarce at West Point, and the prospects daily growing more alarming. The magazines in Forts Clinton, Putnam, and some other of the most important works, had reserves of the best provisions, which were not to be touched; that in case the enemy, by any sudden movement, should invest them, and cut off the communication with the country, the garrisons might be enabled to hold out, until other troops, or the militia of the country, could march to the relief of the besieged; but unfortunately, the scarcity of provisions had become so great that even these reserves were broken in upon, and some of them nearly exhausted; when, after some other representations, our General addressed the following letter to Gen. Washington:

WEST POINT, May 6th, 1781

DEAR GENERAL,

I am honored with yours of the 5th and 6th, to which I shall duly attend. I hoped I should not have been compelled again to represent our situation on account of provisions; but supplies of meat have not arrived—all the Irish beef in the store has been gone for some days—we are at last forced in upon the reserves; that in Fort Clinton has all been taken out this day—the pork which was ordered to be reserved is all issued, except about 16 barrels—the boats are now up from below for provisions, with representations that they are out; the reserves will be gone in a few days if relief does not arrive, and hunger must inevitably disperse the troops. If the authority of our country will not order on supplies, I will struggle to the last moment to maintain the post: but regard to my own character compels me to be thus explicit—that if any ill consequences happen to this post or its dependencies through want of provisions, I shall not hold myself accountable for them.

I have the honor to be, etc.
(Signed) W. HEATH.

His Excellency Gen. WASHINGTON.

To which the Commander in Chief wrote the following answer:

HEADQUARTERS, NEW WINDSOR, May 8th, 1781

DEAR SIR,

Distressed beyond expression at the present situation and future prospects of the army, with regard to provisions, and convinced with you, that, unless an immediate and regular supply can be obtained, the most dangerous consequences are to be apprehended—I have determined to make one great effort more on the subject, and must request that you will second and enforce my representations to, and requisitions upon the New England States, by your personal application to the several Executives, and even Assemblies, if sitting, as I suppose they will be in the course of this month.

From your intimate knowledge of our embarrassed and distressed circumstances, and great personal influence with the eastern States, I am induced to commit the execution of this interesting and important business to you, and wish you to set out on this mission as early as may be convenient.

(Signed) GEO. WASHINGTON.

Maj. Gen. HEATH,

On the next day our General received the following letter of instructions from the Commander in Chief, viz:

HEADQUARTERS, NEW WINDSOR, May 9th, 1781

DEAR SIR,

You will be pleased to proceed immediately to the several eastern States, with dispatches addressed to the Governors of Connecticut, Rhode Island, Massachusetts Bay, and the President of New Hampshire, on the subject of supplies for the army. The present critical and alarming situation of our troops and garrisons, for the want of provisions, is (from the nature of your command) so perfectly known to you, and your personal influence with the New England States is so considerable, that I could not hesitate to commit to you a negotiation, on the success of which the very existence of the army depends.

The great objects of your attention and mission are, 1st—An immediate supply of beef cattle. 2nd—The transportation of all the salted provisions in the western parts of Connecticut and Massachusetts; and 3rd The establishment of a *regular, systematic, effectual* plan for feeding the army through the campaign. Unless the two former are effected, the garrison of Fort Schuyler must inevitably, that of West Point may probably, *fall*, and the whole army be disbanded: without the latter, the same perplexing wants, irregularities and distress which we have so often experienced, will incessantly occur, with eventual far greater evils, if not final ruin.

With regard to the particular mode of obtaining and transporting supplies, I will not presume to dictate; but something must now be attempted on the spur of the occasion. I would suggest whether it would not be expedient for a Committee from the several States (consisting of a few active, sensible men) to meet at some convenient place, in order to make out, upon a uniform and great scale, all the arrangements respecting supplies and transportation for the campaign. In the mean time, to avoid the impending dissolution of the army, the States must individually comply precisely with the requisitions of the Quarter-Master and Commissary upon them.

As the salted provisions which have been put up for the public in the eastern States (except in the western parts of Connecticut and Massachusetts) cannot at present be transported to the army, you will obtain accurate official returns of the quantity that has been procured in the respective States, at what places, and in whose charge it actually is; and if it should not all be collected and lodged in the deposits that have been pointed, out, you will urge this immediately to be done; and that the provisions should be repacked, stored, and taken care of in such a manner as to prevent the hazard of its being tainted or lost by the approaching hot season.

I omit entering into the detail of particulars which it may be necessary to state to the respective Executives (or Legislatures if in session) to enforce the present requisition, because you are as well acquainted with the circumstances of our distress, the prospects before us, and the only resources from whence we can derive relief, as it is possible for you to be. Previous to your departure you will obtain from the Quarter-Master-General and Commissary with the army, the proper estimates of supplies and transportation to be required of the several States, together with all the light and information concerning their department, which may be requisite to transact the business committed to you.

After having delivered the dispatches with which you are charged, and made such further representations as you may judge necessary, you will not cease your applications and importunities, until you are informed officially, whether effectual measures are or will be taken, to prevent the army from starving and disbanding. What supplies in general, and particularly of beef cattle, may certainly be depended upon, to be delivered at fixed regular periods (monthly or weekly) at the army, during the whole campaign. When you shall have seen this business put upon the surest footing and in the best train of execution (which you will endeavor to have effected as early as possible) you will be pleased to report to me, without delay, the success of your proceedings.

I heartily wish you success and a pleasant journey, and am, etc.

(Signed) G. WASHINGTON.

P.S.—I wish attention may be paid to learn what quantity of rum is in store, at what places, and in what manner it may be forwarded. In transportation the arrangements should be made with the States, so as to have the articles brought entirely through to the army, without having them stopped on the road. You will also be pleased to urge the forwarding the summer clothing. G.W.

Maj. Gen. HEATH.

During the month of April, a large number of recruits from the Eastern States, to fill up their respective battalions, arrived at West Point.

May 9—The Commander in Chief visited West Point.

May 11—In the morning, our General left West Point, and proceeded up the river to New Windsor where he received from the Commander in Chief the dispatches addressed to the several executives of the New England States; and in the afternoon crossed the Hudson, on his journey eastward. On his reaching Fishkill, he found that Governor Clinton of New York was making every exertion in his power for the relief of the army—that he had issued impress warrants to take flour and other provisions where they could be found, etc.

May 14—He arrived at Hartford, where he found the Legislature in session. The dispatches to Governor Trumbull were immediately presented to him, with an earnest request for speedy relief. This venerable patriot gave assurance of his immediate attention and exertions, and accordingly laid the dispatches from Gen. Washington before the Legislature, who also discovered the same noble patriotism. They inquired into the state of their treasury, and finding that it was destitute of money, except a sum appropriated to another purpose, they ordered this money to be taken, and directed Col. Champion,[16] one of their number (a gentleman remarkable for his knowledge in the state of provisions in all the towns, skill in purchasing, and expedition in forwarding) immediately to purchase and forward on to the army 160 head of beef cattle, and 1000 barrels of salted provisions from their stores; and resolved to make every other exertion in their power to comply with the requisitions of the Commander in Chief, as they respected both fresh and salted provisions, by appointing a committee for a general arrangement of supplies.

May 16—Our General left Hartford, and on the 18th reached Greenwich, in the State of Rhode Island, where he waited upon Gov. Greene, and presented the dispatches from Gen. Washington. The Legislature of the State were not then in session, but Gov. Greene made the most satisfactory assurances that the State of Rhode Island would adopt every measure recommended by the Commander in Chief. Our General left Greenwich the same day, and arrived at his house in Roxbury on the evening of the 19th, and the next day waited upon Gov. Hancock at Boston, and presented the dispatches with which he was charged. The new Legislature of Massachusetts were to convene on the last Wednesday of the month. Gov. Hancock gave the fullest assurances that in the interim the Executive would do everything in his power for the immediate relief of the army, by directing the several contractors of provisions in the State to forward all in their power with the utmost expedition.

May 21—Intelligence was received at Boston that the State ship-of-war, *Protector*, of 28 guns, commanded by Capt. Williams, had been taken and carried to New York. The next day intelligence was received that on the 13th, Col. Greene, of the Rhode Island regiment, who was doing duty on the lines of the American army, was surprised by a body of the enemy's horse, supposed to be about 150 dragoons, and that the Colonel, Maj. Flagg,[17] and two Subalterns and 27 men were killed and several wounded. Col. Greene was a brave and intrepid officer, and his loss was much regretted. The Colonel had taken post above and near to Croton River, at a place where the river was fordable, to prevent the enemy passing up by this ford to ravage the country. He had practiced the greatest vigilance in guarding this, ford in the nighttime, taking off the guards after sunrise, apprehending that the enemy would never presume to cross the river in the daytime; but the enemy, having learnt his mode of doing duty, on the morning of the 13th effected his overthrow, by crossing the ford soon after the guards had come off, and surrounding their quarters before they had an idea of any enemy being near them. In this situation, the utmost exertion could not avail them.

May 23—Our General left Roxbury on his way to New Hampshire, arrived at Exeter on the evening of the 24th, and delivered to the Hon. Mr. Weare[18] the dispatches addressed to him. The Legislature of New Hampshire was not then in session. The next day, he had an interview with the Honorable President and the Council of Safety, when such representations (in addition to the requisitions of the Commander in Chief) were made to them, as the exigencies of the case required; and the fullest assurances were received, that every aid in the power of the State should be afforded.

May 26—Our General left Exeter on his return, and on the 27th arrived at his house in Roxbury. On the 29th he again waited on Gov. Hancock, and requested that the requisitions of the Commander in Chief of the army might be predominant in all the public objects. The 30th was the General Election Day in Massachusetts, and it appeared that his Excellency John Hancock was re-elected Governor, who, as soon as the two Houses were organized, laid the requisitions of Gen. Washington before them.

June 2—Our General was heard before a Committee of both Houses on the subject of his mission. The zeal and patriotism of the several Executives and Legislatures of the New England States, to relieve and amply supply the army with provisions, were so conspicuous on this occasion that it is not possible to say which, or whether any of them exceeded the other; each was for making every exertion in its power; and, to insure success to their resolutions, they all fell in with the recommendation of the Commander in Chief, and appointed committees to meet in Convention to digest and systematize the business. The Committees met accordingly at Providence, in Rhode Island, and were so fortunate in their arrangements, that the most ample supplies of meat were afterwards furnished for the main army, and a surplus of 100 head of beef cattle weekly sent on after Gen. Washington towards Virginia, until he ordered a discontinuance of that supply, as will appear in the sequel. While the New England States were thus intent in supplying meat for the army, the State of New York was equally assiduous in furnishing flour and forage.

June 4—Intelligence was received by a vessel from the West Indies, that the Count de Grasse, with a French fleet of upwards of 20 sail of the line, had arrived in that quarter. The same day there was a confirmation of this news, and that the fleet, with troops on board, was seen coming this way. The same day intelligence was received that there had been an action[19] at the southward, between Gen. Greene and the British army in that quarter. Gen. Greene, having reconnoitered Camden, did not think it expedient to storm the enemy's works, but retired a little back, with a view to draw the enemy out; in this he succeeded, and an action commenced. The Maryland troops being attacked under some disadvantage, an attempt was made to change their position; this was unfortunately taken by Gen. Greene's army for a retreat, and the whole army retreated accordingly. Gen. Greene had 17 men killed; his retreat was about two or three miles, and the troops were in high spirits. It is always a dangerous maneuver to change a position in the face of an enemy; but necessity sometimes requires it. Gen. Phillips, of the British army, had died in Virginia of a fever.

June 6—The Continental frigate *Alliance* arrived in Boston harbor from France.

The *Alliance* had taken six prizes; two West Indiamen, two sloops of war, and two privateers. In the engagement with the sloops of war, both of which engaged the *Alliance* in a calm, Capt. Barry was wounded in the shoulder by a grapeshot; the Captain of Marines, and eight or nine men killed, and about 20 wounded.

June 9—Orders came on from Gen. Washington, to forward with all possible dispatch all the cannon, mortars, powder, shot, shells, and other military stores belonging to the United States, which were then in Massachusetts and Rhode Island, and also requesting the loan of some heavy artillery, powder, etc. of the State. The most spirited measures were taken for completing the Continental battalions, and raising a body of militia to be in readiness to march when called for. The General Assembly of Massachusetts, in their session, at this time, passed resolutions for settling with the troops of their line to the last of the year 1780, making good the depreciation of their pay, etc.

June 21—Intelligence was received that the British had formed a junction of their principal force at the southward in Virginia, by which means Gen. Greene would deprive them of all their posts in South Carolina; that on the 10th of May, Lord Rawdon[20] was compelled to evacuate Camden with precipitation, leaving behind him three of his officers and 58 privates, who had been dangerously wounded, and were unable to be removed. He burnt part of the town, and some of his baggage. On the 11th of the same month, the strong post of Orangeburg surrendered to Gen. Sumter[21]; a Colonel, several officers, and upwards of 80 men were made prisoners. On the 12th, the garrison of Fort Motte,[22] consisting of seven officers, 12 non-commissioned officers, and 165 privates, surrendered by capitulation to Gen. Marion.[23] On the 15th, Fort Granby capitulated to Lt. Col. Lee; one Lt. Colonel, two Majors, six Captains, six Lieutenants, three Ensigns, one Surgeon, two Sergeant-Majors, 17 Sergeants, nine Corporals, and 305 privates surrendered; large quantities of provisions and some military stores were taken at some of the posts. At the same time the posts of Augusta and Ninety-Six were invested by Gen. Pickens, and Gen. Greene on the 16th had determined to march the army to expedite their reduction.

June 23—Intelligence was received that some time before, the barracks at Fort Schuyler had taken fire and were burnt down; and that afterwards the fort was dismantled and evacuated. The same day it was reported that the Spaniards had taken Pensacola from the British. The marine mortars, and a number of heavy iron cannon, 18- and 24-pounders, were removing from Boston to the North River, New York. The British forces in Virginia, after their junction, were said to be about 6000. The invalids, who had been doing duty in Boston, received orders to march to West Point, where the whole corps was to be collected, and compose a part of the garrison of that post.

June 28—His Excellency the Commander in Chief was pleased to communicate to our General, that in the arrangement of the main army the command of the right wing had been assigned to him.

June 29—A vessel arrived at Boston from Cadiz, with a quantity of clothing for the United States. This vessel brought an account, that the British had again succored the garrison of Gibraltar, but that the Spaniards continued the siege.

June 30—His Most Christian Majesty's frigate, the *Surveillante* arrived in Boston harbor from the West Indies; on her passage had a warm engagement with a British ship-of-war, when some damage was sustained on both sides. This frigate brought news that the French had taken the island of Tobago, and had blocked up Admiral Rodney's fleet at Barbados.

July 4—Was celebrated at Boston, being the Anniversary of the Declaration of American Independence.

July 6—Information was received that Gen. Washington had ordered the American troops from their several cantonments, and that the whole had assembled, and were encamped near Peek's Kill. Some of the enemy's cruisers from Penobscot were cruising in the Bay, where they took several vessels; one within a league of the lighthouse.

July 11—Intelligence was received that there had been a skirmish between the Americans and the British, between White Plains and King's Bridge, but no particulars were received.

July 12—Our General set out from his house in Roxbury for the army.

July 19—The enemy's shipping, which were up the North River, ran down; there was a brisk cannonade at Dobbs' Ferry.

July 21—The American field artillery, which had for some days been on board vessels in the North River, proceeded downwards to the nearest landing to the army. When the enemy's shipping passed Dobbs' Ferry, on the 19th, a box of powder on board the *Savage* ship-of-war took fire, supposed by the bursting of a howitzer shell, on which a number of the crew, apprehending that the ship would blow up, jumped overboard into the river. An American, who was a prisoner on board, jumped overboard at the same time, and swam on shore, relating what had happened; he also reported that the *Savage* was several times hulled by our shot, and must have suffered considerable loss. The late skirmish near King's Bridge was occasioned by the American army's moving down, in order to gave the French officers a view of the British outposts near the bridge. A number of Americans were killed and wounded by long shot from the Jägers of the enemy, who kept up a popping fire whenever they could reach our troops.

July 27—Our General arrived at the army, which was encamped at Phillipsburg, in two lines; the park of artillery in the center of the second line. Accounts had been received from the southward that the enemy had no footing in Georgia, except Savannah, nor in South Carolina, except at Charleston. The position which the American army now occupied was between the lines the preceding campaigns; consequently the roads and commons, as well as the fields and pastures, were covered with grass; while the many deserted houses and ruined fences depicted the horrid devastations of war. The French army, under Gen. Rochambeau, was encamped at a small distance, on the left of the Americans, in one line.

July 29—A forage was made towards Phillips's, conducted by Col. Scammell. It was said that some of the British troops had returned from the southward to New York; and that those in Virginia were collected at Portsmouth.

August 3—About 11 o'clock at night, the British and American guard-boats met in the river, near Dobbs' Ferry, when a considerable firing ensued; we had one man badly wounded, who died soon after. The damage sustained by the enemy was not known.

August 6—The Commander in Chief, attended by a number of the General Officers, reconnoitered towards King's Bridge, covered by strong detachments of cavalry and infantry. Three ships and a galley lay in the river between Fort Washington and Spuyten Duyvil Creek. The enemy did not make any movements. The morning of the 7th, about two o'clock, the army was awakened by the firing of cannon at Dobbs'

Ferry; it appeared that two of the enemy's gunboats had come up as high as the ferry, probably to endeavor to seize some vessels or boats; on finding that they were discovered, they fired four cannon, but to no effect. Four cannon were discharged at the boats from the battery, on which they went down the river. Two days before, Delancey's corps ventured as far above King's Bridge as Phillips's.

News was received that the great French Financier, Necker, had resigned, and that Monsieur Fleury had been appointed in his room. Capt. Saltonstall,[24] formerly of the frigate *Warren*, who was dismissed the service on account of his conduct in the Penobscot expedition,[25] about this time behaved most gallantly in a privateer, on a cruise against the enemy. The American army at this time continued in the same position at Phillipsburg. The Connecticut and Rhode Island lines, and six regiments of the Massachusetts line, composed the front line; the New Hampshire line, four regiments of Massachusetts, Crane's and Lamb's regiments of artillery, with the sappers and miners, the second line; the right wing commanded by Maj. Gen. Heath, the left wing by Maj. Gen. Lord Stirling; the advance of the American army on a height a little advanced of Dobbs' Ferry, under the command of Col. Scammell, and Sheldon's dragoons near Dobbs' Ferry. The French army in one line on the left of the Americans, with their legion under the Duke de Lauzun, at White Plains. Gen. Waterbury,[26] with the militia under his command, towards New Rochelle. The camps at this time swarmed with flies, which were very troublesome.

August 11—Robert Morris, Esq. the American Financier, and Richard Peters, Esq.[27] one of the members of the Board of War, visited the army. The same day, the advance of the army took a position a little more to the northward, and the dragoons were added to Col. Scammell's command. A fleet arrived at New York from England; they brought over between two and 3000 Hessian recruits.

August 14—Col. Hazen's and Col. Van Schaick's regiments joined the army. A French frigate arrived about this time at Rhode Island, supposed to have brought news of the approach of the Count de Grasse. A few nights before, Gen. Schuyler came very near being taken and carried off from his house in Albany. In the general orders of the 15th, the army was directed to hold itself in the most perfect readiness to march on the shortest notice.

August 16—It was whispered that the Count de Grasse, with 28 sail of the line, besides frigates, with a number of land forces on board, might soon be expected on our coast, and these, with the squadron under the command of the Chevalier de Barras,[28] would make a fleet of 36 sail of the line, a force probably superior to any the British could assemble in these seas.

Under prospects so flattering, the Commander in Chief determined to strike the enemy a capital blow in some quarter. To strike at their very root in New York, was a most desirable object; but the situation of New York with Long Island, and Staten Island and the adjacent country, was such as would require a very large army to effect a complete investiture, and give a proper security against the sallies of the enemy, which, from situation, might be easily and frequently made—that such an army must be composed, in a very considerable degree, of militia, to whom the continuing long in camp had often been found disagreeable, and the French were not without apprehensions that if their fleet entered the harbor of New York, and became warmly engaged with the British ships and batteries, in the course of those maneuvers which it might be necessary to make, some of their heavy ships, through the want of a competent knowledge of all parts of the bay, might get aground or be damaged; while all these inconveniences would be avoided in case Lord Cornwallis, with the British army in Virginia, were made the object, and his capture would be almost certain, while the American main army might be left in sufficient strength to act on the defensive against Sir Henry Clinton, and effectually cover the important posts in the Highlands of New York.

August 17—Gen. Washington was pleased to communicate to our General (in confidence) his intentions, at the same time intimating to him that he should give him the command of the main army during his absence. The whole of the French army, with the two regiments of New Jersey, first regiment of New York, Col. Hazen's regiment, Col. Olney's regiment of Rhode Island, Col. Lamb's regiment of artillery, and the light troops under the command of Col. Scammell, were detached for the expedition against Lord Cornwallis, and the army under his command, at Yorktown, in Virginia.

August 18—Some of the corps began to move towards the ferries. The next day, the Commander in Chief was pleased to honor our General with the following:

To Major General HEATH,

SIR,

You are to take command of all the troops remaining in this department, consisting of the two regiments of New Hampshire, ten of Massachusetts, and five of Connecticut infantry, the corps of invalids, Sheldon's legion, the 3rd regiment of artillery, together with all such State troops and militia as are retained in service of those which would have been under my own command.

The security of West Point, and the posts in the Highlands, is to be considered as the first objects of your attention; in order to effect this, you will make such dispositions as in your judgment the circumstances shall from time to time require, taking care to have as large a supply of salted provisions as possible, constantly on hand; to have the fortifications, works, and magazines repaired and perfected as far as may be; to have the garrison at least, in all cases, kept up to its perfect strength; to have the minutes, plans and arrangements, for the defense and support of this important post perfectly understood and vigorously executed in case of any attempt against it. Ample magazines of wood and forage are to be laid in, against the approaching winter; the former should be cut on the margin of the river, and transported to the garrison by water; the latter ought to be collected from the country below the lines, in the greatest quantities possible, and deposited in such places as you shall judge proper.

The force now put under your orders, it is presumed, will be sufficient for all the purposes above mentioned, as well as to yield a very considerable protection and cover to the country, without hazarding the safety of the posts in the Highlands; this is to be esteemed as it respects the friendly inhabitants and resources of the country, an extremely interesting object; but when compared with the former, of a secondary nature. The protection of the northern and western frontier of the State of New York, as well as those parts of that and other States most contiguous and exposed to the ravages and depredations of the enemy, will claim your attention; but as the contingencies which are to be expected in the course of this campaign, may be so various, unforeseen, and almost infinite, that no particular line of conduct can be prescribed for them—upon all such occasions you will be governed by your own prudence and discretion, on which the fullest confidence is placed.

Although your general rule of conduct will be to act on the defensive only, yet it is not meant to prohibit you from striking a blow at the enemy's posts or detachments should a fair opportunity present itself. The most eligible position for your army, in my opinion, will be above (that is, on the north side) of the Croton, as well as for the purpose of supporting the garrison of West Point, annoying the enemy and covering the country, as for the security and repose of your own troops.

Waterbury's brigade (which may be posted towards the Sound), Sheldon's corps, the State troops of New York, and other light parties may occasionally be made use of to hold the enemy in check, and carry on the *petit-guerre* with them; but I would recommend keeping your force as much collected and compact as the nature of the service will admit, doing duty by corps instead of detachments, when ever it is practicable; and above all exerting yourself most strenuously and assiduously, while the troops are in camp of repose, to make them perfect in their exercise and maneuvers, and to establish the most perfect system of discipline and duty. The good of the service and emulation of corps will, I am persuaded, prompt the officers and men to devote their whole time and attention to the pleasing and honorable task of becoming masters of their profession.

The uncertainty which the present movement of the army will probably occasion with the enemy, ought to be increased by every means in your power, and the deception kept up as long as possible. It will not be expedient to prevent the militia, which were ordered, from coming in, until the arrival of the Count de Grasse, or some thing definite and certain is known from the southward; and even these circumstances may (but of this you will be advised) render it advisable to keep the enemy at New York in check prevent their detaching to reinforce their southern army, or to harass the inhabitants on the seacoasts.

The redoubt on the east side of Dobbs' Ferry is to be dismantled and demolished; the platforms to be taken up, and transported up the river, if it can be conveniently done. The block-house on the other side to be maintained, or evacuated and destroyed as you shall judge proper. The water-guards and other precautions to prevent surprise, you will be pleased to take into your consideration, and regulate in such a manner as you shall judge most expedient.

You will be pleased to keep me regularly advised of every important event which shall take place in your departments. Given under my hand at headquarters, near Dobbs' Ferry, this 19th day of August, 1781.

(Signed) GEO. WASHINGTON

P.S.—By the act of Congress of the 3rd of Oct., 1780, a return is to be made to them annually, on or before the first of September, of the troops belonging to the several States, that requisitions may be made for completing the same. This you will please to have done by the troops under your command. The preservation of the boats is a matter of very great importance, to which you will attend. Let all the new boats, and such others as are not absolutely necessary, and allotted to the service of the garrison, be hauled up, and put under the care of a guard, so that the person to whom they are committed shall be accountable for every boat. The abuses committed by people belonging to commissioned whale-boats on Long Island ought to be inquired into and suppressed, especially as Congress have ordered those commissions to be revoked.

G. W.

August 19—About noon, His Excellency Gen. Washington left the army, setting his face towards his native State, in full confidence, to use his own words, "with a common blessing" of capturing Lord Cornwallis and his army; while our General was left to watch Sir Henry Clinton, and guard against those attempts which it was probable he would make to succor Cornwallis direct, or by making such other movements as might tend to induce Gen. Washington to give up his object, or avail himself of some important posts in his absence. Sir Henry Clinton was consequently on the rack, to devise something which should effect his purpose; a stroke at the posts in the Highlands, Connecticut, New Jersey, Albany and Philadelphia, was contemplated. Against all this had our General to guard—let impartiality judge, and candor decide on his conduct.

On the morning of the same day, the French army marched from their encampment towards King's Ferry, where they were to cross the river. The American park of artillery, Col. Olney's regiment, and the New York regiment decamped and moved the same way.

August 20—A little after noon, our General ordered off the baggage to the strong ground near Young's, which at about six o'clock was followed by the army, marching by the left in one column, which took a strong position during the night. The pickets after dusk were drawn back a little to the northward of the former encampment. The advanced parties under Maj. Scott were ordered to join their respective regiments, and Sheldon's horse to patrol in the front.

Lt. Gen. Charles Cornwallis, 2nd Earl Cornwallis.

August 21—Col. Putnam, with 320 infantry, Col. Sheldon's horse, and two companies of the New York levies, were ordered to form an advance for the army, and remain at or near their present ground. About 12 o'clock at noon, the army took up its line of march, and halted at night on the lower parts of North Castle. Two regiments had been detached on the march to Sing-Sing church, to cover a quantity of baggage belonging to the French army, assisting removing it, etc. and a detachment was sent to the New Bridge, to secure a quantity of flour lodged near that place.

August 22—The army marched from North Castle, and encamped at Crom Pond; all the French stores at Tarrytown and Sing-Sing had been secured.

August 23—The army marched from Crom Pond, and took a strong position at Peek's Kill; the first line encamping before the village, and the second behind it. After the troops were encamped, 80 wagons were sent off to assist in forwarding the stores of the army with Gen. Washington. Intelligence was received that a frigate and storeship had arrived at Boston from France, with military stores, etc. for the United States.

August 24—The French troops had not all passed the Ferry—150 Americans were sent to aid them, and at evening 150 more. Intelligence was received that a large French fleet had been seen standing for the continent.

August 26—The whole of the French army had crossed the river. Gen. Washington was as far as Ramapo in the forenoon. Six deserters came in from the enemy, and three prisoners of war belonging to Delancey's corps were sent up; they had taken and were driving off about 30 sheep, which were recovered.

August 27—Dispatches were sent off to Gov. Trumbull at Hartford, and Gov. Hancock at Boston. A heavy cannonade was heard towards New York, from early in the morning till two in the afternoon, supposed to be off at sea.

August 30—At evening a detachment consisting of 250 men, marched towards the New Bridge, where wagons were collected for the grand forage, which was to be covered by this detachment and the troops on the lines—the whole under the command of Col. Greaton. By the last accounts Gen. Washington was as far as Chatham, in the Jersies.

August 31—Colonel Laurens passed the army on his way from Boston to Philadelphia; he had brought from France a large sum in specie for the United States. Col. Laurens reported the friendly disposition of the European powers towards the United States; that Great Britain continued to stand without a single ally, nor could she obtain one in the war in which she was engaged.

September 1—The foragers returned with 42 loads of hay. A Hessian rifleman came in with his rifle. The same day letters were received from Gen. Washington, dated at Trenton, the 29th ult. mentioning that a British fleet of 15 sail of the line had arrived at Sandy Hook from the West Indies. The same evening, about 40 Indians, from the Oneida and other neighboring tribes, came to the army, on their way after Generals Washington and Rochambeau.

September 2—Intelligence was received from New York that a fleet, under the command of Admiral Sir Samuel Hood, had arrived at Sandy Hook from the West Indies, consisting of 14 sail of the line, three 44 gun ships, one of 28, sloop and fire-ship. The ships of the line were, *Barfleur*, of 90 guns, *Princess, Invincible, Alcide, Alfred, Ajax, Resolution, Centaur, Intrepid, Terrible, Montague, Shrewsbury, Belliqueax*, and _____, 74 guns each. It was said that the first battalion of Royals, 13th and 69th British regiments came in the fleet.

September 3—Intelligence was received, that General Washington was at Philadelphia the preceding Friday, and that his army was to march from Trenton, as yesterday.

September 4—Intelligence was received from New York that the British fleet had sailed to counteract the French. The day before, the southern post-rider, with the mail, was stopped near Pompton in the Jersies, and the mail carried off; the horse was left in the road. The same day a fleet of 26 sail, some of which were large, passed Stamford to the eastward.

September 6—Intelligence was received from New York that an embargo was laid on the shipping there and that 6 British transports had been taken by the French. The enemy's shipping in the North River above Fort Washington had all gone down.

September 7—Intelligence was received from New York, that the Count de Grasse had arrived in the Chesapeake on the 31st ultimo; that a 64-gun ship and a frigate had entered York River; that Lord Cornwallis was preparing for a vigorous defense; and that six sail of victuallers had been taken by Admiral Barras. A heavy cannonade was heard the day before towards the Hook. The same day there was much passing between the city and Fort Washington, which occasioned a great rising of dust, visible at a great distance; and there was rumbling of carriages in the night. Mr. Rivington, in his paper, observed the present to be the most interesting and critical era of the war. The same evening a detachment marched from our army for a grand forage.

September 8—Two companies of Col. Weissenfel's[29] regiment were ordered to Albany to cover that city against the designs of the enemy. The same evening, our General received a letter from Gen. Washington, dated at the Head of Elk the preceding day, in which he observes, "I have it now in my power to congratulate you on the arrival of Count de Grasse with 28 ships of the line and some frigates, in the Chesapeake, with a body of land forces on board, which he debarked immediately on his arrival. On his passage, he took Lord Rawdon, who was bound from Charleston to England. This arrival, with Col. Laurens, from France, must fill the United States with the most happy prospects and expectations.... I am thus far on my way to Virginia with the troops under my command; we are now embarking the heavy baggage, stores, and some of the troops.... I must beg of you not to forget sending the quantity of beef I requested, as I must at present altogether depend on that supply."

The same day intelligence was received that the enemy's fleet, which had sailed up the Sound on the 4th, had made a descent on New London. At evening, Maj. Tallmadge, with 20 cavalry and 200 infantry, was ordered to move immediately towards the Sound. The preceding day, about 30 sail of the enemy's vessels passed the Sound towards New York. On the morning of the 9th the foragers returned with 28 loads of hay.

September 10—Intelligence was received from Governor Trumbull, that the enemy had made a descent[30] on New London, on the evening of the 6th with about 2000 infantry and 300 light horse. Their fleet consisted of about 40 sail of ships-of-war and transports; they plundered the inhabitants of property to a large amount, and burnt a great part of the town. The militia behaved very gallantly, and a number of very valuable citizens were killed; among others, Col. Ledyard,[31] Captains Saltonstall and Richards.[32] The enemy, in three assaults on the fort on Groton side of the river, were repulsed, but on the fourth attempt carried it. The militia collecting in greater numbers, with some pieces of artillery, the enemy retreated on board their shipping. Part of the American shipping in the harbor were scuttled and some were run up the river. In Governor Trumbull's letter, the enemy were charged with behaving in a wanton and barbarous manner; and that of between 70 and 80 men who were killed, three only were killed before the enemy entered the fort, and the garrison had submitted; that on Col. Ledyard's delivering his sword reversed to the commanding officer who entered the fort, the officer immediately plunged it in the Colonel's body, on which several soldiers bayoneted him. It is also asserted, that upon the foregoing taking place, an American officer, who stood near to Col. Ledyard, instantly stabbed the British officer who stabbed the Colonel; on which, the British indiscriminately bayoneted a great number of Americans.

This expedition was commanded by Arnold. The British loss was very considerable in killed and wounded; among the former was Major Montgomery. Arnold himself continued on the New London side, and while his troops were plundering and burning, was said to have been at a house where he was treated very politely; that while he was sitting with the gentleman regaling himself, the latter observed that he hoped his house and property would be safe; he was answered that while he (Arnold) was there it would not be touched; but the house, except the room in which they were, was soon plundered, and found to be on fire. During the plunder of the town, the British (as is always the case in a plunder) were in great confusion, setting their arms against trees and fences, while they were collecting and carrying off their plunder; in this situation they might have been easily defeated; nor would it have been the first time that an army in possession of victory lost it in this way; hence, by the articles of war, "If any officer or soldier shall leave his post or colors to go in search of plunder, he is liable to suffer death for the offence."

It is not meant to exculpate or to aggravate the conduct of the enemy on this occasion—but two things are to be remembered: first, that in almost all cases the slaughter does but begin when the vanquished give way; and it has been said, that if this was fully considered, troops would never turn their backs, if it were possible to face the enemy: Secondly, in all attacks by assault, the assailants, between the feelings of danger on the one hand, and resolutions to overcome it on the other, have their minds worked up almost to a point of fury and madness, which those who are assailed, from a confidence in their works, do not feel; and that consequently when a place is carried, and the assailed submit, the assailants cannot simultaneously curb their fury to reason, and in this interval many are slain in a way which cool bystanders would call wanton and barbarous, and even the perpetrators themselves, when their rage subsided would condemn; but while the human passions remain as they now are, there is scarcely a remedy.

September 11—Arnold's fleet was still in the Sound, and further depredations were expected; they were this morning at Killingsworth, and about noon 50 sail of vessels came to anchor between Norwalk and Stamford. Major Tallmadge, who was returning, upon supposition that the enemy had returned to New York, was ordered back immediately. Maj. Knapp[33] was detached with 100 men to reinforce Col. Putnam on the lines; and Brig. Gen. Huntington, with the first Connecticut brigade and a detachment of artillery was ordered to march towards the Sound. The same day the army moved from its encampment at Peek's Kill and took a very strong position on Bald Hill, where it encamped in one line, the second line forming in the center of the first; and the 8th Massachusetts regiment was ordered to march from the army, and reinforce the garrison at West Point.

September 13—Intelligence was received that on the enemy's anchoring off Stamford, Maj. Tallmadge advanced towards the town; Gen. Huntington had advanced as far as Bedford; and that the preceding morning the enemy's fleet came to sail and stood principally to the westward; some of the fleet at the same time standing over to Huntington Bay, Long Island. Major Tallmadge[34] was to remain at or near Canaan for the protection of the inhabitants; Gen. Huntington to return to the army.

The Hessian recruits, which had a little time before arrived at New York, were very sickly, and many died. The fleet which had arrived at New York were in bad condition. The *Prudente* and *Robuste* lay at the shipyard; the *Roebuck* had been sent to Halifax to repair, and had not returned. Mr. Rivington, in his paper, talked of another fleet coming out, under Admiral Digby.

September 15—The enemy had still a number of troops on board their transports in the harbor. The same day intelligence was received from Canada, that the enemy were preparing a number of canoes and small batteaux at St. John's, baking hard bread at Montreal and forwarding it to St. John's, etc. The Cork fleet had arrived at Quebec. The same day about 40 sail of the enemy's vessels passed in the Sound to the eastward.

September 17—Intelligence was received that a brigade of troops had lately come to St. John's, from whence an incursion on our northern frontier might be expected;

on which the whole of Weissenfels' regiment was ordered for Albany immediately; notice was also given to the eastern Governors, and the Brigadiers commanding the militia of the counties of Hampshire and Berkshire, in Massachusetts, requested to lend their aid, if it should be found necessary.

September 18—A deserter came in from New York; he reported that when he left the city about 20 sail of vessels were falling down to the Hook, said to have troops on board.

September 19—The 2nd and 5th Massachusetts regiments were ordered to go into garrison at West Point, and the 7th regiment to join the army; it had before been in garrison. The same day, intelligence was received from New York, that there had been a naval engagement off the Chesapeake[35] between 19 sail of British men-of-war, and 24 French ships of the line: the story was so badly told in New York, that there was good grounds to conclude that the British had received a severe drubbing. On the 17th, when a packet arrived at New York, 3000 people were said to be waiting on the wharves to learn the news, but not a word transpired nor did the countenance of the officer who landed appear to beam with smiles of fortune. The enemy had taken a number of heavy cannon from the grand battery, which were put on board ship. The troops still remained on board the transports and had fallen down to the Hook. A mortal sickness prevailed in Delancey's corps at Morrisania, which was much reduced in its numbers.

September 22—Intelligence was received that the British fleet had been pretty severely handled by the French, and some of the ships were considerably damaged; that the inhabitants were in great consternation in New York; many were packing up their goods; that Arnold's loss at New London, in both killed and wounded was very considerable; that the 38th, 47th and 50th regiments were on that expedition, and then considered as unfit for duty. Gen. Sir Henry Clinton was said to be embarked with the troops, report said from 7 to 8 thousand; among them the British and Hessian grenadiers, light infantry, 42nd regiment, etc.

September 24—A grand forage was made below the lines. The British fleet returned to the Hook on the 20th. The *Prudente* of 64 guns, had gone down in a miserable condition to join the fleet; and the *Robuste* of 74 guns had hauled down nearly opposite to the city. The heavy cannon had been taken from Fort Washington as well as the grand battery.

September 25—Forty-six loads of forage were brought off from below the lines. Mr. Rivington published another account of the naval engagement between the fleets on the 15th; he acknowledged that several ships were much damaged, and that two which had come from the West Indies leaky, were more so after the engagement; that in particular, the *Terrible* was so much damaged as occasioned the taking out her guns, etc. and setting her on fire; after which the fleet returned to the Hook, finding it impracticable to succor Lord Cornwallis. It was said that the troops which had embarked (about 6000) had debarked on Staten Island. Other accounts stated their number not more than 4000—they were impressing and collecting wagons.

September 27—Three deserters came in from Col. Wurmb's corps with their arms, etc.

September 28—Apprehending that the enemy might have intentions of crossing over from Staten Island to the Jersies, a detachment of 300 infantry, with light artillery, under the command of Col. Swift,[36] were ordered to cross the ferry the next morning and move as far as Ramapo, to be on hand to aid the militia, in case the enemy should land in the Jersies.

September 29—Intelligence was received from the northward that a small party had been sent from St. John's to Saratoga, to take a prisoner or two, for the purpose of obtaining information, but that five of the party, with the instructions of the British commandant at St. John's were taken and brought in by Captain Dunham.[37]

September 30—Intelligence was received that Admiral Digby arrived at New York on the 25th inst. with three sail of the line and one frigate. Prince William Henry,[38] the King of England's third son, came in this fleet. It was said in New York that Lord Cornwallis's force in Virginia consisted of 5000 regular troops, and 3000 levies; but that behind him was a numerous Continental army—before him a powerful French fleet. The troops on Staten Island were at this time suspected to be planning some secret expedition; and Congress, from some intelligence which they had received, were not without apprehensions that Philadelphia might be their object. The militia of Pennsylvania were held in readiness for instant service, and our General was notified to hold the army in readiness to move, if necessary. The enemy were carefully watched. Sir Henry Clinton was endeavoring to devise some means whereby he might relieve Lord Cornwallis, but nothing would have diverted Gen. Washington from capturing him. The New York papers were filled with addresses and adulations to their young Prince; but these could not retard the advances of a Washington or defend Cornwallis. The fleet of Count de Grasse made several captures.

October 3—At three o'clock a.m. Major Trescott,[39] with a detachment of 100 men from Maj. Tallmadge's command, crossed the Sound to Long Island and completely surprised the enemy's Fort Salonga,[40] making two Captains, one Lieutenant, and 18 rank and file prisoners; of the enemy, two were killed and two wounded; of the Americans, none were killed, and but one wounded. Two double fortified four-pounders, found in the fort, were damaged. One brass three-pounder, with a number of small arms, ammunition, clothing, British goods, etc. were brought off. This enterprise was conducted with address and gallantry.

October 4—The foragers returned with upwards of 40 loads of hay.

October 5—A detachment of dragoons were sent towards Boston, and 100 picked infantry under Maj. Morrill[41] were to march towards Springfield to escort a large sum of money (brought by Col. Laurens) to Philadelphia.

October 6—The enemy were again embarking their troops from Staten Island; they embarked on board the men-of-war. Considering their case as desperate, they were determined to make one desperate attempt. Ten or twelve fire-ships were prepared to sail with the fleets; they were filled with proper materials for the purpose, and, to prevent suspicion, they were new painted, had guns, and the appearance of some of the handsomest ships in the fleet.

October 8—A detachment was sent on a grand forage. The same day, intelligence was received that a party of refugees and Indians from Niagara had burnt a number of houses and barns at Warwarsing[42]; they were pursued by Col. Paulding, but could not be come up with. Sir Henry Clinton, in his orders of the 3rd, directed 3000 regular troops to embark on board the men-of-war as marines; it was supposed that everything would be ready by the 14th. Secret intelligence had been received from Albany, that the enemy had intentions on that city; that they would advance by different routes and on their near approach would be joined by some disaffected people in the country, and the destruction of the city be effected. Brig. Gen. Stark had been in command for some time at the northward.

October 10—Our General ordered the 2nd New Hampshire regiment and a detachment of artillery to the northward. Gen. Stark had executed a Mr. Loveless,[43] sent in by Capt. Dunham as a spy.

October 13—Intelligence was received that the enemy had advanced to this side of Lake George.

October 14—The 1st New Hampshire and 10th Massachusetts regiments, with a detachment of artillery, were ordered to Albany, where matters wore a more serious aspect.

October 15—Intelligence was received that on the 28th ult. Gen. Washington took a position in the neighborhood of York—the enemy gave him no annoyance: on his advancing, a body of horse paraded before the enemy's works; but retired upon the discharge of a few shots at them. September 29th was spent in taking another position as near the enemy's advanced works as could be done without placing the encampment in range of their shot. Some skirmishing happened between our riflemen and the Jägers, in which the former had the advantage. At night the enemy abandoned all their out-posts (some of which were very advantageous) and retired to the town; the Americans occupied the same ground, and made lodgments at a short distance from the enemy's lines. The heavy artillery was to be brought up as soon as possible, and the siege pushed with vigor. On September 30th, Col. Scammell, who was officer of the day, was wounded and taken prisoner by a party of the enemy's horse, as he was reconnoitering one of the works which had just before been evacuated.

Our General had ordered Maj. Gen. Lord Stirling to proceed to Albany, and take command of the troops in that quarter; he set out for the northward about noon on the October 16th. The same day, Col. Tupper, with the 1st New Hampshire and 10th Massachusetts regiments, and a detachment of artillery, embarked at Fishkill Landing, and arrived at Albany in 18 hours afterwards. The same day it was learnt that the enemy's fleet at New York was 24 or 25 sail of the line, and that 5000 or 6000 of the best troops at New York had embarked and were on the point of sailing to attempt to relieve Earl Cornwallis; it was also said that Cornwallis was short of bread, and that his meat provisions would not last him more than the month out, at farthest he had received fresh provisions but once after he was blockaded.

October 17—In the morning, a horse-guard belonging to Gen. Howe's division, consisting of a Sergeant, nine privates and eight wagoners, with 30 horses, were taken by Delancey's horse a little below Croton River, where the horses had been put to pasture contrary to orders. A Court of Inquiry was ordered to investigate the matter.

October 18—It was learnt that on the preceding Saturday, a British 74 gun ship was struck by the lightning at New York, and sustained considerable damage.

October 22—Gen. Greene's official letter to Congress, announced that his battle on the 8th, near Eutaw Springs, was well fought; that on the field he obtained the victory, drove and pursued the enemy for several miles, when the enemy, throwing themselves into a three-story brick house, a stockaded garden and thick brush, renewed the action, when, after some efforts to dislodge them, Gen. Greene thought it advisable to call off his troops, which was done, and the wounded brought off, except such as were under the fire of the house. Four brass six-pounders having had their horses killed, were also left near the house, in possession of the enemy. This was somewhat similar to what took place at Germantown battle, and now very probably saved the British from a total defeat.

The close of this action barred its being called a complete victory, although its effects proved it such. General Greene of Continental State troops and militia, had one Lieutenant-Colonel, one Major, six Captains, eight Subalterns, eight Sergeants, and 114 rank and file killed—five Lieutenant-Colonels, 13 Captains, 25 Subalterns, 32 Sergeants, and 300 rank and file wounded one Sergeant and 40 rank and file missing— one Brigadier-General of militia wounded. Of the enemy, 500 prisoners, including the wounded, which the enemy left behind them, were taken, and it was supposed that the killed and other wounded of the enemy must be nearly 600 more. Perhaps troops never fought better than the Americans did in this battle; and of the British, General Greene observed, "the enemy fought with equal spirit, and worthy of a better cause."

By a letter from Gen. Washington of the 6th, it appeared that the operations against Earl Cornwallis had then gone on but slowly, but that the trenches were to be opened that night. The same letter observed that some misunderstanding, which had subsisted in Vermont, was settled, and that Gen. Enos and the troops under his command were to be subject to the orders of our General. The army in the Highlands were at this time short of flour, occasioned by the dry season, and consequent want of water for the mills.

October 24—A letter was received from Gen. Washington, dated at York, in Virginia, the 12th, by which it appeared that the trenches were opened on the night of the 6th, without being discovered by the enemy until daylight. The approaches were carried on within 600 yards of the enemy's works without any loss—the 7th and 8th were employed in erecting batteries—on the 9th, two batteries, one on the right, and the other on the left, were opened. The next morning, four other batteries being completed, the whole opened a heavy fire of cannon and mortars, which soon became so warm as to drive the enemy from their guns and their fire was almost totally silenced— very little return was made afterwards. The *Charon* of 44 guns, with one transport, took fire from our shot or shells, the evening of the 10th, and were both consumed. The 11th, another ship was destroyed in the same manner. The same night, the second parallel was advanced within less than 400 yards of the enemy's lines. This approach was also affected without annoyance; and on the 12th, the fatigue men were securely covered while they were completing the works. The same evening there was a flying report, which seemed to gain credit, that Earl Cornwallis and his army surrendered on the 17th, and that Count de Grasse had gone out to meet Admiral Digby.

October 25—Intelligence was received of the advance of the enemy at the northward.

October 26—Col. Francis, with the specie from Boston, passed the river; the money was escorted by 40 horse of Sheldon's regiment, and 150 infantry, and Lt. Col. Millen[44] was ordered with a detachment of infantry, to move on the lower road as far as Morristown, keeping between the escort and the enemy.

October 28—In the afternoon, a letter from Gen. Washington to our General announced the pleasing and highly important news of the complete capture of Earl Cornwallis and his whole army on the 19th. Our General had assured the army that the moment he received the certain intelligence of the capture of Cornwallis, it should be announced to them by the discharge of 13 cannon near his quarters; these were now the heralds to the army, and were instantly answered by a like number of field-pieces in every brigade on the ground.

The surrender of British forces at Yorktown, October 19, 1781 (Library of Congress).

On the 15th, two of the enemy's redoubts were stormed, one by the Americans and the other by the French troops, and soon carried with but little loss. The possession of these redoubts gave the allied army in a great measure the command of the other works of the enemy, who on the 17th beat a parley, and on the 19th, surrendered: 3500 regular troops laid down their arms; 2000 more were sick and wounded in the hospitals. These were exclusive of sailors, Negroes, etc. Earl Cornwallis was to go to England on parole, and remain a prisoner until exchanged. The officers and men were to be exchanged as far as the garrison of Charleston would extend; the remainder were to remain prisoners of war; the British were to retain their private baggage. It was said that more than 100 vessels were taken from the enemy. A detail of the prisoners taken, was stated as follows: one Lt. General, one Brig. General, two Colonels, 14 Lt. Colonels, 16 Majors, 97 Captains, 180 Lieutenants, 55 Ensigns, four Chaplains, six Adjutants, 18 Quartermasters, 18 Surgeons, 25 Mates, 385 Sergeants, 197 Drummers and Trumpeters, 6039 rank and file, 189 in Commissary's department—sailors in the pay of the King, 840—killed during the siege, 309—deserters, 44—75 brass cannon, 169 iron do., 5743 muskets with bayonets, 915 muskets without bayonets, and 1136 damaged muskets were among the trophies of victory. Thus was the principal force of the enemy crushed in the south. At the northward the enemy were advancing, both by the way of the Lakes and by the Mohawk River. Col. Willett,[45] with his regiment of New York levies, and some militia of New York, and from the western parts of Massachusetts, were advancing to meet Maj. Ross,[46] who, with from 500 to 700 men, principally British troops, was making his way towards Albany through the settlements on the Mohawk.

October 29—Intelligence was received that an action[47] took place the preceding Thursday, near Johnstown, between the troops under the command of Col. Willett and Maj. Ross. Col. Willett having advanced until he had arrived near Maj. Ross detached Maj. Rowley of Massachusetts with a body of militia, by a circuitous movement, to get in the rear of the enemy, with orders that as soon as he heard the firing in the front, to fall on them. Maj. Rowley performed his maneuver accordingly, and as soon as Col. Willett judged that the Major had gained the rear of the enemy, he made a vigorous charge on their front when they immediately gave way, and to all appearance the Colonel was nearly in the grasp of victory, when, all at once, without any visible occasion, the levies came to a stand and then immediately began to fall back, the enemy facing about and charging vigorously; the Colonel's brass field-piece and ammunition tumbrel fell into the hands of the enemy, and a rout seemed to be taking place, when Maj. Rowley, not knowing what had taken place in the front, commenced a brisk attack on the enemy's rear; this instantly threw them into confusion, the levies rallied in the front and fought with redoubled bravery; the field-piece and tumbrel were retaken, and the enemy put to a most complete rout and pursued until the levies, militia, and some Oneida Indians who were with Col. Willett were worn down with fatigue.

It was not possible to ascertain the number of the enemy's slain; for, to use the words of the reporting officer, "Unless the swamps and rivers in which they fell were to report the killed, it was impossible to make a return of them." Major Butler,[48] so frequently a troublesome partisan officer on the frontiers, was killed by the Indians as he was passing a river. Fifty- two prisoners were taken and brought in; and Major Ross went off in a direction into the woods where he and his troops must have suffered extremely for provisions, etc. Of the levies and militia with Col. Willett, one Lieutenant and 12 rank and file were killed; one Captain, two Lieutenants, and 20 rank and file were wounded; one Captain, one Lieutenant and three privates missing. Thus were the designs of the enemy also frustrated in the north.

The Corporation of the city of Albany were so much impressed with the seasonable and effectual exertions made by our General to save their city from destruction, that they sent him the following very polite address:

ALBANY, October 22nd, 1781

SIR,

Threatened as this city and the frontiers of the State have been with destruction from an enemy who, forgetting the rights of humanity and customs of war adopted by civilized nations, have hitherto waged it with all the spirit of the most savage barbarism, we cannot reflect but with pleasure and gratitude on the alacrity with which you have pursued the intentions of the Commander in Chief, in affording with so much dispatch a competent support to oppose the enemy; permit us, therefore, to render to you our unfeigned thanks, and to assure you that the corporation of the city of Albany can never be unmindful of your attention; and we entertain not the least doubt but that similar sentiments influence every inhabitant who has experienced the advantage of your generous exertions.

We are, Sir, with the greatest respect and esteem, your most obedient, humble Servants,

By order of the Corporation,
(Signed) ABRA. TEN BROECK, Mayor.

The Hon. Maj. Gen. HEATH.

October 31—The army in the Highlands celebrated the glorious victory obtained over Lord Cornwallis. The whole army was under arms in one line; the artillery interspersed with the brigades to which it was attached; at 12 o'clock, the army was reviewed by the General; at one, a grand *feu-de-joy* was fired, after which, all the officers dined together at a table spread in the field, and formed a great square, where great festivity and social mirth prevailed. The soldiery had an extra boon on the occasion, and, to crown the whole, in the midst of the joy around the table, an officer approached our General, and informed him that, at the request of the prisoners in the provost (who were pretty numerous) he was desired to represent that their hearts expanded with joy on account of the glorious victory obtained by their illustrious Commander in Chief—that they lamented they could not express it with their comrades in arms, but that they did it heartily in their confinement, and solicited the General's goodness in an order for something to cheer their spirits.

This was instantly done, with an additional order to the officer of the provost guard to set every prisoner in confinement at liberty. The promulgation of this order drew a shout of approbation from the whole body of the officers at the table, and probably had a better effect on the discipline of the army than a continuation of confinement and exemplary punishment of the culprits could have produced. The general order of the day directed that, "As soon as the *feu-de-joy* is over, the arms, ammunition, etc. are immediately to be put in perfect order for instant action. All guards, pickets and sentinels to be vigilant and alert on their posts;" which, notwithstanding the joy of the day, was strictly observed.

On this occasion there were rejoicings in all parts of the United States. One instance seems to be worthy of notice: the company collected had determined to burn Gen. Arnold in effigy for his treachery at West Point; just as they were going to commit the effigy to the flames, one of the company observed that one of Arnold's legs was wounded when he was fighting bravely for America, that this leg ought not to be burnt, but amputated; in which the whole company agreed, and this leg was taken off and safely laid by.

November 3—At night the escort with the southern mail, who had put up at Col. Cooper's in Clark's Town, were attacked by a gang of villains who fired into the house and killed the Sergeant dead on the spot and wounded Capt. Champion of Connecticut, who had put up at the same house, in the shoulder; the Corporal of the escort behaved well, threw the mail behind a bed, and defended the house the assailants made off. The same day the foragers returned from below the lines with a large quantity of forage, and two prisoners, taken near Col. Phillips's.

November 5—A Hessian Jäger came in with his horse and equipments complete.

November 7—Two deserters came in from New York; they left the city the evening before—they were very intelligent; by them it was learnt that the British fleet returned to Sandy Hook the preceding Saturday was a week—that no action happened while they were at sea—that the troops were disembarked from the men-of-war, but remained on board the transports—that Gen. Sir Henry Clinton landed on Long Island and came across to the city.

November 8—Intelligence was received from the northward that the enemy did not establish a post at Ticonderoga, but were returning towards Canada; and the militia which had been called out were dismissed. The British at New York at this time, wished to strike some of the posts in the Highlands, but did not attempt any of them. The army was short of flour, but amply supplied with meat.

About this time our General received a letter from Gen. Washington, dated at York (Virginia) October 27, 1781, in which, among other things, the Commander in Chief observes: "There will be no occasion for forwarding on any more beef cattle from the northward for this army. Should there be a greater quantity of cattle sent from the New England States than the daily consumption of your army shall require, I would wish the surplus might be salted (if practicable) at some convenient place on the North River; otherwise, it might be necessary for you to give orders to the Agents and Commissaries to prevent their sending more cattle than you shall have occasion for." This was the good fruit of the systematic arrangement.

November 12—Gen. Glover, with his own brigade, marched for the lines in order to cover a grand forage.

November 13—Lt. De Forest[49] of the Connecticut line, with 25 Continental soldiers, and Capt. Lockwood, with 15 volunteers, including Lieutenants Hull[50] and Mead,[51] of the Connecticut State troops, took an armed slope of 10 carriage-guns with 25 soldiers on board. Lt. De Forest and those with him, behaved with great address and gallantry.

November 16—Brig. Gen. Glover returned from the grand forage; during the forage one of the enemy was killed and two taken prisoners; a quantity of corn, hay, etc. and about 40 swine, were brought off.

November 17—The 3rd Massachusets brigade moved to their ground of cantonment, south of the north redoubt, where they built their huts.

November 19—Admiral Digby remained at New York with seven sail of the line, five of 74 and two of 64 guns, two fifties, two frigates, one 20 gun ship, and two sloops of war; the remainder of the British fleet under the command of Admiral Graves, sailed from Sandy Hook the preceding Monday for the West Indies; a great number of shipping, perhaps 300 sail, were lying in New York harbor; the enemy and inhabitants appeared much dejected.

November 20—Col. Tupper, with the 10th Massachusetts regiment, a detachment of artillery, etc. arrived at West Point from Albany.

November 23—The Connecticut line marched to their cantonment back of Constitution Island, and the corps of artillery to West Point. The same day, Maj. Gen. Lord Stirling returned to the army from Albany.

November 24—Our General removed his quarters from the Continental Village to Robinson's Farm, for winter quarters. The army in want of flour and forage.

November 28—The 1st Massachusetts brigade moved to their cantonment back of West Point.

December 2—The militia which had been called out for three months, were returning home. They had served with much reputation, and done good service for their country.

December 4—Capt. Sacket[52] of the New York levies, near Harrison's Purchase, below the lines, having gone a small distance from his detachment on the morning of the 2nd, was taken prisoner by a party of the enemy. The enemy afterwards attacked Lt. Mosher,[53] to whom the command of the detachment fell; Lt. Mosher and the detachment behaved with great bravery, repulsed the enemy, killed one of them and two horses and wounded eight of the enemy; among them a Capt. Kipp,[54] said mortally; Colonel Holmes and Capt. Kipp had their horses killed under them. The levies had not a man killed or wounded.

The army were now busily employed in building their huts, which they prosecuted with great expedition, and soon rendered them comfortable as to shelter; but many of the troops were in a most naked and distressed condition as to clothing; but relief was daily arriving from the eastward.

December 8—The officers and soldiers who had been in Virginia were now returning to the army. Some of the soldiers, brought the small-pox with them.

December 12—The river was frozen down to Fishkill Landing. The 13th was a general Thanksgiving Day; a large company of the officers of the army dined with our General.

December 24—The Clothier-General was issuing the new clothing to the regimental Paymasters—a most necessary piece of business. Congress about this time, by resolutions which they passed, called upon the Legislatures of the respective States to complete their quotas of the army by the first of March ensuing, Congress being determined to push the late successes until the enemy were driven from America. The preceding day, viz. the 23rd, Capt. Williams[55] of the New York levies (stationed on the lines) with 25 volunteer horse, made an excursion to Morrisania, where they took and brought off prisoners, one Captain, one Lieutenant, and seven privates of Delancey's corps, with out the loss of a man. Capt. Williams conducted this enterprise with address and gallantry. Capt. Pritchard moved down with a detachment of Continental troops to cover the horse, if necessary, but the enemy did not come out.

December 26—Five deserters came in from Arnold's corps, with their horses, etc. complete; they were a patrol to a foraging party near Col. Phillips's. An embarkation of troops was taking place at New York for Charleston and Savannah; Gen. Leslie having written, that without a reinforcement he could not maintain his posts.

December 27—Free Masons celebrated the feast of St. John, etc.

December 31—The river was a little freed of the ice. Thus closed the year 1781, a year which will be memorable in the annals of the United States of America for the capture of Earl Cornwallis and his army for several well-fought battles in the south by General Greene and the British, in that quarter for the Count de Grasse's having visited our coast with the most formidable fleet ever before in these seas and for general successes on the American arms, under the smiles of Divine Providence in every quarter. May the New Year be rendered more auspicious in the completion of the American warfare, and in the establishment of the United States in the full acknowledgment of independence, peace and happiness.

CHAPTER 8

1782

January 1—A new mode of supplying the army by contract commenced under the conduct of Comfort Sands & Co., contractors.

January 7—Nine soldiers had then died of the small-pox; it was spreading, and it was determined to inoculate such as had not had the distemper, which took place in the Connecticut line on the 11th.

January 11—Capt. Honeywell[1] of New York, with a number of volunteer horse, covered by Maj. Trescott with a detachment of Continental troops, made an excursion to Morrisania, took and brought off prisoners Capt. Totten and three privates of Delancey's corps; it was the intent to have captured the Colonel, but he was absent from his quarters. A party of the enemy's horse collected and pursued Capt. Honeywell but they were checked by Major Trescott, and no injury was sustained.

January 14—It was learnt that on the 4th, a fleet of 25 sail of victuallers arrived at New York from Cork under convoy of the *Quebec* frigate; ten sail more were left at Charleston, where the whole touched.

January 16—The river was hard frozen again, and was passable on the ice from West Point to Constitution Island. The same day a sergeant and four dragoons came in from Arnold's corps, with six horses and furniture complete. The sixth dragoon would not come off, on which the others took from him his horse, cloak, sword, etc. They deserted from a foraging party and reported that a great part of the corps would desert when the opportunity offered.

January 17—Three dragoons came in from Arnold's corps with their horses, etc. complete, and one prisoner taken by our guides near Morrisania, was sent up.

January 18—Lt. Hiwell,[2] crossing the river on the ice, fell through, but fortunately got out again.

January 19—It was communicated that about the month of the preceding October, one was offered two thousand guineas to take Gen. Washington, and five hundred to take and bring in Gov. Reed.

January 20—News was received that the Marquis de Bouillé,[3] Governor of Martinique, had recaptured the Island of St. Eustatia, where he made prisoners of 670 men. The Count de Grasse, with 31 sail of the line, had arrived at Martinique before the 6th of December. The British fleet from New York had arrived at Barbados.

January 24—Some uneasiness having taken place on account of the issues of provisions under the contract, the officers commanding brigades were ordered, on the part of the army, to endeavor an adjustment with the contractors, who went for that purpose.

January 28—A man and his horse fell through the ice near West Point; several soldiers lent their assistance, but in vain both were drowned.

January 31—The whole of the troops who had not before had the small-pox, were then under the operation of inoculation—their number near 2000; several had died, but in general it was very favorable.

February 8—News was received that the Duke de Lauzun, who carried to France the news of the capture of Earl Cornwallis, arrived in France in 23 days after he left the Chesapeake; that there were great rejoicings in France on the occasion, and also for the birth of a Dauphin.[4]

February 10—The river had been passable on the ice for several days at King's Ferry. On the preceding Thursday, about 50 of Delancey's horse came out within four miles of Chappaqua, where they halted. On the 8th, they moved towards North Castle, but turned off by Wright's Mills; from thence to King Street, and towards Horseneck; they fell in with a small guard of Gen. Waterbury's—killed one and made four prisoners; they also took two or three inhabitants, plundered two houses, and returned. About this time, a detachment from the Jersey line made an attempt on the refugee post at Bergen, but were repulsed.

February 17—The King of England's speech to his Parliament came to hand; this speech was more moderate than any before had been, and an inclination to pacification was discernible.

February 20—Two deserters came in from Arnold's corps and also two Hessians; ten had come in during the course of two or three days.

February 21—The enemy were out towards Bedford. About this time, nine or ten thousand stand of arms and a large quantity of powder brought from France by Col. Laurens, were brought from Boston to Fishkill.

February 23—A detachment, consisting of 150 men, properly officered, under the command of Maj. Maxwell, marched for Stamford to cover that part of the country.

February 27—Col. Sumner arrived from Massachusetts; he brought on about 2000 suits of clothes for the army. The day before, a Mr. Dyckman,[5] one of our guides on the lines, with 13 volunteer horsemen, made an excursion to Morrisania, took five prisoners of Delancey's corps and five horses; on their return they were pursued by a party of the enemy's horse, who coming rather too near, the brave volunteers faced about, charged vigorously, and took one man prisoner with his horse, and put the rest to flight. The enemy again appeared in some force at a distance, but dared not to renew the attack. About this time, a fleet of transports sailed from New York to the southward; it was conjectured to bring away troops.

March 3—The river was so freed of ice that the General's barge crossed to West Point. Two prisoners of war taken from Delancey's corps were sent up. Accounts from Massachusetts announced an uneasiness among the people respecting the burden of taxes, and that there had been Conventions in the counties of Hampshire and Berkshire.

March 4—Capt. Honeywell, with a body of volunteer horse, backed by the infantry under the command of Maj. Woodbridge, made an excursion to Morrisania. The horse proceeded down between the British fort No. 8 and the cantonment of Delancey's corps, and having turned the cantonments between day-break and sunrise, they entered pell-mell. The enemy were completely surprised and fled in every direction; some were cut down on the spot, others so badly wounded as not to be able to be removed. Some of the enemy availed themselves of positions where the horse could not assail them, from whence they began to fire on the horse; this occasioned the firing of the alarm guns at No. 8. The horse having nearly accomplished their design, moved off, taking the East Chester road, on which Maj. Woodbridge had posted the infantry in ambuscade. Capt. Honeywell had brought off one Subaltern and 20 men prisoners, and 20 horses. The enemy in the vicinity collected a number of horse, backed by light infantry, and pursued Capt. Honeywell until he came to Maj. Woodbridge. The enemy were drawn into the ambuscade, who made one or two discharges on them, on which they broke and retired, but soon returned to the charge; skirmishing ensued, and continued to a considerable distance. Of the Americans, two privates were killed—Mr. Dyckman, one of the guides, a brave and active man, mortally wounded, and three privates slightly wounded.

The enemy at New York were now contemplating means for their own defense against the next campaign, and it was determined to open a canal and strong lines from the Hudson to the East River, at some distance from the city. The canal was to be deep and wide; 2000 men were employed on the works on one day, 300 of whom were inhabitants. The same number were to be furnished daily. These preparations were a defensive shield for the time of approaching negotiation, for, from the debates and speeches in the British Parliament, the olive-branch was evidently putting forth its buds.

Maj. Gen. Benjamin Lincoln.

March 10—Two soldiers belonging to the 6th Massachusetts regiment, having some words respecting their mess, one of them struck the other with his fist a blow on the head and killed him dead on the spot. About the same time, an inhabitant, apprehending that some soldiers were about to rob his henroost, discharged a musket out of a window, by which a soldier was killed.

March 13—Maj. Gen. Lincoln, Secretary at War, arrived at the army on his way to Philadelphia. At this time it was learnt that on the 13th of the preceding December there were strong debates in the British House of Commons respecting the carrying on of the war in America. When Sir James Lowther[6] made a motion that the mode which had been pursued was ineffectual, many Members spoke for and against the motion; when it was put, there was against the motion, 220; for it, 179; majority, 41.

March 14—Lt. Harris, with six men belonging to Capt. Vermilyea's[7] company of militia, having obtained intelligence of a party of Delancey's corps being at a house near Mile-Square, had the address to surprise the whole party, consisting of 12, killed one and made four prisoners.

March 21—A duel[8] was fought at West Point between Capt. _____ and Lieut. _____, when the former was killed and the latter wounded: they fought with pistols, at about ten feet distance. The Lieutenant absconded.

March 25—News was received that the islands of St. Christopher's and Nevis surrendered to the arms of His Most Christian Majesty on the 12th of the preceding February. The terms granted by the French commandants were truly noble, and reflect the highest honor on them.

March 26—About this time, putrid fevers were prevalent among the American troops, and in some instances proved mortal. About this time an embarkation of about 800 troops took place at New York; their destination not publicly known.

March 28—The whole army were ordered to be in readiness for instant action, or to march to such place or places as might stand in need of aid. An additional company was ordered to the lines, and another to Smith's Clove, for the safety of the Commander in Chief, who was on his way from Philadelphia to Newburgh, and was to pass the Clove on the succeeding Saturday or Sunday. News was received that the citizens of London and Westminister had petitioned the King, in the strongest terms, to relinquish the American war.

March 29—Five deserters came in from Arnold's corps with their arms, etc. complete. The enemy were busily employed on their canal and lines: a number of heavy cannon had been put on board ship at New York. About this time the British cruisers were but too successful against the Americans at sea. A ship of 18 guns had, for some time, taken a station off Spuyten Duyvil Creek.

March 31—His Excellency Gen. Washington arrived at Newburgh; he had been absent from the main army since the 19th of the preceding August, having spent the winter at Philadelphia after the capture of Earl Cornwallis.

April 2—Our General went up to Newburgh to pay his respects to the Commander in Chief, where he dined, and returned at evening; Gen. Washington established his quarters at Newburgh. On the night of the 1st, a party of Capt. Pray's men, from the water-guard, being on shore, on the east side of the Hudson, fell in with a party of our own militia, who, in the dark, attacked each other; four of the latter were wounded, and eleven (being the whole of the party) were taken prisoners before the mistake was discovered. An express, on his way from St. John's to New York, with several letters, one in cipher, had been taken.

April 4—The following extract was published in the general orders:

HEADQUARTERS, NEWBURGH, April 4th, 1782

The Commander in Chief having returned and resumed the command of the main army, presents his thanks to Maj. Gen. Heath and the troops which have been employed under his orders, for having preserved the important posts committed to his charge and covered the country so successfully against the depredations of the enemy during the absence of the General.

April 6—The Commander in Chief visited West Point, and reviewed the first Massachusetts brigade. On his arrival at the Point, he was saluted by the discharge of 13 cannon.

April 8—Four deserters came in, three from the 42nd British regiment, and a seaman from the ship *Venger*; this ship stationed in the North River, mounted 24 guns, and had two gun-boats with her. The enemy continued at work on their canal and lines, which they were making very strong. An incredible number of fascines had been made during winter on Long Island and Staten Island, strongly bound with eight bands; these were placed in the face of the work with five pickets in each fascine.

April 9—The Commander in Chief reviewed the 3rd Massachusetts brigade and 10th regiment, and dined with our General. The same day, two deserters came in from the ship in the river. The same night, an armed brig, and three boats, full of men, came up the Hudson, and came to anchor a little above the place where our guard-boats rendezvous at Nyack; they were early discovered and the alarm given. The soldiers landed at Haverstraw about one o'clock on the morning of the 10th and took three or four militiamen. It was supposed that their design was to have taken our whale-boats; they were refugees and sailors. Not knowing but that this might have been a feint to an attack on the lines, 200 men were detached for their support, if necessary. The enemy returned down the river in the afternoon, having, in addition to the militia above mentioned, taken two of Capt. Pray's men who were out burning coal, and two others who were over at Tarrytown fishing, and destroyed some seines. It was learnt from the northward that the enemy were repairing and building boats at St. John's, and bringing up provisions to that place; this rendered it probable that the enemy would be troublesome in that quarter the ensuing campaign. Several parties of Indians had been skulking about on the Mohawk River, had killed a soldier and a lad, and taken a soldier prisoner, and burnt a building.

April 14—Three deserters came in from Robinson's corps; they made their escape from Long Island by crossing the Sound in a canoe. They reported that the enemy were under great apprehensions of an attack, and were making every preparation for defense; that 62,000 fascines had been made on Long Island during the winter and spring. A fleet of transports had arrived at New York from Charleston. Lines were traced out on Long Island from the great fort to the marsh, near McGowan's mill dam.

April 18—It was learnt that the enemy had laid an embargo on the shipping at New York. News was received that Holland had formed an alliance with France, and that a Spanish fleet had arrived in the West Indies.

April 19—The General Officers, and officers commanding brigades and regiments, met at our General's quarters, in consequence of orders from the Commander in Chief, to give an opinion what measures ought to be adopted in consequence of the horrid and brutal murder of a Capt. Huddy,[9] who had commanded a block-house at Tom's River, in the Jersies, and had been taken prisoner by the enemy and carried to New York, where he was closely confined, under guard, and in the sugar-house, and on board a vessel, in irons and then carried over to Bergen, in the Jersies, and hanged by the refugees, a Capt. Lippincott[10] directing the execution. This was done under the pretense that Capt. Huddy had been concerned in the death of one Philip White, although White was killed by the guard, from whom he endeavored to make his escape, and Capt. Huddy was at the same time a prisoner with the enemy. Huddy was left hanging on a tree with the following label fastened on his breast: "Up goes Huddy for Philip White."

This wanton and cruel act so exasperated the inhabitants of New Jersey, that they drew up a petition, signed by a vast number of respectable citizens, claiming of Gen. Washington, as the Military Guardian of their country, the obtainment of justice for this horrid act, or *retaliation* in case justice was refused. Indeed, painful as the idea of retaliation must be to the feelings of humanity, it seemed now to be the only preventative of more horrid murders. Gen. Washington with his wonted prudence and talent for investigation, free of all bias, ordered the officers to assemble as before mentioned, and directed our General to state to them the occasion of their being convened, and then the following questions: "Shall there be retaliation for the murder of Capt. Huddy? On whom shall it be inflicted? And how shall the victim be designated?" The officers assembled were forbidden to converse on the questions submitted to them, each one was to write his own opinion, seal it up, and address it to the Commander in Chief. By this mode of procedure, all the influence which some officers might have on others was prevented, and the spontaneous feelings of every individual officer collected. Col. Humphreys[11] and Col. Trumbull of the General's family, attended the Council, and every direction of the Commander in Chief was most strictly observed. It was found that the officers were unanimous in their opinion that retaliation ought to take place; that it should be inflicted on an officer of equal rank, viz. a Captain; not under Convention or capitulation, but one who had surrendered at discretion; and that in designating such a one, it should be done by lot.

The Commander in Chief was pleased to approve of the opinion of the officers, and wrote to the British commander demanding justice for the wanton murder of Capt. Huddy, informing the British General at the same time that if justice was not obtained retaliation would most assuredly take place. At the same time arrangements were put in train for retaliation; the names of several British officers of equal rank and circumstances were thrown together, and a fair and impartial lot was drawn, when young Capt. Asgill[12] was taken; he was of a noble family, his father was dead, and on him were the fond hopes of his mother, Lady Asgill, placed. Indeed, a more affecting scene than this can scarcely open; an innocent young man doomed to suffer for the wanton offence of another, which deed, no doubt, his soul despised; and the tender breast of a mother rent in twain on the fate of her darling son. Nor were the feelings of the great Washington unmoved on this occasion; they were too manifest not to be observed, and could only be curbed by the invariable resolution in every exigence, to exhibit the administrator of justice. It was months before this tragic business closed, and that the reader may have the whole narrative together, it will be carried forward to such periods as will render a return back to the proper chain of events necessary.

Gen. Sir Guy Carleton, who had come into the command in chief at New York, wrote to Gen. Washington, assuring him of the fullest satisfaction. Sir Guy ordered a Court-Martial for the trial of Capt. Lippincott, who was charged with the murder of Capt. Huddy. The Court-Martial had set and given in their proceedings to Gen. Carleton, who wrote a letter to Gen. Washington requesting a passport for Chief Justice Smith to repair to the headquarters of the American army, in order to lay before the Commander in Chief the proceedings of the Court-Martial, with other documents which he (Sir Guy) had no doubt would give full satisfaction. Upon Gen. Washington's receiving the letter from Sir Guy Carleton, he informed our General that he should not consent to, or give a passport to Mr. Chief Justice Smith, to come up with the proceedings of the Court-Martial on Lippincott; but that he would send him (Gen. Heath) down to Col. Phillips's, near King's Bridge, to meet such officer of equal rank as Sir Guy Carleton might think proper to send out to meet him, with the proceedings of the Court-Martial, etc.; and on the 30th of July the Commander in Chief wrote to our General as follows:

HEADQUARTERS, 30th July, 1782

DEAR SIR,

For your information and that you may know the object of your mission, I enclose to you a transcript of my letter to Sir Guy Carleton, which is herewith committed to your care to be forwarded as soon as possible. Before the time of your going to Phillips's house, I shall have the pleasure of seeing you, or conveying to you in writing my sentiments more fully on the subject of your meeting.

With great regard, etc.
(Signed) G. WASHINGTON

Maj. Gen. HEATH.

Copy

HEADQUARTERS, July 31st, 1782

Sir,

In reply to your letter of the 25th, I have to inform your Excellency that Maj. Gen. Heath, second in command, with two Aides-de-Camp, will have the honor of meeting an officer of equal rank of your Excellency's appointment, at the house of Mr. Phillips, on the 5th day of August next. At that time Gen. Heath will receive from your officer the proceedings of the Court-Martial on Capt. Lippincott, for the murder of Capt. Huddy, together with such other documents as you shall think proper to communicate. The assurance which your Excellency has given me of the fullest satisfaction in this matter, is as pleasing as it is interesting.

Your Excellency's propositions, contained in your letter of the 7th, have been communicated to Congress, and are now under the consideration of that honorable body; as soon as I am favored with their determination, your Excellency may be assured I will do myself the honor to communicate it.

I have the honor, etc.
(Signed) G. WASHINGTON.

SIR GUY CARLETON.

Maj. Gen. Sir Guy Carleton, KB.

By his Excellency George Washington, Esq., General and Commander in Chief of the forces of the United States of America:

To Maj. Gen. HEATH.

SIR,

His Excellency Sir Guy Carleton, having requested a passport for Chief Justice Smith, to repair to the headquarters of the American army, in order to lay before me the proceedings of a Court-Martial, on the trial of Capt. Lippincott for the murder of Capt. Huddy, with other documents and explanations, which lie says, "he has no doubt will give full satisfaction:

I do, therefore, from an earnest desire to proceed with candor and deliberate justice, appoint you to meet an officer of equal rank, at the house of Col. Phillips, on Monday the 5th instant, or at any other time or place which you may think more convenient, for the purpose of receiving the proceedings and documents above mentioned, with such explanations in writing as he may think proper to communicate. The papers you shall receive, you will transmit to me as soon as your business is concluded, together with a report of your proceedings therein.

Given at head-quarters, this 3rd day of August, 1782.

(Signed) G. WASHINGTON.

By His Excellency's command.

The following instructions accompanied the foregoing commission:

To Maj. Gen. HEATH,

SIR,

Having desired you to meet an officer from Sir Guy Carleton for the purpose mentioned in your appointment and authority, you will proceed to execute said business, in the course of which you may inform the officer you meet that, as I have no connection with, or control over any person in the line in which Mr. Smith walks; as the question before us is in my opinion purely of a military nature, and reducible to this single point, whether the perpetrator of the wanton and cruel murder of Huddy is to be given up, or a British officer to suffer in his place, that I could see no propriety or necessity in an interview with the Chief Justice.

If you should find that the design of Sir Guy Carleton is to procrastinate this business, to envelope it in as much intricacy and difficulty as possible, or that he means to justify it by recrimination and law cases, thereby attempting to avert our purposes of retaliation, you may assure him (unless you shall judge it expedient to leave me more at liberty) if not explicitly, at least by strong insinuation, that he will miss his aim; and that my deliberate and dispassionate proceedings in this case are intended to give him, as he now has had, full time to determine whether the guilty person or an innocent officer shall be made the subject of retaliation.

You will be particularly cautious, that whatever passes in the conference you are to have, which is to be considered as official, be committed to writing, that no omissions or misconceptions may be plead hereafter; and you will inform the officer in explicit terms, if you find the matter is not likely to end as justice dictates and we could wish, that all oral conversation will be excluded from the official report of these proceedings now, or any share in the account of them hereafter, or the recital of them will be considered as unfair, and an evident departure from that line of rectitude which we wished to pursue, for an unbiased world to judge by.

If, notwithstanding my letter to Sir Guy Carleton, requesting his appointment of an officer of your rank to meet you on this business, he should send Mr. Chief Justice Smith, you may, at your discretion, either receive the proceedings of the Court, and such other documents as he is merely the bearer of, without going into any explanation with this gentleman, or refuse the whole, as the circumstances of the moment shall dictate to you. Or if this gentleman should be an attendant on the officer aforementioned, you may refuse to admit him at your conference. In the first case you may either return with the proceedings, etc. or you may write to Sir Guy Carleton that you will wait a given time for an officer, agreeable to the purport of my letter to him of the 30th of last month.

Given at headquarters, Newburgh, August 3rd, 1782.

(Signed) G. WASHINGTON.

In the afternoon of the same day, our General received the following letter from the Commander in Chief:

HEADQUARTERS, August 3rd, 1782

DEAR SIR,

   By the contents of Sir Guy Carleton's letter, which came enclosed in yours of this day, I find it is unnecessary for you to proceed to Phillips's house. Disappointed in not obtaining a passport for Mr. Chief Justice Smith to come out, he will not, he says, trouble an officer of your rank to be the bearer of a bundle of papers only; but adds, they shall be sent out in the ordinary course of conveyance. Your letter to Col. Trumbull, covering the new adopted system of issues, etc. is received.

(Signed) G. WASHINGTON.

Maj. Gen. HEATH.

   Not long after, the proceedings of the Court-Martial on Capt. Lippincott for the murder of Capt. Huddy were sent out; Lippincott was acquitted by the Court, and it appeared that the British Commanders in Chief, both Sir Henry Clinton and Sir Guy Carleton, disapproved the act. It seemed that a kind of Board of Directors who had a subordinate direction of the refugee operations, were somehow concerned in this business, and that *argument* and some *artifice* were necessary to smooth it over. However, Gen. Washington, painful as his task was, was not to be diverted from justice or retaliation; but execution was suspended. Lady Asgill, learning the unhappy situation of her darling son, with much policy, and equal success, applied to the Count de Vergennes,[13] then Prime Minister of France, who spread the matter before the King and Queen: indeed, it was a subject that needed no extra coloring to fix it on the mind of humanity. The King and Queen listened to the request, and Congress was addressed in a representation, that the French, as well as American arms, were victorious at York, and that the former seemed to have some share in the prisoners; and hinted that it would be pleasing to the French Court if young Asgill was pardoned—which Congress complied with; and although reparation for the wanton murder of Capt. Huddy was not fully obtained, yet it is highly probable, that the firm and determined conduct of Gen. Washington on the occasion put a final stop to any further repetition of the kind.

   Sir Guy Carleton was probably the greatest General which the British had in America during the war, and it was fortunate for the Americans that he was so long kept within the limits of Canada. In him were combined many of those great qualifications which form the General. When Sir Guy visited the American prisoners in confinement in Canada, he addressed them with all the tenderness of a father; he observed to the young prisoners that he did not blame them, it was the fault of the designing men of their country that had led them into difficulty; that he would not hold them in confinement, but would send them home to their fathers and friends.

See here the soothing art that could not fail to cool the ardor of the young warrior in the cause of his country.

To Gen. Waterbury of Connecticut, when he showed him his commission, Sir Guy observed, "Your commission is from the proper authority of your Colony (Connecticut had not changed her form of government); you are no rebel, Sir; you shall go home to your family." Soon after Sir Guy Carleton came into the command at New York, a Connecticut soldier, who had been a prisoner, came out to our army, and requested a pass to go home, informing that he had given a parole to Sir Guy not to serve again during the war; but he was ordered to join his regiment, which disappointed the soldier exceedingly. Gen. Washington ordered the Commissary of Prisoners to credit the British for one man exchanged; and informed Sir Guy that this practice would not be allowed. Many soldiers were at that time very uneasy in the American army—had a conduct of this sort been allowed, many soldiers on the outposts and otherwise, might have gone to the enemy, have pretended they were taken, and have come out under parole and have gone home, to the unspeakable injury of the army, but it was nipped in the bud—only one other having come out in the same way before it was put a stop to. We now return to take up the chain of events from which we digressed.

April 20—Two prisoners of war, taken near King Street, were sent up by Major Oliver.[14]

April 21—A Sergeant-Major deserted and came out; he reported that an enterprise was contemplating at New York and a number of large boats were collecting at Turtle Bay.

April 24—Two deserters came in from the *Adamant* man-of-war, of 50 guns, which lay in the East River, against New York. Admiral Digby's flag was then hoisted on board the *Centurion*. The seamen on board the ships very sickly. The latter end of April, the *Duke of Cumberland* packet, Capt. Dashwood, arrived at New York, in six weeks from England with the March mail, by which it was learnt that the debates in the British Parliament on the American war, grew more and more interesting; that a motion had been made by Gen. Conway, for bringing in a bill, empowering the King to make peace with America. The beginning of May, the British cruisers were very successful against the Americans; eleven sail of vessels from Philadelphia were taken and carried into New York with near 9000 barrels of flour.

May 4—This evening exhibited the most extraordinary *aurora borealis* ever before seen by those who observed it.

May 5—It was learnt that the merchants of Edinburgh at a meeting on the 7th of the preceding January, declared and published their sentiments and wishes for peace with America and a renewal of friendship. It was also further learnt that it was the prevailing sense of the British House of Commons, as a first step to an accommodation with America, to change the mode of carrying on the war, and to act only on the defensive, on the Continent; and that the person who should advise to offensive operations against the Americans, should be considered as an enemy to the King and nation. At the same time, France and Holland appeared to be making great preparations for a vigorous campaign.

May 6—Symptoms of a dangerous mutiny were discovered in the Connecticut line; it had been conducted with so much address as to have been nearly matured before it was divulged. Under the pressure of real or supposed grievances, the soldiers of the whole line had determined at reveille the next morning to have marched from their cantonment with arms, etc. complete, for Fishkill, where they were to take a number of field- pieces and such ammunition and provisions as might be necessary and then proceed to Hartford and there demand of their new General Assembly that justice which they supposed was their due. Just as the officers were going to bed, a faithful soldier who was waiter to an officer came to his room, and told the officer that he could not go to rest until he divulged to him an event which would assuredly take place the next morning at break of day; and that everything was then in readiness for it—and laid open the whole secret. The matter was immediately communicated to the principal officers of the line, and several soldiers were seized and confined, and one suffered. The whole design was frustrated. Mutiny is a most horrid offence in an army, which, without strict order and discipline, is but a rope of sand. On the other hand, human nature can bear but to a certain degree, and no further; hence any trial of human nature, beyond such a degree, is impolitic, and unjustifiable. Of this line, it may with strict justice be said, that their whole conduct through the war was highly meritorious.

May 7—A stop was put to the inoculation with the smallpox.

May 8—A prisoner was sent up, and a deserter came in.

May 9—News was received that there had been a total change of the British Ministry, and that Fort St. Philip and the whole island of Minorca surrendered to the Spaniards on the 6th of the preceding February, by capitulation.

May 15—Eleven trusty Sergeants were sent to Massachusetts to march on the recruits to the army from that State.

May 17—Two deserters came in, who reported that a packet had arrived at New York from England.

May 24—Near 100 old and decrepit soldiers were collected from the different regiments, and many of them discharged. About this time a packet arrived at Boston in 25 days' passage from France; the letters were immediately forwarded to Congress.

May 26—The 1st Massachusetts brigade was ordered to move out of its cantonment and encamp near the German Huts. The United States of Holland acknowledged the independence of the United States of America, the 28th of the preceding March. There was a great talk of peace in New York. In the American army great preparations for some time had been making to celebrate the birth of the Dauphin of France. At least 1000 men a day were employed, under the direction of the engineers and other artists, in constructing a most superb arbor, decorated with every emblem and device descriptive of the occasion, and the alliance between France and America, which ingenuity could invent; and perhaps for anything of the kind, constructed in the field, was never surpassed.

May 31—The birth of the Dauphin of France was celebrated by the American army. An elegant dinner was provided by order of the Commander in Chief, of which the officers of the army and a great number of ladies and gentlemen, invited from the adjacent country, partook. Thirteen toasts were drunk, announced by the discharge of cannon. At evening there was a grand *feu-de-joy*, opened by the discharge of 13 cannon, three times repeated. The *feu-de-joy*, being fired in the dusk, had a pleasing appearance to the eye, as well as the ear, and was so ordered for that purpose. The army was not formed in line, but each brigade was drawn up in front of its own cantonment, or camp, on both sides of the river, and thus were in a circle of several miles circumference, in the center of which the Commander in Chief and the spectators were placed. After the *feu-de-joy* there was an exhibition of fire-works, etc.

June 2—Information was received that the Island of New Providence and its dependencies were taken by the Spaniards on the 11th of the preceding May. The garrison, which consisted of about 200 men, were sent to Europe. The new frigate *South Carolina*, built in Europe, arrived about this time in the Delaware; she was an exceeding fine ship, mounting 28 42-pounders on one deck, and 12 12-pounders on her quarter and fore-castle. She was commanded by Commodore Gillon.[15]

There had been a bloody engagement in the West Indies the 12th of the preceding April, between the Count de Grasse and Admiral Rodney; but all the accounts had been very vague. The British now published their account, and that they took from the French the *Ville de Paris*, of guns, and 1300 men; *Le Glorieux*, *Le Cesar*, and *Le Hector*, of 74 guns each; and *Le Ardent*, of 64 guns, and sunk one ship of the line. They acknowledged to have had 236 men killed, and 779 wounded; among whom were several officers. They also boasted of having obtained a very signal advantage in the European seas, over Admiral Kempenfelt.[16]

June 5—It was reported that a French fleet had been seen on the American coast. A fleet about this time sailed from New York eastward through the Sound, conjectured to be destined to Penobscot. The brigades of the American army daily maneuvered, and fired to great acceptation.

June 14—The British had been removing a number of heavy cannon and ordnance stores from their works at the north end of New York island, and placing light pieces in the room of them. A number of deserters daily came in.

June 24—The Commander in Chief sent the following letter to our General:

HEADQUARTERS, NEWBURGH, June 24th, 1782

DEAR SIR,

I am at this moment setting out for Albany and shall be absent a few days. I give you this information for the regulation of your own conduct; and request, in the meantime, you will give me any intelligence you may receive which you shall deem of sufficient consequence for communication by express.

(Signed) G. WASHINGTON.

Maj. Gen. HEATH.

June 26—It was learnt from Canada, that several armed vessels and a number of batteaux had come up Lake Champlain; there were probably about 300 men. A much larger force (report said 3000) was gone or going towards Lake Ontario, to establish a post at Oswego.

June 27—Another ship came up the North River and took a station near Spuyten Duyvil Creek.

July 2—The Commander in Chief returned from Albany.

July 4—The army fired a grand *feu-de-joy*, it being the anniversary of the declaration of American Independence.

July 11—At evening, the Commander in Chief wrote our General the following letter:

HEADQUARTERS, July 11th, 1782

DEAR SIR,

I have at this moment received a letter from Count de Rochambeau (by one of his Aides, in 5 days from Williamsburg) informing me that he is on his way to Philadelphia; that he will be there the 13th or 14th, and wishes for an interview with me; for this purpose I shall set out in the morning, very early, and have only to request your usual attention.

(Signed) G. WASHINGTON.

Maj. Gen. HEATH.

July 13—Two prisoners of war were sent up, and three German deserters came in, and the next day a dragoon with his horse, etc. complete. About this time the southern mail was taken between Philadelphia and Morristown.

July 18—It was learnt that on the 21st of the preceding May, Gen. Wayne obtained a considerable advantage over the enemy, with very little loss on his side, near Ogeechee, in Georgia; the enemy retired into Savannah. About this time, a Corporal and eight men deserted from our block-house at Dobbs' Ferry.

July 21—Three deserters came in. About this time a fleet of about 40 sail arrived at Sandy Hook under convoy of two frigates; they were supposed to be from Ireland.

July 22—Three deserters came in from the British grenadiers; two others deserted at the same time, but had not got in. The same day four deserters came in from the *Hussar* frigate, and the next day three soldiers. At this time the cow thieves and refugees were lurking in the Highlands, and detachments were sent out to patrol them.

July 26—Information was received that a party of the enemy to the number of 400 or 500 had appeared on the Mohawk River, advancing towards Herkimer. They killed a Continental soldier.

July 27—Gen. Washington returned to Newburgh from Philadelphia.

August 2—The British May and June packets had arrived at New York. Admiral Barrington had taken a French man-of-war of 74 guns, and several transports destined for the East Indies. The next day it was learnt that a French fleet, consisting of 12 or 13 sail of the line, and three frigates, had arrived in the Chesapeake. On the 29th ult. a bloody engagement took place off the Chesapeake between the French frigate *Amazone* of 36 guns, and the British frigate *Margaretta*, which terminated in favor of the latter.

August 6—Information was received that the British had evacuated Savannah in Georgia.

August 8—Four deserters came in from the enemy.

August 10—The prospect of an approaching peace brightened. Gen. Sir Guy Carleton and Admiral Digby informed Gen. Washington that Mr. Grenville had gone over to France on the negotiation for peace, and that the independence of America was to be acknowledged previous to, or as an opening of the negotiation. The refugees at New York were greatly alarmed at the prospect of peace. Sir Guy Carleton had notified the inhabitants to meet him; and, in Rivington's paper of the 7th, there appeared a proclamation advising the refugees to continue their loyalty and make themselves easy until the event of the negotiation was known.

August 12—A large stone magazine, capable of containing 1000 barrels of gun powder, was begun to be erected on Constitution Island; it was built upon the principles of Monsieur Vauban,[17] and under the direction of Maj. Villefranche.[18]

August 15—It was learnt that the French fleet, which had been at the Chesapeake, had arrived at Boston. The British troops evacuated Savannah the 11th of July, leaving the town and works uninjured. Previous to the evacuation, the refugees sent out to Gen. Wayne, to know if they might depend on protection in their persons and property; they were answered in the affirmative, until they were delivered over to the civil authority, who, they were informed, must decide on their case. When the British left the town near 200 of the inhabitants immediately entered the American service in the Georgia battalion.

August 19—Three prisoners of war were sent up; they were taken near East Chester. Several deserters came in about the same time.

August 22—The light infantry of the American army moved down, and encamped near Peek's Kill.

August 24—Maj. Gen. Knox was in the general orders appointed to the command of West Point. The artillery, sappers and miners, 10th Massachusetts regiment, and the corps of invalids, for the garrison. From the 25th to the 27th, inclusive, seven deserters came in; they reported that the sick of the British army were ordered to be sent on board the hospital ships, and not to the hospitals on shore. The heavy baggage was also ordered to be put on board the shipping; the officers to retain on shore no more than what was of absolute necessity.

August 29—An order of encampment and battle for the American army was published. The army was to encamp in one line with a reserve; the New Jersey and New York troops were to form a division under the command of Maj. Gen. St. Clair; the Connecticut troops, a division under Maj. Gen. McDougall; these two divisions to form the right wing, to be commanded by Maj. Gen. Gates; the New Hampshire brigade and the first brigade of Massachusetts, to form a division under the command of Maj. Gen. Lord Stirling; the 2nd and 3rd Massachusetts brigades, a division under the command of Maj. Gen. Howe; these two divisions forming the left wing under the command of Maj. Gen. Heath. The 2nd Connecticut and 3rd Massachusetts brigades to form the reserve; and when the ground would admit, form at 200 paces in the rear of the army. Maj. Gen. Lord Stirling was ordered to Albany to take command of that part of his division which was then in that quarter.

August 31—As many of the army as could be carried in the boats embarked at their respective brigade landings, and the whole of the boats being formed in order, fell down the river to Verplank's Point, where the troops disembarked and encamped. They made a most beautiful appearance when in the boats and in motion. The remainder of the army marched down by land.

September 1—Information was received that the British were on the eve of evacuating Charleston, South Carolina. The season was remarkably dry, both to the eastward and southward; it was with difficulty that the army could obtain a supply of water. About this time an embarkation of Hessian troops took place at New York.

September 7—There was a grand review and maneuver of the army, which gave great satisfaction. The July packet arrived at New York about this time; it appeared that the Marquess of Rockingham[19] had died, that Mr. Fox[20] and Lord Cavendish[21] had resigned their places, and that Lord Shelburne[22] was appointed one of the Secretaries of State.

September 14—The American army was under arms to receive Gen. Count de Rochambeau; after his reception, the army denied before him, and returned to their respective encampments. The French army was now arriving from the southward; they encamped to the south of Peek's Kill as they arrived.

September 16—The enemy made a grand forage near Valentine's Hill; Sir Guy Carleton was out in person, as was the young prince. The covering party, it was said, consisted of 5000 or 6000 men; a number deserted. The American army at this time was in great want of forage, occasioned by the dry season.

September 18—The last of the French army arrived.

September 20—Gen. Washington reviewed the French army; the troops made a fine appearance. A French frigate had been run on shore in the Delaware and taken by the enemy.

September 21—The American army maneuvered before the Commander in Chief, Gen. Rochambeau, and many other officers. The troops made a handsome appearance and maneuvered well.

September 22—It was learnt that the ships of war and transports at New York were watering and preparing for sea, and a number of regiments were under orders for embarkation. A little before this time, Congress had authorized and empowered Gen. Washington to adjust and finally settle the accounts subsisting between the United States and the British government respecting the support of the prisoners of war on both sides; and to provide, by a general cartel, for their greater comfort and exchange, under the great seal ratifying what he, the Commander in Chief of their army, should agree to. Gen. Washington transferred this power to Major-Generals Heath and Knox, whom he appointed Commissioners for the purpose, and instructed them not to proceed to business unless the British Commissioners were found to be equally empowered to bring the business to a final issue. The time and place of meeting were agreed to by the two Commanders in Chief, and was to be on the 25th of September, at Tappan.

September 24—The American Commissioners sent down two of their Aides-de-Camp to take up the necessary quarters, and make other preparations, and a company of light infantry was ordered to Tappan to furnish guards and sentinels.

September 25—The American Commissioners embarked on board their barges at King's Ferry and fell down the river to Tappan Landing, where they arrived about two o'clock, p.m. In less than half an hour the British Commissioners, in two vessels wearing flags, came up the river, and cast anchor off the Landing. The American Commissioners waited at the shore, and sent off their barges to aid in bringing the British Commissioners on shore, the river being at that time very rough; on their reaching shore, it was found that Lt. Gen. Campbell[23] and the Hon. Mr. Elliot,[24] who had been Lt. Governor of New York, were the Commissioners on the part of the British. The whole dined together, an elegant dinner having been ordered by the American Commissioners, and politeness and great sociability took place, and mutual arrangement for the daily support of the table was agreed on, as it was expected that the business would not be completed in less than three or four weeks, if the whole object was adjusted.

September 26—The Commissioners interchanged copies of their respective powers; these were to be considered until the next day, when answers were to be given in writing whether the powers were satisfactory on both sides. On examining the powers given to the British Commissioners, it appeared that their doings would not be conclusive until confirmed, and were very short of those held by the American Commissioners, whose agreement and signature were to be final.

September 27—The American Commissioners stated to the British Commissioners that the powers with which they were vested were inadequate to effect the expectations of the government of the United States, and that therefore the negotiation must be broken off. Of the great difference of the powers the British Commissioners were fully convinced. The American Commissioners thought it to be their duty when they gave their note of objections to the British delegated powers, to hand with it a very pointed protest, in behalf of the United States, against that conduct on the part of the British, which had so long delayed the settlement of the accounts for the support of the prisoners of war which were in the power of the United States. The Commissaries of Prisoners on both sides were present, to present and support their respective accounts; and a settlement would not only have been just, but also very interesting to the United States.

September 28—About 12 o'clock at noon the Commissioners parted with the same politeness and good humor with which they had met, and which had invariably continued during the time they were together. Our General sent orders to the commanding officer at Dobbs' Ferry to permit the British flags to pass down the river, and the American Commissioners returned to camp. The day before (the 27th) Gen. Washington, covered by the dragoons and light infantry, reconnoitered the grounds on the east side of the river, below the White Plains, and on the 29th, about noon, returned to camp.

October 3—It was learnt that the enemy had evacuated Lloyd's Neck, and destroyed their works at that place; their works at Bergen Point, in the Jersies, had been destroyed before that time.

October 5—Maj. Gen. Gates arrived at camp. At this time the horses of the army were suffering for want of forage.

October 6—Intelligence was received from the southward that on the 27th of August, Col. Laurens[25] was killed in a skirmish[26] with the enemy; the loss of this brave young officer was much regretted. The enemy, previous to their leaving Charleston, desired to purchase some provisions, and Gen. Leslie[27] had intimated to Gen. Greene that if this could not be permitted, he must take the provisions by force. The former being denied, the latter was attempted, and Col. Laurens fell; 24 or 25 others were killed, wounded, or taken prisoners, and one howitzer fell into the hands of the enemy.

October 7—Intelligence was received that Maj. Gen. Lee had died, a little before, at Philadelphia; he had just before sold his estate in Virginia for £6,100 sterling.

October 8—The weather beginning to grow cold and blowing, all the bowers (which were numerous and very salutary, during the hot season) were ordered to be pulled down and removed, to prevent accidents by fire, and to admit the benefit of the sun.

October 12—Intelligence was received from Europe by the arrival of a vessel in 34 days from Amsterdam, that the negotiation for peace was going on, and that additional Ministers and Envoys had gone to attend; that the combined fleets were all in port; that the siege of Gibraltar was continued, and that there had been an obstinate engagement in the East Indies, between the French and English fleets, in which both fleets had suffered much, but no ships were taken by either side. The insurrection in South America had been quelled.

October 15—A new contract for supplying the army with provisions, under Messrs. Wadsworth and Carter, took place.

October 16—A grand maneuver was performed by eight picked battalions, preparatory to a grand review, which was to be the next day. On the 19th (several preceding days having been stormy) the grand maneuver was performed by the eight picked battalions. The evolutions and firings were performed with regularity and exactness, much to the credit of the troops, and general satisfaction of the numerous spectators of the American and French armies.

October 20—The Secretary of War arrived at camp. The enemy were demolishing their works at No. 8, Morrisania. Intelligence was received that the besiegers of Gibraltar had made a nearer approach to the place, and were playing upon it with 200 pieces of artillery.

October 22—The first division of the French army moved eastward; they were to halt at Hartford, in Connecticut, where the whole were to rendezvous. The American army was put under orders to be ready to move at the shortest notice. The August packet from England arrived at New York the day before.

October 24—The whole American army maneuvered before the Hon. the Secretary of War. The Commander in Chief, in the orders of the day, expressed his own as well as the Secretary of War's fullest approbation.

October 26—At reveille, the left wing of the American army, under the command of our General, struck their tents and marched from the encampment as far as the wood near the north redoubt, in the Highlands, where they remained during the night; the day and night were rainy, and the troops had no covering but the heavens.

October 27—The troops crossed the Hudson in boats to West Point, the whole having crossed by half past 12 o'clock. In the afternoon, the troops took up their line of march, and ascended Butter Hill, a tedious march, and halted and passed the night on the northern descent of the hill, in the open field.

October 28—At seven o'clock a.m. the troops resumed their march from Butter Hill, and reached the ground on which they were to build their huts, in New Windsor, at about half past 10 o'clock, a.m. Upon this ground, and its vicinity, the army passed the ensuing winter. The cantonment, for its nature and kind, was regular and beautiful. Upon an eminence, the troops erected a building handsomely finished, with a spacious hall, sufficient to contain a brigade of troops on Lord's days, for public worship, with an orchestra at one end; the vault of the hall was arched; at each end of the hall were two rooms, conveniently situated for the issuing of the general orders, for the sitting of Boards of Officers, Courts Martial, etc. and an office and store for the Quartermaster and Commissary departments. On the top was a cupola and flag-staff, on which a flag was hoisted occasionally for signals, etc. In this cantonment the army spent the winter very comfortably, and it proved to be their last winter quarters.

October 30—It was learnt that on the 26th or 27th, fourteen British men-of-war of the line, one 44 gun ship, seven frigates, three large transports, and ten or twelve brigs and schooners sailed from New York, it was conjectured for the West Indies. They were observed to sail nearer under Long Island than usual, and came to near the place where Gen. Howe landed in the year 1776, where it was conjectured troops now embarked.

On the 7th of the preceding August, Congress passed resolutions directing the Secretary of War, on or before the 1st day of January following, to cause the non-commissioned officers and privates belonging to the lines of the several States, to be arranged in such a manner as to form complete regiments, agreeable to the acts of Congress of the 3rd and 21st of October, 1780, of regiments of not less than 500 rank and file, the junior regiments to be drafted to fill the senior regiments. The regiments so formed to be completely officered; the officers to agree and determine who should stay in service; or if this could not be affected by agreement, the juniors who were supernumerary of each grade were to retire, retaining their rank, and be entitled to the emoluments to which the officers were entitled who retired under the resolutions of the 3rd and 21st of October, 1780. In consequence of these resolutions, the Commander in Chief on this day (30th of Oct.) ordered the regiments of the Massachusetts line to be reduced to eight regiments of 500 rank and file each, or as near as could be to that number; and the Connecticut line to three regiments of similar strength, with three Field Officers, nine Captains, 19 Subalterns, one Surgeon, and one Mate each; and the regiments were formed accordingly.

November 1—It was learnt from Europe that the *Royal George*, a first-rate English man-of-war, of 110 guns, had been overset near Spithead by a sudden flaw of wind as she lay heeled to repair a leak on the other side; that she sunk in about eight minutes, having on board 12 or 1300 souls, about 900 of whom perished.

November 5—Our General left the army, and commenced his journey to the eastward, and arrived at his house in Roxbury on the 11th.

November 12—There was a transit of Mercury over the northwest limb of the sun's disk. The preceding week, one of the French men-of-war in Portsmouth harbor (N. H.) was struck by lightning and her foremast damaged. The French army were now on their march towards Boston. The *America*, a fine new 74 gun ship, the first of her rate built in the United States, and which had not long before been presented by Congress to his most Christian Majesty, was launched at Portsmouth on Tuesday, the 5th instant.

November 18—The field artillery of the French army reached Boston. The same day it was reported that the British troops had left Charleston, South Carolina.

November 21—The French discharged their artillery horses to the number of several hundreds.

November 27—Intelligence was received from Spain that the British had relieved Gibraltar and taken a Spanish 70 gun ship; several of their gun-boats were also destroyed. Had Spain long before this given over the siege of Gibraltar and employed her naval and land forces against the British in some quarter more vulnerable, solid advantage might have accrued, much money and many lives have been saved.

November 28—General Thanksgiving throughout the United States. The French fleet, under the command of the Marquis de Vaudreuil,[28] was at this time in Nantasket Road, except a few ships which were at Portsmouth, New Hampshire.

December 2—Maj. Gen. Baron Viomenil, commander of the French army (Count Rochambeau not coming this way) arrived at Boston from Providence. The troops were coming forward in divisions, at one day's march distance from each other. The first division arrived at Boston on the 5th in the morning.

December 6—In the morning, a ship lying in Boston harbor, laden with masts, destined to the West Indies, by some accident took fire and burnt down to the water's edge; the loss was very considerable. Advice was received from Europe that the Commissioners for settling peace were sitting at Paris; that matters were in forwardness;

several articles had been agreed to, etc. A reinforcement of French ships and troops had arrived in the West Indies from France. This day the last division of the French army reached Boston. These troops embarked on board the men-of-war, were much crowded, and in danger of growing sickly if continued long on board. About this time, the American officers had been very uneasy respecting their great arrears of pay, etc., and soon after addressed Congress on the subject, and appointed a committee from the army to present their petition and support it.

December 11—The town of Boston presented an address to the French General and officers.

December 22—The French fleet had fallen down below the Castle and were in readiness to proceed to sea. The markets were at this time extremely high; flour at eight and some at nine dollars per hundred; butter was sold at 2s. 4d. per pound, etc.

December 24—His most Christian Majesty's fleet, under the command of the Marquis de Vaudreuil, came to sail in King and Nantasket Roads, and went out to sea, having the army under the command of Gen. Viomenil on board. The fleet was first to stand to the northward until it was joined by the ships from Portsmouth; they were then to tack and stand to the southward, and take with them the *Fantasque*, armed en-flute from Rhode Island, and proceed to the West Indies.

December 25—It was learnt that near 3000 refugee inhabitants had gone from Charleston, South Carolina, to Jamaica, and about the same number to Augustine. The exorbitant prices of provisions fell immediately after the sailing of the French fleet.

December 26—Authentic accounts were received from Europe that Monsieur de la Perreuse, in the ship *Sceptre*, with two frigates, had returned to France from a successful enterprise against the British settlements in Hudson's Bay, having entirely destroyed the establishments and property of the English on that coast, estimating the damage at ten millions of livres.

December 31—Intelligence was received that the British homeward-bound West India fleet, on their way to England, met a violent storm, in which two 74 gunships, the *Ramillies* and the *Centaur* were said to have foundered; and that a number of the merchantmen had been taken by French and American cruisers and carried into France that four prizes had been taken by the American frigate *Alliance*, Capt. Barry, having 1200 hhds. of sugar and 400 hhds. of rum on board.

CHAPTER 9

1783

January 1—Intelligence was received that a terrible fire happened in the city of Constantinople in the month of the preceding August, in which a large part of the city was consumed and about 5000 lives lost. The fire was supposed to have been kindled by the malefactors in six different places.

January 4—Intelligence was received that Great Britain had acknowledged the independence of the United States, collectively and severally, and that a commission had been sent to Mr. Oswald,[1] one of the British Commissioners at Paris, to treat with the American Commissioners accordingly. Some further accounts of the terrible fire in Constantinople stated that near 200,000 inhabitants were burnt out of their habitations that the fire continued to burn sixty-two hours, and at some times with a front a mile in width.

January 8—Intelligence was received that the *Charleston* man-of-war, belonging to the State of South Carolina, a remarkable fine ship, commanded by Commodore Gillon, was taken by the British and carried into New York. In this month the inhabitants of Massachusetts, in their several religious societies, made voluntary contributions to the inhabitants of the town of Charlestown, to enable them to rebuild a meeting-house in the room of that which was destroyed by fire by the British troops during the Battle of Bunker Hill, on the 17th of June, 1775.

January 24—News was received that Maj. Gen. Lord Stirling had lately died at Albany; he was a brave officer in the American army.

January 25—Intelligence was received that the British troops left Charleston, in South Carolina, the 14th of the preceding December, and the Bar the 17th, and that Gen. Greene had taken possession of the city. It had been previously agreed that the Americans would not molest the British in quitting the place, and on their part they were not to injure the city.

Maj. Gen. William Alexander, Lord Stirling.

January 28—It was learnt that Gen. Clark[2] had been very successful against the Shawanese Indians, and had destroyed a number of their towns. From France it was learnt that though there was the greatest prospect of peace, yet all the powers at war were straining every nerve to be prepared for the opening of the next campaign. The damage sustained by the British homeward-bound West India fleet was greater than at first supposed; among the disabled ships was the *Ville de Paris* of 110 guns, and several others.

January 29—A prize ship, taken by Capt. Manley, arrived in Boston harbor, having about 1800 barrels of provisions on board.

February 5—News was received that the British had reinforced the garrison at Penobscot—that the whole garrison consisted of nearly 900 men—that a further reinforcement was expected—and that the British were endeavoring to extend their influence in that quarter.

February 6—Intelligence was received that a number of Loyalists had gone from New York to Nova Scotia; that Gov. Franklin,[3] in England, had written to his friends in New York that peace would certainly take place. About this time, the articles of a treaty of amity and commerce between the United States of America and Holland was published by Congress. In the month of the preceding December, Congress passed a spirited resolution respecting the conduct of the government of Vermont, and about this time the Council of Vermont presented to Congress a remonstrance against the resolution as interfering with their internal police. About this time Gen. Washington and Gen. Sir Guy Carleton had an interview on the lines of the two armies.

February 20—Intelligence was received that Don Solano,[4] with ten sail of Spanish men-of-war had arrived at the Havana, and that the Count D'Estaing had arrived with a French fleet at Martinique; that an attack on the island of Jamaica was soon expected to take place, in consequence of which seven British regiments were to go from New York to the West Indies. The refugees at New York were selling off their effects at auction, and preparing for a sudden removal to Nova Scotia.

February 21—The British King's speech to his Parliament appeared in a handbill. The speech breathed reconciliation throughout. The King informed his Parliament that he had gone the utmost lengths the power granted to him would allow, and that he hoped soon to lay before them the articles of peace, which were in great forwardness, and such as he apprehended they would approve; that he hoped the two countries would still be in friendship—that religion, language, interests, etc. urged this—that he devoutly prayed Great Britain might not experience any of those calamities which might be feared from such a dismemberment of the Empire, and then extends some compassionate expressions to America. Alas, O King! It might have been happy for both countries if a due consideration had been early exercised; then might much blood and much treasure have been saved. Let it be a warning to other nations to be wise and just! Nature will have her own way, and do her own work in her own time. America, of course, would be independent and sovereign, but a mistaken policy in Great Britain hurried on an event to her own loss, long before nature had ripened it for her own consummation. The public expectation now was high, and the period when peace should be announced supposed to be even at the door, and diverse premature accounts were at different times circulated.

February 25—It was learnt that Lt. Col. Barber of the New Jersey line had a little before been killed, together with his horse, near the army, by the unexpected fall of

King George III (Library of Congress).

a tree which a soldier was cutting. By this event a brave officer and valuable citizen was lost, who had frequently distinguished himself in action; his fall, therefore, in this manner, and at the very grasp of the harvest of his toils, was rendered the more affecting.

February 27—Intelligence was received from Virginia that the House of Delegates of that State had recommended to their constituents not to choose into places of power and trust men who had not been attached to the cause of liberty, and only such as had given early and decided proof of their friendship.

February 28—It was found that the British cruisers from New York had taken a number of American vessels, among them several from Boston to Virginia.

March 3—Accounts were received from Europe that in an assault made by the Spanish troops on the garrison of Gibraltar, in the month of September, the besieged, with their cannon loaded with grape-shot, made great havoc among the assailants, but that this did not check their ardor; but that upon a near approach to the walls, they were stopped and thrown into great confusion by several engines throwing scalding water upon them. Some were scalded almost to death, and others had their eyes put out a new mode of defense, but a powerful one.

March 6—Intelligence was received that not long before, the French frigate *Sybille* had been taken by some of the British cruisers and carried into New York.

March 20—It was learnt from Philadelphia that the *Washington* packet, Capt. Barney, had arrived at that place from L'Orient in France, which place she left the 17th of January. The public dispatches brought by this vessel, although they did not announce a peace to be concluded, yet informed that the negotiations were going on; everything was settled between America and Great Britain, and matters looked favorable towards France; but difficulties were subsisting between Great Britain, Spain and Holland. Several of the outlines of the articles of the treaty between Great Britain and the United States of America were published and in general were thought to be favorable to the latter. The same packet brought dispatches for Gen. Sir Guy Carleton and Admiral Digby, which were forwarded to New York.

March 22—It was learnt that a great uneasiness had discovered itself in the American army, on account of the great arrears of pay which was due, and some doubting apprehensions as to the real intention of the public to fulfill their promises to the army, and in particular that of half pay. An anonymous notification and two addresses to the officers made their appearance about ten days before, couched in very firm and decided language; these produced an address from the Commander in Chief, a meeting of the officers, a representation to Congress, and their resolutions respecting the army at that time.

The evening of the 28th a letter was received from Philadelphia purporting that a vessel had arrived there from Europe with the intelligence that the preliminary articles of peace were signed on the 20th of the preceding January. Hostilities were to cease in Europe the 20th of February, and in America on the 20th of this month. The public dispatches had not now arrived, but were momently expected.

April 2—It was learnt that a very valuable prize was carried into Salem.

April 7—Our General set out from his house in Roxbury and arrived at the headquarters of the American army at Newburgh, on Hudson's River, on the 14th, in the forenoon.

April 16th, in the general orders of the day, our General was directed to take the immediate command of the army, during the absence of Maj. Gen. Gates. Congress had published their proclamation suspending hostilities.

April 18—The Commander in Chief addressed the army on the happy cessation of hostilities as follows:

"The Commander in Chief orders the cessation of hostilities between the United States of America and the King of Great Britain to be publicly proclaimed tomorrow at 12 o'clock, at the New Building; and that the Proclamation which will be communicated herewith, be read tomorrow evening at the head of every regiment and corps of the army; after which, the chaplains, with the several brigades, will render thanks to Almighty God for all his mercies, particularly for his over-ruling the wrath of man to his own glory, and causing the rage of war to cease amongst the nations.

Although the proclamation before alluded to extends only to the prohibition of hostilities, and not to the annunciation of a general peace, yet it must afford the most rational and sincere satisfaction to every benevolent mind, as it puts a period to a long and doubtful contest—stops the effusion of human blood—opens the prospect to a more splendid scene—and, like another morning star, promises the approach of a brighter day than hath hitherto illuminated this western hemisphere! On such a happy day—a day which is the harbinger of peace—a day which completes the eighth year of the war, it would be ingratitude not to rejoice: it would be insensibility not to participate in the general felicity.

The Commander in Chief, far from endeavoring to stifle the feelings of joy in his own bosom, offers his most cordial congratulations on the occasion to all the officers of every denomination—to all the troops of the United States in general, and in particular to those gallant and persevering men who had resolved to defend the rights of their invaded country so long as the war should continue; for these are the men who ought to be considered as the pride and boast of the American army, and who, crowned with well-earned laurels, may soon withdraw from the field of glory to the more tranquil walks of civil life.

While the General recollects the almost infinite variety of scenes through which we have passed, with a mixture of pleasure, astonishment and gratitude—while he contemplates the prospects before us with rapture—he cannot help wishing that all the brave men, of whatever condition they may be, who have shared in the toils and dangers of effecting this glorious revolution, of rescuing millions from the hand of oppression, and of laying the foundation of a great empire, might be impressed with a proper idea of the dignified part they have been called to act (under the smiles of Providence) on the stage of human affairs; for happy, thrice happy, shall they be pronounced hereafter, who have contributed any thing, who have performed the meanest office in erecting this stupendous fabric of Freedom and Empire on the broad basis of independency; who have assisted in protecting the rights of human nature, and establishing an asylum for the poor and oppressed of all nations and religions.

The glorious task for which we first flew to arms being thus accomplished—the liberties of our country fully acknowledged and firmly secured by the smiles of Heaven on the purity of our cause, and the honest exertions of a feeble people determined to be free, against a powerful nation disposed to oppress them; and the character of those who have persevered through every extremity of hardship, suffering and danger, being immortalized by the illustrious appellation of the *Patriot Army*—nothing now remains but for the actors of this mighty scene to preserve a perfect, unvarying consistency of character through the very last act; to close the drama with applause; and to retire from the military theatre with the same approbation of angels and men, which have crowned all their former virtuous actions.

For this purpose, no disorder or licentiousness must be tolerated; every considerate and well-disposed soldier must remember it will be absolutely necessary to wait with patience, until peace shall be declared, or Congress shall be enabled to take proper measures for the security of the public stores, etc. As soon as these arrangements shall be made, the General is confident there will be no delay in discharging, with every mark of distinction and honor all the men enlisted for the war, who will then have faith fully performed their engagements with the public. The General has already interested himself in their behalf, and he thinks he need not repeat the assurances of his disposition to be useful to them on the present, and every other proper occasion. In the meantime, he is determined that no military neglects or excesses shall go unpunished while he retains the command of the army.

The Adjutant-General will have such working-parties detailed to assist in making the preparation for a general rejoicing, as the Chief Engineer, with the army, shall call for; and the Quarter-Master-General will also furnish such materials as he may want. The Quarter-Master-General will, without delay, procure such a number of discharges to be printed as will be sufficient for all the men enlisted for the war; he will please to apply to headquarters for the form. An extra ration of liquor to be issued to *every* man tomorrow, to drink perpetual peace, independence, and happiness to the United States of America."

April 18—In the afternoon, a schooner, _____ Cottle, master, from Nantucket, with fish, oil, rum, etc. came up the Hudson to Newburgh. This was the first American vessel which had come up the river since the British took possession of New York, in the year 1776.

April 19—At noon, the Proclamation of Congress for a cessation of hostilities was published at the door of the New Building, followed by three huzzas; after which a prayer was made by the Rev. Mr. Gano, and an anthem (*Independence*, from Billings) was performed by vocal and instrumental music. The same day, Gen. Washington went for Ringwood, to meet the Secretary at War, on some business of importance.

April 20—At evening the Commander in Chief returned to headquarters.

April 21—Permission was given for such persons as might choose it, to go to New York with provisions, etc. A vessel was loading with flour to go down the river; and one laden with rum, porter, cheese, beef, etc. came up from New York. Thus, as we have seen how the rage of war came on, we now see how by degrees that rage subsided, until the olive sprang up and progressed to full bloom.

April 24—It was learnt from Europe that on the 5th of February, preceding, the *Bedford*, Capt. Morris, made entry at the customhouse in London, being the first vessel that had arrived in the river, belonging to the United States.

April 26—It was learnt that the refugees were embarking in order to leave New York; and many transports were falling down to the watering-place. About this time Congress recommended an impost duty to the several States.

April 27—Intelligence was received that the Indians had recently committed some outrages on the western frontier; had killed and scalped 17 persons near Wheeling Creek.

May 1—Congress had expressed their opinion in a resolution which was this day published, that the term for which the men engaged for the war are to serve, does not expire until the definitive treaty is received; and that then those engaged for the war, and who so continue, shall have their arms and accoutrements as a present, for their long and faithful services.

May 2—The next morning the Commander in Chief was to go down the river to Dobbs' Ferry to meet Gen. Sir Guy Carleton. Four companies of light infantry marched this morning for that place, to do the duty of guards. Sir Guy was to come up the river in a frigate.

May 3—In the forenoon, the Commander in Chief and Gov. Clinton, with their suites, etc. went down the river.

May 7—It was learnt that several vessels had arrived at Boston from Europe, Halifax, etc. with merchandise; in consequence of which the price of goods had much fallen and the inhabitants of the eastern States were fitting out a great number of fishing vessels.

May 8—It was said that 11,644 American prisoners had died during the war, in the prisons and on board the prison ships at New York; a surprising number, and evidences that if their treatment was not severe, they were too much crowded or not properly attended to in other respects. Those who have seen know, and others can easily conceive that where men are closely confined in great numbers in prison-ships or in gaols, that without frequent airing and cleaning the air in such places becomes putrid and poisonous, and produces almost certain death. How much care then ought to be exercised by every humane commander in the appointment of provost officers, to be assured that those whom they appoint are not only firm and resolute (necessary qualifications in such officers) but that they also are considerate and humane; and that such commanders themselves take care to know, and, if necessary, correct any abuses which may exist. Such conduct towards the confined and distressed would add a laurel to the hero's brow equal to the triumphs of victory, and more lasting; for if the merciful man be merciful even to his beast, how much more ought a great and brave man to feel for the unfortunate of his own species!

May 9—At evening the Commander in Chief returned to headquarters, having had an interview with Sir Guy Carleton.

May 15—The Commander in Chief went for Poughkeepsie. A letter from Gen. Sir Guy Carleton to Gov. Clinton had rendered an interview between the Governor and the Commander in Chief necessary.

May 16—At evening the Commander in Chief returned to headquarters.

May 28—The army about this time were badly supplied with provisions, and much uneasiness was discovered, both by the officers and soldiers.

May 31—It was learnt that Congress had passed a resolution to furlough the men engaged for the war. This mode appeared to be marked with policy in several respects.

June 2—The general orders of the day announced that the men engaged for the war should be immediately furloughed, with a proportion of the officers. They were to be discharged as soon as the definitive treaty arrived; they were to be marched home in divisions. Those men that remained engaged for other periods, were to be formed into complete corps. The officers to agree who should stay, and in cases where they could not agree, seniority was to decide.

June 3—The Maryland battalion was put under orders to march to the southward.

June 5—The Maryland battalion marched from the cantonment. The same day, the general officers, and officers commanding regiments and corps in the cantonment on Hudson's River, having, by their committee for that purpose appointed, prepared an address to the Commander in Chief—it was accordingly presented in the words following:

Sir,

It is difficult for us to express the regret we feel at being obliged again to solicit your Excellency's attention and patronage. Next to the anguish which the prospect of our own wretchedness excites in our breasts, is the pain which arises from a knowledge of your anxiety on account of those men who have been the sharers of your fortunes, and have had the honor of being your companions through the various vicissitudes of the war. Nothing, therefore, but necessity could induce us to a representation which we know must give you concern.

Your Excellency has so intimate a knowledge of the condition of the army as to render a particular delineation unnecessary. As you have been a witness of our sufferings during a war uncommon in its nature, and unparalleled in many circumstances attending it; so you are now, Sir, no less a witness of the unequal burden which has fallen upon us, from the want of that provision to which, from our assiduous and unremitting services, we conceive we are entitled. Having recently expressed our sense of what was due to our distress; having repeated to your Excellency the confidence we had, that our accounts would be liquidated, the balances ascertained, and adequate funds provided for payment previous to our being dispersed or disbanded; having seen with pleasure the approbation which Congress gave our reliance, it is with a mixture of astonishment and chagrin, that we view the late resolve of Congress, by which the soldiers for the war and a proportionate number of officers are to be furloughed without any one of those important objects being accomplished; and, to complete the scene of woe, are to be compelled to leave the army without the means of defraying the debts we have necessarily incurred in the course of service, or even of gratifying those menials in the pittance which is their due; much less to carry with us that support and comfort to our families, of which, from our long military services, they have been deprived. No less exposed then to the insults of the meanest followers of the army, than to the arrests of the sheriff—deprived of the ability to assist our families, and without an evidence that any thing is due to us for our services, and consequently without the least prospect of obtaining credit for even a temporary subsistence, until we can get into business—to what quarter can we look? We take the liberty to say, Sir, only to your Excellency; and, from the sincerity of our hearts, we do it no less from a persuasion of the efficiency of your further efforts in our favor, than from the kind assurances you have been pleased to give us of your support.

To your Excellency, then, we make our appeal, and in the most solemn manner, from that abhorrence of oppression and injustice which first unsheathed our swords; from the remembrance of the common dangers through which we have passed; and from the recollection of those astonishing events, which have been effected by our united efforts—permit us to solicit your further aid and to entreat that the order of the 2nd instant, founded on the act of Congress of the 26th of May last, may be suspended or varied in its operation, so far as that no officer or soldier be obliged to receive a furlough until that honorable body can be apprized of the wretched situation into which the army must be plunged by a conformity to it; that your Excellency will endeavor to prevail on Congress—nay, that on the principles of common justice you will insist that neither officer or soldier can be compelled to leave the field until a liquidation of accounts can be effected, till the balances are ascertained, certificates for the sums due given, including the commutation of half-pay to the officers and gratuity of 80 dollars to the soldiers, and until a supply of money can be furnished sufficient to carry us from the field of glory with honor to ourselves and credit to our country. We still wish to believe that that country to which we have been so long devoted will never look with indifference on the distress of those of her sons who have so essentially contributed to the establishment of Freedom, the security of property, and the rearing of an empire.

In the name and behalf of the Generals and officers commanding regiments and corps, in the cantonment on Hudson's River,

I have the honor to be, With the highest respect,
Your Excellency's Most obedient servant,
W. HEATH, Maj. Gen. *President.*

June 5, 1783.

To the foregoing address, Gen. Washington was pleased to return the following answer, viz:

HEADQUARTERS, June 6th, 1783.

SIR,

Before I make a reply to the subject of the address of the Generals and Officers, commanding the regiments and corps of this army, presented by yourself, yesterday, I entreat that those gentlemen will accept my warmest acknowledgment for the confidence they have been pleased to repose in me; they may be assured it shall never be abused; and I beg they will be persuaded, that as no man can possibly be better acquainted than I am with the past merits and services of the army, so no one can possibly be more strongly impressed with their present ineligible situation, feel a keener sensibility at their distresses, or more ardently desire to alleviate or remove them. But it would be unnecessary, perhaps, to enter into a detail of what I have done, and what I am still attempting to do, in order to assist in the accomplishment of this interesting purpose. Let it be sufficient to observe, I do not yet despair of success; for I am perfectly convinced that the States cannot without involving themselves in national bankruptcy and ruin, refuse to comply with the requisitions of Congress; who, it must be acknowledged, have done everything in their power to obtain ample and complete justice for the army; and whose great object in the present measure undoubtedly was, by a reduction of expense, to enable the Financier to make the three months' payment to the army, which on all hands has been agreed to be absolutely and indispensably necessary. To explain this matter, I beg leave to insert an extract of a letter from the Superintendent of Finance, dated the 29th ult.

It is now a month since the committee conferred with me on that subject, and I then told them no payment could be made to the army but by means of a paper anticipation; and unless our expenditures were immediately and considerably reduced, even that could not be done. Our expenditures have nevertheless been continued, and our revenues lessen, the States growing daily more and more remiss in their collections. The consequence is, that I cannot make payment in the manner first intended; the notes issued for this purpose would have been payable at two, four, and six months from the date, but at present they will be at six months, and even that will soon become impracticable, unless our expenses be immediately curtailed.

I shall cause such notes to be issued for three months' pay to the army; and I must entreat, Sir, that every influence be used with the States to absorb them, together with my other engagements, by taxation. Three days ago a messenger was dispatched by me to urge the necessity of forwarding these notes with the greatest possible expedition. Under this state of circumstances, I need scarcely add, that the expense of every day in feeding the whole army will increase very considerably the inability of the public to discharge the debts already incurred, at least for a considerable time to come.

Although the officers of the army very well know my official situation; that I am only a servant of the public, and that it is not for me to dispense with orders which it is my duty to carry into execution; yet, as furloughs, in all services, are considered as a matter of indulgence and not of compulsion—as Congress, I am persuaded, entertain the best disposition towards the army—and, as I apprehend in a very short time the two principal articles of complaint will be removed—I shall not hesitate to comply with the wishes of the army, under these reservations only, that officers sufficient to conduct the men who choose to receive furloughs will attend them, either on furlough or by detachment. The propriety and necessity of this measure must be obvious to all; it need not, therefore, be enforced; and with regard to the non-commissioned officers and privates, such as from a peculiarity of circumstances wish not to receive furloughs at this time, will give in their names by 12 o'clock tomorrow to the commanding officers of their regiments, that on a report to the Adjutant- General, an equal number of men, engaged for three years, may be furloughed, which will make the saving of expenses exactly the same to the public.

I cannot but hope the notes will soon arrive, and that the settlement of accounts may be completed by the assistance of the Pay-Masters in a very few days. In the meantime, I shall have the honor of laying the sentiments of the Generals and Officers commanding regiments and corps, before Congress; they are expressed in such a decent, candid, and affecting manner, that I am certain every mark of attention will be paid to them.

I have the honor to be, with great esteem, Sir,

Your most obedient Servant,
(Signed) GEO. WASHINGTON.

Maj. Gen. HEATH.

The two preceding papers were enclosed in the following letter from the Commander in Chief to his Excellency the President of Congress:

HEADQUARTERS, NEWBURGH, June 7th, 1783.

SIR,

I have the honor to enclose to your Excellency the copy of an address to me from the Generals and Officers commanding regiments and corps, together with my answer to it. These enclosures will explain the distresses which resulted from the measures now carrying into execution, in consequence of the resolution of the 26th of May; but the sensibility occasioned by a parting scene under such peculiar circumstances, will not admit of description!

The two subjects of complaint with the army appear to be the delay of the three months' payment which had been expected, and the want of a settlement of accounts. I have thought myself authorized to assure them Congress had and would attend particularly to their grievances; and have made some little variation respecting furloughs, from what was at first proposed; the Secretary of War will be able to explain the reason and propriety of this alteration.

While I consider it a tribute of justice, on this occasion, to mention the temperate and orderly behavior of the whole army, and particularly the accommodating spirit of the officers in arranging themselves to the command of the battalions which will be composed of the three years' men, permit me to recall to mind all their former sufferings and merits, and to recommend their reasonable requests to the early and favorable notice of Congress.

I have the honor to be, etc.

A little before this time, the officers of the army beginning to realize that the dissolution of the army was drawing nigh, and wishing to perpetuate that friendship which numerous hardships, sufferings, and common dangers had inspired in their breasts—resolved to form themselves into a Society, by the name of the *Cincinnati*. Several meetings were had for the purpose, and an Institution was digested and completed; and although our General presided at one of the meetings, and cheerfully, at the request of his brother officers, transmitted copies of the Institution, covered by a letter, to the officer commanding the southern army, and to the senior officers of the respective State lines, from Pennsylvania to Georgia—yet he had serious objections to the Institution as it stood, and refused for some time to sign it. He wished, as much as any one in the army, to perpetuate the happy friendship cemented in the breasts of the officers by an eight years' common danger and sufferings, but he thought this would be best done by simply forming a Society, to meet annually in their respective States, for the purpose of a social hour, and to brighten the chain of friendship, with a fund for the relief of the unfortunate of their brethren; but he was opposed to any idea of any thing that had any resemblance of an order, or any insignia or badge of distinction, asserting that it would only serve to mark them in an unfavorable light with their fellow-citizens: but the prevailing opinion of the officers was otherwise.

Our General was finally induced to sign the Institution, from the following consideration—(but not until all the officers were appointed, and he nearly ready to leave the army) conversing with an officer of rank, who was of the same opinion with him, they parted in the resolution not to sign the Institution; but the next morning the officer called upon him, and observed that one consideration, not before mentioned, had occurred to him, viz.: that it might happen in the days of their posterity, in case they did not sign, that the descendant of one who was a member might happen to fall in company with the descendant of one who was not; that the latter, on observing the badge, might inquire what it was, and whats its intention—upon its being answered that it was the insignia of a Society, of which his ancestor who served in the American army during the revolution, was a member—the other might reply, my ancestor too served during that war, but I never heard any thing of such a badge in our family; to which it might probably be answered, it is likely your ancestor was guilty of some misconduct, which deprived him of it. Upon this our General broke out—"I see it, I see it, and spurn the idea;" which led him to sign the general Institution: and he subscribed to the State fund 166 dollars, being one month's pay, as was stipulated in the Institution.

He, however, never met with the Society, although no one has cherished a warmer affection for every member of the army. After the revolution in France, finding that the insignias of distinctions were doing away, it led him anew to review the distinction which the badge of the Society to which he belonged, if not in fact, yet in appearance seemed to exhibit, and brought to mind all his former objections, which induced him to write to the Secretary-General to erase his name from the Institution; but that his subscription to the fund should remain so long as it was applied to the purpose for which it was given—the relief of the unfortunate.[5]

June 6—In the forenoon, the Jersey line marched from the cantonment to their own State, where they were to be disbanded. The same day, the first New York regiment made a present of their standards and band to Governor Clinton; they were escorted to Poughkeepsie by the light-infantry company of the regiment.

June 8—The men for the war, belonging to the Maryland, New Jersey, New York, and New Hampshire lines, having marched from the cantonment, a division of the Massachusetts men marched on this day.

June 9—A division of the Suffolk and Worcester furloughed men marched for their own State, and so on, a division each day, until the whole had marched.

June 10—Our General was General of the Day. In the after orders of the Commander in Chief on this day it was expressed, "The strength of the army in this cantonment being considerably diminished by the number of men lately furloughed, the order of the 16th of April, directing a General, Field Officers, and Quartermaster to be of the day, and also a regiment to parade every day for duty, is dispensed with. For the present there will be one Field-Officer, and an Adjutant of the day; and the guards only will form on the grand parade at nine o'clock in the morning." It is here a little remarkable that our General, by whose orders, and under whose direction the first guard in the American war mounted at the foot of Prospect Hill, on the evening of the 19th of April, 1775, after the battle of that day, should happen, in the course of service, to be the last General of the day in the American main army, on the 10th of June, 1783, to inspect, turn off, and visit the guards. At the first period, the roads were full of militia, pressing towards Boston, to commence and prosecute a dubious war; they were now filled with veteran soldiers, covered with laurels, returning form the field to their peaceful abodes.

June 11—About two o'clock, p.m. the wind freshened from the west; there were several thunder showers, with large hail-stones, some of which were supposed to be two inches long. The lightning struck the flagstaff of the New Building, entered the house, and ran down the south side of it, doing some damage, and stunning several soldiers near the door. In the general orders of this day it was announced that the levees were to be discontinued.

June 13—The men who had enlisted for three years, and for shorter periods not expired, were formed, those belonging to Massachusetts into four regiments, and were to be commanded by Colonels Michael Jackson, Henry Jackson, and Joseph Vose, and Lt. Col. Commandant Sprout. On the morning of the 16th, these regiments incorporated, and were formed into two brigades, the one commanded by Brig. Gen. Patterson, and the other by Brig. Gen. Greaton.

June 19—A number of officers of the army, viz.: several general officers, and officers commanding regiments and corps, met at the New Building, and elected his Excellency Gen. Washington, President General; Gen. McDougall, Treasurer; and Gen. Knox, Secretary, *pro tempore*, to the Society of the Cincinnati.

June 20—The Massachusetts State Society of the Cincinnati met, and made choice of Maj. Gen. Lincoln for their President; Maj. Gen. Knox, Vice-President; Col. John Brooks, Secretary; Col. Henry Jackson, Treasurer; and Capt. Heywood, Assistant-Treasurer. The same day the troops at the cantonment were put under orders to be ready to march for West Point on the succeeding Monday.

June 22—Our General issued his last order, which finished as follows: "The long wished for period having arrived, when the din of war ceases, the olive-branch of peace is displayed, the toils and fatigues of the field are drawing to a close, a part of the army have already mingled with their fellow-citizens, and others will probably ere long join them—Maj. Gen. Heath being about to leave the army, and this being the last opportunity which will remain in his power to express that affection for his brother officers and soldiers, which more than eight years of service has established in his breast, he cannot depart without leaving his best wishes for the health, prosperity and happiness of those whose lot it is a little longer to continue in the field—invoke every blessing on them, and bid them an affection ate farewell."

June 23—The Massachusetts regiments marched to West Point. The morning of the 24th our General was to commence his journey homeward; but the Commander in Chief wished him not to proceed until the afternoon. On his arrival at headquarters, Col. Humphreys, one of the Aides-de-Camp of the Commander in Chief, gave him a sealed letter,[6] observing to him to read at his leisure. On opening it, in General Washington's own handwriting it was as follows:

(Private)

HEADQUARTERS, June 24th, 1783.

DEAR SIR,

Previous to your departure from the army, I wish to take an opportunity of expressing my sentiments of your services, my obligations for your assistance, and my wishes for your future felicity. Our object is at last attained; the arrangements are almost completed, and the day of separation is now at hand. Permit me, therefore, to thank you for the trouble you have lately taken in the arrangement of the corps under your orders, as well as for all your former cheerful and able exertions in the public service. Suffer me to offer this last testimony of my regard to your merits; and give me leave, my dear Sir, to assure you of the real affection and esteem with which I am, and shall at all times, and under all circumstances, continue to be

Washington's farewell to his officers, December 4, 1783. Engraving after painting by Alonzo Chappel.

Your sincere friend, and Very humble servant,
(Signed) G. WASHINGTON.

Maj. Gen. HEATH.

In the afternoon, the general officers were in Council at headquarters, in consequence of an express from Philadelphia. Four or five hundred men of the Pennsylvania line, of those who had been furloughed on or about the 20th, grew very mutinous, refused to obey orders, entered the city of Philadelphia, seized some public stores, surrounded the place where Congress and the Supreme Court of the State were sitting, and made several demands and occasioned some consternation, which caused a representation to the Commander in Chief. The Continental regiments were to be put under marching orders immediately. It was judged inexpedient to call out the militia.

At about five o'clock p.m. our General took his leave of his beloved General, and commenced his journey for Massachusetts, and arrived at his house in Roxbury on the first day of July, at two o'clock, p.m. where he gave evidence that an eight years' military life had not divested him of the feelings or manners of a citizen.

October 30—It was learnt that the definitive treaty of peace was signed the 3rd of the preceding September; and that dispatches were sent off to the different Courts in Europe, to America, the East and West Indies, etc. with an account of this happy event. Congress, by a proclamation which bore date of the 18th of this month, discharged from further service such soldiers as were engaged for the war, and officers who were absent by derangement and furlough. The discharges to take place the 3rd of November, ensuing.

November 2—Gen. Washington issued his last and farewell orders to the federal armies, taking an affectionate leave of them, and giving them his best advice.

November 4—Gen. Washington, by proclamation, in compliance with a resolve of Congress of the 29th of the preceding October, discharged all the troops in the service of the United States, that were then in Pennsylvania or to the southward thereof, except the garrison of Fort Pitt. The British troops having left New York, on the 25th of November, at one o'clock, p.m. a detachment of the American army took possession of the city; after which, his Excellency General Washington, and Governor Clinton, made their public entry, properly escorted, etc. The Governor gave a public dinner at Fraunces Tavern.

December 2—There was a grand exhibition of fireworks in celebration of the peace, at the bowling green, in Broadway. The magnificent fireworks far exceeded any before exhibited in the United States. On the 4th, at noon, a great number of American officers of distinction met at Fraunces Tavern, to take their leave of their great Commander, Gen. Washington, who, on filling a glass of wine, addressed his brave compatriots as follows:

> With a heart full of love and gratitude, I now take leave of you—I most devoutly wish that your latter days may be as prosperous and happy, as your former ones have been glorious and honorable.

The dissolution of the American army (excepting a small detachment of artillery and of infantry) took place a few days after; and General WASHINGTON, ere long, retired to his seat at Mount Vernon, covered with every laurel with which his own victorious conduct, and a grateful country, could adorn him; and with the applause of an admiring world.

Chapter Notes

Preface

1. "To George Washington from William Heath, 17 April 1797," Founders Online, National Archives (http://founders.archives.gov/documents/Washington/06-01-02-0072, ver. 2014-02-12). Source: *The Papers of George Washington*, Retirement Series, vol. 1, 4 March 1797–30 December 1797, ed. W. W. Abbot (Charlottesville: University Press of Virginia, 1998, 103–104).

2. "From George Washington to William Heath, 20 May 1797," Founders Online, National Archives (http://founders.archives.gov/documents/Washington/06-01-02-0118, ver. 2014-02-12). Source: *The Papers of George Washington*, Retirement Series, vol. 1, 4 March 1797–30 December 1797, ed. W. W. Abbot (Charlottesville: University Press of Virginia, 1998, 148–150; Heath sent a copy of the book to Washington after it was published in 1798. While it is unknown whether Washington read it, Heath's book was in Washington's library at Mount Vernon at the time of his death in 1799.

3. William Abbatt (1851–1935) was an author, magazine publisher, and editor based in New York during the first half of the twentiethth century. His work concentrated on the American Revolution, and included several publications on John André and Benedict Arnold. In addition to his work with scholarly manuscripts, Abbatt edited and published *The Magazine for History with Notes and Queries*. Abbatt's papers are now located at the University of Michigan.

4. William M. Fowler, Jr., *American Crisis: George Washington and the Dangerous Two Years After Yorktown, 1781–1783* (New York: Walker, 2011), 53–54.

5. Bud Hannings, *American Revolutionary War Leaders: A Biographical Dictionary* (Jefferson, NC: McFarland, 2006), 166; "William Heath," in *Dictionary of American Biography*, vol. VII, ed. Allen Johnson and Dumas Malone (New York: Charles Scribner's & Sons, 1946), 491.

6. Paul David Nelson, "William Heath," in *American Revolutionary War: A Student Encyclopedia*, vol. II: E-L, ed. Gregory Fremont-Barnes and Richard Alan Ryerson (Santa Barbara, CA: ABC-CLIO, 2007), 862–864

7. William A. Crafts, "A General of the Revolution," in *New England Magazine: An Illustrated Monthly*, vol. 3, (Boston: New England Magazine Corporation, 1891), 513–519.

8. John R. Galvin, *The Minute Men: The First Fight: Myths and Realities of the American Revolution* (Dulles, VA: Potomac, 2006), 215.

9. Richard L. Blanco, "William Heath," in *The American Revolution: An Encyclopedia*, vol. 1: A-L, ed. Richard L. Blanco (New York: Garland, 1993), 750.

10. Crafts, "A General of the Revolution," 519.

11. See "To Thomas Jefferson from William Heath, 25 February 1801," Founders Online, National Archives (http://founders.archives.gov/documents/Jefferson/01-33-02-0063, ver. 2014-02-12). Source: *The Papers of Thomas Jefferson*, vol. 33, 17 February–30 April 1801, ed. Barbara B. Oberg (Princeton: Princeton University Press, 2006), 65–66.

Introduction

1. Hannings, *American Revolutionary War Leaders*, 166; various sources list his exact birth date as either March 2, 7, or 13. However, General Heath states in his memoirs that he was born on March 2 using the "Old Syle" (O.S.) calendar.

2. Amos Blanchard, "William Heath," in *American Military and Naval Biography* (Cincinnati, OH: A. Salisbury, 1832), 208.

3. Ibid.

4. David Hackett Fischer, *Paul Revere's Ride* (New York, NY: Oxford University Press, 1994), 247.

5. Ibid.

6. Blanchard, *American and Naval Biography*, 208.

7. Harold. E. Selesky, ed., "William Heath," in *Encyclopedia of the American Revolution*, vol. 1 (Detroit, MI: Charles Scribner's & Sons, 2006), 497–498.

8. Thomas Wilson, "William Heath," in *The Biography of Principal American Military and Naval Heroes*, vol. 1 (New York: John Low, 1817), 136.

9. Blanchard, *American Military and Naval Biography*, 208.

10. Of the various Massachusetts Militia generals, Heath lived closest in proximity to the battlefield, and was therefore able to get there the fastest.

11. Nathaniel Philbrick, *Bunker Hill: A City, a Siege, a Revolution* (New York: Viking, 2013), 151; Paul

Lockhart, *The Whites of Their Eyes: Bunker Hill, the First American Army, and the Emergence of George Washington* (New York, NY: Harper, 2011), 24.

12. See Philbrick, *Bunker Hill*, 154–155.

13. Ibid., 155.

14. See Fischer, *Paul Revere's Ride*, 247–248; Galvin, *The Minute Men*, 215.

15. Galvin, *The Minute Men*, 216.

16. Nelson, "William Heath," 862–863.

17. Selesky, *Encyclopedia of the American Revolution*, 498.

18. Wilson, *The Biography of Principal American Military and Naval Heroes*, 139.

19. William Abbatt, ed., *Memoirs of Major General William Heath* (New York: William Abbatt, 1901), 16.

20. Ibid.

21. Selesky, *Encyclopedia of the American Revolution*, 498.

22. Nelson, "William Heath," 863.

23. Nelson, "William Heath," 863; Wilson, *The Biography of Principal American Military and Naval Heroes*, 141–146.

24. Selesky, *Encyclopedia of the American Revolution*, 498.

25. Wilson, *The Biography of Principal American Military and Naval Heroes*, 147.

26. Abbatt, *Memoirs of Major General William Heath*, 100–101.

27. George Washington to William Heath, February 4, 1777, John C. Fitzpatrick, ed., *The Writings of George Washington from the Original Manuscript Sources: 1745–1799* (Washington, D.C.: Reprint Services, 1931–1944), Vol. 7, 100.

28. Nelson, "William Heath," 863.

29. John Adams to Abigail Adams, February 21, 1777, L.H. Butterfield, ed., *Adams Family Correspondence* (Cambridge, MA: Harvard University Press, 1963), vol. 2, 165.

30. William Heath to George Washington, February 6, 1777, John C. Fitzpatrick, ed., *The Writings of George Washington*, 96.

31. Ibid.

32. Abbatt, *Memoirs of Major General William Heath*, 105.

33. Heath was married to Sarah Lockbridge Heath and had five children (Samuel, William Jr., Sarah, Joseph, and Henry).

34. Selesky, *Encyclopedia of the American Revolution*, 498.

35. Theodore P. Savas and J. David Dameron, eds., *The New American Revolution Handbook* (New York: Savas Beatie, 2010), 15.

36. Brendan Morrissey, *Saratoga 1777: Turning Point of a Revolution* (Oxford, UK: Osprey, 2000), 86–87.

37. The Convention Army was not released from captivity until the end of the war in 1783.

38. Wilson, *The Biography of Principal American Military and Naval Heroes*, 151.

39. Ibid., 152.

40. See Abbott, *Memoirs of Major General William Heath*.

41. Wilson, *The Biography of Principal American Military and Naval Heroes*, 153.

42. Ibid.

43. Ibid., 154.

44. Selesky, *Encyclopedia of the American Revolution*, 498.

45. Wilson, *The Biography of Principal American Military and Naval Heroes*, 155–156.

46. Ibid., 157.

47. Ibid., 157–158.

48. Ibid., 158–159.

49. Ibid., 160.

50. Fowler, *American Crisis*, 60.

51. Ibid.

52. Charles E. Bennett and Donald R. Lennon, *A Quest for Glory: Major General Robert Howe and the American Revolution* (Chapel Hill: University of North Carolina Press, 1991), 142.

53. Fowler, *American Crisis*, 61.

54. Bennett and Lennon, *A Quest for Glory*, 142–144.

55. Selesky, *Encyclopedia of the American Revolution*, 498.

56. Francis Samuel Drake, *The Town of Roxbury: Its Memorable Persons and Places, Its History and Antiquities, with Numerous Illustrations of its Old Landmarks and Noted Personages* (Boston, MA: Alfred Mudge and Son, 1878), 389.

57. Nelson, "William Heath," 864.

58. Selesky, *Encyclopedia of the American Revolution*, 498.

59. James Thatcher, *A Military Journal During the American Revolutionary War, from 1775 to 1783, Describing Interesting Events and Transactions of This Period; with Numerous Historical Facts and Anecdotes from the Original Manuscript* (Boston, MA: Cottons & Barnard, 1827). Retrieved on 10/14/2011 from http://threerivershms.com/journalheath.htm.

60. Heath garnered 43.6 percent of the vote, while William Eustis came in with only 0.6 percent.

61. Nelson, "William Heath," 864.

62. Thatcher, *A Military Journal*.

63. Nelson, "William Heath," 864.

64. Drake, *The Town of Roxbury*, 390.

65. Ibid.

66. Nelson, "William Heath," 864.

67. Abbatt, *Memoirs of Major General William Heath*, VI; General Heath is buried in Forest Hills Cemetery in the Jamaica Plain section of Boston.

Chapter 1

1. General Heath's immigrant ancestor was his great-great grandfather, William Heath (1591–1652), who came from the community of Ware in Hertfordshire, England. In 1632 he immigrated from Nazeing, England, to the Massachusetts Bay Colony aboard a ship called the *Lyon*.

2. This is a reference to Lt. Gen. John Manners (1721–1770), who was a top British commander during the Seven Years' War and was the eldest son of the 3rd Duke of Rutland. Since General Manners did not outlive his father, he was known during his lifetime by his father's subsidiary title, Marquess of Granby.

3. Established in 1638, the Ancient and Honor-

able Artillery Company of Massachusetts is the oldest charted military organization in North America and the third oldest chartered military organization in the world. It was founded as a citizen militia but in more modern times has become a social and ceremonial group.

4. Sir Francis Bernard, 1st Baronet (1712–1779), served as governor of New Jersey from 1758 to 1760 and was governor of Massachusetts from 1760 to 1769.

5. Thomas Hutchinson (1711–1780) served as acting governor of Massachusetts in 1760 and was governor from 1769 to 1774.

6. Brig. Gen. Jedidiah Preble (1707–1784) of Maine was a soldier, judge, and legislator. He declined the commission offered to him by the Massachusetts Provincial Congress in February 1775. One of his sons, Edward Preble (1761–1807) went on to serve as a commodore in the U.S. Navy.

7. John Whitcomb (1720–1812) of Lancaster, Massachusetts, was a widely admired veteran of the French and Indian War. During the early stages of the Revolution, he served as a militia commander and was commissioned a brigadier general in the Continental Army in 1776. He resigned from active service shortly thereafter due to advancing age.

8. Menotomy was founded in 1635 as a village near Cambridge. The word means "swift running water" in Algonquin. The town was renamed Arlington, Massachusetts, in 1867.

9. Azor Orne (1731–1796) of Marblehead, Massachusetts, was a prominent politician and businessman who served as an officer in the Massachusetts Militia. He would go on to earn the rank of major general in the Militia.

10. Jeremiah Lee (1721–1775) of Marblehead, Massachusetts, was America's largest colonial ship owner, with an inventory of more than 21 vessels. He was also considered to be one of the most successful and affluent businessmen in America prior to the Revolution.

11. Probably Capt. Adam Wheeler (1732–1802) of Hubbardston, Massachusetts. A deacon and French and Indian War veteran, he saw action in several battles such as Lexington, Bunker Hill, and White Plains.

12. Francis Smith (1723–1791) would go on to become a major general in the British Army.

13. Hugh Percy, 2nd Duke of Northumberland (1742–1817), was a brigadier general during the Battles of Lexington and Concord. He would later become a lieutenant general before resigning his command in 1777.

14. Dr. Eliphalet Downer (1743–1806) of Roxbury, Massachusetts, was a prominent physician and ardent patriot. He later served as a ship's surgeon but was captured by the British and imprisoned in England. However, he ultimately managed to escape.

15. Joseph Ward (1737–1812) of Newton, Massachusetts, was a school master who went on to serve as a colonel in the Continental Army as well as a state legislator following the war.

16. The HMS *Lively* was a 20-gun post ship of the Royal Navy. She was captured by the French in 1778, but recaptured by the British in 1781.

17. Col. William Prescott (1726–1795) of Groton, Massachusetts, was best known for his famous order during the Battle of Bunker Hill: "do not fire until you see the whites of their eyes."

18. The British and American casualty figures given by General Heath are generally consistent with other published accounts.

19. The date and order of their appointment determined each general's level of seniority within the Continental Army.

20. Col. Richard Gridley (1710–1796) of Boston, Massachusetts, served as chief engineer for the Eastern Department for much of the war. He was highly regarded by General Washington as well as many other officers.

21. Rufus Putnam (1738–1824) of New Braintree, Massachusetts, was a skilled engineering officer who went on to become a brigadier general in the Continental Army. He was influential in helping to settle the Northwest Territory (modern-day Ohio) following the war.

22. Col. David Brewer (1731–1799) of Framingham, Massachusetts, commanded the 9th Massachusetts Regiment at the Battle of Bunker Hill.

23. Capt. Jeduthan Baldwin (1732–1788) of Massachusetts. He was later promoted to colonel.

24. Benjamin Tupper (1738–1792) and John Crane (1744–1805) both went on to become brevet brigadier generals in the Continental Army.

25. A *halbert* was a long-handled weapon of which the head had a point and several sharp edges.

26. A *pistareen* was a small silver coin used in America and the West Indies during the eighteenth century.

27. Joseph Vose (1738–1816) went on to become a colonel in the Continental Army, commanding the 1st Massachusetts Regiment.

28. Originally from Dracut, Massachusetts, James Varnum (1748–1789) later became a brigadier general in the Continental Army and a major general in the Rhode Island Militia.

29. Col. Daniel Hitchcock (1739–1777) later commanded the 2nd Rhode Island Regiment and was thanked publically by General Washington for his efforts at the Battles of Trenton and Princeton.

30. The Kennebec River is a 170-mile river located entirely in Maine.

31. The Chardière River is a 115 mile river in southeast Quebec, Canada.

32. Dr. Benjamin Church (1734–1778) of Boston, Massachusetts, was chief physician and director general of the Continental Army's medical service from July to October 1775. Dubbed "the first American traitor," he was tried and convicted for sending secret information to British Gen. Thomas Gage.

33. Col. Ebenezer Bridge (1742–1823) of Massachusetts.

34. Lt. Col. William Bond (d. 1776), who served in Garnder's Massachusetts Regiment.

35. John Glover (1732–1797) of Marblehead, Massachusetts, went on to serve as a brigadier general in the Continental Army.

36. Capt. Thomas Waite Foster of Massachusetts.

37. In this context, *inure* means to get accustomed to something unpleasant.

38. This was the Battle of Great Bridge, fought on December 9, 1775, in what is now Chesapeake, Virginia.

39. John Murray, 4th Earl of Dunmore (1730–1809) was governor of New York from 1770 to 1771 and governor of Virginia from 1771 to 1775. He was the last royal governor of Virginia.

Chapter 2

1. Joseph Frye (1712–1794) of Andover, Massachusetts, was a militia officer who served in both King George's War and the French and Indian War. Following those conflicts he settled in Maine. During the early stages of the Revolution, he served as a major general in the Massachusetts Militia and briefly as a brigadier general in the Continental Army before resigning due to advancing age.
2. These officers were Capt. Edward Payson Williams (d. 1777), Capt. Jacob Could (1752–1816), and probably Capt. William Wyman (1752–1809).
3. These officers were probably Lt. Samuel Foster (d. 1778), Lt. Samuel Shaw (1754–1794), either Lt. David Patterson of the 14th Massachusetts Regiment or William Patterson of the 15th Massachusetts Regiment, Lt. Joshua Trafton, and Ensign James Cheeney of the 3rd Massachusetts Regiment
4. Thomas Knowlton (1740–1776) of West Boxford, Massachusetts, later settled in Connecticut and served in the French and Indian War. During the Revolution, he commanded an elite force of troops that carried out reconnaissance and intelligence-gathering missions. Rising to the rank of lieutenant colonel, he was later killed during the Battle of Harlem Heights on September 16, 1776. Knowlton is considered to be America's first intelligence professional.
5. These were probably Brigade-Major David Henley and Brigade-Major Richard Cary, who later served as an aide-de-camp to George Washington.
6. Charlestown is the oldest neighborhood in Boston. The Charlestown Neck was later eliminated through landfill operations.
7. Today, the site of Dorchester Neck is located within the South Boston section of Boston. The narrow neck itself was later eliminated through landfill operations.
8. A *sally* is an attack by the defenders of a town or fortress under siege against a besieging force.
9. Rev. Abiel Leonard (1740–1777) of Danbury, Connecticut, was a chaplain in the Continental Army.
10. Now known as Lechmere Square in Cambridge, Massachusetts, Lechmere's Point was the landing point for British troops en route to the Battles of Lexington and Concord.
11. Col. Paul Dudley Sargent (1745–1828) of Salem, Massachusetts, commanded the 8th Massachusetts Regiment during the Siege of Boston. He later served as a militia officer and settled in Maine following the war.
12. Probably Elihu Lyman (1741–1823) of Belchertown, Massachusetts, who went on to serve as a captain in the Continental Army.
13. Probably Col. Jedediah Huntington (1743–1818) of Connecticut, who was later appointed a brigadier general in 1777.
14. An *abattis* is afield fortification obstacle formed of branches of trees laid in a row, with the sharpened tops directed outwards toward the enemy.
15. Ebenezer Learned (1728–1801) of Oxford, Massachusetts, was a French and Indian War veteran who went on to serve as a brigadier general in the Continental Army.
16. *Viz.* is an adverb that means "as follows."
17. These officers were John Greaton, John Stark, John Paterson, William Bond, and Charles Webb.
18. Now known as Castle Island and located in South Boston, "Castle William" served as the main base of military operations for the British until they destroyed it in March 1776 while evacuating Boston.
19. On cannons, *trunnions* are protrusions from the sides of the barrel that rest on the carriage.
20. William Thompson (1736–1781) of Carlisle, Pennsylvania, was an Irish immigrant who served during the French and Indian War. He was appointed colonel of the 1st Pennsylvania Regiment in 1775 and promoted to brigadier general shortly thereafter. The promotion was opposed by George Washington, who apparently had doubts about Thompson's abilities in the field.
21. William DeHart (1746–1801) of Morristown, New Jersey, was a lawyer by trade who went on to serve as a lieutenant colonel in the Continental Army.
22. Esek Hopkins (1718–1802) of Scituate, Rhode Island, was a privateer, colonial legislator, and militia officer who served as the first commander-in-chief of the Continental Navy.
23. Enoch Poor (1736–1780) of Exeter, New Hampshire, was a shipbuilder and merchant who went on to serve as a brigadier general in the Continental Army.
24. John Thomas (1724–1776) was a doctor and militia officer who went on to serve as a major general in the Continental Army. He died of smallpox in Canada on June 2, 1776.
25. Now known as Randall's Island, it is situated in the East River and part of the Borough of Manhattan in New York City.
26. Timothy Bedel (1737–1787) of Salem, New Hampshire, was a prominent military and political leader in New Hampshire prior to the Revolution. He served as a colonel in the New Hampshire Militia during the Revolutionary War and was also a staff officer under Generals Philip Schuyler and Horatio Gates.
27. Henry Sherburne of Rhode Island, who was later promoted to colonel.
28. Captain Seth Harding of the Massachusetts State cruiser *Defence*, captured the armed transports *Annabella* and *Howe*, on board of which were 200 of the 71st Highlanders as well as then–Col. Campbell.
29. Sir Archibald Campbell (1739–1791) would remain a prisoner of war until 1778, when he was exchanged for Patriot hero Col. Ethan Allen. Campbell went on to become a major general in the British Army and serve as Royal Governor of Jamaica.
30. These officers were Col. John Shee of Pennsylvania and Col. Robert Magaw (1738–1790) of Pennsylvania.
31. David Wooster (1711–1777) of Stratford, Connecticut, was a French and Indian War veteran who served as a major general in the Continental Army.

He died following the Battle of Ridgefield on May 2, 1777.

32. John Durkee (1728–1782) of Windham, Connecticut, was a French and Indian War veteran who distinguished himself in battle at Bunker Hill. He was known as the "Bold Bean Hiller," which apparently referred to his place of residence.

33. William Shepard (1737–1817) of Westfield, Massachusetts, served as colonel of the 4th Massachusetts Regiment and was later a militia general. Following the war, he served in the U.S. House of Representatives from 1797 to 1802.

34. Lt. Col. James Paterson served as adjutant general of Gen. Sir William Howe's army from April 1776 to July 1777. Later in the war he rose in rank to brigadier general.

35. Jonathan Holman (1732- 1814) of Sutton, Massachusetts, was a French and Indian War veteran who rose to the rank of colonel in the Continental Army, commanding the 5th Massachusetts Regiment.

36. Horn's Hook is now located in the vicinity of 88th Street, East River, New York.

37. Edward Hand (1744–1802) was an Irish immigrant from Lancaster, Pennsylvania. Following pre-war service as an officer in the British Army, he joined the Patriot cause and went on to command the 1st Pennsylvania Regiment. He later served as adjutant general under George Washington and concluded the war as a major general.

38. Morris Graham of New York commanded the 1st Duchess County Militia.

39. This was the Battle of Long Island, fought on August 27, 1776. It is also known as the Battle of Brooklyn or the Battle of Brooklyn Heights.

40. The officers here not previously mentioned were Col. Daniel Broadhead (1736–1809) of Pennsylvania and Col. Samuel Miles (1740–1805) of Pennsylvania.

41. *Videttes* are mounted sentries in advance of the outposts of an army.

42. John Chester (1747–1809) of Connecticut served as a colonel in the Continental Army and was present at Bunker Hill.

43. Now known as Kip's Bay, it is a neighborhood in the New York City Borough of Manhattan.

44. James Chapman (1734–1826) of New London, Connecticut, served as a major in the 1st Continental Regiment.

45. Brigadier-Major John P. Wyllys. He was killed at the Battle of the Miami in 1790.

46. Capt. Micajah Gleason (1740–1776) of Framingham, Massachusetts.

47. Maj. Andrew Leitch (d. 1776) of Prince William County, Virginia, served in the 1st Virginia Continental Regiment.

48. Samuel Holden Parsons (1737–1789) of Lyme, Connecticut, was a prominent judge who saw extensive service during the American Revolution. He was later promoted to the rank of major general in the Continental Army.

49. Probably Gen. Thomas Scott of the Massachusetts Militia.

50. John Haslet (1727–1777) was an Irish immigrant and French and Indian War veteran who settled near Milford, Delaware, in 1764. During the Revolution, he was commissioned a colonel and commanded the 1st Delaware Regiment, considered to be one of the finest units in the Continental Army. Haslet was killed in action at the Battle of Princeton in January 1777.

51. Samuel John Atlee (1739–1786) of Lancaster, Pennsylvania, served as colonel of the Pennsylvania Musketry Battalion. He was later captured by the British during the Battle of Long Island and exchanged in 1778.

52. Probably Roger Morris (1717–1794), who served as a colonel in the British Army during the French and Indian War. An avowed Loyalist, he returned to his native England with his family in 1776. His house, now known as the Morris-Jumel Mansion and located in Manhattan, served as a headquarters for both sides during the Revolution.

53. Maj. Samuel Logan of the 5th New York Regiment.

54. Capt. John Wisner (1737–1811) of New York served in the Orange County Militia.

55. Col. Robert Rogers (1731–1795) was a controversial British officer and Massachusetts native who commanded the famous Rogers' Rangers during the French and Indian War. During the early stages of the Revolution, he was offered a command by the Continental Congress but declined on the grounds that he was a British military officer. Instead, he commanded a ranger type unit for the British and assisted in the capture of Patriot spy Nathan Hale in September 1776.

56. Now known as Ward's Island. It is situated in the East River in New York City.

57. This area is now located in Yonkers, New York.

58. Capt. Jotham Horton of Knox's Artillery.

59. Capt. Edward Crafts of Knox's Artillery.

60. This was the inventor David Bushnell (1740–1826) who developed the famous *Turtle* submarine. Piloted by Sgt. Ezra Lee of the Continental Army, it attempted to attack the HMS *Eagle* in New York Harbor in September 1776, but was unsuccessful.

61. This is Maj. Gen. Alexander McDougall (1731–1786) of New York with whom General Heath had a bitter feud during the war's later stages.

62. Peleg Wadsworth (1748–1829) of Duxbury, Massachusetts, was a Harvard graduate and educator who served as a brigadier general in the Massachusetts Militia during the Revolution.

63. John Fellows (1735–1808) of Sheffield, Massachusetts, was a French and Indian War veteran who served as a brigadier general in the Massachusetts Militia during the Revolution.

64. These officers were Col. William Shepard (1737–1817) of Massachusetts, Col. Joseph Read (1732–1801) of Massachusetts, Col. Loammi Baldwin (1744–1807) of Massachusetts, and Brig. Gen. John Glover (1732–1797) of Massachusetts.

65. Col. Jonathan Brewer of Massachusetts was a French and Indian War veteran and innkeeper who led a regiment named after him at the Battle of Bunker Hill.

66. This officer was Col. John Haslet (1727–1777) with his own Delaware regiment and a detachment of Maryland troops.

67. William Malcolm (1745–1791) was a prominent

New York City merchant and legislator. During the Revolution, he commanded Malcolm's Additional Continental Regiment and was also an aide to Maj. Gen. Horatio Gates. By the end of the war, he served as a brigadier general in the New York Militia.

68. Lt. Ephraim Fenno of Knox's Artillery.

69. These officers were Col. John Tyler of Connecticut, Col. Jedediah Huntington of Connecticut, and Col. Dyer Throop of Connecticut.

70. Col. Joseph Reed (1741–1785) of Trenton, New Jersey, was an aide-de-camp to George Washington as well as adjutant general of the Continental Army during the war's early stages. He later served in the Continental Congress and was President (Governor) of Pennsylvania.

71. Col. John Lasher (1726–1805) commanded a regiment in the New York Militia.

72. Lt. Daniel Jackson of Knox's Artillery.

73. Maj. Israel Keith (b. 1744) of Bridgewater, Massachusetts, later served as an aide-de-camp and deputy adjutant general to General Heath from 1777 to 1778. He concluded the war as a lieutenant colonel.

74. Maj. Jonathan Pollard of Massachusetts.

75. Col. Levi Pawling (1721–1782) of Ulster County, New York, was a prominent judge and New York Militia officer during the Revolution.

76. Col. Richard Cary of Virginia.

77. For this incident, Major Austin of Col. Brewer's regiment was court-martialed and dismissed from the service.

78. Fort Montgomery was a fortification built by the Continental Army in 1776 on the west bank of the Hudson River. The site was declared a National Historic Landmark in 1972.

79. Capt. John Gooch of Massachusetts.

80. Capt. William Treadwell of Knox's Artillery.

81. Pollopel's is the modern spelling.

82. Ebenezer Huntington (1754–1834) of Norwich, Connecticut, was a brother of Brig. Gen. Jedediah Huntington (1743–1818). He served in the 1st and 3rd Connecticut Regiments during the Revolution and concluded the war as a lieutenant colonel. Huntington later served as a brigadier general in the 1790s and was a U.S. Congressman from 1810 to 1811 and from 1817 to 1819.

83. Alexander Scammell (1747–1781) was a Harvard-educated attorney from Massachusetts who served as an officer on the New Hampshire line during the early stages of the Revolution. He later rose to the rank of colonel, serving as an assistant adjutant general for Maj. Gen. Charles Lee and later as adjutant general of the Continental Army. Scammell was the highest ranking American officer killed during the Siege of Yorktown.

84. James Bowdoin (1726–1790) was a prominent Patriot leader in Massachusetts who later served as governor of that state from 1785 to 1787.

85. Probably Col. Elisha Porter of Massachusetts.

86. The Rev. Dr. Charles Inglis, rector of New York City's Trinity Church, was a prominent Loyalist.

87. Col. A. Hawkes Hay of the Haverstraw Militia Regiment.

88. This officer was William Harcourt, 3rd Earl Harcourt (1743–1830) of the British Army, who at the time commanded the 16th Light Dragoons. For capturing General Lee, Harcourt was promoted to full colonel as a reward. He went on to become a field marshal during the reign of King George IV (1820–1830).

89. This Loyalist officer was probably Lt. Col. Abraham Buskirk of New Jersey.

90. Kakaat is now Ramapo. It and Clarkstown are in Rockland County, New York.

91. Col. Nathan Sparhawk of the Massachusetts Militia.

Chapter 3

1. James Ewing (1736–1806) of Lancaster, Pennsylvania, was a prominent legislator and militia officer prior to the Revolution. During the war, he served as a brigadier general in the Pennsylvania Militia. Following the war, Ewing served as vice president (lieutenant governor) of Pennsylvania from 1782 to 1784.

2. John Cadwalader (1742–1786) of Philadelphia, Pennsylvania, was a merchant who served as colonel of the Philadelphia Associators, a volunteer militia unit founded by Benjamin Franklin in 1747.

3. Col. Robert Rogers (1731–1795).

4. Probably Capt. John Graham of the 1st New York Regiment.

5. *Inst.* refers to in or of the present month; "your letter of the 10th inst."

6. Probably Josiah Whitney (1731–1806) of the Massachusetts Militia. He was promoted to brigadier general in 1783.

7. *Waldeckers* were German mercenaries who served with the British Army.

8. Jonathan Moulton (1726–1787) of North Hampton, New Hampshire, was a prominent solider and political leader. A veteran of King George's War and the French and Indian War, he commanded the 3rd New Hampshire Militia during the Revolution and was later promoted to brigadier general.

9. This could have been either Col. David Gilman or Col. Nicholas Gilman.

10. Philip Van Cortlandt (1749–1821) of Westchester County, New York, was a surveyor, landowner, and politician. During the Revolution, he commanded the 2nd New York Regiment in the Continental Army. Following the war, he served in the New York State Legislature and the U.S. House of Representatives (1793–1809).

11. A *chandeller* was a wooden frame, filled with fascines, to form a traverse in sapping.

12. A *fascine* is a rough bundle of brushwood or other material used for strengthening an earthen structure.

13. Delancey's Mills were in what is now Bronx Park in New York City.

14. Abraham Ten Broeck (1734–1818) of Albany, New York, was a prominent politician and businessman of Dutch descent who served as a brigadier general in the New York Militia during the Revolution.

15. Hart's Island is just below City Island in Long Island Sound.

16. Probably Col. William Humphrey of the 5th Duchess County Regiment.

17. Roger Enos (1729–1808) of Hartford, Connecticut, was a French and Indian War veteran who served as lieutenant colonel of several Continental Army regiments during the Revolution. In 1776, he moved to Windsor, Vermont, and was appointed colonel of a militia regiment from that area.

18. This was Col. Charles Armand Tuffin, Marquis de la Rouërie (1751–1793). He was an exiled French nobleman who served with the Continental Army, later earning promotion to brigadier general.

19. Philippe Hubert Preudhomme de Borre (1717–1791) was a French nobleman and military leader who served as a military expert for the Continental Army. He was quickly promoted to brigadier general but later resigned in disgrace following a poor performance at the Battle of Brandywine in September 1777.

20. Col. James Wesson of the Continental Army's 9th Massachusetts Regiment.

21. Col. Edward Wigglesworth of the Continental Army's 13th Massachusetts Regiment.

22. Col. John Bailey of Hanover, Massachusetts. He commanded the 2nd Massachusetts Regiment in the Continental Army.

23. John Crane (1744–1805) of Braintree, Massachusetts, was a French and Indian War veteran and participant in the Boston Tea Party. He moved to Providence, Rhode Island, in 1774. During the Revolution, Crane commanded the 3rd Continental Artillery Regiment and was awarded a brevet promotion to brigadier general in 1783.

24. Philippe Charles Tronson du Coudray (1738–1777) was a French brigadier general and artillery expert who went on to serve as an inspector general in the Continental Army. He drowned in a horse riding accident in 1777.

25. Col. Return J. Meigs, Sr. (1740–1823), of Middletown, Connecticut, commanded several Continental Army regiments during the Revolution and was distinguished for his leadership in the 1777 Meigs Raid and the 1779 Battle of Stony Point.

26. John Manley (1733–1793) of Marblehead, Massachusetts, was a Continental Navy officer who was successful in capturing several British ships over the course of the war.

27. Now known as New Brunswick, New Jersey.

28. This could have been either Capt. Thomas Clouston of Massachusetts or Capt. John Clouston of New York. Both were privateers during this period.

29. This quote is actually widely attributed to Maj. Gen. William Phillips (1731–1781) of the British Army.

30. Maj. Gen. William Phillips (1731–1781) of the British Army.

31. Maj. Gen. Arthur St. Clair (1737–1818) of Pennsylvania. He was court-martialed for surrendering Ticonderoga but was later exonerated and returned to duty. However, St. Clair held no other field commands after that point and served instead as an aide-de-camp to George Washington.

32. This was Col. Ebenezer Francis (d. 1777) of Massachusetts, who commanded the 11th Massachusetts Regiment.

33. William Barton (1748–1831) of Warren, Rhode Island, was a colonel in the Continental Army as well as adjutant general of the Rhode Island Militia.

34. Located in Newport, Rhode Island, this home is now known as the Nichols-Overing House.

35. Barrimore Matthew "Barry" St. Leger (1733–1789) was a British Army officer who saw service in the French and Indian War. During the Revolution, he commanded the 34th Regiment of Foot during the Quebec and Saratoga Campaigns and was later brevetted a brigadier general.

36. This was the famous Jane McCrea (1752–1777), who was purportedly slain by Native Americans aligned with Lt. Gen. John Burgoyne.

37. This was Lt. Col. Friedrich Baum (1727–1777), a Hessian who was mortally wounded and captured at the Battle of Saratoga.

38. This was Lt. Col. Heinrich von Breymann (d. 1777), a Hessian officer who was killed by one of his own men during the Battle of Saratoga.

39. Nicholas Herkimer (1728–1777) of New York's Mohawk Valley was a brigadier general in the New York Militia. He was mortally wounded at the August 1777 Battle of Oriskany.

40. Located in the northeast corner of Maryland, Head of Elk is now known as Elkton.

41. Capt. Jonathan Haraden (1744–1803) of Gloucester, Massachusetts, was a highly successful privateer during the Revolution, leading several attacks on British shipping vessels.

42. Col. William R. Lee (1745–1824) of Salem, Massachusetts, commanded Lee's Additional Regiment in the Continental Army. He was supposedly a distant relative of Maj. Gen. Charles Lee (1732–1782).

43. This was Charles Grey, 1st Earl Grey (1729–1807), who was then a major general in the British Army. Following the 1777 Battle of Paoli, where Grey had collected the flints from his soldiers' muskets before ordering a bayonet attack, he became known as "No-Flint Grey."

44. This was the Battle of Paoli, fought on September 20, 1777. As it was a nighttime surprise attack, it was later dubbed (from the American perspective) the "Paoli massacre," even though American casualties were relatively light.

45. This was the first Battle of Saratoga, which ended in a pyrrhic British victory.

46. These officers were Lt. Col. Winborne Adams of the 2nd New Hampshire Regiment and Lt. Col. Andrew Colburn of the 3rd New Hampshire Regiment.

47. This officer was Lt. Col. John Brown of the Berkshire Militia.

48. A *bateaux* is a long, light flat-bottomed boat that was used extensively across North America during the colonial period.

49. This was the second Battle of Saratoga, which ended in a decisive American victory.

50. This officer was Brig. Gen. Simon Fraser (1729–1777), who was mortally wounded by an American sniper named Timothy Murphy (1751–1818).

51. Later spelled Peploop's or Peplap's.

52. Esopus is a town in Ulster County, New York.

53. This officer was Lt. Col. Thomas Musgrave of the 40th Regiment of Foot.

54. This home, known as Cliveden or the Benjamin Chew House, is now a U.S. National Historic Landmark.

55. Francis Nash (1742–1777) of Hillsborough, North Carolina, was an attorney, court clerk, and colonial legislator prior to the Revolution. Following service in the North Carolina Provisional Congress, Nash was promoted to brigadier general on February 5, 1777.

56. This was Brig. Gen. James Agnew (1719–1777), who was killed by an American sniper during the Battle of Germantown.

57. This may be the Jason Russell House, located in Arlington, Massachusetts. It is now on the U.S. National Register of Historic Places.

58. This was Brig. Gen. William Whipple, Jr. (1730–1785), of the New Hampshire Militia. He was also a signer of the U.S. Declaration of Independence as a representative from New Hampshire.

59. Maj. Joseph Swasey (d. 1817) of Col. William R. Lee's regiment.

60. Count Carl Emil Ulrich von Donop (1732–1777) of Hesse-Kassel.

61. Brig. Gen. William Irvine (1741–1804) of Pennsylvania.

Chapter 4

1. This was Adm. Richard Howe, 1st Earl Howe (1726–1799) of the British Royal Navy.

2. This was probably the HMS *Eagle* of the British Royal Navy. It was in operation from 1774 through 1812.

3. David Henley (1748–1823) of Charlestown, Massachusetts, was a Continental Army officer who served as George Washington's intelligence officer and as prisoner of war commandant. This situation began when he stabbed an insolent but unarmed British prisoner. The court-martial proceedings were held at Cambridge from January 20 to February 25, 1778, and Henley was acquitted. Afterwards, General Burgoyne challenged him to a duel, which was to take place in Bermuda. Although Colonel Henley accepted the challenge, the duel never took place.

4. These officers listed (and not previously mentioned in the book) were probably Lt. Col. Dudley Coleman of the 13th Massachusetts Regiment; Lt. Col. John Popkin of the 3rd Continental Artillery; Maj. William Curtis of Henley's Additional Continentals; Capt. Thomas Randall of the 3rd Continental Artillery; Capt. John Langdon of Jackson's Continentals; Capt. Stephen Sewell of Lee's Additional Continentals; Capt. John Hastings of Lee's Additional Continentals. In addition to those officers, Continental Army Judge Advocate General William Tudor was also present.

5. Nicholas Cooke (1717–1782) served as governor of Rhode Island from 1776 to 1778.

6. A *fusee* was an old term for "flintlock rifle."

7. In this context, a *wag* refers to someone who jokes or does pranks.

8. This was Sir Robert Pigot, 2nd Baronet (1720–1796), then a major general in the British Army.

9. Silas Deane (1737–1789) of Connecticut served as the United States' first foreign diplomat, lobbying the French Government for aid. His service as a diplomat was highly controversial, and he was accused by the Continental Congress of administrative carelessness as well as possibly being a spy.

10. These were essentially supply ships.

11. William Tryon (1729–1788) was a British colonial governor of North Carolina (1765–1771) and of New York (1771–1780). During the Revolution, his authority in New York was very limited and was applicable only to British-occupied areas.

12. Jonathan Trumbull, Sr. (1710–1785), was both governor of the Connecticut Colony (1769–1776) and governor of Connecticut (1776–1784). He was one of the only British colonial governors who went on to support the patriot cause.

13. Emer de Vattel (1714–1767), as Swiss philosopher, legal expert, and diplomat, was most famous for his seminal work, *The Law of Nations*, first published in 1758.

14. Baron Samuel von Pufendorf (1632–1694) was a German jurist and political philosopher who was best known for his comments and revisions of the natural law theories of Thomas Hobbes and Hugo Grotius.

15. Hugo Grotius (1583–1645) was a Dutch jurist and political philosopher who laid the foundations for modern international law, based largely on natural law.

16. Henry Harnage (1739–1826) of the 62nd British Infantry was one of the officers captured following the Battle of Saratoga. He had also been severely wounded during the battle. His two highlighted letters were part of a lengthy correspondence initiated by Harnage to get exchanged or paroled on account of his wife's illness. The exchange of letters eventually included such figures as George Washington, Horatio Gates, and Benjamin Franklin. The request for a parole was eventually granted.

17. A *xebeck* was a Mediterranean sailing ship that was used mostly for trading.

18. A *matross* was a soldier of artillery, ranking below a gunner. They assisted gunners in loading, firing, and sponging the cannons.

19. A *snow* is a type of two-masted sailing vessel.

20. This was Maj. Thomas Bumstead (1739–1828) of Massachusetts. Following the war, he went on to establish a coach shop, reportedly selling one to Abigail Adams herself.

21. Lt. Zaccheus Dunnell of the 3rd Continental Artillery.

22. This was the John Hancock of Continental Congress fame. His brief tenure as a military commander was a fiasco.

23. A *glass* (nautical term) is a half-hour sand glass. Thus, "three glasses" would be an hour and a half.

24. Solomon Lovell (1732–1801) of Abington, Massachusetts, was a brigadier general in the Massachusetts Militia.

25. The Hon. John Byron (1723–1786) was a vice admiral in the British Royal Navy during the later stages of the Revolution. He was commander-in-chief of the British fleet in the West Indies from 1778 to 1779 and was later commander-in-chief for the North American Station. Byron was known as "Foul-Weather Jack" because of his frequent encounters with bad weather at sea.

26. This was Brig. Gen. Johann Friederich Specht (d. 1787), who commanded the 1st Brigade of Brunswick troops at the Battle of Saratoga.

27. Louis Antoine de Bougainville (1729–1811) was a French admiral, general, and explorer who saw action at the Battle of the Chesapeake (1781) as well as at the Battle of the Saintes (1782). Bougainville was best known as being the first Frenchman to circumnavigate the globe.

28. Col. Ichabod Alden (1739–1778) of Duxbury, Massachusetts, commanded the 7th Massachusetts Regiment stationed at Cherry Valley, New York. He was a great-grandson of *Mayflower* pilgrim John Alden. The surprise attack of Native Americans at Cherry Valley was retaliation for their defeat at the Battle of Oriskany a year earlier.

29. Joseph Ward (1737–1812) of Newton, Massachusetts, was a schoolmaster and teacher prior to his service in the Continental Army. During the early stages of the Revolution, he served as a secretary and aide for Maj. Gen. Artemas Ward. Following the war, he was a state legislator and judge.

30. William Bradford (1755–1795) of Philadelphia, Pennsylvania, was a lawyer and judge who went on to serve as U.S. Attorney General from 1794 to 1795.

31. Vice Adm. James Gambier (1723–1789) of the British Royal Navy served as commander-in-chief of the North American Station from 1770 to 1771 and again from 1778 to 1779.

Chapter 5

1. Henry Mowatt (1734–1798) was a British Royal Navy officer who commanded ships in northern New England during the Revolution. He was best known for his attack on Falmouth, Massachusetts, (present-day Portland, Maine), in October 1775.

2. A *picaroon* is another term for pirate ship.

3. Located on England's southern coast, Gosport is a town on the western side of Portsmouth Harbor opposite the City of Portsmouth.

4. Dr. Eliphalet Downer (1743–1806) was known as the "fighting surgeon," serving with both the Continental Army and Navy.

5. Dr. Downer had been captured while serving on an American privateer in the English Channel. Although he had been severely wounded, he and some comrades escaped the British prison by tunneling forty feet under the prison walls. Their only digging tool was a jack knife.

6. This is a reference to the First Battle of Savannah (sometimes called the Capture of Savannah), fought on December 29, 1778.

7. Robert Howe (1732–1786) was a major general in the Continental Army from North Carolina. He was once suspected of possible treason (by supposedly giving information to the British), but this charge has never been proven.

8. These charges were related to Arnold's rumored war-profiteering as military commander of Philadelphia.

9. This was William Tryon (1729–1788), the British colonial governor of New York. Along with his political appointment, Tryon was also commis-sioned a major general in the British Army (in America only) in 1778. In that capacity, he conducted a series of raids on towns along the Connecticut coast in 1779.

10. William Maxwell (1733–1796) was a brigadier general in the Continental Army from New Jersey. Originally from County Tyrone in Northern Ireland, he was sometimes called "Scotch Willie."

11. Samuel Elbert (1740–1788) of Savannah, Georgia was a highly respected Continental Army officer who was later brevetted a brigadier general. He was captured by the British at the Battle of Brier Creek and later exchanged for Brig. Gen. James Inglis Hamilton. Elbert later served as Governor of Georgia from 1785 to 1786.

12. Edward Winslow (1746–1815) of Plymouth, Massachusetts, was a Loyalist officer who served with the British Army during the Revolution. Following the war, he and his family settled in Canada, where Winslow was instrumental in the creation of the Province of New Brunswick.

13. George Leonard (1742–1826) of Plymouth, Massachusetts, was a noted Loyalist who commanded a fleet of ships that raided coastal towns in 1779. Following the war, he and his family lived in Nova Scotia and New Brunswick.

14. Capt. Tobias Fernald of the 18th Continentals.

15. Goose Van Schaick (1736–1789) of Albany, New York, was a colonel in the Continental Army who was later brevetted a brigadier general. He was best known for leading this 1779 expedition against the Onondaga Indians, for which he received the thanks of Congress.

16. Edward Mathew (1729–1785) was a brigadier general in the British Army during the Revolution as well as an aide-de-camp to King George III. He was father-in-law to Jane Austen's brother (James), and was supposed to have inspired the character General Tilney in her novel *Northanger Abbey*.

17. Sir George Collier (1738–1795) was a vice-admiral in the Royal Navy.

18. These forces were commanded by Lt. Col. Banastre Tarleton (1754–1833) and Lt. Col. John Graves Simcoe (1752–1806).

19. Lt. Col. Thomas Grosvenor (1744–1825) of the 3rd Connecticut Regiment.

20. This is probably a reference to Dunderberg Mountain near Stony Point, New York.

21. Col. Elisha Sheldon commanded the 2nd Continental Light Dragoons. In 2006, this regiment's battle flag (captured by Lt. Col. Banastre Tarleton's forces in 1779) sold for $12.3 million in a Sotheby's auction.

22. Col. Josiah Starr (1740–1813) of the 1st Connecticut Regiment.

23. Note that there are two "General Howes" being discussed in this section of the memoirs, Maj. Gen. Robert Howe of the Continental Army and Gen. William Howe of the British Army.

24. Col. Francis McLean (1717–1781) of the British Army.

25. Stephen Moylan (1737–1811) of Philadelphia, Pennsylvania, had several positions in the Continental Army, including muster-master general, quartermaster general, and personal aide to George Washington. He was also a cavalry officer and commanded the 4th

Continental Light Dragoons. He was brevetted a brigadier general in November 1783.

26. This was Lt. Col. Andreas Emmerich (1737–1809), a German who had served for many years with the British Army.

27. Anthony Walton White (1750–1803) of New Jersey commanded the 3rd New Jersey Regiment and later the 1st Continental Light Dragoons. He was later promoted to colonel in 1780.

28. This was Anne-César, Chevalier de la Luzerne (1741–1791), who served as the second French minister to the United States from 1779 to 1784.

29. The Genesee Country has since become famous for its orchards.

30. *Sieur* is a title of respect used by the French and is similar to "Sir." Conrad Alexandre Gerard de Rayneval (1729–1790) was the first French diplomatic representative to the United States.

31. Lt. Erasmus Gill (1752–1807) of Moylan's Dragoons. He was later promoted to major.

32. Joseph Yorke, 1st Baron Dover (1724–1792) was a British soldier, politician, and diplomat. He served as British ambassador to the Netherlands for thirty years (1751–1781).

33. Probably Capt. Jonathan Hallett of the 2nd New York Militia.

34. Maj. Amos Waldbridge of the 2nd Connecticut Regiment.

35. Probably Col. Philip Burr Bradley (1738–1821) of Fairfield, Connecticut. He was commander of the 5th Connecticut Regiment.

36. Simcoe was later exchanged for Col. Thomas Reynolds of the 2nd Burlington County (N.J.) Militia Regiment.

37. This was Maj. Elias Van Benschoten (1728–1815) of Lt. Col. Albert Pawling's New York Levies.

38. John Armstrong, Jr. (1758–1843), of Carlisle, Pennsylvania, served as an aide-de-camp to Generals Hugh Mercer and Horatio Gates. After the war, he was a U.S. senator (1801–1804) as well as U.S. secretary of war (1813–1814).

39. Probably Maj. Mansfield Bearmore, who was a Loyalist officer serving with the British Army.

40. This was another term for "provost guard."

41. Ludwig von Wurmb (1736–1813) later became a lieutenant general and served during the Napoleonic Wars.

42. This officer was Lt. Miles Oakley of the 4th New York Regiment.

43. Joseph McKeel (1750–1816) was a Loyalist military operative who fled to Canada following the war. He and his family eventually settled in Kings County, New Brunswick, where he was granted land in 1785 in recognition of his British military service.

44. John Harris Cruger (1738–1807) was a wealthy New York Loyalist who served as a lieutenant colonel in the First Battalion of DeLancey's Brigade. He was later appointed to the command of Ninety-Six, a fortified, British-held village in South Carolina. Following the war, he and his family fled to London, where he died in exile.

45. This was probably Lt. Col. Ezra Newhall (1733–1798) of Massachusetts, who served with the 5th Massachusetts Regiment earlier in the war.

Chapter 6

1. Daniel Lyman (1756–1830) of Durham, Connecticut, was an aide-de-camp to General Heath. Following the war, Lyman settled in Newport, Rhode Island, and served as chief justice of the Rhode Island Supreme Court from 1802 to 1816.

2. Ebenezer Sproat (1752–1805) of Middleborough, Massachusetts, served with several Massachusetts regiments (including the 2nd, 3rd, 4th, and 12th) and was respected by both officers and enlisted men alike. His wife was the daughter of Commodore Abraham Whipple (1733–1819) of the Continental Navy. Following the war, he and his family settled in Ohio. His surname is also spelled "Sprout."

3. Probably Capt. Seth Drew (d. 1824) of the 2nd Massachusetts Regiment.

4. Col. John Mead of the 9th Connecticut Militia.

5. In this context, *levies* refer to a unit of conscripted soldiers.

6. Capt. Samuel Keeler of Col. P.B. Bradley's regiment of Connecticut State Troops.

7. Capt. Samuel Lockwood of the 2nd Continental Artillery.

8. Isaac Hatfield of New York was a Loyalist serving with the British Army.

9. John Paterson (1744–1808) of New Britain, Connecticut, was a lawyer and colonial legislator who was a brigade commander in the Continental Army. He was brevetted a major general in 1783 and settled in New York after the war. Paterson served in the U.S. House of Representatives from 1803 to 1805.

10. Col. Joseph Thompson of the 10th Massachusetts Regiment.

11. Capt. William Watson of the 9th Massachusetts Regiment.

12. Capt. Moses Roberts of the 15th Massachusetts Regiment.

13. Capt. Orange Stoddard of the 1st Massachusetts Regiment.

14. Capt. Lt. Michael Farley of Wesson's Regiment.

15. Capt. James Cooper of the 14th Massachusetts Regiment.

16. This was probably Col. Ichabod Norton (1736–1825) of Farmington, Connecticut, who was a prominent soldier and legislator during the period.

17. Lt. William Burley of the 11th Massachusetts Regiment.

18. Lt. Jonathan Maynard of the 5th Massachusetts Regiment.

19. Ensign Stephen Fowler of the 6th Massachusetts Regiment.

20. Ensign Levi Bradley of the 4th Massachusetts Regiment.

21. Ezra Badlam (1746–1788) of Milton, Massachusetts, was a lieutenant colonel with the 2nd Massachusetts Regiment. His brother, Stephen Badlam (1748–1815) was a brigadier general in the Massachusetts Militia.

22. This was Thomas Langhorne Byles of the 3rd Pennsylvania Regiment.

23. "Latouche" was in reference to Captain de la Touche-Tréville.

24. This was later celebrated as Dark Day throughout New England.

25. Dr. James Craik (1730–1814) was physician general of the Continental Army as well as George Washington's personal physician.

26. Jabez Bowen, Jr. (1739–1815), of Providence, Rhode Island, was a deputy governor of Rhode Island, militia officer, and chief justice of the Rhode Island Supreme Court.

27. Col. Israel Angell (1740–1832) of the 2nd Rhode Island Regiment.

28. Louis-Dominique Ethis Corny (1736–1790) was a French military official and commissary attached to General Rochambeau's forces.

29. An *en flûte* is a French naval expression from the Age of Sail to designate a warship used as transport, with a reduced armament.

30. Brig. George Godfrey (1720–1793) of the Massachusetts Militia.

31. These officers were Col. Nathan Tyler, Col. Abner Perry, and probably Maj. Moses Bullard of the Massachusetts Militia.

32. This is a reference to London's famous 1780 Gordon Riots, which were aimed to trying to stop British Parliamentary movement toward partial Catholic emancipation.

33. Lord George Gordon (1751–1793) was a British politician and president of the Protestant Association who helped instigate the Gordon Riots in June 1780.

34. Silas Talbot (1751–1813) of Dighton, Massachusetts, was an officer in both the Continental Army and Navy, later rising to the rank of commodore. Along with being a U.S. congressman from 1793 to 1795, he was best known for commanding the USS *Constitution* from 1799 to 1801.

35. Luc Urbain de Bouexic, Comte de Guichen (1712–1790), was a French admiral who led a squadron of ships in the West Indies during the American Revolution.

36. John Jameson (1751–1810) of Culpeper, Virginia, was a colonel in the Continental Army. He was instrumental in exposing Benedict Arnold's treasonous plot at West Point, but also inadvertently allowed Arnold to escape.

37. Lt. Col. John Brown of Massachusetts.

38. Also known as the *Hudson River Chain*, it prevented British ships from sailing up the Hudson River.

39. Lt. Col. Jean Baptiste Gouvion (1747–1792) was General Rochambeau's chief of artillery. He was later promoted to brigadier general and was killed in battle during the French Revolution.

40. This officer was Capt. John Buchanan (d. 1803) of the 1st Pennsylvania Regiment.

41. François-Jean de Chastellux (1734–1788) was a French major general who served on General Rochambeau's staff. He was the principal liaison between Rochambeau and George Washington.

42. This was probably Louis Marc Antoine de Noailles (1756–1804), a French Army officer who served under the Marquis de Lafayette.

43. This was Joseph-François-Louis-Charles de Damas (1758–1829), who took part as a colonel in the American Revolution from 1780 to 1781. He later became a general and received a dukedom in 1825.

44. Thomas-Antoine de Mauduit du Plessis (1753–1791) was a French lieutenant colonel who took part in many battles during the American Revolution. He was killed by his own troops during the 1791 Haitian Revolution.

45. The Marquis de Laval was a French nobleman and colonel who commanded a French Army regiment supporting the Continental Army.

46. Adam Philipe, Comte de Custine (1740–1793), was a colonel in General Rochambeau's expeditionary force and later rose to the rank of lieutenant general in the French Army. He was executed during the French Revolution in 1793.

47. François de Fleury (1749–1799) was a French nobleman who volunteered to fight with the Continental Army during the American Revolution. He later became a general and was badly wounded during the French Revolutionary War, prompting his resignation from the army.

48. Maj. Hugh Maxwell of the 15th Massachusetts Regiment.

49. Antoine de Sartine (1729–1801) was a French statesman who served as secretary of state for the Navy from 1774 to 1780. He was eventually dismissed by King Louis XVI.

50. The Marquis de Castries (1727–1801) was a French nobleman and marshal. He served as Secretary of State for the Navy from 1780 to 1787.

51. Probably Maj. Thomas Huggeford, who commanded a unit of Loyalist light horsemen.

52. William Hull (1753–1825) of Derby, Connecticut, served as a lieutenant colonel in the Continental Army and was also a close friend of the famed Revolutionary hero Nathan Hale. Hull went on to serve as a general in the War of 1812.

53. Probably Capt. Roger Welles of the 9th Connecticut Regiment.

54. Lt. John Hart of the 9th Connecticut Regiment.

55. Capt. Thomas Pritchard of the 5th Massachusetts Regiment.

Chapter 7

1. This was probably Christian Graf von Forbach (1752–1817), later known as Christian Marquis de Deux-Ponts. He was an officer in the French Army and later served as a general in the Prussian and Bavarian Armies. During the American Revolution, he served in General Rochambeau's expeditionary force.

2. Hans Axel von Fersen (1755–1810) was a Swedish count and army general who served with the French Army during the American Revolution. He was later an alleged lover of Queen Marie Antoinette of France.

3. Col. Sheldon was a French officer of English extraction.

4. This was the Battle of Cowpens, fought on January 17, 1781.

5. This was Seth Warner (1743–1784) of Roxbury, Connecticut. He later moved to Vermont and commanded the Green Mountain boys during the Revolution. In 1778, he was commissioned a brigadier general in the Vermont Militia.

6. Probably Col. Moses Ashley of the 5th Massachusetts Regiment.

7. This was Jean B.L.P.F. d'Olliéres, Count de Saint Maime.

8. Jean-Joseph Sourbader de Gimat (b. 1743) was a volunteer French officer who served as an aide to the Marquis de Lafayette. In 1781, he saw action during the Battle of Green Spring and during the Siege of Yorktown .

9. L'Orient (or Lorient) is a seaport in the Brittany region of France.

10. Capt. John Pray (d. 1812) of the 12th Massachusetts Regiment.

11. This was Brig. Gen. Andrew Pickens (1739–1817), the famed partisan militia leader who would go on to serve in the U.S. House of Representatives from 1793 to 1795. He is the 7th great-grandfather of former U.S. senator and 2004 vice presidential candidate John Edwards.

12. This was the prominent cavalry commander Henry Lee III (1756–1818), better known as "Light-Horse Harry" Lee. He is best remembered in history as being the father of Confederate Gen. Robert E. Lee.

13. Capt. Isaac Pope of the 4th Massachusetts Regiment.

14. This was the Battle of Guilford Courthouse, fought on March 15, 1781.

15. This was Pierre Francois Beville, Quarter Master General of the French Army in America.

16. Col. Henry Champion II (1723–1897) of East Haddam, Connecticut served as Commissary General for the Eastern Department of the Continental Army. His sons Epaphroditus and Henry III were also officers in the Connecticut Militia and Continental Army respectively.

17. Ebenezer Flagg, Jr. (1747–1781), of Newport, Rhode Island, served in the 1st Rhode Island Regiment, which was composed mostly of African-Americans.

18. Meshech Weare (1713–1786) of Seabrook, New Hampshire, served as the first president (governor) of New Hampshire from 1776 to 1785.

19. This was the Battle of Hobkirk's Hill, fought on April 25, 1781, which was considered a tactical British victory but strategic American victory. It is sometimes referred to as the Second Battle of Camden.

20. This was Maj. Gen. Francis Rawdon-Hastings, 1st Marquess of Hastings (1754–1826), who would go on to serve as Governor-General of India from 1813 to 1823 and Governor of Malta from 1824 to 1826.

21. This was the famed partisan leader Thomas Sumter (1734–1832) of South Carolina, who held commissions in Continental Army as well as the South Carolina Militia over the course of the war. Following the war, he served in both the U.S. House of Representatives (1797–1801) and the U.S. Senate (1801–1810).

22. The site of Fort Motte is located in what is now Calhoun County, South Carolina.

23. This was the famed partisan leader Francis Marion (1732–1795) of South Carolina, who held commissions in both the Continental Army and the South Carolina Militia. He was best known by his nickname, the "Swamp Fox."

24. This was Dudley Saltonstall (1738–1796) of New London, Connecticut, who was a successful merchant captain and privateer. He served as a captain in the Continental Navy before being court-martialed

and dismissed from the service for his poor performance during the 1781 Penobscot expedition.

25. The Penobscot expedition was a failed attack against a British-held stronghold in Penobscot Bay, Maine, that took place in the summer of 1779. Capt. Dudley Saltonstall was criticized severely for his poor performance as a commander in this military operation.

26. Brig. Gen. David Waterbury (1723–1801) of Stamford, Connecticut, commanded a brigade of Connecticut State Troops during the Revolution.

27. Richard Peters, Jr. (1744–1828), of Philadelphia, Pennsylvania, was a prominent attorney who served as Commissioner of the Board of War for much of the Revolution. He later served in the Continental Congress from 1782 to 1783.

28. Jacques-Melchior Saint Laurent, Comte de Barras (1719–1793), was an admiral in the French Navy who commanded a squadron of ships based at Newport, Rhode Island, during the American Revolution. He later served under Admiral de Grasse in the West Indies.

29. Frederick, Baron de Weissenfels (1738–1806), was a Prussian-born British officer who settled in New York prior to the Revolution. During the war, he supported the Patriot cause and served as lieutenant colonel of the 4th New York Levies.

30. This operation was led by Benedict Arnold, who by this time was a brigadier general in the British Army.

31. William Ledyard (1738–1781) of Groton, Connecticut, was a lieutenant colonel in the Connecticut Militia during the Revolution. He commanded Fort Griswold and was killed by the British following their takeover of that fort in September 1781. This battle is sometimes referred to as the Battle of Groton Heights. The town of Ledyard, Connecticut, is named in his honor.

32. Capt. Peter Richard s of the Massachusetts Militia.

33. Maj. Moses Knapp (d. 1809) of the 10th Massachusetts Regiment

34. Benjamin Tallmadge (1754–1835) of Setauket, New York, was a major with the 2nd Continental Light Dragoons. He was later appointed chief intelligence officer for George Washington with the rank of colonel. Following the war, Tallmadge served in the U.S. House of Representatives from 1801 to 1817.

35. This was the Battle of the Chesapeake (sometimes called the Battle of the Capes), fought on September 5, 1781. It was a decisive French victory that prevented the British from resupplying or reinforcing Lord Cornwallis' forces at Yorktown, Virginia.

36. Heman Swift (1733–1814) of Cornwall, Connecticut, served as a colonel in the Connecticut State Troops during the Revolution. He was later brevetted a brigadier general in September 1783.

37. Capt. George Dunham of the 2nd Massachusetts Regiment.

38. Following a career in the British Royal Navy, Prince William Henry (1765–1837) went on to rule Great Britain as King William IV (1830–1837). While the Prince was stationed in New York, George Washington authorized a proposed mission to kidnap him. However, the British were made aware of this opera-

tion and assigned several bodyguards to protect the Prince. Thus, the plan never came to fruition.

39. Maj. Lemuel Trescott (1751–1826) of the 16th Massachusetts Regiment.

40. The site of Fort Salonga is located on the north shore of Long Island in Suffolk County, New York.

41. Maj. Amos Morrill (1748–1810) of the 2nd New Hampshire Regiment.

42. Wawarsing is located in Ulster County, New York.

43. Thomas Lovelace was hung near the present Schuylerville, New York. He was a noted Loyalist marauder.

44. Lt. Col. James Millen of the 4th Massachusetts Regiment.

45. Marinus Willett (1740–1830) of Jamaica, New York was a French and Indian War veteran who was later active with the Sons of Liberty. He was a highly respected soldier who served as a colonel in both the Continental Army and the New York Militia. Following the war, he served as mayor of New York City from 1807 to 1808.

46. Maj. John Ross of the King's Royal Regiment of New York.

47. This was the Battle of Johnstown, fought on October 25, 1781, which ended in an American victory.

48. This was William Butler (1752–1781), a prominent New York Loyalist who was despised by the Patriots. This hatred stemmed from his involvement in the 1778 Cherry Valley Massacre.

49. Lt. Samuel De Forest of the 5th Connecticut Regiment.

50. Probably Lt. Abner Hull of the 7th Connecticut Regiment.

51. Probably Lt. Jasper Mead of the 5th Connecticut Regiment.

52. Capt. Samuel Sacket of the 4th New York Regiment.

53. Lt. John Mosher of the 8th Massachusetts Regiment.

54. Capt. Samuel Kipp (d. 1781) was a noted New York Loyalist.

55. Capt. Daniel Williams of the New York Militia.

Chapter 8

1. Capt. Israel Honeywell, Jr., of the 1st Westchester Militia.

2. Lt. John Hiwell (d. 1788) of the 3rd Continental Artillery.

3. François Claude Amour, marquis de Bouillé (1739–1800) was a French general who led French forces in the West Indies during the American Revolution. In later years, he was a committed Royalist during the French Revolution and was forced to go into exile. He is mentioned as a hated Royalist in the French national anthem, *La Marseillaise*.

4. The *Dauphin* of France was a title given to the heir apparent to the throne of France from 1350 to 1791 and 1824 to 1830. The word is French for dolphin, and in this case was a reference to Louis Joseph de France (1781–1789), who was the second child and elder son of King Louis XVI of France. He died of an illness during the early stages of the French Revolution.

5. Abraham "Brom" Dyckman (1754–1782) was a New York Militia soldier and guide for the Continental Army. He had served as a guide for General Heath during the failed January 1777 attack on Fort Independence, and was highly respected for his skills. Dyckman was mortally wounded in March 1782 following a skirmish with New York Loyalist forces.

6. This was probably Sir James Lowther, 1st Earl of Lonsdale (1736–1802), who served as a Member of Parliament from 1757 to 1784.

7. Capt. Benjamin Vermilyea of the 1st Westchester Militia.

8. The participants in this duel were Capt. Luke Hitchcock of the 1st Massachusetts Regiment and Lt. Nathan Stone of Jackson's Massachusetts Regiment.

9. Joshua "Jack" Huddy (1735–1782) of Salem County, New Jersey, commanded both a militia unit and privateer ship during the Revolution. His execution by British forces led to a major international incident known as the Asgill Affair.

10. Richard Lippincott (1745–1826) of Shrewsbury, New Jersey, was a Loyalist officer who was best known for his part in the execution of Capt. Joshua Huddy. He was ultimately court-martialed for authorizing the execution but was later cleared of the charges. Following the war, Lippincott settled in what is now Toronto, Canada.

11. David Humphreys (1752–1818) of Derby, Connecticut, was a lieutenant colonel in the Continental Army. Following service as an aide for Generals Israel Putnam and Nathanael Greene, Humphreys served as George Washington's aide-de-camp from 1780 until the end of the war. Following the war, he became a diplomat and served as U.S. minister to both Portugal and Spain.

12. Sir Charles Asgill, 2nd Baronet (1762–1823), was the only son of one-time Lord Mayor of London Sir Charles Asgill (1713–1788). During the Revolution, the younger Asgill served as a captain in the British Army and was later captured following the Surrender at Yorktown. Following the famous Asgill Affair discussed by General Heath, Asgill went on to become a general in the British Army.

13. Charles Gravier, comte de Vergennes (1717–1787), was a French statesman and diplomat who served as Foreign Minister from 1774 to 1787.

14. Maj. Robert Oliver of the 3rd Massachusetts Regiment.

15. Alexander Gillon (1741–1794) of Charleston, South Carolina, was a merchant and seaman who served as a commodore in the South Carolina Navy. Following the war, he served in the U.S. House of Representatives from 1793 to 1794.

16. Richard Kempenfelt (1718–1782) was a rear-admiral in the British Royal Navy. He is best remembered for defeating the French with a vastly inferior force at the 1781 Battle of Ushant.

17. Jacques Anne Joseph Le Prestre de Vauban (1754–1816) served as General Rochambeau's aide-de-camp during the American Revolution. He later became a general in the French Army.

18. This was Jean-Louis-Ambroise de Genton, chevalier de Villefranche (1747–1784).

19. Charles Watson-Wentworth, 2nd Marquess of Rockingham (1730–1782), served as British prime minister from 1765 to 1766 and in 1782.

20. Charles James Fox (1749–1806) served as British secretary of state for foreign affairs in 1782, 1783, and in 1806.

21. William Cavendish-Bentinck, 3rd Duke of Portland (1738–1809) had served as Lord Lieutenant of Ireland prior to his resignation. He later served as British prime minister in 1783 and from 1807 to 1809. He also served as chancellor of the University of Oxford.

22. William Petty, 2nd Earl of Shelburne (1737–1805), served as British prime minister from 1782 to 1783. His government oversaw the peace negotiations with the Americans that culminated in the 1783 Peace of Paris.

23. John Campbell of Strachur (1727–1806) was a British general and Scottish clan chief. He commanded British forces during the 1781 Siege of Pensacola and later succeeded Sir Guy Carleton as British commander in chief in North America.

24. Andrew Elliot (1728–1797) of Pennsylvania was a staunch Loyalist who served as lieutenant governor of New York from 1780 to 1783. He served briefly as acting colonial governor of New York in 1783 until the British evacuation.

25. John Laurens (1754–1782) of Charleston, South Carolina, was a soldier and statesman who served as a lieutenant colonel in the Continental Army. He was also an aide-de-camp to George Washington. Unlike many of his Southern colleagues, Laurens was critical of slavery and proposed recruiting slaves to fight for their freedom as soldiers.

26. This was the Battle of Combahee River, fought on August 26, 1782.

27. This was Maj. Gen. Alexander Leslie (1731–1794) of the British Army. He had replaced Lord Cornwallis as commander in the South in 1782.

28. Louis-Philippe de Vaudreuil (1724–1802) was a French admiral who was second in command of the French fleet in North America during the American Revolution.

Chapter 9

1. Richard Oswold (1705–1784) of Scotland was a merchant and British Government advisor who served as the British Peace Commissioner in Paris. He is best remembered for helping to negotiate the 1783 Peace of Paris.

2. This was Brig. Gen. George Rogers Clark (1752–1818) of Virginia. His younger brother William was one of the leaders of the Lewis and Clark Expedition (1804–1806). General Clark's campaign against the Shawanese Indians was in response to the British-Indian victory at the Battle of Blue Licks in August 1782.

3. This was the noted Loyalist William Franklin (1730–1814)—son of Benjamin Franklin—who had served as Royal Governor of New Jersey from 1763 to 1776.

4. José Solano y Bote, Marquess of Socorro (1726–1806), was a senior Spanish naval officer who later served as General Captain of the Spanish Royal Navy.

5. Several of General Heath's direct descendants went on to represent him in the Society of the Cincinnati. As the most recent one passed away in 1986, General Heath has not been represented in the Society since that time.

6. This letter went on to become one of General Heath's most prized possessions. In the years following the war, he proudly presented it whenever he had visitors to his Roxbury home.

Bibliography

Abbatt, William, ed. *Memoirs of Major General William Heath*. New York: William Abbatt, 1901.

Abbot, W.W., ed. *The Papers of George Washington*, Retirement Series, vol. 1, 4 March 1797–30 December 1797. Charlottesville: University Press of Virginia, 1998.

Bennett, Charles E., and Donald R. Lennon. *A Quest for Glory: Major General Robert Howe and the American Revolution*. Chapel Hill: University of North Carolina Press, 1991.

Blanchard, Amos. "William Heath." In *American Military and Naval Biography*, p. 208. Cincinnati, OH: A. Salisbury, 1832.

Butterfield, L.H., ed. *Adams Family Correspondence*, vol. 2. Cambridge, MA: Harvard University Press, 1963.

Crafts, William A. "A General of the Revolution." In *New England Magazine: An Illustrated Monthly*, vol. 3, 513–519. Boston: New England Magazine Corporation, 1891.

Drake, Francis Samuel. *The Town of Roxbury: Its Memorable Persons and Places, Its History and Antiquities, with Numerous Illustrations of its Old Landmarks and Noted Personages*. Boston: Alfred Mudge and Son, 1878.

Fischer, David Hackett. *Paul Revere's Ride*. New York: Oxford University Press, 1994.

Fitzpatrick, John C., ed. *The Writings of George Washington from the Original Manuscript Sources:1745–1799*, vol. 7. Washington, D.C.: Reprint Services, 1931–1944.

Fowler, William M. Jr. *American Crisis: George Washington and the Dangerous Two Years After Yorktown, 1781–1783*. New York: Walker, 2011.

Galvin, John R. *The Minute Men: The First Fight: Myths and Realities of the American Revolution*. Dulles, VA: Potomac, 2006.

Hannings, Bud. *American Revolutionary War Leaders: A Biographical Dictionary*. Jefferson, NC: McFarland, 2006.

Heath, William. *Memoirs of Major-General Heath. Containing Anecdotes, Details of Skirmishes, Battles, and Other Military Events, During the American War*. Boston: I. Thomas and E. T. Andrews, 1798.

Johnson, Allen and Dumas Malone, eds. "William Heath." In *Dictionary of American Biography*, vol. VII, 491. New York: Charles Scribner's Sons, 1946.

Lockhart, Paul. *The Whites of Their Eyes: Bunker Hill, the First American Army, and the Emergence of George Washington*. New York: Harper, 2011.

Morrissey, Brendan. *Saratoga 1777: Turning Point of a Revolution*. Oxford, UK: Osprey, 2000.

Nelson, Paul David. "William Heath." in *American Revolutionary War: A Student Encyclopedia*, vol. II: E-L, edited by Gregory Fremont-Barnes and Richard Alan Ryerson, 862–864. Santa Barbara, CA: ABC-CLIO, 2007.

Oberg, Barbara B., ed. *The Papers of Thomas Jefferson*, vol. 33, 17 February–30 April 1801. Princeton: Princeton University Press, 2006.

Philbrick, Nathaniel. *Bunker Hill: A City, a Siege, a Revolution*. New York: Viking, 2013.

Savas, Theodore P., and J. David Dameron, eds. *The New American Revolution Handbook*. New York: Savas Beatie, 2010.

Selesky, Harold E. "William Heath." In *Encyclopedia of the American Revolution*, vol. 1, edited by Harold E. Selesky, 497–498. Detroit: Charles Scribner's Sons, 2006.

Thatcher, James. *A Military Journal During the American Revolutionary War, from 1775 to 1783, Describing Interesting Events and Transactions of this Period; with Numerous Historical Facts and Anecdotes from the Original Manuscript*. Boston: Cottons & Barnard, 1827. Retrieved on October 14, 2011 from http://threerivershms.com/journalheath.htm.

Wilson, Thomas. "William Heath." In *The Biography of Principal American Military and Naval Heroes*, vol. 1, 136. New York: John Low, 1817.

Index